Holy Ghost Fire!

~ Including ~

Prayers and Poems to God

by

Almighty God's Servant, Don Diaz

I have baptized you with water unto repentance, but he (Jesus) shall baptize you with the <u>Holy Ghost</u>, and with <u>Fire!</u> {Matthew 3:11}

On the day of Pentecost, suddenly there came a sound from heaven as of a rushing mighty wind, and it filled all the house where they were sitting. And there appeared unto them cloven tongues of <u>Fire</u>, and it sat upon each of them. And they were all filled with the <u>Holy Ghost</u>!
{Acts 2:1}
All power is given unto me in Heaven and in Earth, go ye into all the world and preach the Gospel to every creature and nation, baptizing them in the name of the Father, and the Son, and the Holy Ghost!
"<u>Feed my Sheep!</u>" ~ "**Jesus Christ**"

January 2017

Holy Ghost Fire
Don Diaz

Copyright © Don Diaz
January, 2017

Published By Parables
January, 2017

All Rights Reserved. No part of this book may be reproduced or utilized in any form or by any means, electronic or mechanical, including photocopying, recording, or by any information storage and retrieval system, without permission in writing from the author.

Unless otherwise specified Scripture quotations are taken from the authorized version of the King James Bible.

ISBN 978-1-945698-14-9

Printed in the United States of America

Readers should be aware that Internet Web sites offered as citations and/or sources for further information may have been changed or disappeared between the time this was written and when it is read.

Holy Ghost Fire!

~ Including ~

Prayers and Poems to God

by

Almighty God's Servant, Don Diaz

I have baptized you with water unto repentance, but he (Jesus) shall baptize you with the <u>Holy Ghost</u>, and with <u>Fire!</u>   {Matthew 3:11}

On the day of Pentecost, suddenly there came a sound from heaven as of a rushing mighty wind, and it filled all the house where they were sitting. And there appeared unto them cloven tongues of <u>Fire</u>, and it sat upon each of them. And they were all filled with the <u>Holy Ghost!</u>
{Acts 2:1}

All power is given unto me in Heaven and in Earth, go ye into all the world and preach the Gospel to every creature and nation, baptizing them in the name of the Father, and the Son, and the Holy Ghost!

"<u>Feed my Sheep!</u>" ~ **"Jesus Christ"**

January 2017

~ Dedication to God ~

I want to humbly thank, and dedicate this book, "Holy Ghost Fire" to Our Father God who art in Heaven, Our Lord and Savior, Jesus Christ; and The Holy Spirit; my Guide, Comforter, Teacher, and Protector! To my Father God: The One and Only True Living Jehovah God in All of the Universe, and in All of Existence!!! I Thank You Almighty God for even allowing a wretched flea and worm such as me, to enter into your magnificent holy Awesome Presence! To kneel before you, to Pray and tremble at your feet; to Worship and Praise You! The Great "I AM", Creator of the Universe, The Giver of all Life, The Author of all Truth and Light, all wisdom, knowledge, and understanding! Heavenly Father, the splendor of thy magnificent glory and power radiates across the entire universe you have created! The very touch of thine almighty hand shows the light and life of **Jehovah God!** The Entire Universe can never contain your Awesome Power and Glory! Father God, I want to sincerely Thank You for all, all, all; that you have done for me and all of mankind; and all of the spiritual and the physical Universe! I Thank You!!! Father God, since the day I read in Ezekiel 22:30, when you said, "I sought for a man among them, to make up the hedge, and Stand Up in the Gap before me for the land, that I should not destroy it! But I found none!" Those words ripped my heart out, and caused me much pain and anguish! Our Father God who created us, could not FIND ONE MAN Among Them, at that time, to pray, and cry out, and to intercede before him; for the human race, to save us and deliver us from evil; may God have mercy on us all! It became my sincere desire and goal, to kneel at God's feet, and truly learn from God how to pray and intercede in the spirit and in truth! And to stand up in the gap and make up the hedge before God for the hearts and souls of a lost and dying world, that my Lord Jesus died on the cross to Save! To the Mighty Lord Jesus Christ: I Thank You Lord Jesus! For every single Drop of your Precious Holy Blood that washes away sin, and sets men's souls Free! I thank you for the crown of thorns, and the nails of Pain! I thank you for dying on the cross to set mankind free, and rising again on the third day! Your resurrection is our salvation! Without you Mighty Lord Jesus, we would all be lost! And to the Holy Spirit: thank you for being so patient with me, you are my best friend, guide teacher, and comforter! You taught me more about God, Jesus, Truth, Prayer, and living and walking in the spirit than anyone! I Love you! God's servant, Don Diaz

Holy Ghost Fire! ~ Including:
Prayers and Poems to God ~ Table of Contents

1. ~ Almighty God - Creator of the Universe!
2. ~ Opening Introduction
3. ~ 50 Prayers and Poems to God
4. ~ Scripture Page - The Apostle Paul
5. ~ Preface: A Word from the Author
6. ~ God's New Covenant Page
7. ~ Faith and Trust in God
8. ~ God's Love, Grace, and Mercy
9. ~ Holy Fire and Holy Ground!
10. ~ The Basic Rules Page
11. ~ The Basic Foundation of God
12. ~ Spiritual Warfare Page
13. ~ Holiness, Prayer, and Spiritual Warfare!
14. ~ The Fruits of the Holy Spirit
15. ~ The Works and Sins of the Flesh
16. ~ Sermon Message - "Be Ye Perfect!"
17. ~ A Completion, Summation, and Conclusion!

~ PRAYER TO GOD ~

"O'Heavenly Father, we praise you and thank you for your Precious Son Jesus Christ, and Holy Spirit! Please give us wisdom, knowledge, and spiritual understanding! Give us spiritual <u>ears</u> to <u>hear</u> and <u>know</u> your <u>voice</u>! A sharp, clear, <u>mind</u> to understand exactly what <u>you</u> are saying to us! And most of all Lord, a Soft, Tender, Pure, Holy <u>heart</u>, that will <u>Receive</u> and <u>Do</u> your <u>Perfect will</u>! O' Lord God, Consume us with your Holy Ghost Fire! And <u>Teach</u> us to walk, pray, and <u>Live</u> in the Spirit; as a <u>Faithful</u> and <u>Fruitful</u> part of the body of <u>Jesus Christ</u>! Holy Spirit purify and sanctify us to be your Holy Temple Forever!" God's Servant, Don Diaz

Almighty God - Creator of the Universe!

Almighty God is the All Seeing, All Knowing, and All Powerful, Creator of the Universe! God's Omnipotence, Wisdom, and Intelligence, Is Far Beyond Any Puny Human Intellect, comprehension, or capability of understanding. God is Ever-present, Omnipresent, Forever! Throughout the Ages and Aeons of Time and Space; Far Beyond the Unseen Realms of the Physical and Spiritual Universe, that Encapsulate all of Existence and Creation! **God Rules** over All the Kingdoms of Heaven and Earth, of Men and Angels! To **Almighty God** Alone, belongs **The Kingdom, The Power, and The Glory!!!** Forever and ever and ever, Eternally! God has No Beginning! God has No End! God's Presence, His All-Seeing, All Knowing Perception; Engulf, Contain, and Encapsulates all of the Entire Universe; and all of Existence! Including Time and Space, and the Physical and Spiritual World, in One Brief Glance of an Instant! Almighty God Sees and Perceives, the Nether Regions and Realms of Infinity, Yet to Be Created! God Has No Boundary's, No Perimeters, No Confines, No End of Resources, No Restrictions or Limitations of His Will, His Capabilities and Creative Powers! Absolutely Nothing is Beyond Almighty Gods Awesome Ability and Reach! The Unlimited Power of The One True Living Jehovah God, The Alpha and Omega, The Great I AM, The Creator of all Creation! Is Far Beyond the Knowledge, Perception, or Understanding of Man; by Any Measurement, or by any Numerical Value of Any Human Calculation! Almighty God is not Bound by the Fabric of Time and Space, or the Physical Boundary's of Created Matter like Man Is. The Unlimited Reach of His Arm, His Sight and Perception is Far Beyond Billions and Trillions of Light-Years Across the Entire Universe, a Million Times Over! Our **God** is Ever-Present, Omnipresent, Throughout all of the Ages! **Almighty God** is Perpetually Here and Everywhere all at Once! There is no Location Where God is Not Present, Not Then, Not Now, Not Ever! In Him We Live and Breathe and have our Being. All the Heavens Cannot Contain Him, and Yet He came to Earth as a Humble Man, **Jesus Christ**! And was Obedient unto Death, Even the Death of the Cross! To Save Us, and Free Mankind from Sin and Evil! Jesus Took the Keys of Hell and Death from Satan, and Rose from the Grave 3 Days Later! Because it was Never, Ever, Possible, that Hell or Death or the Grave could Ever Hold Him! **Jesus Ascended into Heaven**, and is Seated at the Right Hand of God, He is our Great High Priest in the Holy of Holies! The Mighty **Lamb of God**, that Taketh Away the Sins of the World! Jesus is my Lord, my Savior, my Rock, my Fortress, my Deliverer, my God, My Everything! In "**Jesus Christ**" Do I Trust my Heart, my Soul, my Spirit, my Very Being! God's "**Holy Spirit**" Lives Inside Me, He Guides Me, He Teaches Me, HE LOVES ME!!! God the Father, his Son Jesus Christ, and The Holy Spirit, are Worthy to Receive Glory and Honor, Praise and Worship, for all of Eternity! I Love them Forever! Gods servant, Don Diaz

Opening Introduction

To All my beloved brothers and sisters, who believe that Jesus is the Christ; in every Race, Country, and Nation. Grace and Peace from God the Father, and our Lord and Savior Jesus Christ! The Lamb of God that Taketh away the Sin of the World! I hope this opening letter finds you well, and in good health and spirit. Almighty God, who at different times in the past, and in various manners, spoke unto the fathers by his Prophets! Has in these last days spoken unto us by his Holy Son **Jesus Christ!** Who God has appointed heir of all things, (either in heaven or in earth) by whom he also made the worlds! All things were created by God through Jesus Christ, and nothing was made without him! {John 1:1-3} In him was life, and the life was the light of men! Who being the brightness of God's glory, and the express image of his person, (and character) and upholding all things by the word of his power! **Jesus himself**, purged our sins, and sat down at the right hand of the Majesty of God on High! When he gave himself for our sins, that he might deliver us from this present evil world, according to the will of God! Jesus was wounded for our transgressions, bruised for our iniquities; and by his stripes we are healed! For God so loved the world, that he gave his only begotten son, that whosoever believes in him, should not perish but have **Eternal Life!** God did not send Jesus into the world to condemn the world, but that the world through him, might be saved! For if you confess with your mouth the lord Jesus Christ, and believe in your heart that God raised him from the dead, thou shalt be saved! {John 3:16, Romans 10:9} Billions and Billions of people, confess with their Mouth, that Jesus Christ is their Lord and Savior; but the Truth is that their Heart is far from him! Because billions and billions of people come To the Cross of Jesus Christ! But they Never get **on the Cross!** Now, does this mean that we are to build a wooden cross, and nail ourselves to it? No, it means that if Jesus Christ is truly your Lord and Savior! You must truly give Jesus and the Holy Spirit **Full Control** of your Life and all the things that you do! Jesus must be your Lord! (the only one in command and control!) Before he can Be Your Savior!!! Going to church means very little if you are not doing God's will! Jesus said, why do you call me Lord, Lord, and do not do the things that I say? (what I said to do!) Behold, to **obey** is **better** than sacrifice! People in every religion pray! And then some of them get up and strap a bomb to their body, and kill thousands in the name of Allah! But the One True Living Jehovah God Most High, says to everybody! Thou shalt Not Kill! And it is at the Feet of **Jesus Christ,** the only Begotten Son of **Jehovah God!** That **Every Person who ever Lived, WILL BOW**, and confess that **Jesus Christ is Lord!** Because, as "it is written," We must all appear before the Judgment Seat of Christ, that Every One may (answer) and receive, for the things done in his body, according to all that he hath done, weather it be good or bad. Therefore Knowing the **Terror of the Lord!** (the Terrifying prospect of having to Stand Before and **Answer To** the One True Living **Almighty Jehovah God of the Universe!**) "We Persuade Men!" (to prepare for the coming judgment!) {2 Corinthians 5:10} "For it is written, As I Live, saith the Lord, That at the name of Jesus every knee **Shall bow**, of things in heaven, and things in earth, and under the earth; and every tongue **shall confess** that **Jesus Christ is Lord!!!** To the glory of **God the Father!!!** So then Every One of Us shall give an account of himself to God! {Philippians 2:10 & Romans 4:11}

Opening Introduction

It is my utmost and sincere prayer, that these writings would cover you in God's Love and Grace! And ignite a Holy, All-Consuming Fire in your Soul, and a unquenchable Hunger for God and Jesus Christ! In your Heart! Because everything else on this earth is only temporary! Absolutely nothing else should be More Important to You than your Personal Relationship with Almighty God, and his only begotten son Jesus Christ! And the **Eternal State of Your Soul!!! NOTHING!!! Your Soul** is the only thing you have that will Last Forever! Your **Soul** is you, the very essence of your being; your thoughts, your feelings, and all of your memories! And those memories will last Forever! In Jesus parable, about the Rich man and Lazarus, Abraham said to the rich man,"remember, in thy lifetime, thou receivedst good things! And Lazarus suffered evil things! But now he is comforted, and thou art tormented!" The Rich man could remember his whole lifetime! You'll remember every time someone told you about Jesus, or invited you to church, or prayed for you! The **Truth** and absolute Fact is that **God is Real! Jesus** is his Son! I can Personally Testify and **Guarantee** to you, from my own personal, intimate, relationship and my own personal dealings, that I myself have had with Almighty God the Father, his Son Jesus Christ, and the Holy Spirit who **Lives Inside Me!** I Personally Pray to, and **Talk to God**, Every Single Day! And **God Talks to Me!** I hear **God's** Voice! I Watch and See the things God says to me, come to pass! I have personally had Jesus speak my name, audibly into my physical ear! For me it's such an easy "No Brainer," to Know without a shadow of a doubt that Almighty **God is Real!** And **God is Awesome!!!** I Trust **God**, more than I trust anybody else in existence! Forever! God will Not and cannot Lie! Ever! For Me it's so easy and simple, because I spend lots of quality time, alone with God! Imagine if some one walked up to you and said to you, "Your **Father is not Real**, He does not exist!" And you said to them, Don't be ridicules,"**I Talked to Him this Morning!**" People who Can't See **God** are so blind, as to not **See the Sun in the Sky at High Noon!** In the summer, on a Clear Day! Do You **Want Proof!!!** Consider this Fact! Right now, as I am writing this Page, the Year is 2015 A.D. And do you know why it's 2015 A.D. Because **Jesus Christ was Born** around two thousand and fifteen Years ago! The whole **Earth's Yearly Time Measurement "Rotates AROUND JESUS CHRIST BIRTH!!!"** Just Like the **earth rotates around the Sun!** On the day that Jesus Christ was born, mankind already had thousands of years of recorded history firmly established on an accepted historical dateline! Then the birth of one man, **Jesus Christ (the Messiah) changed everything on the whole planet earth**! Now, all the years before **Jesus Christ Birth** are recorded as B.C. or Before Christ! And All the years after **Jesus Christ birth** are recorded as A.D. or Anno Domini, which is Latin for,"The year of our Lord" announcing the **birth of Jesus Christ!** And Jesus was born in between that time span, and **All** the years **Re-adjusted** around **Jesus** birth! Either before or after! Tell me, what are the **Chances** that in the future, a man will be born, and the Whole Earth will screech to a halt, and all mankind will say stop the presses! Now, all the Thousands of years before his birth, will count down to zero at His birth! And the years will restart at "**ONE**"on the year of His birth! And climb back up from there! It will **Never, Ever, happen Again!** Because **Jesus Christ** is the **Messiah** and the **Son** of the **One True Living Almighty Jehovah God!!!** That's Why! Almighty God and his Son Jesus Christ, Created the Universe! Just OPEN YOUR EYE'S!

Opening Introduction

These writings are bathed in Prayers and tears, and forged in the Furnace of God's Holy Fire! From the Truth of **God's** word, **The Holy Bible!** And Inspired by a close, personal, relationship with **Almighty God the Father**, his only begotten Son **Jesus Christ**, and the **Holy Spirit**, who Lives Inside of me! The Holy Spirit helps me, guides me, strengthens, and teaches me, every step of the way! {John 16:13} The meek will he guide in judgment and teach his way! For thou art my Rock and Fortress, therefore lead me and guide me for thy name's sake! I will instruct thee and teach thee in the way which thou shalt go, I will guide thee with mine (all seeing) Eye! For (Almighty) God is our God for ever and ever and He will be our guide even unto death! (and for all eternity!) Thou shalt guide me with thy Council, and afterward receive me into glory! {Psalms 25:9, 31:3, 32:8, 48:14, 73:24} **Jesus** said, "I AM the Light of the World!" He that followeth **ME**, shall not walk in darkness, but shall have the light of life! I AM the Way, the Truth, and the Life! No man cometh unto the Father, but by Me! {John 8:12, 14:6} For there is **one God**, and **one** mediator between God and men, the man **Jesus Christ!** {1Timothy 2:5} I ask you humbly and sincerely, to please read this Whole Book, Entirely and Completely! Carefully and Prayerfully, from the First page to the Last Page! And keep this in mind, In a Legal Trial, all of the Jury is seated and sequestered for the Entire time that the case is carefully brought before them to consider and make a decision on! They listen to the opening statements, and introduction on the case and matter at hand! **Uninterrupted!** They must sit and Patiently Listen to all of the facts in the case! They must look at and see! All of the Evidence brought before them in the trial! And then they must Listen to and Hear All of the Closing Arguments! Before they can even Go into the Jury Chambers! And begin to thoroughly consider the matter, and begin to form or make a decision! And this is a very, very, **Important Matter** that I am bringing before You! I would ask you to Please Hear Me Out fully, patiently, carefully, and completely! Especially because the Issue and matter at hand is the **ETERNAL STATE OF YOUR SOUL!!! FOREVER!!!** And the Information, Testimony and Biblical Scripture that I am bringing before you; in Love, and compassionate care, and concern; is All for You! It's Your **Defense!!! YOU are the VERY SUBJECT and THE DEFENDANT IN THIS TRIAL CASE!!!** So how much the more, should **You** hear all the facts and arguments in this matter, very patiently and carefully! Because it concerns the very **Eternal State and Destination of Your Soul! Permanently!** I Cannot Possibly Stress this One Point Enough To YOU! **"YOU" MUST STAND BEFORE THE JUDGMENT SEAT OF ALMIGHTY GOD!!! There Are ABSOLUTELY -NO- EXCEPTIONS! YOU WILL PERSONALLY STAND BEFORE GOD!!!** Let these words sink deep down into your ears, until they reach your very heart and soul! Almighty **God** is the most Powerful Being in the whole entire Universe! And All of Existence! **DO NOT EVER TAKE ALMIGHTY GOD LIGHTLY!!! IT IS THE MOST FATAL MISTAKE YOU WILL EVER MAKE!!!** Even **Jesus Christ**, God's only begotten Son, said in no uncertain terms,"I will tell you who **You** should Fear!" "**FEAR GOD!!!**" "Do not fear them that can only kill the body. But Fear Him that has the Power to Destroy both Body and Soul, **IN HELL!!! Forever!!!** Yea, I say unto You, **FEAR HIM!!!** (**GOD!**) {Matthew 10:28} It's a fearful thing to fall into the hands of the Living God! Knowing the Terror of God! We warn men!

Opening Introduction

Jesus said,"The hour is coming (Judgment day is on the Way!) and now is, (because Jesus has already been Resurrected) when the dead shall hear the voice of the son of God, and they that hear shall Live! For as the Father (God) hath life in himself; so hath he given to the son (Jesus) to have life in himself! God has given Jesus, the authority to execute the Judgment, because He is the son of man! (God in the Flesh) For the Father judgeth no man, but hath committed all Judgment unto the son! (Jesus) That all men should honor the son, (Jesus) even as they honor the Father! Truly, I say unto you, he that heareth my word and believes on him that sent me, hath everlasting life, and shall not come into condemnation but is passed from death unto life! Do Not be surprised, (or caught off guard, because the day of Jesus return, will be hidden like a thief in the night) and the hour is coming when all who are in the Graves! (every person who ever lived on the Planet Earth!) Shall all hear Jesus voice, and shall all come Forth! They that have done **Good**, unto the Resurrection of **Life!** And they that have done **Evil**, unto the Resurrection of **Damnation!**{John 5:22-29} For we must all appear before the judgment seat of Christ that every single person shall Answer for, and Receive his reward or punishment, according to all the things (actions and deeds) that he or she did in their body! (in their lifetime) weather it be good or bad! {2 Corinthians 5:10} Jesus also said, that we will have to answer for all the words that come out of our **Mouth!** "O' Generation of vipers, how can ye, being evil, speak good things? For out of the abundance of the heart the mouth speaketh! A good man out of a good, holy, pure, heart; speaks good things! (the Truth) But a evil man, out of a evil, wicked, heart, speaks evil things! (curse words, lies, and Gossip) But I say unto you, that every idle word that men shall speak, they shall give an account for on the day of judgment! For by thy (good truthful) words, thou shalt be justified, and by thy (evil wicked) words thou shalt be condemned!"{Matthew 12:34} And when you stand before God on Judgment Day! And the books are opened, showing all the things you did, and the life you lived, good or bad! The way you treated others, and if you obeyed **God**, and lived a Holy, Pure, Loving, Sanctified life! Or if you lived just like the devil, lying, stealing, cursing, murdering, committing adultery, fornication, homosexuality drunkenness, drugs, coveting, whoremongering, promiscuous, lusting, gossiping, slandering, Atheist! It will all be exposed on the **Great and Terrible Day of Judgment!** Even the hidden thoughts of mens Hearts and Minds will all be Revealed, by the Light and Revelation of Gods Holy Son, **Jesus Christ!** When All of Mankind shall kneel before **ALMIGHTY HOLY GOD!!!** "For there is nothing covered that shall not be revealed, or hidden, that shall not be known! What I tell you in darkness, that speak ye in the light! And what ye hear in the ear, that, preach ye upon the housetops! "Jesus" {Matthew 10:26} When the Lord (Jesus) comes, he will bring to the light, both the hidden things of darkness, and will make manifest (and reveal) the counsels (or desires) of the hearts!{1 Corinthians 4:5} For mine Eyes are upon all their ways, they are not hid from my face; neither is their iniquity hidden from mine Eyes! {Jeremiah 16:17} O'God, you know my foolishness, and my sins are not hid from **thee**! {Psalms 69:5} That is **Why Jesus** said,"**Repent**, for **Kingdom of Heaven** is at Hand! Repent from all of your Sins, and turn from your wicked ways, so **Jesus Blood** can wash you clean and **God's Grace** can cover you, **Before Judgment Day!** Repent ye, and be converted, that Your Sins may be Blotted Out! {Acts 3:19}

Opening Introduction

Blow ye the Trumpet in Zion, and Sound an Alarm in my Holy mountain! Let all the Inhabitants of the land tremble! Because the Day of the Lord cometh, for it is nigh at hand, and as a destruction from the Almighty shall it come! The Earth shall quake, the Heavens shall tremble, the sun and the moon shall be dark, and the stars shall withdraw their shining! And the **Lord** shall utter his Voice before his army, for his camp is very great! And He (**Jesus!**) is Strong that Exccuteth his word! For the day of the Lord is Great and Very Terrible! And who can abide (or stand before) It? So now, therefore, saith the lord, turn ye to me with all your Heart, and with fasting, and with weeping, and with mourning! And Rend Your Heart, and not your garments, and Turn to the Lord your God! Because our God is gracious and merciful, slow to anger, and of great kindness! (repent and God will forgive you) {Joel 2:1,1:15, 2:10} As I Live,"saith the **Lord God**" I have no pleasure in the death of the wicked! But that the wicked turn from his evil way and live! Turn ye, turn ye from your evil ways, for why will ye die? {Ezekiel 33:11} The Lord knoweth how to deliver the godly (these who cry out to Jesus, and hope in God's grace, and mercy, and forgiveness) out of temptations; and how to reserve the unjust (all who love their sins and have absolutely no intentions of repenting, or changing their evil lifestyle) unto the day of judgment to be punished! {2 Peter 2:9} That is why the mighty Lord Jesus, in his great love and mercy, calls all the world to repentance! Because God is longsuffering and not willing that anyone should Perish, but that all should come to repentance! (God) who will have all men to be saved and come unto the knowledge of the truth, about the **saving grace** of our Lord and Savior **Jesus Christ**! {2 Peter 3:9, 1 Timothy 2:4} Beloved, when the Great and Terrible **Day of Judgment** comes, (For it is nigh at hand) if You haven't Truly Repented, and turned from your wicked ways! (it doesn't matter how good you think you are, all our righteousness is filthy rags in God's sight!) If you haven't been washed clean by Jesus's Blood and covered by God's grace and mercy, **YOU WILL NOT BE READY!!!** When the Mighty **Lord Jesus** utters his Voice; for He is Strong that Executeth God's Word, with Eyes that Flame with Fire! Because The Word of **God** is Quick and Powerful, (alive and active) and Sharper than any Two-Edged Sword! Piercing even to the dividing asunder of the **Soul** and **Spirit**, and of the joints and marrow, and is a **Discerner** of the Thoughts and Intents of the Heart! (it will separate the lies from the truth, and expose your **Hearts** True desires and motives) Neither is there Any Creature (physical man or spiritual being) that is not manifest in God's Sight! But All Things are Naked and Opened unto the Eyes of him with whom we have to Do! **Almighty God!!!** {Hebrews 4:12} Absolutely, Positively, **Nothing is Hidden** from Almighty God's, All-Seeing, All-Knowing, **Eyes!!!** No man, no woman, no spirit, no angel, no demon, no secret, no lie, no theft, no sin, no dark room, no deep hidden cave, no planet, no Star in the sky, no place in Time or Space, anywhere in the Physical or Spiritual Universe! **Absolutely Nothing is Beyond the Sight, Power and Reach of The "One" True Living Almighty Jehovah God**! And I cannot possibly with every single fiber in my being, Stress to you and Warn you enough, that You will personally stand before God! Do not take it lightly! No puny human words can ever accurately convey Almighty God's Awesome, Universe Shaking Power! And You will answer to **God** on Judgment Day! It is a fearful thing to fall into the hands of the One True Living God! "Apostle Paul"{Hebrews 10:31}

Opening Introduction

All of Mankind will fall down at Jesus feet on Judgment day, Terrified and Stunned! Every Atheist who ever lived, and said out of their mouths, "there is no God" their tongues will be Silent! Paralyzed with Fear, Gripped with Agony, to the Core of their Souls, that they mistakenly, carelessly, spoke out against **The One True Living Jehovah God of All Creation!!!** To whom they must now answer To! And for what reason did they do such a stupid thing? So they could callously suppress and ignore their own conscience, and appease the sinful, evil desires, of their wicked flesh, without thought or concern for the consequences, before a **Holy God** that they **did not want** to exist! That's why! To all who have Ears to hear, Let them Hear! **God is Alive!!! Forevermore!!!** That Fact will Never, Ever, Change!!! And to every person on the Planet Earth, here is small hint and clue! If You are alive on this very Day, it is only because **GOD IS ALIVE!!!** If God did not exist, You would not exist! Because God created You! And you, dear atheist, are the Living Proof, of the very God, you think you can deny! I challenge every person, who says that there is no God, to try and stand up on Judgment Day! Point their finger at Almighty God, and say,"you're not real" And I guarantee that No one can answer that challenge! Their legs and their tongues will be paralyzed with fear, as their mind races to think of what they will say, to the Almighty God that they claimed did not Exist! I will rest my case on Judgment Day! But their fate will be sealed by then! It's Too Late to try to Repent on Judgment Day! The Lord Jesus said,"If you do not believe that I Am the Christ, You will Die in your Sins! Because you have not believed in the only begotten Son of God!" {John 3:18, 8:24} Today is the day of salvation! Today, Jesus is seated on the Mercy Seat, in the Holy of Holies! Today, You can find Grace, and Mercy, and Forgiveness for Sins, when You truly repent from them! Today, Jesus can save you from your sins, and wash you, and make you clean! On Judgment Day, Jesus will be seated on the **Judgment Seat**, on a **Throne of Justice!!!** Where Jesus will execute the Judgment of the Word of God, with mercy, grace, love and forgiveness, to all who repented from sin and evil; lived holy, pure, clean lives, did the will of God, and that which was good, right, and just! God's children will enter into heaven, Forever! And to all who did Evil, who loved their sins and their wicked lifestyle, lying, stealing, cursing, murdering, adultery, fornication and homosexuality, lusting and partying, like their father Satan, and had no intention to **Stop sinning** and Repenting from their Evil Ways! **Hell and Eternal Damnation!!!** Forever!!! For whosoever was not found written in **God's Book of Life**, was **Cast into the Lake of Fire!!!** {Revelation 20:15} There are only two places where You can go, either in Heaven or in Hell! Forever! These are the only two places where all the souls of men will reside, **For All of Eternity!** There is no purgatory! And the Judge on Judgment Day, Almighty God's only Begotten Son **Jesus Christ**; his **Decision is Final and Forever!** There will be no appeals, no sidebar, no crooked lawyers, no bribes, and no new evidence! All of the Facts from your Life will be laid out right there before you, and all of the words that came out of your mouth! You will want to crawl under a rock, as all the vile, filthy words and lies, that spewed forth out of **your mouth** are read before a Holy God! And the facts of the things **you did in your Lifetime**, you will Answer For and Give an Account to **Almighty God!** Or, you can accept **Jesus as your Lord and Savior** and he will stand before God and say, the Punishment for his sins are Paid for with **My Blood!**

Opening Introduction

Beloved, this is the very purpose for my **Labor of Love!** I Love my **Father God in Heaven!** I Love my Lord and Savior **Jesus Christ!** I Love the **Holy Spirit** who Lives inside Me! And **I Love You**, and I truly care about what happens to your Soul for all of Eternity! You see, I Know God Personally, and there is No Way that I am going to walk through **Heavens Gates**, with a clear conscience, and go Worship God for all of Eternity! Without knowing I did everything in my power, to tell the Real Truth to a Lost and Dying World; that is Blinded by Sin, deceived by Satan, and being spoon fed a whole lot of Garbage and Lies! By T.V. Preachers and Denominations **Begging For Money**, and preaching a Soft, Easy, Marshmallow Gospel of **Forgiveness** without **True**, **Heartrending**, **Soul searching**, **Life Changing**, **Repentance!!!** Which is the only kind of Repentance that will Get You into Heaven! Any Preacher who does not tell you, in no uncertain terms to **Get Out of Your Sins**, does Not Preach the **Real Gospel of Jesus Christ!!!** The very First Words out of Jesus mouth, when He began to Preach the Gospel were, "**Repent, For the Kingdom of Heaven is at Hand!!!**" But, Please don't just take my word for it! It's your very Soul that is on the line! You must get **The Holy Bible**, and Read it yourself! I strongly recommend the King James Version! Here is the very spot! {Matthew 4:17} "From that time Jesus began to preach, and to say, Repent: for the kingdom of heaven is at hand!" The very First word! when Jesus began to Preach, was "**REPENT!!!**" Get Out of Your Sins! Turn from your Evil Ways! Forsake all your Sins and Stop Doing Them! Hate Them! Fight Against Them! Overcome Your Sins at **All Cost!** (Jesus said) Pick Up your Cross, and Crucify your Evil Fleshly Desires, every Single Day, and **Follow Me!** That is **True Repentance** the way that **Jesus Christ** taught It! "And Jesus said to them all, if any man will come after me, let him deny himself, and take up his cross every day, and follow me! For whosoever will save his life shall lose it, but whosoever shall lose his life for my sake the same shall save it! For what is a man advantaged, if he gains the whole world, and loses his own soul! {Luke 9:23-25} If My People, which are called by My Name, shall humble themselves, and Pray, and seek my face, and **Turn from their Wicked ways**! "then!" then will I hear from Heaven, and will **Forgive their Sins!** {2 Chronicles 7:14} Absolutely Nothing in this whole entire World is worth more than Eternal Life in Heaven with Almighty God! **NOTHING!!!** And "**Jesus Christ**" is the Greatest Treasure in all of Existence!!! Because Jesus Christ is **the Only way into Heaven!!!** "Jesus saith unto him, I am the way, the truth, and the life; No Man commeth unto the Father, **But by ME!** {John 14:6} For there is One God, and One mediator between God and men, the man Jesus Christ! {1 Timothy 2:5} And Jesus, the One and Only Way, says **Repent**, humble yourself, Pray and Seek my Face, and turn away from your wicked ways! Deny yourself, take up your cross every day, crucify your sinful fleshly desires, **and follow Me!!!** Walk in the Spirit and you will not fulfill the Lusts of the flesh! For there is no condemnation to them who are in Christ Jesus, who do not walk after the flesh, (fleshly desires) but who walk in the Spirit! (and **obey the Holy Spirit** as he guides them how to **Overcome sin and evil!**) For (the people who are truly) led by the **Spirit of God**, they are the Sons of God! {Romans 8:1-14} You must learn all of the True Gospel! Christianity is not just going to church, a way of thinking, a theology, or a philosophy! Christianity is a "real personal relationship" with God living inside of You!

Opening Introduction

Beloved, If you want to have a <u>Real Personal Relationship</u> with **God!** You have to spend real, quality time, uninterrupted, alone with God! In a quiet and undisturbed place, for Diligent, Sincere Prayer and Bible Study! (turn your cell phone or any other interruptions <u>off</u>) The <u>reward</u> you get out of it, will be equal to the <u>effort</u> that <u>You put into it!</u> Because without **Faith** it is <u>Impossible</u> to please God! For he that cometh to God must **Believe** that he is, (Real) and that **God** is a rewarder of them that **<u>Diligently Seek Him!</u>** And <u>always</u> Go to **God** <u>humbly and Respectfully!</u> Work out your Salvation with fear and trembling! Because **Almighty God Rules over the Entire Universe from Heaven Above!!!** While you and I, my beloved brethren, are just lowly <u>dust and dirt</u>, down here on the earth! "For dust thou art and unto dust thou shalt return." {Genesis 3:19} And <u>Never, Ever, Forget</u>, that you are praying to the **One True Living Jehovah God Most High!** <u>Do Not</u> just carelessly <u>utter</u> anything to <u>Almighty God!</u> The Most Powerful Being in **All of Existence!!!** The One and Only **Real God** who has the <u>Power</u> to <u>Save your Body and Soul</u> for <u>all</u> of Eternity, or <u>Destroy your Body and Soul in **Hell** for all of Eternity!</u> On <u>Judgment Day!</u> So, **Pray to God Humbly!** Jesus spake this parable unto certain men which trusted in themselves that they were righteous, and despised others. "Two men went up into the temple to pray, the one a Pharisee, (a member of a high Religious order) and the other a publican. (a tax collector) The Pharisee stood and prayed thus with himself, "God, I thank thee, that I am not as other men are, extortioners, unjust, adulterers, or even as this publican. I fast twice in the week, I give tithes of all that I possess." And the publican, standing afar off, would <u>not so much as</u> lift up his eyes unto heaven, but <u>smote</u> upon his breast, saying, <u>"God, be merciful to me a sinner."</u> I tell you, this man (publican) went down to his house justified rather than the other! For every one that <u>exalteth himself</u> shall be abased, and he that humbleth himself shall be exalted! (and received before God) The Pharisee thought that by his puny human efforts, he could, (by his own efforts) earn favor with God! The Jewish religion, (under the Old Testament) are <u>still</u> trying to be <u>Justified</u> by <u>the Law</u>, <u>To this very Day!</u> Beloved, It's <u>Impossible!</u> The Apostle Paul told them, "Anyone who seeks to be <u>Justified by the Law</u>, ye are all <u>fallen from</u> **Grace!**" The blood of Jesus Christ is <u>Not covering you!</u> Because **You** are relying on your <u>own righteousness,</u> **Not His!** For we through the <u>Spirit</u>, wait for the hope of **Righteousness by Faith!** In **Jesus Christ!** {Galatians 5:4} Because "we are <u>all unclean,</u> and <u>our</u> righteousness is as <u>filthy rags</u>" in God's sight! {Isaiah 64:6} The Scripture hath concluded that <u>all</u> (mankind is) under sin! That the promise by **Faith** in Jesus Christ might be given to <u>them</u> that <u>Believe in Him!</u> But before Faith came, we were kept under the Law, shut up unto the Faith which should afterwards be revealed. Wherefore the Law was our schoolmaster <u>to bring us unto Christ,</u> that we might be Justified by **Faith!** But after that Faith is come, we are no longer under a schoolmaster. {Galatians 3:22-25} (but that schoolmaster served as our <u>teacher</u> to show us that **we could not save ourselves!** By our <u>own</u> efforts! And that <u>we needed a</u> **Savior!**) For by the deeds of the Law, <u>no flesh</u> (man) shall be justified, for by the Law is the knowledge of sin! For <u>all have sinned,</u> and come short of the glory of God! {Romans 3:20-28} We seek to be found <u>in him,</u> (part of the body of Christ) <u>not</u> having <u>our own</u> righteousness, which is of <u>the Law!</u> But that which is by <u>the Faith of Christ</u>, the righteousness which is of <u>God</u> by <u>Faith!</u> {Philippians 3:9}

Opening Introduction

Beloved, when Jesus Christ preached the Gospel, he preached about Sin and Repentance, he preached about Holiness and righteousness, he preached about Faith, obedience, and doing God the Fathers will, he preached about how evil liars, and thieves, and murders, were the children of Satan! Jesus preached about love and grace, mercy and forgiveness; he preached about the wrath of God and Judgment Day! Jesus said that, in my Fathers house (in Heaven) were many mansions, and that he was going there to prepare a place for us,(God's children) and that he is going to return again and bring us to the Marriage Supper of the Lamb! Jesus also preached about Hell and Destruction and the Punishment of Sinners! Jesus spoke directly about **Hell** 15 different times, and Damnation or Destruction 7 different times, in the four Gospels! (Matthew, Mark, Luke, and John) In Those teachings, is One of the most Important Prophetic and Visionary Teachings in the History of Mankind, that only **Jesus**, "God in the Flesh!!!" Could know and warn the Human Race about! Every Person on the Planet Earth should study and take heed to Jesus Warning about the **Coming Judgment Day!!!** "Enter ye in at the strait gate: For Wide is the gate, and Broad is the way, that leadeth to Destruction, and Many there be which **Go In There!** Because Strait is the gate, and Narrow is the way that **Leadeth to Life** and Few there be that Find It! {Matthew 7:13} And, one day a man asked Jesus, "Lord, are there many that be saved?" And Jesus said unto them, "Strive to Enter into the strait gait, for many, I say unto you, will Seek to Enter In and **Will Not Be Able!**" {Luke 13:23} First, lets take a close look at the word "strive" in the original text or language, the Greek root word, "agonize" was used. so we will look at the definition for both words. **Strive**: to struggle or compete for a prize; to contend with an adversary; to fight fiercely
and ferociously to obtain; to labor fervently for something!
Agonize: a violent life or death struggle; to suffer pain in a massive struggle for ultimate victory!
So Jesus was saying that we have to strive, agonize, and fight ferociously to Enter into Heaven! Now, I'll take these two Verses on the same subject, put them together and clarify them in modern english for easy understanding. "One day, A man asked Jesus,"Lord, how many people will actually make it into Heaven? And Jesus told them to Strive diligently, and Fight ferociously, to Enter into the narrow path that leads to Heaven, because many people will try to enter into that narrow path, and will not be able to make it in! Because **Wide** is the path, and **Broad** is the road that leads to Hell and Destruction, and there will be **Many People** which Go into that wide path! Because narrow is the path and Strait is the road that lead to Eternal life in heaven! and only a few People will be able to enter into that narrow Path! "**No One**" (that ever lived on earth!) knows more about **Heaven and Hell** than **Jesus Christ!!!** Because **JESUS IS GOD in the FLESH!!!** With his All Seeing and All Knowing **Prophetic Eyes!!! Jesus** knows and see's everything that is going to Happen! Forever! Jesus told them that the Temple would be torn down, Jesus told Peter, that he would deny him 3 times before the rooster crowed! God showed Daniel, Isaiah, and Jeremiah, the things that happened decades and centuries before they did! In Revelations, Jesus showed the Apostle John, what would happen at The End of the World! Beloved, **Jesus knows Everything! HE IS GOD!** Jesus said, many people will go into the path to Destruction! And only a **Few** will **Enter into Heaven!** "For many are called, but few are chosen!"{Matthew 22:14}

Opening Introduction!

Beloved, this is an an earth shattering revelation, and a most Important matter to think about carefully! Did you just let **Jesus** Prophesy, (That **Will shortly be Fulfilled!**) Go in one Ear and Out the Other! Jesus said, **Many** people will go to Hell, and only a **Few** people make it into Heaven! That many will Seek to Enter In, but **Will Not Be Able!!!** Let these words sink deep into your Ears, Mind, and Soul! This is **God** talking directly to You, and Warning You of What is Coming! So that You will prepare your Heart and Soul For **Judgment Day**, where **You will Kneel at Jesus Feet!!!** Because my beloved brethren, **Almighty God Loves You and WANTS YOU TO MAKE IT INTO HEAVEN!!!** This is the very Reason why Jesus told us Exactly what is going to Happen! So that you would turn from your wicked ways, and Live Your Life according to this Knowledge! You absolutely **must** Strive diligently, and Fight Ferociously, to **Enter into the Strait and narrow Path** that leads through Heavens Gates!!! Because If you don't Strive and Fight Hard, **You Will Not Make It In!!!** You must Focus every day to **Do** and **stay** in God our Father's will, and keep yours eyes on Jesus! Beloved, you must have a close personal, intimate, relationship with the **Holy Spirit**, every day! Communicating with the Holy Spirit and being sensitive to him, so that if and when you are about to Do or say anything outside of God the Fathers will, You will feel him pulling you back and warning you that you are about to grieve God our Father! Remember what the scripture says, "For as many as **are led by the Spirit of God**, they are the sons of God!"{Romans 8:14} And,"Let **No Corrupt Communication** proceed out of your mouth, and **Do Not Grieve** the Holy Spirit of God, whereby ye are sealed (and covered) unto the day of your redemption!"{Ephesians 4:29} My beloved, **Prayer is our Lifeline to God!!!** We **Must Pray** in the Spirit, and Walk in the Spirit, every single day of our Lives! Jesus Christ **IS** God in the flesh! And he still had to pray to God the Father, Every Single Day, Constantly!!! Jesus, our Lord and Savior, easily out prayed his disciples! And admonished them, to watch and Pray, that ye enter not into temptation! Remember Peter, James, and John, (in the garden of Gethsemane) Jesus said, what, could ye not watch with me for one hour? the spirit indeed is willing, but the flesh is Weak! And I ask You, beloved, Do You Watch and Pray at least **One Hour** every single day? If the answer is **no**, Do You really believe that you are **Striving diligently** and **Fighting ferociously** to **Enter into the Strait and Narrow Gate!** If **One Hour** of Prayer is to much to ask? How many hours do you spend watching the filth on T.V.? And You wonder Why? You can't overcome Sin and Temptation! Beloved, it's **your soul** on the Line! The Prophet Daniel, made the small effort to Pray 3 times a day; and **God** sent the arch-angel Gabriel to Him, and the angel told him Thou Art Greatly Beloved! The effort you make to seek God is so very Important, not only for your soul, but your family's as well! My Brethren, Do Not Neglect to Pray!!! Beloved, Praying is one part, **Obeying is the other!** Jesus told them,"Not every one that saith unto me, Lord, Lord, shall Enter into the Kingdom of Heaven, but they that **Do the will of my Father** which is in Heaven! Many will say to me in that day, Lord, Lord, have we not prophesied in thy name? And in thy name have cast out devils? And in thy name done many wonderful works? And then I will Profess unto them, I never knew you; depart from me, **Ye that work iniquity!** {Matthew 7:21} Elijah Prayed, and God sent Fire! Peter prayed, and God raised the Dead! God knew them!!! Does God know You?

Opening Introduction

Beloved, it is God's will that you learn all of the Council of the Holy Bible, and all of the truth that's in God's word! A Real Man of God, "Will Tell You" what the "Holy Spirit of God" wants him to Say! And 99.9 % percent of the time, that is exactly what Your Flesh does Not Want to Hear! Because it's going to be the same thing that Jesus taught US! Take up your cross and crucify your fleshly desires! And this is nothing New! Korah and Dathan rebelled against the word of the Lord through Moses, and were swallowed up by the earth and consumed, 3500 years ago! The children of Israel told the Prophet Isaiah, See not, (the Truth) Do not Prophesy unto us, the Right (word of God), Tell us Smooth, Easy Things, Prophesy (lies) and Deceits! And people do the same thing today! But Beloved, I Love You, and I know that only the Truth will set you Free! I Fear God, and I don't want anyone's Blood on my Hands when I stand before Him! So I Kneel humbly at God's feet and ask the Holy Spirit, please take 1000% percent Full Control at All Times, and let my tongue speak Every Word that You want said! Not my will, but Thy Will Be Done in my Life!!! Therefore, hear ye the word of the Lord! "Now go, write it before them in a table, and note it in a book, that it may be for the time to come and Forever!" Woe to the rebellious children, saith the Lord, that take Council, but not of me; and that cover with a covering, but not of my Holy Spirit! That they may add sin to sin! For this is a Rebellious People, sinful, lying children; children that will not hear the Law of the Lord! Which say to the seers, See not; and tell the Prophets, prophesy not unto us right things, speak unto us smooth things, prophesy deceits! {Isaiah 30:1, 30:8-10} This is Exactly what is happening in the World today! The United States justice system, which was Founded on the Principals in the Bible! Will Not Allow the Ten Commandments to be displayed in Front of a Courthouse! We can't say a prayer to God or Jesus in our schools, asking him to Deliver us from Evil! But the wicked men in charge, can't figure out why the devils kids keep bringing in guns and killing, in the same schools, that they won't allow prayer for God's Help In! Duh! God completely Destroyed Sodom and Gomorrah, but now if you preach the truth that homosexuality is a Sin, they want to throw you in jail! And in the Church, most of the Preachers and Denominations preach a soft, Smooth, Easy Gospel of forgiveness! Not the Real, True, Life changing, Heart searching Repentance! That might Interfere with your Sinful Lifestyle, ruffle your feathers, or Offend your Evil Wicked little Heart! Oh No, they would Never Do That! Because then you would Stop Giving Them Your MONEY!!! And the Real Truth Is that most of the Preachers, Churches, Ministries, and World Wide Denominations, are Just Money Making Businesses! And The Earth is their Fat Cash Cow! To Rake in Millions and Billions of DOLLARS, All over the world, Every Year! That is their TRUE MOTIVE and PURPOSE! And when these Charlatans, and Thieves, Stand Before Almighty God! They are going to wish that they had Never Been Born! Almighty God will burn them in the Deepest Parts of Hell! Because Satan is using them to Push Lost Souls away from God! All the People who see them, and know that they are just greedy thieves, now don't trust or believe that the gospel is real! Beloved, God is Real!!! And I don't want your Money! I Love You, and I only want You to know the Real Truth about Jesus and God! "I want you to make it into Heaven!" Beloved, that is what I want!

Opening Introduction

Everyone needs to know the Full, Complete, Unadulterated, True Gospel of **Jesus Christ!** Everyone! Because He is **the only Way** you will ever get into Heaven! You need to have a Personal Relationship with **God**, by accepting Jesus Christ as your Lord and Savior! And Inviting **the Holy Spirit** into your Heart and Soul! Through **Faith** and **Belief** that **Jesus is the Christ**, the only Begotten Son of God! That Jesus Christ is the Messiah and Lamb of God that taketh away the Sin of the world! Who died on the **Cross of Calvary**, and shed his Blood for the Forgiveness of our Sins! And he was **Resurrected** on the third day and ascended into Heaven, where he is now seated at the right hand of God! You must be **Born Again** through the **Holy Spirit** into the **Body of Christ**, where you will be covered by **God's** grace and mercy! And receive the spirit of his son into your heart whereby we cry Abba, Father, being an adopted son and heir of God through Christ! Becoming the abode or the **Temple of Almighty God**, whereby you are sealed with the Holy Spirit of promise unto the day of your redemption! Beloved this is the only way that you can be filled with the knowledge of his will, in all godly wisdom and spiritual understanding! And personally receive a true Spiritual revelation from God, to strengthen and exercise your senses to discern between Good and Evil, darkness and light, rightly dividing the Word of Truth! Beloved, the best way that I can describe a real spiritual revelation from God; it is like someone trying to tell a blind man what the sun and the sky, the moon and the stars, the mountains and the oceans look like with words; and suddenly his eyes are opened and he can now see what words can never describe! A Revelation from God enlightens your understanding like no words ever can! Where the Scriptures and the **Love and Knowledge of God** are **Illuminated** in your **Heart**, and **Mind**, and **Soul**! With all Spiritual Wisdom, Knowledge and Understanding, as the Light of God shines into your heart and soul! That he would grant you according to the riches of his glory, to be strengthened with might by his holy spirit in the inner man! That Christ might dwell in your heart by faith; that ye, being firmly rooted and grounded in Love! Might be able to comprehend with all saints, what is the breadth, and length, and depth, and height; and to know the Love of Christ, which passeth knowledge! That Ye might be Filled with all the Fullness of God! Who is able to Do Exceeding Abundantly above all that we ask or think, according to his Mighty Power that Worketh in Us! Unto **Almighty God** be all the glory in the church by **Jesus Christ** throughout all Ages, world without End, Amen. Beloved, the Almighty, Holy God of heaven and earth, extends an olive branch of repentance and forgiveness through Christ Jesus our Lord to all of mankind! (the goodness of God leadeth thee to repentance) So that you might receive of Gods grace, and mercy, and Love, and forgiveness of sins, towards all sinners! (when you truly repent from all of your sins) Whereby you would be Protected and Covered by Jesus Blood, and Sanctification, in the Spirit, as a Living Member of the Body of Christ! (the Only Safe Place in the Universe!) Thereby Preparing you for the Judgment Day, of the Almighty, Holy, One True Living God's, wrath against sin and wickedness of Evil men, who shall be punished with Everlasting Destruction from the presence of the Lord! (if you're not in the book of life, you will be cast into the lake of fire! Rev.20:15) I want You to be prepared and ready to stand before Almighty God on Judgment Day! Because **God's** Decision is **Final! Complete! Finished!** There will be No appeals, No new trials, For **All of Eternity! Forever!!!**

Opening Introduction

Beloved, when a man joins the Marines, the Army, or the Navy, first they send the new recruit to boot camp, to build up his physical conditioning, through rigorous training and exercise! Then if he passes and qualifies, they will send him through specialized training, like Green berets or Navy Seals! Where the physical and mental training and preparation, are Much tougher and demanding on the mind and body! Through legendary, heartrending, physical challenges of endurance and testings like "hell week" that push a soldier to the absolute limits of physical and mental endurance! And then they push them Even Further and Harder! More and more and more, Harder and Harder! And they Do This to show them, that their Physical, Mental, and Emotional Endurance Limits are much greater and capable than they ever thought that they were in their own minds! And they do this for a **Most Important Reason!** So that they will be the most Completely and Utterly Trained, Conditioned, and Prepared as **Humanly Possible!!!** For the **Life or Death Battle** and **War** that They are going to **Have to Fight Through!!!** Against an Evil Enemy who is **Hell Bound** on **Killing and Destroying YOU!** So your Drill Sergeant and Instructor, (Minister and Teacher) Pound You, and Drill You, and Temper You, and Sharpen You, Like a Hardened Steel Sword! Forged and Purified in **A Furnace of Fire!!!** So that when You reach the Real Battlefield, on **Judgment Day!!! YOU WILL LIVE AND NOT DIE** or be **DESTROYED FOREVER!!!** So, my Beloved brothers and sisters, Whom I deeply Love and Care For! When I, (your humble servant, and brother in the Lord) with as much Love and Tenderness, Kindness and very Human Compassion, (having been in the same Fiery Furnace for years) Because **I Truly Love You!!!** And Really, Sincerely, with many Prayers and tears, want you to make it into **Heaven!** Take the Sharp and Powerful, Flaming Truth of **God's Holy Word**,(from Genesis to Revelation) and use it to the very best of my **God given** talent and abilities! To Pound out every **Sin and Iniquity** and any **Evil Fleshly Desire**, or Spot of **Wickedness** in every **Heart and Soul** that I can Reach, through the **Grace of God!** It is only to Help You Overcome our Evil Enemy Satan, who Will Do everything in his Power to drag us all to Hell with Him! And to Prepare you (my Beloved Brethren) to Stand Before Almighty God on the coming Judgment Day! So that You can, and will, Enter into Heaven! It is only because "I Love You" so very much, and cannot bear the thought of one single soul, (that Jesus Died for) Not going to Heaven, because I Did Not Make Every Effort to Reach You, And Pray for you, and tell you the True Gospel of **Jesus Christ!** That God wants to Save You, and Forgive Your Sins, and Wash You Clean! And Bring **You to Heaven with Him! For all of Eternity!** (that's why God created us in his Image!) **To be his Family!** I have to know, with all my heart, when I kneel at the Judgment seat of Christ, and answer to God for my life! That when I walk into Heavens Gates and Worship God for all of Eternity! That I Truly and Sincerely, Tried with all my Heart, to tell the whole world that **Jesus Christ** can and will **Save You!** If you will Let Him! And that I tried to warn the whole world of the coming Judgment Day! Preaching the Full and Complete **Gospel** and **Word of God**, Just like my Lord and Savior Jesus Did It! Because, my beloved brethren, It is better to Preach the whole Gospel, at Full Power, Burning Hot, with **Holy Ghost Fire!** Than a Luke-warm, watered down milk message, that Jesus would Reject! I would rather drive you ten miles into heavens gates, than to have you fall A foot short of Entering in!

Opening Introduction

This then is the message which we have heard of him, (Jesus) and declare unto you, that God is Light, and in him is no darkness at all! If we say that we have fellowship with him, (God) and we walk in the darkness, we lie, and do not the truth! But "**If**" **we walk in the Light**, as He is in the Light! (then) We have fellowship (with God), and the **Blood** of **Jesus Christ his Son**, cleanseth us from **all Sin!** If we say that we have no sin, we deceive ourselves, and the truth is not in us. If we confess our sins, he is Faithful and just to Forgive us our Sins, and to cleanse us from all unrighteousness! If we say that we have not sinned, we make him a liar, and his word is not in us. Beloved brethren, I write these things unto you, that ye sin not! And if any man sin, we have an advocate with the Father, **Jesus Christ** the Righteous! And he is the propitiation for our Sins, and not for ours only, but also for the sins of the whole world! And this is how we can be sure that we know him, if **We keep God's Commandments**! He that saith, I know him, but does not keep God's commandments, is a liar and the truth is not in him! But whoever keeps God's word, in him the love of God is truly perfected! This is how we know that we are in him! (walking with God in the Light) He that saith that he abideth in him (Jesus) he himself ought to walk, even as he (Jesus) Walked! {1 John 1:5-10, 2:1-6} Every Man (who says) he has this hope in (Jesus) Purifieth himself, even as he (Jesus) is pure! Whosoever committeth sin transgresseth also the law; for sin is the transgression of the law. And ye know that he (Jesus) was manifested to take away our sins, and in him is No Sin! Whosoever abideth **in him sinneth not!** Whosoever sinneth hath not seen him, neither known him! Little children, let no man deceive you; he that doeth righteousness is righteous, even as he is righteous. He that committeth **sin is of the devil!** For the devil sinneth from the beginning! For this purpose the Son of God (**Jesus**) was manifested, that he might **Destroy the works of the devil! Whosoever is Born of God doth not commit Sin!** For his seed remaineth in him, and he cannot sin; because He is Born of God! In this (by this you can tell who) the children of **God are** manifest, and (who are) the children of the devil! Whosoever doeth not righteousness, (does not live holy, pure, sanctified lives) is **not of God!** Neither he (anyone) who **does not** love his brother! (Mankind) For this is the message ye have heard from the beginning, that we should love one another! {1 John 3:3-11} We know that we have passed from death unto life, because we love the brethren! He (anyone) that does not love his brother **abideth in Death!** (is still dead in sin and is **Not Born Again**) Whosoever hateth his brother **is a Murderer!** and ye know that No Murderer hath ETERNAL LIFE abiding in him! {1 John 3:14} Whosoever believeth that **Jesus is the Christ** is born of God! Every one who loves **God**, also loves God's only begotten son, **Jesus Christ!** By This we know that we love the children of God, when we love God, and we keep his Commandments! And God's commandments are not grievous. (to us) For whatsoever is Born of God, Overcometh the world; and this is the victory that overcometh the world, even our **Faith!** Who is he that overcometh the world? He that believeth that **Jesus is the Son of God!!!** {1 John 5:1-5} Behold, Now is come Salvation, and Strength, and the Kingdom of our God, and the Power of his Christ! Because the Devil, who accused all of our brethren day and night, before our Father God! The Devil (named Satan} is **Cast Down!** And God's Children **Overcame him** by **the Blood of the Lamb**, and by the **word** of their **Testimony!**{Revelations 12:10}

Prayers & Poems To God

Draw Nigh Unto God,
And He Will Draw Nigh Unto You!
James 4:8

The Eyes of The Lord Look To & Fro,
Throughout The Whole Earth;
To Show Himself Strong, on Behalf of Them;
Whose Heart is Perfect Towards Him!
2 chronicles 16: 9

Ask and it Shall be given you, Seek and Ye Shall Find,
Knock and It Shall Be Opened unto You!
Matthew 7:7

I Am The Resurrection, and The Life;
He That Believeth In Me, Though He Were Dead,
Yet Shall He Live! "Jesus Christ" John 11:25

By: Don Diaz

Prayers and Poems to God by Don Diaz

1. Sound The Alarm!
2. Prayer to be with Jesus
3. Servants Prayer
4. Prayer to God
5. Prayer Warriors
6. Prayer for God's Help
7. Questions
8. A Heart for God
9. A Living Sacrifice
10. A Holy Man of Prayer
11. The Power of Prayer
12. A Man of God
13. God's Champion
14. Called by God
15. Hope for the Hopeless
16. Are You Ready?
17. Hallowed Be Thy Name
18. God Help America
19. I Hate Sin
20. Judgment Day
21. Marriage Supper of the Lamb
22. Which Path?
23. Prayer for Lost Souls!
24. Our Heavenly Father
25. Battle Prayer!
26. Thy Perfect Will
27. Who Will Fight For God?
28. Latenight Prayers
29. Prevailing Prayer
30. Prayer for Holiness
31. The Battle of Good and Evil
32. The Path to Heaven
33. The Holy Judge
34. Prayer for Holy Fire
35. The Crucifixion of Jesus Christ
36. The Anointed Messiah
37. No Sunday Christian
38. Tried and Tested
39. My Closest Friend
40. Trust in God
41. Prayer for Strength
42. Together for Eternity
43. One Day
44. Live Through Me
45. The Victory is God's
46. Forever Worthy!
47. Jesus is the One and Only Way!
48. Heavens Gates
49. The Battle is Won!
50. Our God is a Consuming Fire!

To all my Beloved Brothers and Sisters in Christ Jesus, Across America and throughout the whole World. Who Trust and Believe in our Lord and Savior, Jesus Christ; in truth and sincerity. Who Believe God's Word "The Holy Bible" is <u>Completely and Totally</u> <u>True</u>!!! Fervently with a Pure Heart; who Do God's Perfect will! To <u>All</u> who wait patiently with Prayer and Fasting, the coming of Jesus Christ!   All these Writings were Born in Prayer and Holy Ghost Fire!!! Almighty God gets all the Praise! Without <u>God</u> none of this would be possible! **"Hallelujah" "Glory to God in the Highest"**   Jesus Christ's Servant,

Don Diaz

Sound The Alarm!

O' Watchman, Watchman, Up On The Wall;
                                   Blow Thy Trumpet, Sound The Call!
Till All The Earth Can Hear The Cry,
                                   Judgment Day Is Drawing Nigh!
The Kingdom Of Heaven Is At Hand,
                                   For **Jesus** You Must Make Your Stand!
Repent, Repent, From Every Sin,
                                   So Heaven, You Can Enter In!
Do God's Will, Obey His Word;
                                   To Do, Not Just Hear, The Truth You've Heard!
Holy, Holy, God Most High;
                                   Hath No Pleasure When The Wicked Die!
He Sent **Jesus Christ**, To Set Us Free;
                                   He Is The Only Way, For You And Me!
Judgment, Judgment, Drawing Nigh;
                                   The Wicked Gnash Their Teeth And Cry!
The Lake Of Fire Lies In Wait,
                                   For Evil Men Of Sin And Hate!
Repent, Repent, Please Make Your Stand;
                                   The Kingdom Of Heaven Is At Hand!

"Blow Ye the Trumpet in Zion!" "Sound the Alarm in my Holy Mountain!" "Let all the inhabitants of the land tremble! The Great and Terrible day of the Lord commeth, for it it nigh at hand!" {Joel 2:1}
"From that time, Jesus began to preach, and to say, Repent: for the kingdom of Heaven is at Hand." {Matthew 4:17}
"Not every one that saith unto me, Lord, Lord, shall enter into Heaven, but he that does the will of "God" my Father! But be ye Doers of the word, and not Hearers only, deceiving your own selves." {Matthew 7:21 & James 1:22}
"And they were judged every man according to their works. And whosoever was not found written in the Book of Life, was cast into the Lake of Fire! {Revelations 20:13 & 15}

"For the time is come that Judgment must begin at the House of God! And if it first begin with us, what shall the End be of them, that Do Not obey the gospel of God? And if the righteous scarcely be saved! Where shall the ungodly and the sinner appear? {1 Peter 4:17}
"The Lord Jesus shall be Revealed from Heaven with his mighty Angels, in flaming Fire, taking vengeance on them that Do not know God, or obey the Gospel of Jesus Christ! Who shall be punished with Everlasting Destruction! {2 Thessalonians 1:7}

Almighty Gods Watchman,
                         Don Diaz

Prayer to be with Jesus

I Ask You Not For Riches Lord,
                              Neither For Fortune or Fame.
But To Be With You, In Gods Kingdom;
                              And To Praise Your Holy Name!
No Treasure, Earth Could Ever Hold;
                              Or Prize That Man Can Own.
Compares To You, You Are The One;
                              Your Presence is My Home!
There, In All Your Awesome Might;
                              Your Power and Your Glory.
I'll Bend My Knees and Tremble,
                              There Before the Lord of Glory!
For Many Long Years I've Waited Lord;
                              To Look Into Your Eyes.
To Thank You For Your Love,
                              And Grace & Mercy in my Life!
If the Prayer of Just this Humble Man,
                              Can Bring Joy to my Lords Heart!
I Gladly Offer Up My Prayer,
                              With Praise and Thanks of Heart!

To The One, Hell and Death Could <u>Not</u> Hold!
                                            "Jesus Christ"

"I go to prepair a place for you, and I will come Again and recieve You unto Myself; That where I Am, There Ye may be also."
{John 14:3}   "Jesus Christ"

                                  Thy Humble Servant,
                                            Don Diaz

Servants Prayer

O'Jesus Lord, Thou Great High Priest;
        I Pray To Be The Very Least!
To Kneel and Wash My Brethrens Feet;
        And Be A Man of God Complete!
Full of Thy Spirit, and Thy Power;
        To Be Prepaired at Every Hour!
So When You Lord, Do Split the Skys,
        I Won't Be Taken By Suprise.
But With My Candle Burning Bright,
        Your Everlasting Holy Light!
Clothed in White, And Unashamed;
        To Speak Thy Precious Holy Name!
Founded on Thy Solid Rock,
        From Which No Storm Could Ever Knock!
To Through Thy Holy Fire, Stand;
        And Enter in The Promised Land.
To Worship You At Thine Very Throne,
        Forever Mine Eternal Home!

        Almighty Gods Servant,
                Don Diaz

Prayer to God

Thou Most High God of Holiness,
        Thine Precious Name my Lips do Bless!
Send Holy Fire Down on Me,
        Burn Any Part That's Not Like Thee!
My Heart, My Lips, My Tongue, My Love;
        Till I Reflect Thee, Up Above.
Till I Am Dead, Upon the Cross;
        And Jesus is Both Lord and Boss!
Till in my Heart, Thine Light Doth Dwell;
        And Burn it in the Face of Hell!
Till Satan Walks Away in Shame;
        Unable to cause me, To curse thy Name.
Behold, I Pray Both Day and Night;
        Illuminate Me, With Thy Light!
Endue with Power, From on High;
        For Souls of the Lost, I Plead and Cry!
Look right here Lord, Look and See;
        The Gap is where I Long to Be!

Job 1:8-12, 2:5
Ezekiel 22:30

        Jesus Christ's Servant,
                Don Diaz

Prayer Warriors

O'Where are the Men, Who Refuse to Sin;
                                                And Resist the Devil down Bold!
Who Follow the Lord, and Desire his Ways;
                                                More than all Silver and Gold!
Who Pray Down the Fire, of Holy Desire;
                                                And Tear Down the Very Gates of Hell!
Whom Demons Proclaim, And Call out His Name;
                                                And Say "I Know This Man as Well."
Who march through the Land, With Gods Sword in their Hand;
                                                And Set the Captives All Free!
Who Fight for the Lost, No Matter the Cost;
                                                Although Trials and Persecution there Be!
Who Victoriously Win, Overcoming this World and its Sin;
                                                And Before Whom, the Devil Doth Flee!
Who Shine The Lords Light, In the Darkest of Night;
                                                Lord Jesus, Please Make One of Me!

"Upon This Rock I Will Build My Church, And The Gates of Hell Shall Not Prevail Against It!"
{Matthew 16:18}   "Jesus Christ"

"And there appeared unto them Cloven Tongues of Fire, And it Sat Apon Each of them;
And They Were All Filled With The Holy Ghost"   {Acts 2:3-4}

"Submit yourselves unto God;   "And the Evil Spirit Answered and said,
Resist the Devil, and He Will   "Jesus I Know, And Paul I Know"
Flee from You" {James 4:7}   But Who Are <u>Ye</u>?" {Acts 19:15}

Jesus Christ & Almighty God's Servant,
                                                Don Diaz

Prayer For Gods Help

O' God my Father of the Light,
                Please Storm the Gates of Hell Tonight!
It's not by Power, nor by Might;
                But by Thy Spirit Wins the Fight!
Please Send Thine Holy Fire Down,
                and Burn the Altar to the Ground!
Till Not One Single Priest of Baal,
                Against thy People doth Prevail.
Lord Jesus Died on Calvary,
                And Shed His Blood to Set Us Free!
Then He Rose on the Third Day,
                And Opened up a Strait True Way.
So Loosen stiff necks, And Soften hard hearts;
                Make Blindness From our Eyes Depart!
Please Cause our Ears to Hear thy Word,
                And Understand What We Have Heard!
I Will Not Cease To Pray for Light,
                Till Thou Set Free more Souls this Night!
Ten Legions of Angels I ask of Thee,
                To Fight and set more Captives Free!
God Rend The Heavens and Come Thou Down,
    Till The Mountains Flow Away and the Lost Be Found!
In Jesus Name I Ask and Plea,
                Please Draw Lost Souls "God" unto Thee!
To The Great "I AM" Father God,
                Thy Servant, Don Diaz

Questions ?

Are The Demons Afraid, When You Fall On Your Knees?
Do They Sit Back and Laugh, Full of Comfort and Ease?
Are You So Full of Sin, God Won't Move on Your Prayers?
Does It Sound Good Down Here, But Go Undone Up There?
Do You Walk Just Like Jesus? Are Lost Souls Your Desire?
Do You Tear Down Hells Gates, Full of Holy Ghost Fire?
Do You Do Gods Perfect Will? Is the Father Well Pleased?
Do The Demons All Flee When You Fall On Your Knees?
Do You Fight For Gods Kingdom?
                             Are You Feared Down in Hell?
If Satan Were Questioned, <u>Your</u> Name Would He Tell?
Well One Thing's For Certain, Gods <u>Fire</u> Will Tell!
       If You Fought For Heaven, Or You Fought For Hell!
Just One Last Question, I Will Ask Of Thee.
               That Question Is, Whose Servant Are Ye?

"Now there was a day when the sons of God came to present themselves before the lord, and Satan came also among them. And the Lord questioned Satan, saying to him; "Have you considered my servant Job? That there is none like him in the earth, a perfect and upright Man. One that fears God, and escheweth (Avoids) Evil." {Job 1:6-8}

"The Lord is far from the wicked; but he heareth the Prayer of the righteous" {Proverbs 15: 29}

"The Eyes of the Lord are over the Righteous, and his Ears are open unto their Prayers: but the face of the Lord is Against them that <u>Do</u> <u>Evil</u>! { 1 Peter 3:12}

"Every Man's work shall be made Manifest: for the day shall declare it, because it shall be revealed by Fire; and the <u>Fire</u> shall try every man's work of what sort it is. If any man's work abide which he hath built in Christ, he shall receive a reward. If any Man's work shall be burned, he shall suffer loss: but he himself shall be saved, yet so <u>as</u> <u>by</u> <u>Fire</u>!" {1Corinthians 3:13}

The effectual fervent prayer of a Righteous man Availeth much! {James 5:16}

Almighty Gods Servant,
                Don Diaz

A Heart For God

Great Father God in Heaven, Lord; Please Hear My Prayer To You.
Create In Me, A Heart O' God; That's Holy, Pure and True!
A Heart That Can't Be Sifted, A Heart That Will Not Fail!
A Heart That Loves You Without End, A Heart That Will Prevail!
A Heart That Fights All Evil, A Heart That Will Not Sin!
A Heart That Treasures Heaven Above, and Your Holy Spirit Within!
A Heart That Seeks You Always, A Heart That Loves Your Ways!
A Heart To Stand Your Test O'God, And Still Will Give You Praise!
A Heart That's Always Diligent, A Heart That Loves Your Word!
A Heart That Studies Day & Night, And Lives The Truth I've Heard!
A Heart That Stands Through Fire, Consumed By Love For You!
A Heart That Last The Test Of Time, No Matter What You Do!
A Heart That' Full Of Mercy, A Heart That's Full Of Grace!
A Heart That"s Washed In Jesus Blood, And Longs to See His Face!
A Heart That Fears No Evil, A Heart That Trust In You!
A Heart That Loves Your Holy Fire, Cleansing Through & Through!
A Heart That's Soft Before You , A Heart that Does your Will!
A Heart That Does Your Perfect Plan, Forever To Fulfill!
A Heart That Hold's No Hatred, A Heart That Will Forgive!
A Heart That Longs To Be With You, For All The Days I Live!
A Heart That Gives <u>You</u> Glory, Through Every Trial By Fire!
A Heart To <u>Praise</u> You Without End, This Is My Hearts Desire!

Ye Hypocrites, well did Isaiah prophesy of you, Saying;"This people draweth nigh unto me with their mouth, But their <u>Hearts</u> are <u>far</u> from <u>Me</u>!" But in vain do they worship me, Teaching for doctrines the commandments of men.
{Matthew 15:7-9}   "Jesus Christ"

"Blessed Are The Pure In Heart, For They Shall <u>See God</u>!"
"Jesus Christ" {Matthew 5:8}

Heavenly Father, <u>You</u> are my Heart!
Jesus Christ's Servant,

Don Diaz

A Living Sacrifice

Almighty God in Heaven, Lord;
                        Please Hear My Prayer Tonight!
I Tell You Lord, With All My Heart:
                        I Want To <u>Do</u> It <u>Right</u>!
I Want To Speak With Boldness,
                        Every Word You Want Me To!
And Not to Do or Say Lord,
                        Any Thing That Won't Please You!
I Want My Prayers Lord,
                        Crystal Clear and Pure Before Your Throne!
As if You Wrote Them Down for Me,
                        And I Spoke Them as Your Own!
Please Take the Coals From Off Thine Altar,
                        And Touch My Lips and Heart.
Please Fill Me With Thy Holy Spirit,
                        And Set my Life Apart!
Forge Me By Thy Mighty Hand,
                        The Very Man That You Have Planned.
My Life Upon Your Altar Lay,
                        In Your Image Make Me, Lord I Pray!

I Saw the Lord sitting upon a throne, High and lifted up; and his train filled the Temple! Above it stood the seraphims with six wings each, covering their faces and feet. And one cried to another and said; Holy, Holy, Holy, is the lord of Host. The whole earth is full of his Glory. The post of the door moved and the house was filled with smoke. Then I said, woe is me, I am undone, for I am a man of unclean lips, and mine eyes have seen the King. Then flew one of the seraphims unto me with a live coal from off the altar in his hand. And he laid it upon my mouth, and said; lo, this hath touched thy lips; and thine iniquity is taken away, and thy sin purged. {Isaiah 6:1-7}

I beseech you therefore brethren, by the mercies of God,
That ye present your bodies a Living Sacrifice, Holy
Acceptable unto God." {Romans 12:1}

                        Jesus Christ Servant,
                              Don Diaz

A Holy Man of Prayer!

Although I Preach A Thousand Sermons, Satan Doth Not Care!
      As Much As He Fears One Single Night, A Holy Man In Prayer!
And Though I See Ten Million Faces, And Reach The Ears of Man!
      My Words Are Dead And Powerless, Without God's Mighty Hand!
And Though I Teach Every Single Scripture, The Holy Bible Said!
Unless They Are Brought To Life By God,
      Every Single Word Is Dead!
Until I Do The Will of God, And Pray God's Fire Down!
My Words Will Fall Dead Off My Lips,
      And Plummet To The Ground!
Unless My Life, I Live In True Holiness;
      And Purity In My Heart!
My Words Will Be Blanks That Make A Noise,
      But Never Hit The Mark!
Unless There's Fire In My Bones,
      And God Sends His Spirit Down!
I Can Yell And Scream At The Top of My Lungs,
      But No Lost Souls Will Be Found!
And You May Not Agree With This, But Here I Make My Stand!
      It's Better To Reach The Ears of God, Than A Million Ears of Man!
Although I Preach A Thousand Sermons, Satan Doth Not Care!
      As Much As He Fears One Single Night, A Holy Man in Prayer!

"Not By Might, Not By Power, But By My Spirit, Saith The Lord of Host" {Zechariah 4:6}

Who also hath made us able ministers of the new Testament; not of the letter, but of the Spirit, for the letter killeth, but the Spirit giveth Life!
{2 Corinthians 3:6}

"Now when Solomon had made an end of Praying, the Fire came down from heaven, and the glory of the Lord filled the house. and the priest could not enter the house because of the glory of the lord. And all Israel saw the Fire and the Glory fill the Lords house, And they bowed themselves with their faces on the ground to the pavement and Worshipped." {2 Chronicles 7:1}

Jesus Christ's Servant & God's Intercessor,

      Don Diaz

The Power of Prayer

Under Starlit Night, The Battle I'll Fight:
                                        And Cry Out To The Lord!
Till Lightning Throws, And Thunder Blows;
                                        And He Unsheathes His Mighty Sword!
Till Chains He'll Smack, And Shackles Crack;
                                        And The Captives Are Set Free!
Till Demons Flee In Misery, And Race Into The Sea!
Till Jesus Blood, His Precious Blood; Covers Me Head To Toe!
Till Sin Is Gone, And There Is Not One;
                                        Not Washed as White as Snow!
Till God Will Hear Me Crystal Clear,
                                        And His Spirit Fills My Soul!
Till His Fire Falls And Purifies All,
                                        No Spot That's Not Made Whole!
Till Obedience Grows And Holiness Glows;
                                        And My Father Is Well Pleased!
Till Satans Calls and Accusations Fall,
                                        He'll Have No Place In Me!
Till Jesus Comes, Gods Holy Son;
                                        In Whom I Trust My Soul!
Till He Carries Me, Forever Free;
                                        To Gods Eternal Home!

    To The Messiah, Jesus Christ,
    and Our Father God in Heaven,
                                Thy Humble Servant,
                                            Don Diaz

A Man Of God!

Thou One True Living God Most High,
                                              In Jesus Name, Please Hear My Cry!

With Holy Ghost Fire, Mine Heart Thou Fill;
                                              Till I Live And Breath, To Do Thy Will!

A Burning and A Shining Light,
                                              To Brighten The Darkest, Blackest Night!

A Man Of God, Holy, Pure And True;
                                              So When They Look at Me, They Only See You!

A Light That Brightens All The World,
                                              Every Man and Woman, Every Boy and Girl.

A Holy Light Before Their Eyes,
                                              That Exposes All of Satan's Lies!

A Man Of God That Feeds Thy Sheep,
                                              Pure Holy Words, Their Souls to keep!

Every Thought Into Captivity,
                                              The Obedience of Christ Thou Forge in Me!

Precept Upon Precept, Line Upon Line;
                                              Till With Pure Clean Heart, Thine Light Doth <u>Shine</u>!

To <u>Do</u> And <u>Teach</u> Thy Commandments All,
                                              To Rich or Poor, To Great Or Small!

To Bear Much Fruit From Every Tree
                                              And Glorify <u>God</u>, For All To See!

To Let No Evil Leave My Tongue,
                                              It Will Grieve Thee God, And Hurt Thy Young!

To Love Thy Brethren Fervently,
                                              So the World Can "Jesus Disciples" See!

"Ye are the light of the world, A city that is set on a hill cannot be hid. Let your light so shine before men, That they may see your good works And glorify your Father which is in heaven."
"Jesus Christ" {Matthew 5:14}

Almighty God's Servant, Don Diaz

God's Champion

Almighty God, for whom I Stand,
                 Unsheath Your Sword With Mighty Hand!
Set The Battle In Array,
                 And Remove The Giants Head Today!
Though I Walk Through The Vally of the Shadow of Death,
                 I Do Not Fear The Face of Death!
Lord <u>Jesus</u> Is My Strenth And Shield,
                 <u>God's</u> Holy Spirit <u>Rules</u> The Field!
<u>NO</u> Wepon Formed, Can Face Thy Light!
                 Jesus Put To <u>Shame</u> The Army of Night!
Satan, He Shall Feel The Sting,
                 of Jesus Christ Sword; The King Of KINGS!
The Host of Demons Run and Flee;
                 Their Leader <u>Slain</u>, The Captives Set FREE!
Before God's Throne, I'll Worship and Praise;
                 Ten Million, Billion, Trillion Days!
O'Grave Where IS Thy Victory?
                 O'Death Where IS Thy Sting?
Both Hell And Death Are Swallowed UP;
                 By My LORD And KING!
To The Mighty Lamb of GOD, Jesus Christ,
Who Took the Keys of Hell and Death From Satan;
And <u>Rose</u> Again, Because it was <u>Never</u> Possible that
<u>Death</u> or the <u>Grave</u> Could <u>Hold</u> <u>Him</u>! For HE ALONE
Could <u>Take</u> The Book of <u>Life</u> From GOD'S Hand,
And Brake Loose The Seven Seals Thereon! AMEN!
                 Jesus Christ's Humble Servant,
                         Don Diaz

Called By God

One Night A Young Man Sat Alone,
        In The Back Yard Of His Chalmette Home.
When The Holy Spirit, Spoke Inside;
        "I AM GOD" His Voice Replied!
"I AM REAL and YOU ARE HEALED,"
        Gods Holy Spirit Then Revealed!
That Night, That Young Man's Life Was Changed;
        And He Would <u>Never</u> Be The Same!
Thousands of Prayers, He'd Weep and Pray;
        And Send Them Up To God Each Day.
Repenting Sincerely, From Every Sin;
        Untill There Was Not One Within.
Crying Out To God Each Night,
        For Your Kingdom Lord, I Want To Fight!
The Gates of Hell, They <u>SHALL NOT STAND</u>!
        While There is Breath Within This Man!
Lord Jesus Died, To Set <u>US FREE</u>!
        Lord Jesus, I Give My <u>Life</u> To Thee!

" Who hath believed our report? And to whom is the arm of the Lord revealed?" {Isaiah 53;1}

"But His Word Was in Mine Heart as a Burning Fire Shut Up In My Bones!" {Jeremiah 20:9}

"Let Every Thing That Has Breath Praise the Lord, Praise Ye The Lord" {Psalm 150:6}

"Fear not, little flock: For it is your Father's good pleasure to give you the Kingdom" {Luke 12:32}

"As he saith also in Isaiah," I will call them my people, which were not my people. And it shall come to pass, there shall they be called the children of the living God." {Romans 9:25} {Isaiah 65:1}

to the Risen Savior, Jesus Christ;
now seated at the right hand of God;
and our Father God, the Great "I AM"
Thy Humble Servant,

        Don Diaz

Hope For The Hopeless

Has Your Body Been Eaten By Cancer?
                                  Or Maybe You're Getting Old And Gray.
My Friend I Don't Care What Problem Your Facing,
                                  I Tell You There's A Beautiful New Day!
Do You Feel Like Your Lost Hurt And Lonely,
                                  Like No One In The World Seems To Care.
Get Down on Your Knees, And Cry Out To God;
                                  I <u>Guarantee</u> You, He Really Is There!
Have You Lost A Close Friend Or A Loved One?
                                  For Your Pain, Is There No End In Sight?
Please Know There's A Bright And Glorious Day,
                                  At The End Of Each Long Dreadful Night.
God <u>Sees</u> Every Trial You Are Facing,
                                  He <u>Feels</u> Every Pain In Your Heart.
God <u>Wants</u> You To Know, That When This Life's Over;
                                  It's Not Just The End, It's The <u>Start</u>!
You See <u>Jesus</u> "Really Is" The Messiah!
                                  There's A Heaven, It <u>Really Is True</u>!
I Have Seen Jesus Christ, I Have Seen The New World;
                                  And He's Coming Back One Day For You!
So If You Think That Your Life Is All Over,
                                  And That All You Have Waiting Is Death.
There's Eternal Salvation, In The Mighty <u>Son</u> Of God!
                                  <u>In</u> Him There Is <u>LIFE</u> Over <u>DEATH</u>!

"Let not your heart be troubled, ye believe in God, believe also in Me. In my Fathers house are many mansions: I go to prepare a place for you. I <u>will</u> come again, and receive you unto myself; that where I am, there ye may be also" "Jesus Christ" {John 14:1}
It Is <u>Impossible</u> for God to lie! {Hebrews 6:18}

"I am the <u>Resurrection</u>, and the <u>Life</u>!" He that <u>Believeth</u> in <u>Me</u>, though He were Dead; yet shall He <u>Live</u>!" "Jesus Christ" {John 11:25}

Almighty God's Servant,
                            Don Diaz

Are You Ready ?

One Day They Will Lower, Your Body into the Ground!
And even if you've made billions,"with you" not a penny will be found!
Your House, Your Boat and Car, will all be Worthless as the Dust!
On that Day You'll Realize, It was in God you should have Trust!
But did you live God's holy word, or did you mock and curse his name?
Will you stand clean before his throne, or stink of Sin and Shame?
Did you Serve the Mighty Lord Jesus,
        Full of Gods Holy Cleansing Fire?
Or Did You Serve Evil Satan,
        That Thieving Sin Filled Liar?
Did You Stand for Truth and Love,
        And God's Pure Holy Light?
Or Did you Stand for Evil and Lies,
        And Wickedness in the Night?
Did You Fight for God's Holy Kingdom,
        And Worship God on his Throne?
Or Did You Fight for Evil Cursing and Hatred,
        And Satan as his Own?
And as You Go Into the Ground,
        Will You THEN Try to Scream and Yell?

"PLEASE GOD, GIVE ME ANOTHER CHANCE"
        "I DON'T WANT TO BURN IN HELL!!!"

   Jesus Christ and Almighty God's Servant,
             Don Diaz

Hallowed Be Thy Name

Almighty, Holy, God Most High:
>> Creator Of The Earth and Sky!
The Universe, From End To End;
>> At Thy Word The Heavens Rend!
Beneath Thy Feet, The Mountains Shake;
>> At Thy Presence, The Earth Doth Quake!
Thy Lightning Reacheth Across The Sky,
>> Mere Fingertips Of El-Shaddai!
As Thunder Roars, Thy Mighty Power;
>> Satan And His Demons, Tremble And Cower!
O'Father God, Thou Great I AM;
>> <u>NO</u> <u>ONE</u> Can Stay Thine Awesome Hand!
Nothing In Existence, Compares With Thee;
>> Throughout All Of Eternity!
Arch-Angels Bow, Before Your Glory;
>> The Whole Earth Knows Your Sons True Story!
He Died On The Cross, And Has Risen Again!
>> He Ascended into Heaven at Your Right Hand!
Jesus Christ Put Satan, To Open Shame!
>> Lord Hallowed Be Thy Holy Name!

~ Almighty God ~ Elohim ~
To Adonai-Yahweh (Lord Jehovah),
& His Son Jesus Christ (Messiah);

>> Thy Humble Servant,
>> Don Diaz

God Help America!

The Evil Vile Filth of America, Hath Piled up to God on High!
The Wicked Preachers Teach that "Sin is O.K.", I Hang my Head and Cry!
As Gays and Lesbians Stand up in the Pulpit, and say "I Walk with God."
And Bring Upon Us Swift Destruction, You Unholy Reprobate Clod!
Our Bankers Steal From the Poor and Homeless, with just one stroke of the Pen!
They Destroy Our Banks And Institutions, But take Million Dollar Bonuses In!
We have Murdered over Fifty Million Babies, and throw their small bodies away!
Those Evil Doctors and Mothers Will All, Stand Before God one Day!
As Alcohol Flows through Millions of Homes, From Countless Liquor Stores!
With Drugs and Pills and the Millions it Kills, Car crashes and Overdoses Galore!
All the Evil Lies and Four letter Words, That Spew out from our Tongues!
And Yet We Look Puzzled at the next Generation, and say;
"What's happened to our Young?"
As Adultery and Fornication Rage, Nothing is Sacred in Our Eyes!
And Yet We wonder Why Our Marriages Fail? People It Is No Surprise!
As Sex and Lust Fill Our T.V. Screens, and Pornography Rages Strong!
Countless Little Children are Abducted and Killed, America It Won't Be Long!
It Won't Be Long Before Almighty God, Brings Swift Destruction from on High!
But Still The Evil Preachers Teach "Sin is O.K.", I Fall To My Knees and Cry!

Now, thou son of man, wilt thou judge, wilt thou judge the bloody city? yea, thou shalt shew her all her abominations. Then say thou, Thus saith the Lord God, The city sheddeth blood in the midst of it, that her time may come, and maketh idols against herself to defile herself. Her Priest have violated my law, and have profained mine holy things: They have put no difference between the Holy and the profane, neither have they shewed the difference between the unclean and the clean. They have hid their Eyes from my commandments, and I am Profained among them. In thee Have they taken gifts to shed blood; thou has taken usury and increase, thou hast greedily gained of thy neighbours By extortion, and hast forgotten Me, saith the Lord God. Thou art become guilty in thy blood that thou hast shed; and hast defiled thyself in thine Idols which thou hast made; and thou hast caused thy days to draw near, and art come even unto thy years: Therefore I have made thee a reproach unto the heathen, and a mocking to all countries. Behold therefore I have smitten mine hand at thy dishonest gain which thou hast made, and at thy blood which hath been in the midst of thee. Can thine heart endure, or can thine hands be strong, in the days that I shall deal with thee?
" I the Lord God have spoken it, and will do it!"   {Ezekiel 22:2-4, 12-14, 26}

"Thou shall not lay with mankind,
as you do with womankind, (men with men)"   "Be ye Holy, For I am Holy" {1 Peter 1:16}
"It is an Abomination!" {Leviticus 18:22}

Jesus Christ and Almighty Gods servant,

Don Diaz

I Hate Sin!

I Hate Every Sin O'Lord, I Hate It With All My Might!
Because It Separates Me From <u>You</u>! I Want Your Holy Light!
O'God, Please Cut Every Shackle of Sin;
                                                   Unchain Me From The Grave!
I Trust You Jesus, With All My Heart;
                                                   Because Only You Can Save!
Please Take Thy Holy Spirit Scalpel, Cut Evil O<u>ut</u> My Heart!
Give Me A Holy Heart of Flesh, This Stone One Must Depart!
Only thy mighty Holy Spirit, can tear these walls of Sin Down!
Sound thy Trumpet Seven Times, till not One Brick Is Found!
Take Thy Mighty Finger O'God,
                                               Engrave Your Name Upon My Heart!
Because I Belong To You O'God, Purify Me; Every Part!
Till No Devil or Demon in Hell,
                                             Can Keep Me From Doing Thy Will!
I Want To Walk Like Jesus, O'God;
                                             And Thine Every Word Fulfill!

"A New Heart also will I give you, And A New Spirit Will I Put Within You: And I Will Take Away The Stony Heart Out of Your Flesh, And I Will Give You A Heart of Flesh. And I Will Put My Spirit Within You, And Cause You To Walk In My Statutes, And Ye Shall Keep My Judgments, And Do Them."   {Ezekiel 36: 26-27}

"Ye Are Our Epistle Written in Our Hearts, Known and Read Of All Men: Forasmuch As Ye Are Manifestly Declared To Be The Epistle Of Christ Ministered By Us, Written Not with Ink; but with the Spirit of the Living God: not in Tables of Stone, but in fleshly Tables of the Heart. And Such Trust Have We Through Christ To God-ward."   {2 Corinthians 3:2-4}

"What? Know Ye not your body is the Temple of The Holy Ghost which is in You, Which Ye have of God, and Ye are not your own? For Ye are bought with a Price: therefore glorify God in Your Body, And In Your Spirit, Which Are God's."   {1 Corinthians 6:19-20}

                                            Almighty God's Servant,

                                                  Don Diaz

Judgment Day!

There is a Great and Mighty <u>God</u>, who rules from Heavens throne!
The Kingdom, Power and the Glory; Forever <u>He</u> Will Own!!!
The Angels and All the Host of Heaven, Bow down at His Feet!
One Day We <u>All</u> Shall also <u>Bow</u>, Before His Judgment Seat!!!
To Answer For All the Things We've Done, the Evil and the Good.
We'll wish that we could turn back time, and change it if we could!
Because there before Gods Awesome sight, No secret can be hid!
You see Gods Powerful Holy Light, Shows everything You Did!
You must Repent from Every Sin, and Believe in Jesus Name!
To let his <u>Blood</u> wash you Clean, or you'll stink of Sin and Shame!

    Heavens Gates Are Waiting,

                  For Those Who <u>Do</u> <u>Gods</u> <u>Will</u>!

    But Hell and Darkness Lie in Wait,

                  For Evil Men to Fill!!!

"Not every one that saith unto me, Lord, Lord; shall enter into the kingdom of Heaven; but <u>he</u> that doeth the will of my Father which is in Heaven" "Jesus Christ" {Matthew 7:21}

"For if ye live after the flesh, ye shall die:but if ye through the spirit do mortify the deeds of the body ye shall live. For as many as are led by the spirit of God, they are the sons of God." {Romans 8:13-14}

"Why call ye me, Lord, Lord; but do not <u>do</u> the things that I say? "Jesus Christ" {Luke 6:46}

"Walk in the spirit and ye shall not fulfil the lust of the flesh" {Galatians 5:16}

"Now the works of the Flesh are these; Adultery, fornication, uncleanness, lasciviousness; Idolatry, witchcraft, hatred, variance, emulations, wrath, strife, seditions, heresies; Envyings Murders, Drunkenness, revelings, and such like: of the which I tell you that they who <u>Do</u> such things as these, <u>shall</u> <u>not</u> Inherit the Kingdom of God." {Galatians 5:19-21}

Now to the Almighty, Immortal, Invisible, One True Living God;
The most powerful being in <u>all</u> of existence; creator of the universe!
Whose Kingdom goes on Forever! Be All Glory and Honor, Praise
and Holy Majesty for all of Eternity!   Jesus Christ Servant,
                "Amen"   Don Diaz

The Marriage Supper of the Lamb!

Glory, Glory, Hallelujah! I Give my Praise to Thee O' God!

    I am Going to a Marriage, in a <u>White</u> Wedding Garment Shod!

The Marriage Supper of the Lamb, in Heaven Up Above!

    Invited There by <u>God</u>, with His Grace, Mercy, and Love!

It Will Be an Awesome Feast, Such that has Never Been <u>Seen</u> Before!

    All the Saints of the Ages, will be Dancing on the Floor!

Elijah, Moses, Daniel, Look; There Goes The Apostle Paul!

    No Saint is Too Big or Great, and No Soul is Too Small!

We're One Big Happy Family, with Our Father <u>God</u> Above!

    Cleansed by <u>Jesus</u> <u>Blood</u>, His Grace, His Mercy, and His Love!

Come All, The <u>Way</u> is Opened Up, and <u>Jesus</u> is His Name!

    He Defeated Death and Darkness, and Put Them to Open Shame!

Come One, Come All, There's None to Small;

    Don't Be Shy or Awe Struck Smitten!

In God Our Father's <u>Book</u> of <u>Life</u>,

    Your Name It <u>Can</u> Be Written!

<u>All</u> of <u>Mankind</u> is Invited, and The Price It Has Been <u>Paid</u>!

    When Jesus Died Upon the Cross, and Then <u>Rose</u> from the <u>Grave</u>!

Almighty <u>God</u> and All His Angels, will Be There, in The Great Hall!

    The Seraphim's and Cherubim's, and King David at the Ball!

And You'll Find Me Near Jesus, I'll Be Worshiping at <u>His</u> Feet!

    Our Mighty Lord and Savior, has Made Me Whole, Pure, and Complete!

Or I Might Worship The Father First, Because <u>He</u> Sent Jesus Down!

    I'll Kneel Before <u>God's</u> Throne and Praise, and Toss <u>God</u> any Crown!

Glory, Glory, Hallelujah! I <u>PRAISE</u> <u>YOU</u> <u>GOD</u>, The Great <u>I AM</u>!!!

    We've Got an <u>Invitation</u> To The Marriage Of The <u>LAMB</u>!!!

He that <u>Overcometh</u>, the same shall be clothed in White Raiment, and I will <u>not</u> blot his name out of the book of <u>Life</u>, but I will confess his <u>name</u> before my <u>Father</u>, and before his Angels! "Jesus" {Revelations 3:5}

And having spoiled principalities and powers, he (Jesus) made a shew of them openly, triumphing over them in it! {Colossians 2:15}

The marriage of the Lamb is <u>come</u>! And his wife hath made herself ready. To her was granted that she should be in fine linen, clean and white! For the fine linen is the righteousness of saints. Write, blessed are they which are called unto the Marriage supper of the Lamb!!!

If we <u>Walk in the Light</u> as he (God) is in the Light, then the <u>blood</u> of Jesus Christ cleanses us from <u>all</u> <u>sin</u>! {Rev. 19:7 & 1 John 1:7}

God's Servant,

Don Diaz

Which Path?

So There are <u>Two</u> Paths Before You, Tell me which One will <u>You</u> Choose?

Only <u>One</u> Path Leads to Heaven, On the Other Path <u>You</u> Lose!

There are a Million Roads <u>to</u> Hell, But Not <u>One</u> Single Road Leads <u>Out</u>!

No Matter how much You Pray and Cry, or Yell, or Scream and Shout!

Almighty <u>God</u> is Inviting <u>You</u>, To Heaven Up Above!

And Jesus Christ is <u>Calling</u> You, with Grace, Mercy, and Love!

The Holy Spirit Comforts all, who accept Jesus Christ and Pray!

He Guides and Teaches about Jesus, those who Believe, Trust and Obey!

Because Broad is the Path that Leads to Destruction, where many will <u>Go In</u>!

It's the Path that's Filled with Lust and Greed, and Hate, and Death, and <u>Sin</u>!

Because <u>Narrow</u> is the Path and <u>Way</u> that Leadeth Thee to <u>Life</u>!

To the <u>Few</u> there be that Find it, Jesus <u>is</u> the Way to Life!

A Pharisee named Saul was Hell Bound, on the Damascus Road,

When Jesus appeared and said, It's Hard to Kick Against the Goad!

The Point, You <u>Cannot</u> Fight Against <u>God</u>, It's a Battle You Will <u>Lose</u>!!!

So Saul, This Road to Hell, How <u>Can</u> it be the One <u>You</u> Choose?

That Day Saul's <u>Heart</u> was Changed, Illuminated by <u>Jesus</u> Light!

He Became the Apostle Paul, and Began to for God's Kingdom Fight!

He Boldly followed Jesus, and Turned Millions of <u>Souls</u> Away from Hell!

So When <u>Your</u> Life is Over, What's the Story <u>It</u> will Tell?

You Too <u>Can</u> Change Your Path, So Tell Me <u>Which</u> <u>Path</u> will <u>You</u> Choose?

Only <u>One</u> Path Leads to Heaven, on the Other Path You <u>Lose</u>!

Enter ye in at the <u>strait</u> gate, for wide is the gate, and broad is the way, that leads to destruction; and many will go in that wide path! Because strait is the gate, and narrow is the way, which Leads unto Life, and few there be that <u>Find It</u>! "Jesus Christ" {Matt. 7:13} I am the Way, the Truth, and the Life! No Man can get to God the Father, but by <u>Me</u>! "Jesus" {John 14:6} So shall it be at the end of the world; the angels shall come forth, and remove the wicked from among the just; and shall cast them into the furnace of fire! And there shall be <u>wailing</u> and <u>gnashing</u> of teeth! "Jesus" {Matthew 13:49}

As I went to Damascus, I saw a Light from Heaven shining around me; and I heard a voice saying to me Saul, Saul, why persecutest thou me? It is hard for thee to kick against the pricks! (goad, pointed stick) And I said, Who art thou, Lord? And he said, I am Jesus whom thou persecutest! Rise, stand up, I have appeared unto thee for this purpose, to make you a minister and a witness to the gentiles. To open their eyes and turn them from darkness to light, and from Satan to God! So that they may receive forgiveness of sins, and sanctification, by Faith in Me! {Acts 26:12}

Almighty God's Servant,

Don Diaz

Prayer for Lost Souls!

Almighty God of Holiness that Lives Inside of Me,
        O'May I know what thou dost know, and see what thou dost see!
Ignite Your Fire in my Heart and Burn Within my Soul,
        God Breathe your Breath of Life in me, and take Complete Control!
Thy Holy Spirit Knows and See's the Hidden things of God,
        Illuminate your Light to me, Thy Perfect Will O'God!
My Holy Precious Savior, Praying in the Garden Lay,
        Upon his Face to set us Free and Open Up the Way!
O'May I Pray as He doth Pray, and Call God's Fire Down,
        to Ignite the Hearts and Souls of Men, Till God's Love doth Abound!
For 'Tis No Burden Too Great or Steep, to Carry for my God,
        and Take up my Cross where Jesus walked, is the way that I shall trod!
Upon the Mount of Transfiguration, with Burden am I Bound,
        To Lay Upon God's Altar, so that Lost Souls can be Found!
For 'Tis the Path Lord Jesus Took, Shall I Not Tread it Still,
        I'll Bend my Knees in Holy Prayer, and Do my Fathers Will!
To Stand Up in the Gap, so that Lost Souls can be Set Free,
        Please share with me thy Burden God, I'll Pray it Through to Thee!
Because my Prayers can Reach God's Ears, Hells Gates they Shall Not Stand!
        I'll Carry my Savior's Burden, for a Lost and Dying Land!

Know ye not that ye are the temple of God, and that the Spirit of God dwelleth in you? {1 Corinthians 3:16}

And I (God) looked for a man among them that should make up the hedge, and stand in the gap before me for the land, that I should not destroy it; but I found none! {Ezek 22:30}

Jesus breathed on them and said, "receive ye the Holy Ghost and power" when he is come upon you! {John 20:22 & Acts 1:8}

Jesus went to a place called Gethsemane and told his disciples, sit ye here while I go and pray yonder. And he went a little further and fell on his face and prayed! {Matthew 26:36}

Then Jesus taketh Peter, James, and John, and bringeth them up into a high mountain apart, and he was Transfigured before them, and his face did shine as the sun, and his raiment was as white as the Light! Upon this rock I will build my church, and the Gates of Hell shall not prevail against it! "Jesus Christ" {Matthew 17:1 & 16:18}

An angel came and stood at the altar, having a golden censer and much incense, that he should offer it with the prayers of all saints upon the golden altar which was before the throne; and the smoke of the incense with the prayers of the saints ascended up before God! {Revelation 8:3}

I exhort that first of all, prayers, intercessions, supplications, and giving of thanks be made For All Men! {1 Timothy 2:1}

To my Lord and Savior,
Jesus Christ, I Love You!
God's Servant,
Don Diaz

Our Heavenly Father!

O' Father God of All Creation, that made every Man, and Land or Nation!
I Praise Your Hallowed Name this Night, to Worship <u>You</u> is my Delight!
The <u>One</u> True Living <u>God</u> Above, of Holiness, Truth, Power, and Love!
All The Universe Shines Your Magnificent Glory,
           Your Precious Son Jesus preached the Gospel Story!
Peace on Earth, Good will towards Men, into Heaven above you can <u>Enter</u> In!
The Price <u>He</u> has Paid, Upon the Cross, to <u>Raise</u> the Dead, and <u>Save</u> the Lost!
Jesus Blood <u>Can</u> Cleanse the Blackest Soul,
           and Clothe them in <u>White</u>, and make them Whole!
The Holy Spirit of God above; will <u>Guide</u> you to Truth, Holiness, and Love!
Jesus Christ has Laid the <u>Eternal</u> <u>Foundation</u>,
           for Every Man, Woman, and Child, in any Country or Nation!
The Cornerstone of <u>Salvation</u>, come from Heaven Above,
           that showed <u>God</u> the Father's Grace, Mercy, and Love!
Jesus shed his Blood for <u>US</u>, and Died on the Cross,
           to Save Mankind from being, Eternally <u>Lost</u>!
<u>Resurrected</u> the Third Day, Jesus <u>Rose</u> from the Grave,
           He <u>Ascended</u> into Heaven, the Whole World to <u>Save</u>!
Lord Jesus, I Lift your name up on high, let all God's Saints, and Angels Cry!
We <u>Praise</u> you Lord Jesus, the Lamb of God! That takes the worlds <u>sins</u> away!
Glory to God in the Highest!!! Thy Kingdom <u>Come</u> Today! Amen & Amen!

In the beginning, God created the Heaven and the Earth. {Genesis 1:1}

From that time Jesus began to preach, and say, "Repent, for the Kingdom of Heaven is at Hand." {Matthew 4:17}

If we <u>walk</u> in the Light as <u>He</u> (God) is in the Light, the <u>blood</u> of Jesus Christ his son cleanses us from <u>all</u> <u>Sin</u>! Because your sins are forgiven you for his <u>name's</u> sake! {1 John 1:7 & 2:12}

The angel said, I know ye seek Jesus who was crucified, he is not here, for he has risen, as he said! Matthew 28:5

When the (Holy) Spirit of Truth is come, he will <u>guide</u> you into all <u>Truth</u>! "Jesus Christ" {John 16:13}

For <u>no</u> other foundation can any man lay, than the <u>one</u> that is laid, which is Jesus Christ! {1 Corinthians 3:11}

The stone which the builders rejected, (Jesus Christ) is become the head (cornerstone) of the corner! {Mark 12:10}

Then John seeth Jesus walking towards him and said, "Behold the Lamb of God, which taketh away the sin of the world!" {John 1:29}

God's Servant,

Don Diaz

Battle Prayer!

Almighty God of all Creation, O' Heavenly Father, Please Hear my Prayer to You! Thou One True Living God Most High, I ask you in the name of Jesus Christ, your Only Begotten Son! Please avenge me of my Enemy Satan! Curse Satan afresh and anew, this day, this hour, this very minute, this very second! O' Father God of Truth, and Power, and Might! Avenge me of every evil spirit in existence, and every single principality of evil, every single Spiritual Wickedness in high places, every single ruler of the darkness of this world and the prince of the power of the air! Curse them all afresh and anew, especially Satan! Curse them with a very, horrible, and terrible, painful, grievous, Powerful, Powerful; **Evil Destroying curse!** A dreadful curse that crushes the plots and plans of Satan, smashes all the works of hell and darkness, and tears down the very Gates of Hell; and **Delivers Lost Souls from Evil**, Sin, and all bondage! Deliver us from Evil O' my Father God, Free Lost Souls from all over the Planet Earth! **We Need You Almighty Father God!!!** Without you Great Jehovah God, we are Blind, and Miserable, and Naked, and Dead! We are Helpless without You, thou Great I AM, Father God of All Creation! WE - NEED - YOU - GOD!!! For it is Not by Might, it is Not by Power, But it is by Your Holy Spirit O' God!!! That sets the Captives Free! Through Faith in your son Jesus and his Resurrection from the Dead, and his Precious Holy Blood that Cleanses us from All Sin! O' God my Father, take your all Powerful hand, and wield your Mighty Sword in the Spirit and Cut through Chains of Sin, and Shackles of Iniquity and Set the Captives Free! In every Country, in every Nation, in every Color, in every Language on the Earth! You promised us in your word, O' God; that when the enemy comes in like a flood; that You would Lift up a Holy Standard Against him! We Trust You O'Father God! Lead us not into temptation, but deliver us from evil; for thine is the Kingdom, and the Power, and the Glory! For ever and ever! In Jesus Holy Name we Pray! Amen!

And Jesus told a Parable that men ought always to pray, and not to faint! There was a judge in a city that feared not God nor regarded man. And a widow in that city came to him saying, Avenge me of mine adversary!!! And he did not for a while, but then he thought, I fear not god nor regard man; Yet because this widow troubles me, I will avenge her, lest by her constant coming she weary me! Hear what the unjust judge said. And shall not God avenge his own elect, who cry day and night unto him? I tell you that he will avenge them speedily!!! {Luke 18:1-8} "And the Lord God told the serpent, thou art cursed!" {Gen. 3:14}

Truly, I say unto you, Whatsoever ye shall ask the Father in my name, he will (do it) give you! So far, you have asked for nothing in my name, ask and ye shall receive! {John 16:23} When the enemy shall come in like a flood, the Spirit of the Lord shall Lift Up a Standard Against him! {Isaiah 59:19} "It is not by Might, nor by Power, but by my Spirit, saith the Lord!" {Zechariah 4:6}

Jesus Servant,
Don Diaz

Thy Perfect Will

God I Want To <u>Do</u> Thy Perfect Will, I Am Not Here To Play Games!
When You Open Up The <u>Book</u> of <u>Life</u>, I Want To <u>Hear</u> My Name!
I Have Learned That Just One Single Sin, It Makes Me Deaf To You!
But When I Do Thy Perfect Will,
                         Your Voice Comes Scorching Through!
O'Holy Spirit Please <u>Search</u> My Heart, For the Things I Cannot See!
Please Burn Up Every Single Part, Until <u>Jesus</u> is Formed In <u>Me</u>!
God when I <u>Do</u> Thy Perfect Will, Your Flaming Holy <u>Fire</u> Falls Down!
And Makes My Prayers All Feared in Hell,
                         And Smashes Hell's Gates To The Ground!
Because When I Do Thy Perfect Will, God's Angels Stand And Cheer!
And the Demons Flee in Misery, Crying "The Man of God is Here!"
God When I Do Thy Perfect Will, I Am Unchained From the <u>Grave</u>!
And I Shine Your Light to All the World,
                         So That Lost Souls <u>Can</u> Be Saved!
O'God Within Your Perfect Will, Is Not <u>One</u> Single <u>Sin</u>!
And Heaven's Gates are Open Wide, as you say "Well Done, Come <u>In</u>!"
O'God, My Father, I Am Your Son, Send Your Holy Spirit Down!
     Until Within My Sanctified <u>Heart</u>, Your Perfect Will Is <u>Found</u>!

"And be not <u>conformed</u> to this world: but be ye transformed by the renewing of your <u>mind</u>, that ye may prove what is good, and acceptable and <u>Perfect</u> <u>will</u> of God." {Romans 12:2}
          "The Apostle Paul"
"That Ye May <u>Stand</u> <u>Perfect</u> and complete in all the <u>Will</u> of God." {Colossians 4:12}
"Make you perfect in every good work to <u>do</u> His Will." {Hebrews 13:21}

"Solomon my son, know thou the God of thy Father, and serve him with a <u>Perfect</u> <u>Heart</u> and a <u>willing</u> <u>mind</u>: for the Lord <u>searcheth</u> all <u>hearts</u>, and understandeth all imaginations of the thoughts of the <u>heart</u>: If thou <u>seek</u> him, He <u>will</u> be <u>found</u> of thee; but if thou <u>forsake</u> Him, He <u>will</u> <u>cast</u> <u>thee</u> <u>off</u> Forever!"
       "King David" {1 Chronicles 28:9}

Almighty God & Jesus Christ's Servant,

                                    Don Diaz

Who Will Fight For God?

Who Will <u>Wait</u> Before The Lord,
      And <u>Serve</u> Him Day And Night?
Who Will <u>Live</u> His Holy Word,
      And For His Kingdom Fight?
Who Will <u>Walk</u> In All His Ways,
      And <u>Overcome</u> This World?
Who Will Sing And <u>Give</u> Him <u>Praise</u>,
      And <u>Teach</u> The Boys And Girls?
Who Will <u>Break</u> The Devils Hold,
      And <u>Shine</u> <u>God's</u> Light To Men?
Who Will <u>Point</u> Them To The Lord,
      And <u>Lead</u> The Stray Sheep In?
Who Will <u>Stand</u> Up In The Gap,
      Although It's Deep And Wide?
Who'll Bend Their Knees In Holy Prayer,
      And <u>Climb</u> The Mountain Side?
Who'll Stand <u>Tall</u> When Others Fall,
      Through <u>Trials</u> And All Temptation?
And Be <u>Made</u> Into, A Christ Like <u>Man</u>;
      On The Mount Of <u>Transfiguration</u>!

"And I <u>sought</u> for a <u>man</u> among them, that should <u>make</u> up the hedge, and <u>stand</u> in the <u>Gap</u> before <u>me</u> for the <u>land</u>, That I should <u>not</u> <u>destroy</u> it:but I found <u>none</u>!" {Ezekiel 22:30}

"And after six days <u>Jesus</u> taketh with him Peter, James, and John, and <u>leadeth</u> <u>them</u> up unto a <u>high</u> <u>mountain</u> apart by themselves, and he was Transfigured before them." {Mark 9:2}

"Whosoever shall <u>Do</u> and <u>Teach</u> my commandments shall be called great in the kingdom of heaven!" "Jesus" {Matthew 5:19}

Almighty Gods Servant,
    Don Diaz

LateNight Prayers

Heavenly Father, Please Wake Me;
                        Any Hour of The Night!
For On My Knees, I'll Gladly Pray;
                        To, For Your Kingdom Fight!
You Have Done So Much, I Could Never Touch;
                        All That You Have Done For Me!
Your Precious, Holy Son Jesus;
                        Paid The Price On Calvary!
You Have Saved Me By Your Awesome Strength,
                        And Kept Me By Your Power!
Your Mighty Holy Spirit,
                        Guards My Soul At Every Hour!
Guards My Soul, From Hell and Death;
                        And Laughs Boldly At The Grave!
Jesus Washed Our Sin Away,
                        Untold Multitudes, He Did Save!
Great Lamb of God, Please Wake Me;
                        To, For Your Kingdom Fight!
I'll Gladly Bend My Knees and Pray,
                        Any Hour of The Night!

"Know Ye not that your body is the temple of the Holy Ghost, Which is in You; which ye have of God, and ye are not your Own? For Ye are bought with a Price: therefore glorify God in your body, and in your Spirit, Which are God's."
{1 Corinthians 6:19}   "The Apostle Paul"

"Grieve not the Holy Spirit of God, whereby Ye are sealed unto the day of redemption."
{Ephesians 4:30}

"To an Inheritance incorruptible, and undefiled, And that fadeth not away, reserved in Heaven for You; Who are kept by the Power of God through Faith unto salvation ready to be revealed in the last time."
{1 Peter 1:5}

Almighty God's Servant,

Don Diaz

Prevailing Prayer

Just like A Pointed Arrow,
                        My Prayer Seeks To God's Own Throne!
To The One True God of Holiness,
                        And His Son Jesus Christ, Alone!
Sharpened By My Obedience, To Do God's Perfect Will.
        Aimed By Grace and Mercy, God's Own Plan, Me To Fulfill.
Shot By The Fire and Love for God,
                        That Burns Within My Heart!
Washed By Jesus Own Blood,
                        That Makes it Pure, And Reach the Mark!
It Passes Through The Veil, That Jesus Ripped On Calvary!
Ripped By God's Own Love for Us,
                        So That We Could Be Set Free!
To The Only Wise God, Immortal, Invisible;
                        That Could Rule From Heaven's Throne!
To The Awesome God of Power and Glory,
                        The Kingdom, Forever, He Will Own!
To Worship and Praise, To Love and Adore,
                        Great Jehovah on This Hour!
To Thank Him For His Son, His Love,
                        And Holy Spirit Power!

"I indeed baptize you with water unto repentance: But he that cometh after me is mightier than I, Whose shoes I am not worthy to bear: He shall Baptize you with the Holy Ghost, and with Fire!"
"John the Baptist" {Matthew 3:11}

"Jesus, when he had cried again with a loud voice, yielded up the ghost. And behold, the veil of the Temple was rent in two from the top to the bottom; and the earth quaked, and the rocks rent!"
{Matthew 27:50}

To The One That Baptizes with the Holy Ghost,(and with Fire);
The Anointed One, Jesus Christ, (the Messiah) Lamb of God;
And Our Holy Father in Heaven, Almighty God,
                    Your Humble Servant,
                               Don Diaz

Prayer For Holiness

Jesus, Jesus, Lord of All;
                                      We Want To See Your Glory!
And Proclaim To All The World,
                                      Your Resurrection Story!
Please Purge Us, Cleanse Us, Purify Us;
                                      Ready For the Master's Use!
From Every Sin and Evil Thing,
                                      We Want To Be Set Loose!
Heavenly Father, Please Take Us Now,
                                  And Consume Us With Holy Ghost Fire!
Until With Pure and Sanctified Hearts,
                                    Your Will is Our Only Desire!
Holy Spirit, Lead Us Now;
                                    And Cleanse Us From Every Sin!
Until There's Not One Single Trace,
                                    Of Evil Left Within!

"If Ye love me, keep my commandments. If Ye shall ask any thing in my name, I will do it. And I will pray the Father, and he shall give you another comforter, that he may abide with you for ever; Even the spirit of Truth; whom the world cannot receive, because it seeth him not, neither knoweth him: but ye know him; For he dwelleth with you, and shall be in you." {John 14:14}

"When He, the Spirit of truth, is come; He will guide you into all truth. And when he is come, He will reprove the world of sin, and of righteousness, and of Judgment; Of sin because they believe not on me, of righteousness because I go to my Father, of judgment because the prince of this world is judged. {John 16:8}

To Our Heavenly Father, God, The Great I Am;
And His Son, Jesus Christ, The Messiah;
                                      Thy Servant,
                                        Don Diaz

The Battle of Good and Evil

When You Woke Up This Morning,
                Did You Know You Were in a Fight?
Between The Rulers of the Darkness,
                and The Almighty God of Truth and Light!
This Battle Rages Daily for Possession of Your Soul!
                The One That You Obey, is the One That Has Control.
Almighty God is Great and Powerful, He Will Always Win!
                But Unless We <u>Do God's Will</u>, "His Kingdom" We Can't Enter In!
Satan Knows, He Can't Beat God;
                So He Fights Against Us Instead!
To Pull Us From God's Holy Light,
                Into the Darkness of the Dead!
So God Has Sent His Holy Son, To Come and Set Us Free!
He Took the Keys of Hell & Death;
                He's the Way for You and Me.
Just Believe and Trust, In Jesus Christ;
                And Repent from Every Sin!
Because If You Believe and Do God's Will;
                <u>Heaven</u>, You Can Enter In!

"If thou shalt confess with thy mouth the Lord Jesus, and shalt believe in thine heart that God hath raised him from the dead, thou shall be saved. For with the heart man believeth unto righteousness; and with the mouth confession is made unto salvation. For whosoever shall call upon the name of the lord shall be saved." {Romans 10:9, 10 & 13}
"He that believeth on him is not condemned; But he that believeth not is condemned already, because he hath not believed in the name of the only begotten Son of God." {John 3:18}   "Jesus Christ"

"Not every one that saith unto me, "Lord, Lord," shall enter into the kingdom of Heaven; But he that <u>Doeth</u> the will of my Father which is in Heaven." {Matthew 7:21}   "Jesus Christ"
"Jesus answered them, "verily, verily, I say unto you "Whosoever committeth sin is the servant of sin." {John 8:34}
"Except a man be born again, He cannot see the Kingdom of God." {John 3:3}   "Jesus Christ"

Praise to the One True Living God, and his son Jesus Christ;
        God's Humble Servant,
                Don Diaz

The Path To Heaven

Although I Go Through Trial By Fire,
                                        Holy Spirit Lead Me Higher!
Through The Flames I Want to Stand,
                                        Forge Me Now By God's Own Hand!
Purer Than The Purest Gold,
                                        Lamb of God, Me to Behold!
For Me, No Other Path Can Be;
                                        But Up Mount Zion, Straight to Thee!
Although, This Path "The World" May Dread;
                                        This is Where My Master Tread!
I'll Bend My Knees, Endure The Pain;
                                        Knowing Jesus Did The Same!
Spotless Lamb Who Knew No Sin,
                                        So That We Could Enter In!
He Gave His Life, Embraced The Cross;
                                        So You and I Would Not Be Lost!
Look Not To The Left or Right,
                                        On Jesus Christ I've Set My Sights!
For The Prize, "I Know" You See;
                                        My "Lord and King" Waits There For Me!

"But this one thing that I do, Forgetting those things which are behind, and reaching forth unto those things which are before, **I Press Toward the Mark for the Prize of the high calling of God in Christ Jesus!** That I may know him, and the power of his Resurrection, and the fellowship of his Sufferings, being made conformable unto his death; If by any means I might attain unto the Resurrection of the dead." "The Apostle Paul" {Philippians 3:10-14}

Every man's work shall be made manifest: for the day shall declare it, because it shall be revealed by Fire; the Fire shall try every man's work of what sort it is. If any man's work abide which he hath built in Christ, He shall receive a reward. If any man's work shall be burned, he shall suffer loss: but he himself shall be Saved, yet so as by Fire! "The Apostle Paul" {1 Corinthians 3:13-15}

To Jesus Christ, The "Messiah" & "Great High Priest,"
And Our Holy Father God in Heaven,   Thine Humble Servant,
                                                                     Don Diaz

The Holy Judge

Jesus Christ the Righteous, Is About to Split the Skys!
And Catch this Whole Evil World, Completely by Surprise!
He's Filled with Holy Anger, and with Fire in His Eyes!
He'll Execute the Judgment, Exposing Every Sin and Lies!
The Evil Men will all Cry Out, with Fear in Their Voices!
But It will be to Late for Mercy,
                     They've Already Made Their Choices.
They Had the Chance to Repent,
                     But They Cursed and Mocked God Then.
So Now, Here at the Judgment;
                     They Have <u>No</u> Cover for Their Sins!
They Should Have Called on Jesus Christ,
                     To Wash Their Sins Away!
But the Judgment Gavel Falls, There Before Him on that Day!
"<u>Please</u> <u>Hear</u>," The Lord <u>IS</u> Coming; He's Holy, Just and True!
Repent Your Sins, and Serve the Lord; **Before He Judges You!**
         His Word is True and Holy, It Cuts Evil to The Bone!
But Those Found in His Righteousness,
                     Will Praise Him on His Throne!

"And the kings of the earth, and the great men, and the rich men, and the chief captains, and the mighty men, and every bondman, and every free man, hid themselves in the dens and in the rocks of the mountains; and said to the mountains and the rocks, fall on us, and hide us from the face of him that sitteth on the throne, and from the wrath of the Lamb: For the great day of his wrath is come; and who shall be able to stand? {Revelation 6:15-17}

"It is a Fearful thing to fall into the hands of the **Living God!**" {Hebrews 10:31}

"Knowing Therefore **The Terror of the Lord**, We persuade men!" Apostle Paul" {2 Corinthians 5:11}

"The word of God is Quick, and Powerful, sharper than any two edged sword, piercing even to the dividing asunder of the soul and spirit, and of the joints and the marrow, and is a discerner of the thoughts and intents of the heart."{Hebrews 4:11}

To the Holy, Mighty, Eternal;
Judge of all the World; "Jesus Christ"

Thine Humble Servant,
                 Don Diaz

Prayer For Holy Fire

On My Knees, Till Satan Flees;
                                      And God's Fire Falls From Heaven!
Thy Kingdom Come, Thy Will Be Done;
                                      Until My Hearts Unleavened!
The Gates of Hell, They Cracked and Fell;
                                      And Crushed Beneath My Feet!
My Hands I Raised, Jesus Name I Praised;
                                      God's Risen Son Elite!
The Mountains Shook, His Power Look;
                                      It Set's The Captives Free!
The Demons Flee, In Misery;
                                      And Race Into The Sea!
The Hearts Of Men, They Melt Within;
                                      Before God's Mighty Power!
Thy Spirit Lord, Unsheathe Your Sword;
                                      Set Free More Souls This Hour!
No Night Can Hide, Your Light Inside;
                                      Burn Bright Within My Soul!
The Heavens Rend, God's Fire Send;
                                      Give Jesus Full Control!

"This is the word of the Lord unto Zerubbabel, saying; Not By Might, Nor By Power, But By My Spirit; Saith The Lord of Host."   {Zachariah 4:6}

"For as many as are led by the Spirit of God, They are the sons of God." {Romans 8:14}

"Your Glorying is not good, Know Ye not that a little leaven leaveneth the whole lump? Purge out therefore the old leaven, That ye may be a new lump, as ye are unleavened. For even Christ our Passover is Sacrificed For Us.   {1 Corinthians 5:7-8}

"Oh that thou wouldest Rend the Heavens, that thou wouldest come down, that the mountains might flow down at thy presence, as when the melting fire burneth, to make thy name known to thine adversaries, that the nations may tremble at thy presence! {Isaiah 64:1-2}

Jesus Christ & Almighty God's Servant,

Don Diaz

The Crucifixion of Jesus Christ

See Him There Upon The Cross, Without Him All This World is Lost!
Precious Lamb of God Above, Who Died To Show The Fathers Love.
Love For All This Sinful World, Love For Every Boy and Girl.
He Took Our Stripes, He Bore Our Blame;
The Crown of Thorns, The Nails of Pain;
The Soldiers Struck His Holy Face!
Blows Meant For Us, He Took Our Place.
"Crucify Him" the Crowd Cried, They Stuck A Spear into His Side!
Precious Lamb Who Knew No Sin, So That We Could Enter In!
He Shed His Blood On Calvary, So You and I Could Be Set Free!
And Then He Rose on the Third Day, To Get to Heaven, He is the Way!
He Bore Our Sin, Our Guilt, Our Shame!
So We Could Praise God's Holy Name.
Then Heaven's Gates HE Opened Wide!
So That WE Could Walk Inside!
<u>NOW</u> See Him There, Upon The CROSS!
<u>WITHOUT HIM</u>, ALL OUR SOULS ARE LOST!

"He is despised and rejected of men; a man of sorrows, and acquainted with grief; and we hid our faces from him. He was despised, and we esteemed him not. But he was wounded for our Transgressions, He was bruised for our iniquities: the chastisement of our peace was upon him; And with his stripes we are Healed. All we like sheep have gone astray; we have turned every one to his own way; and the Lord hath laid on him the iniquity of us all." {Isaiah 53:3, 5 & 6}

I AM THE WAY, THE TRUTH, AND THE LIFE; NO MAN COMETH UNTO THE FATHER, <u>BUT BY ME</u>! {John 14:6}

"JESUS CHRIST"

To The Incredible, Mighty, Awesome, Powerful LAMB of GOD;
Who Took The Keys of Hell & Death! And Opened The Book of Life!
The King of KINGS, & Lord of LORDS!   "Jesus Christ"
I LOVE YOU!   Your Humble Servant,

Don Diaz

The Anointed Messiah

Mighty Lord Jesus, Great Son of God;
                                       I Praise and Worship You!
Because I Know That You Have Done,
                                       What **No Other Man** Could Do!
You Tore The Temple Veil In Two,
                                       And Opened Up The Way!
You Paid The Price on Calvary,
                                       NO ONE Else Could Ever Pay!
You Washed Us In Your Blood,
                                       And Made Us Clean Before God's Throne!
You Clothed Us With Your Righteousness,
                                       For We Have None of Our Own!
You Took The Keys of Hell & Death!
                                       And Set The Captives FREE!
You Have **Risen From The Grave O' Lord**,
                                       It Had NO Hold On THEE!
You Opened Up, The BOOK of LIFE;
                                       And Broke Loose The Seven Seals!
A Multitude of Names, Contained Inside;
                                       God's Kingdom To Reveal!
You Ascended Up To Heaven,
                                       And Now Sit at God's Right Hand!
The Resurrection, Life & Way, Into The Promised Land!
Jesus Christ & Almighty God's Humble Servant,
                                                                   Don Diaz

{Hebrews 1:3,1:13} {Acts 2:33-34, 7:55-56} {Mark 16:19} {Romans 8:34} {Ephesians 1:20}
{Colossians 3:1} {1 Peter 3:22} {Luke 22:69} {Matthew 26:64} *{Revelations 5:7}*

No Sunday Christian

Thou One True Living God Most High,
        Please Bend Thy Ear, And Hear My Cry!
With Holy Ghost Fire, Mine Heart Thou Fill;
        Till I Live And Breathe, To Do Thy Will!
No Sunday Christian, Will I Be;
        Every Day Give I Unto Thee!
Before No Sin, Will I Retreat,
        Till All Lay Crushed, Beneath My Feet!
The Walls of Jericho, Tear Thou Down;
        Till Not One Brick of Sin is Found!
The Obedience of Christ, Thou Forge in Me,
        Every Thought Into Captivity!
Precept Upon Precept, Line Upon Line;
        Till With Pure Clean Heart, Thine Light Doth Shine!
Glorify Thy Holy Name Through Me,
        To Praise You For All Eternity!
Heavenly Father, I Trust in Thy Awesome Power;
        Please Make Me More Like Jesus, This Hour!
Before Thine Awesome, Mighty Hand;
        <u>NO</u> Enemy Will Ever Stand!
The Universe Was Made By Thee,
        God Rules For All Eternity!

        Jesus Christ's Servant,
                Don Diaz

Tried And Tested

O'Great and Mighty God in Heaven,
                                      I am Trusting in Your Might!
I Am Looking The Devil in the Eye,
                                      And For God's Kingdom Fight!
I Am Standing on Thy Solid Rock,
                                      And Jesus is His Name!
I Am Going To Do God's Perfect Will,
                                      And Watch Satan Flee In Shame!
The Hour Has Come, For This Servant-Son;
                                      To Stand Up In Thy Might!
To Drink The Cup of My Great Lord,
                                      And Overcome the Night!
The Enemy Lies on Every Side,
                                      Like Many Times Before!
But Drink I Will, Till I Am Fill;
                                      This Test I Shall Endure!
For When I Am Weak, Then Am I Strong;
                                      In Weakness I Shall Rejoice!
Through Every Firey Trial, O'God;
                                      I'll Praise You With My Voice!

"Then Was Jesus Led Up By the Holy Spirit into the wilderness to be tempted of the Devil." {Matthew 4:1}

"And all the Churches shall know that I am he which searcheth the reins and hearts; I will give unto every one of you according to your works." {Revelations 2:23}
                "Jesus Christ"

"Beloved, think it not strange concerning the fiery trial which is to try you, as though some strange thing happened unto you; That the trial of your faith being much more precious than of gold that perisheth, though it be tried with fire, might be found unto praise and honour and glory at the appearing of Jesus Christ."
            {1 Peter 1:7 & 4:12}

"And he said unto me,"My Grace is sufficient for thee; For my strength is made perfect in weakness." Most Gladly therefore I will rather glory in my infirmities, that the Power of Christ may rest upon me. Therefore I take pleasure in infirmities, in reproaches, in necessities, in persecutions, in distresses for Christ's sake: For when I am weak, then am I strong."
    "The Apostle Paul"   {2 Corinthians 12:9}

Jesus Christ &
Almighty God's Servant,
                    Don Diaz

My Closest Friend

God You Are My Closest Friend,
>My Love For You Will Never End!

Hated, Rejected and Despised;
>By Everyone, In This Worlds Eyes!

Although, All I Ever Wanted Was Good;
>I Am Always Misunderstood.

All I Want Is To Stand, for Thy Truth;
>And To Help Them All, Both Old and Youth!

For Them All, "Tears & Prayers" To You I Groan;
>But All They Do Is Pick Up Stones!

I Only Want To See Them Free,
>They Only Seem To Throw Stones At Me!

God, Why Do All Thy Servants, They Hate?
>Thy Servants Lead Men, To Heavens Gates!

Forget This World, Use Your Head!
>All Eternity Forever, Lies Ahead!

The Judgment Seat of Christ, Is At Hand!
>For God, You Must <u>Make</u> <u>Your</u> <u>Stand</u>!

Jesus, You Are My Closest Friend;
>My Love For You, Will Never End!

Ye are my Friends, If ye do whatsoever I command you. Henceforth I call you not servants; for the servant Knoweth not what his lord doeth: But I have called you Friends. Remember the word that I said unto you, The servant is not greater than his lord. If they have persecuted Me, they will also persecute you; If they have kept my saying, they will keep yours also." {John 15:14-20}
"Jesus Christ"

These things I command you that ye love one another. If the world hate you, Ye know it hated <u>me</u> before it hated you."   "Jesus Christ"   {John 15:17}

**Almighty God's Servant,
Don Diaz**

Trust In God

Trust In God with All Thy Might,
                              Trust In God, Both Day and Night!
For In His Hands Thy Soul is Held,
                              And In His Arms, You Will Do Well!
Trust Not in the Strength of Man,
                              For Vain is the Help of Man!
Through God We Shall Do Valiantly,
                              For He Shall Tread Down Our Enemies!
From the Ends of the Earth, Unto Thee my Heart Cries;
                              Lead Me To Jesus, Thy Rock most High!
Place My Feet on Holy Ground,
                              For in Thy Strength My Soul Abound!
Safe in the Cover of Thy Wings,
                              With Joy My Heart Rejoices and Sings!
Consume Me with Thy Holy Love,
                              Worship Almighty God, Up Above!
For None Can Stop, His Awesome Hand;
                              Lord Lead Me to Thy Promised Land!
Trust In God with All Thy Might,
                              Trust In God, Both Day and Night!

"Nay, in all these things we are more than conquerors Through him that loved us. For I am persuaded, that neither death, nor life, nor angels, nor principalities, nor powers, nor things present, nor things to come, nor hight, nor depth, nor any other creature, shall be able to separate us from the love of God, which is in Christ Jesus our Lord."   "The Apostle Paul"
{Romans 8:37}

Jesus Christ &
Almighty God's servant,
Don Diaz

Prayer For Strength

Holy, Holy, God Most High;
                    Without You Lord I'd Surely Die!
Turn Me Not Over To Evil Desire,
                    Please Endue Me O'Lord, With Holy Ghost Fire!
Your Spirit and Love That Set Me Free,
                    Please Let It Not Grow Cold in Me!
When This Evil World, Tries to Steal My Love;
                    I Cry out To Jesus, High Above!
I Love Jesus and He Loves Me,
                    With God Is Where I Long To Be!
For God's Kingdom, I Want to Fight,
                    And Be Well Pleasing in His Sight!
Although Trials and Temptations, Shall Test My Love;
                    I Will Not Stop Fighting, For God Above!
When I Finish The Course, My Calling Complete;
                    I'll Toss My Crown At Jesus Feet!
He Already Knows My Heart, You See;
                    To Be With Almighty God, Is the Crown for Me!

"Behold, I send the promise of my Father upon you; But Tarry Ye in the city of Jerusalem, until you be Endued with Power from on High!"
{Luke 24:49}   "Jesus Christ"

"I Have fought a good fight, I have finished my course, I have kept the faith: Henceforth there is laid up for me a crown of righteousness, which the lord, the righteous Judge, shall give me at that day: and not to me only, But unto all them also that love his appearing."
{2 Timothy 4:7}   "The Apostle Paul"

Jesus Christ's Servant,
                    Don Diaz

Together For Eternity

O' Great I AM, Jehovah God;
                      Please Hear my Prayer Tonight!
Deliver Me From Evil, O'God;
                      And Save Me By Thy Might!
For You Alone Lord Jesus, Can Save;
                      A Mortal Man, From A Godless Grave!
O'Holy Spirit, Please Take My Hand;
                      And Lead Me To God's Promised Land!
Almighty God, I Put My Trust in Thee;
                      To Love You For All Eternity!
Lord, From The Grave I Cannot Praise;
                      And Worship You For Eternal Days!
God, From The Grave I Cannot Sing;
                      The Splendor of The King of Kings!
Lord Jesus, I Long To Be With Thee;
                      Together For Eternity!
Please Cover My With Thy Grace and Love,
                      And Cleanse Me With Fire, From Up Above!
I Dream About The Day I'll Bow and Worship at thy Feet!
When I See Your Face, in That Heavenly Place,
                      My Life Will Be Complete!

    To The Magnificent Lamb of God, Jesus Christ;
            Thy Humble Servant,
                      Don Diaz

One Day

My friends the day you leave this world,
                                  What will you have really done?
Did you spend your whole life to please yourself,
                                  Or to serve Gods Holy Son?
At this moment Billions of precious Souls,
                                  Race towards Hell at a Million miles an Hour!
When every One could be set Free,
                                  Saved by Jesus with Holy Ghost Power!
We concentrate on Earthbound things,
                                  To fulfill all our fleshly desires.
And close our eyes to Almighty God,
                                  And The Lake of Hell and Fire!
Your Whole Entire Life is Shorter,
                                  Than One Single Day in Hell!
But yet you Ignore every single warning,
                                  And you think that all is well.
When will the Truth Finally reach your Brain?
                                  That when all is said and done.
That You "<u>YES YOU</u>" Must Stand Before <u>GOD</u>!
                                  And the Judgement Seat of his Holy Son.
With All the Money in All the World,
                                  You can`t buy back One Single Day!
To come back to the earth and Repent your Sins,
                                  Before Gods Judgement Day!
My friend the day you leave this world,
                                  I Pray that what you will have done.
Is Washed your Soul in Jesus Blood,
                                  Gods Holy Precious Son!

"For we must All Appear Before
The Judgment Seat of Jesus Christ."
    {2 Corinthians 5:10}   Almighty Gods Servant,
                                            Don Diaz

Live Through Me!

O'Holy Spirit Live Through Me, And Be the Man I Cannot Be!
To Do the Things I Cannot Do, And See The Things I Cannot See!
To Walk the Walk, I Cannot Walk!
                        And Talk the Talk, I Cannot Talk!
To Teach the Things I Cannot Teach,
                        And Preach the Things I Cannot Preach!
To Pray the Things I Cannot Pray,
                        And Say the Things I Cannot Say!
To Live the Life I Cannot Live,
                        And Give the Things I Cannot Give!
To Shine the Light I Cannot Shine,
                        And Show Thine Heavenly Life Divine!
To Grow Thine Fruits I Cannot Grow,
                        And Show God's Heavenly Holy Glow!
To Use the Gifts Thou Gave to Me,
                        And See God's Children All Set Free!
To Tear Hell's Gates Down to the Ground!
                        So All the Lost Souls can Be Found!
To Worship God, My Father, Up Above;
                        And Send Him All My Heartfelt Love!
To Praise the Lord Jesus, Who on Calvary;
                        He Baptized with, Thou Holy Spirit, ME!
O'Holy Spirit <u>Live Through Me!</u> Till Jesus Christ is All They See!!!

And I will Put my Spirit within You, and Cause you to walk in my statutes, and ye shall keep my Judgments, and Do them! (Ezekiel 36:27)

"When the Spirit of Truth is Come, He will Guide You Unto All Truth!" "Jesus Christ" (John 16:13)
"Take no thought how or what ye shall speak, For it is not ye that speak, But the Spirit of your Father which Speaketh in You!" "Jesus Christ" (Matthew 10:19)

I Indeed Baptize you with Water unto Repentance: But He that cometh after me is mightier than I, whose Shoes I am not worthy to bear; He shall Baptize You with the Holy Ghost, and with Fire! "John the Baptist" (Matthew 3:11)

For as many as are Led by the Spirit of God, they are the Sons of God "The Apostle Paul" (Romans 8:14)

Almighty God's Servant,

Don Diaz

The Victory is God's!

When Jesus Died Upon the Cross, He Washed Our Sins Away!

When He Ascended Up To Heaven, The Holy Spirit Came Down to Stay!

Jesus is Seated Up in Heaven, And so are Me and You!

If You Will Just Abide in Him, His Holy Spirit Will Abide in You!

It's a Work of God from Beginning to End, To Save Both Me and You.

If You'll Just Have Faith, He'll Do What He Said; That's Exactly What He Will Do!

So Stop Fighting in Your Own Strength, and Trust in God's Mighty Power!

He'll Cleanse You, Guide You, Teach You; and Guard Your Soul at Every Hour!

You See It's God's Good Pleasure, To Do What We Cannot Do!

It Gives Him Joy to Set Us Free, Thats What Jesus Came to Do!

The More Impossible the Battle Seems, It Gives God Great Joy and Glory!

To Rise Up in You and Win the Fight, For His Holy Son in Glory!

So if You'll Simply Stand Your Ground, and Trust what God can Do!

He Already Has The Victory, and He'll Win this Fight Through You!

You See When Jesus Died on the Cross, Brothers & Sisters We Died There Too!

And Just Like He Raised Jesus from the Dead, He'll Raise Both Me and You!

Know ye not, that so many of us as were baptized unto Jesus Christ were baptized unto his death? Therefore We are buried with him by baptism into death: that like as Christ was raised up from the dead by the glory of the Father, even so we also should walk in newness of life. For if we have been planted together in the likeness of his death, we shall be also in the likeness of his resurrection: Knowing this, that our old man is crucified with him, that the body of sin might be destroyed; that henceforth we should not serve sin. For he that is dead is freed from sin. Now if we be dead with Christ, we believe we shall also live with him: Knowing that Christ being raised from the dead dieth no more; death hath no more dominion over him. For in that he died, he died unto sin once: but in that he liveth, he liveth unto God. Likewise reckon ye also yourselves to be dead indeed unto sin, but alive unto God through Jesus Christ our Lord. {Romans 6:3-11}

"Fear not, little flock: for it is your Father's good pleasure to give you the kingdom.
   "Jesus Christ"   {Luke 12:32}

But God, who is rich in mercy, for his great love wherewith he loved us, Even when we were dead in sins, hath quickened us together with Christ, (by grace ye are saved;) And hath raised us up together, and made us sit together in heavenly places in Christ Jesus: That in the ages to come he might shew the exceeding riches of his grace in his kindness toward us through Christ Jesus. For by grace are ye saved through faith; and that not of yourselves: it is the gift of God: Not of works, lest any man should boast. For we are his workmanship, created in Christ Jesus!   {Ephesians 2:4-10}

"Abide in me, and I in you. As the branch cannot bear fruit of itself, except it abide in the vine; no more can ye, except ye abide in me. I am the vine, ye are the branches: He that abideth in me, and I in him, the same bringeth forth much fruit: for without me ye can do nothing.   "Jesus Christ"   {John 15:4-5}

"My Heavenly Father, God"
"I am more Astounded by your Awesome, Mighty Power; Each and Every Day!"

Jesus Christ's Servant,

Don Diaz

Forever Worthy!

Behold, The Mighty Lamb of God,

                    That Takes the Worlds Sins Away!

God's Spotless, Holy, Son Divine,

                    And We Are <u>All</u> But Clay!

God The Father's <u>Love</u> He Showed,

                    On The Cross At Calvary!

Jesus Holy' Precious, Blood He Shed,

                    That Cleansed And Set Us Free!

<u>No</u> <u>Words</u> Can Sufficiently, Or Adequately Speak,

                    To The Glory Of Thy Name!

<u>Jesus</u> Clothed <u>Us</u> In His <u>Own</u> Righteousness,

                    And Removed <u>All</u> Our Sin And Shame!

As We <u>Kneel</u> Before Your Cross But <u>Dust</u>,

                    And <u>Fall Trembling</u> At <u>Your Feet</u>!

Your Magnificent, Awesome, Sacrifice;

                    Has <u>Redeemed Us</u> Whole and Complete!

<u>FOREVER WORTHY</u> IS THE LAMB! God's only begotten <u>Son</u>!

<u>FOREVER WORTHY</u> IS THE LAMB!   <u>JESUS</u> IS THE <u>ONE</u>!

<u>FOREVER WORTHY</u> IS THE LAMB!

                    For <u>All</u> Eternity <u>We Will Praise</u>!

God The Father, The Holy Spirit, And The Son!

John seeth **Jesus** coming unto him, and saith, Behold, the Lamb of God, which taketh away the sin of the world! {John 1:29} {Revelation 5:11-14} {1 John 5:7} And I beheld, and I heard many saying with loud voices; Worthy is the Lamb that was slain, to receive power and riches, wisdom and strength, honor & glory, & blessing!

Forever Worthy <u>To Be Praised</u>!
For there are three that bear record in heaven, the Father, the Word, and the Holy Ghost; and these three are <u>one</u>!

Almighty God's humble servant,

                    Don Diaz

Jesus is the One and Only Way!

O' God Our Father of All Creation, Send Forth Thy **Truth**, to Every Nation!
That **Jesus Christ**, Thine Precious **Son**, He Is The Way, The **Only One !!!**
The Keys of Hell and Death of Man, are Held by Him, They are in His Hand!
The Kingdom of Darkness **Is Defeated**, at God's right hand, Jesus Christ is Seated!
On a Wooden Cross, at Calvary, He Shed His Blood, and **Set Mankind FREE!!!**
The Temple Veil, It Has Been Rended, Into Heaven Above, **Jesus** Has Ascended!
He's Seated Now, at **God's** Right Hand, to Cleanse and Free, the Souls of Man!
The **Holy Spirit** Guides the Way, Into **Heavens Gate's**, To **Forever** Stay!
Jesus's Blood Has Cleansed, this Prodigals Son! **Jesus is the Way, The Only One!**
God's Angels Sang, the Precious Words, the Joyful Song, the Shepherd's Heard!
"Peace On Earth,"Good Will Toward Men," your Souls can Now be Born Again!
In Bethlehem, A Savior Born, and the Power of Hell and Death is Shorn!!!
"BEHOLD, THE LAMB," "GOD'S HOLY SON,"
   "JESUS CHRIST IS THE WAY," "THE ONLY ONE!!!"

"I AM The Way, The Truth, and The LIFE!!!" No man can come unto the Father, But By Me!
   "Jesus Christ" {John 14:6}
"For there is one **God**, and one Mediator between God and men, the man Jesus Christ!"
   {1 Timothy 2:5}
"If ye continue in my word, then are ye my disciples indeed, and ye shall know the truth, and the truth shall make you Free!
   "Jesus Christ" {John 8:31}
And there were shepherds in a field, in Bethlehem, watching over their flock by night; and the Angel of the Lord came upon them and said, Behold, I bring you good tidings of great joy, which shall be to all people! This day, a savior is born, which is Christ the Lord! Suddenly, with the Angel, there was an multitude of heavenly host; Praising God and saying,"Glory to God in the Highest," Peace on earth, good will towards men." {Luke 2:8-14}
When he, (the Holy Spirit) has come, (when you are born again) He will Guide You into all truth, & He shall teach you! "Jesus" {John 14:26,16:13}

And they Crucified Jesus on a cross, between two thieves, then said Jesus, "Father, forgive them, for they know not what they do." then Jesus cried with a loud voice, and gave up the ghost. And the veil of the Temple was rent in two, from the top to the bottom! (signifying that the way to **God**, was now open to men) And the Earth Quaked, the rocks rent, and the graves were opened, and many bodies of the saints that slept, arose, went into the holy city after his resurrection! (and were seen by many) When the centurion, and all that were with him, watching Jesus; saw the earthquake, and those things that were done, they feared greatly, saying, Truly, this was The Son of God!
   {Luke 23:34, Matthew 27:50, & Mark 15:37 }
At the grave, on the third day, an Angel said to Mary, I know that ye seek Jesus, who was crucified, he is Not here, for **He is Risen**! **Jesus Christ** has redeemed us from the power of the grave, as it is written,"Death is swallowed up in victory," O' Death, where is thy sting? O' Grave, where is thy Victory? {1Corinthians 15:54}
"Fear Not, **I Am** the First and the Last! **I Am He that Liveth**, and was dead; and, Behold, **I AM ALIVE Forevermore!!!** And have the Keys of Hell and Death!" "Jesus Christ" {Revelation 1:18}

Almighty God's, humble, thankful, servant,
   ~ I Love You Jesus ~   Don Diaz

Heaven's Gates

O' Heaven's Gates, When I Walk In,
                        Because Jesus Cleansed my Soul from Sin!
God will Wipe Every Tear, from my Eyes,
                        Forever to be at my Father's Side!
The Lamb of God has Set Me Free,
                        I'll Worship Jesus for All of Eternity!
His Offering for Sin, of his Blood Red Bright,
                        Has Clothed Me in a Robe of White!
When He Died Upon The Cross for Me,
                        And All of Mankind, to Set Us Free!
Jesus Rose From The Grave, on the Third Day,
                        An Angel Rolled The Stone Away!
God's Holy Kingdom is Drawing Near,
                        In Heaven The Saints and Angels Cheer!
The Precious Lamb, God's Holy Son,
                        Has <u>Conquered Death</u>, The <u>Battle's Won</u>!
Jesus Took The Book from Our Father's Hand,
                        And Opened Heaven's Gates To Man!
<u>Jesus Christ</u> Has Cleansed My Soul from Sin,
                        Into Heaven's Gates, <u>I Will Walk In</u>!!!

And I saw in the right hand of (God) that sat upon the throne, a book sealed with seven seals. And a strong Angel proclaiming with a loud voice, Who is worthy to open the book, and to loose the seals on it? And no man in heaven, nor in earth, neither under the earth, was able to open the book, neither to look on it! And I wept much, because no man was found worthy to open and read the book, or to look upon it! And one of the elders said, weep not, Behold, the Lion of Juda, the root of David, (Jesus) hath prevailed to open the book, and to loose the seven seals upon it! And I beheld the Lamb take the book out of the right hand of God! {Revelation 5:1-7}

God is Light, and in him is <u>no</u> darkness at all! If we say that we have fellowship with him, and (we) walk in the darkness, we lie, and do not the truth! But if we walk in the light, as he (God) is in the light, we have fellowship one with another, and the Blood of Jesus Christ his son, <u>cleanseth us</u> from <u>all sin!</u>   {1 John 1:5}
John seeth Jesus, and saith, Behold the Lamb of God that taketh away the sin of the world! {John 1:29}
The Angel of the Lord descended from heaven, and he rolled back the stone from the grave and said, I know ye seek Jesus, he is not here, he has <u>Risen!</u> {Matthew 28:2}

Almighty God's humble Servant,

                        Don Diaz

The Battle is Won!

O'Holy Father In Heaven Above, I Send Up To You my Praise and Love!

    For Everything That You Have Done, You Gave to Us, Your Precious Son!

The Cornerstone and Sure Foundation, That Paved The Way For Our Salvation!

    The Temple Veil Was Ripped In Two, And Opened Up The Path To You!

Our God and Father who sent Jesus down, the King of Kings who wears the crown!

    To Rule up in Heaven for Eternity, Seated at thy hand O'God, right next to Thee!

The Twenty Four Elders They All Fell Down,

    And Tossed at God's Feet, all of Their Crowns!

Thou Art Worthy O'Lord to Receive Glory and Honor,

    You've Created All Things By Your Awesome Power!

So Let All God's Saints and Angels Sing,

    Worthy, Worthy, Worthy, Is The Lamb That Was Slain!

You've Redeemed Us To God With Your Own Precious Blood!

    And Secured Us A Home Up In Heaven Above!

You're The Lion Of Juda, The Root Of David!

    When You Died On The Cross, The Way Was Created!

There's <u>No</u> Other Name Given For Men To Be Saved!

    Than By Jesus Christ Who Rose From The Grave!

You Took The Book Out of Our Fathers Right Hand!

    And Opened Up Heavens Gates For Every Man!

You're The Only One Worthy, To Break the Seven Seals!

    Satan Is Defeated, God's Kingdom Revealed!

And Death Is Conquered, The Battle is Won!

There's <u>Eternal</u> <u>Salvation</u> In <u>God's</u> <u>Risen</u> <u>Son</u>!

And I saw a Strong Angel proclaim, Who is worthy to open the book, and loose the seals? I beheld, and in the midst of the throne, stood a Lamb as it had been slain, he came and took the book out of the right hand of God, who sat on the throne! when he had taken the book the twenty four elders fell down before the Lamb! Saying, Thou art worthy to take the book, and to Open the Seals thereof: for thou wast slain, and hast redeemed us to God by thy Blood out of every kindred, and tongue, and people, and Nation! "Glory to God!" Revelation Chapter 5

I am the way, the truth, and the life! No man can come to the Father but by <u>me</u>! "Jesus Christ" {John 14:6}

Wherefore God hath highly exalted him, and given him a name which is above every other Name! Neither is there Salvation in any other name under Heaven, Given among men, whereby we must be Saved!<{Acts 4:12} {1 Timothy 2:5}

For there is One God, and One mediator between God and men, Jesus Christ!

Worthy is the Lamb that was Slain, to receive glory and honor, and power, and wisdom, and blessings! I Praise You Lord Jesus!   God's servant, Don Diaz

Our God is a Consuming Fire!

O'Consuming God of Fire and Light,   Holy Spirit Engulf my Soul Tonight!
Let, with Thy Truth, My Mind Be Shod,
>   Without Holiness, "No Man" Can See God!

Your Awesome "Holy Fire" Consumeth All,
>   For at God's Feet, All His Enemies Fall!

The Mighty Sword, Within Thy Hand,   Destroyeth All Evil in Every Land!
The Wicked, they Shall Be Turned into Hell,
>   With Fire and Brimstone their Souls Shall Dwell!

And All the Nations that Forget God,
>   Smite with Fierceness and Wrath of thy Holy Rod!

The "<u>HOLY ONE</u>" of Israel,   Will Cast You into the Depths of Hell!
Will You <u>NOT FEAR ALMIGHTY GOD</u>,
>   O' Sinners in the Hands of an Angry God!!!

He Sent His Son Jesus To <u>Set</u> You <u>FREE</u>,
>   But Instead, thine own Wickedness, shall Correct Thee!

Because, "Men Loved Darkness, Rather than Light,"
>   With, <u>ALMIGHTY GOD YOU CANNOT FIGHT</u>!!!

Despise Thou, The Precious, "LAMB OF GOD,"
>   Who Died for <u>YOU</u>, You Evil Clod!

With Judgment and Wrath, You Shall Be Shorn,
>   Behold, Father God; <u>They Have Been Warned</u>!!!

Let us have grace, to serve God acceptably with reverence and Godly Fear! Because our God is a Consuming Fire! {Hebrews 12:28} Without peace and holiness, no man shall see the Lord! {Hebrews 12:14} The Lord is known by the judgment he Executeth; the Wicked is snared in the work of his own hands! The Wicked shall be turned into Hell, and all the nations that forget God! {Psalms 9:16} The Fear of the Lord is the beginning of wisdom; and the knowledge of the Holy is understanding! {Proverbs 9:10}

Thine own Wickedness shall correct thee, and thy backslidings shall reprove thee; know therefore and see that it is an evil thing and bitter, that thou hast forsaken the Lord thy God, and that my Fear is not in thee, saith the Lord God of hosts!   {Jeremiah 2:19}

And this is the condemnation, that Light is come into the world, and men loved darkness rather than Light, because their deeds were Evil! For every one that doeth Evil hateth the Light!   {John 3:19}

And out of his mouth goeth a sharp Sword, that with it he should smite the nations: and he shall rule them with a Rod of Iron: and he treadeth the winepress of the fierceness and wrath of Almighty God! And whosoever was not found written in the Book of Life, was <u>Cast into the Lake of Fire</u>!!!   {Revelations 19:15 & 20:15}

Almighty God's Humble Servant,   Don Diaz

Therefore if any man be in Christ, He is a new creature: old things are passed away; Behold all things are become new! Yea and doubtless, I count all things but loss for the excellency of the knowledge of Christ Jesus my Lord: for whom I have suffered the loss of all things, and do count them but Dung! That I may win Christ! And be found in him, not having mine own righteousness which is of the law, but that which is through the Faith of Christ, the righteousness which is of God by Faith: That I may know him, and the power of his resurrection, and the fellowship of his sufferings, being made conformable unto his death; If by any means I might attain unto the resurrection of the dead! For I am persuaded that neither death, nor life, nor angels, nor principalities, nor powers, nor things present, nor things to come, nor hight, nor depth, nor any other creature, shall be able to separate us from the love of God, which is in Christ Jesus our Lord! Nay, for in all these things we are more than conquerors through him that loved us! But this one thing I do, forgetting those things which are behind, and reaching forth unto those things which are before, I press toward the mark for the prize of the high calling of God in Christ Jesus!   "The Apostle Paul"

Preface : A Word from the Author

Beloved, this book, "Holy Ghost Fire" was created for <u>one</u> purpose, <u>To Bring You Closer to Almighty Holy God</u> and his <u>Awesome Incredible Son Jesus Christ</u>! Who Love you and want <u>you</u> to be <u>IN Heaven with them</u>! Because <u>That is WHY YOU were Created by God</u>! In the <u>Image of God</u>! To be a member of God's <u>holy family</u> in Heaven for all of Eternity! <u>Forever</u>! So that <u>Gods Holy Spirit</u> can <u>live</u> in your Heart and Soul and Spirit, by Faith and Trust in God! And Faith and Trust in the Mighty Lamb of God, <u>Jesus Christ</u> "that taketh away the sin of the World!" So that you can be <u>Born Again</u> and let the Holy Spirit <u>Rise Up</u> Inside your very Heart and Soul, in his Awesome Mighty Holy Power! You see the <u>Holy Spirit is God</u>! Part of the Holy Trinity! God the Father, God the Son (Jesus), God the Holy Spirit! Because these Three <u>ARE ONE</u>! Joined in Perfect Union and in One Accord! Perfectly and Forever! So the Holy Spirit can cleanse You and Prepare You; so that he can Present <u>You</u> a <u>Spotless Holy Bride</u> to God's son, Jesus Christ! So that He can Guide You and Teach You, Protect and Comfort You! To Transform You and make You <u>Just Like Jesus</u> our Lord and Savior; our <u>Great High Priest</u>! Our Advocate with the Father, Jesus Christ the Righteous who is the Propitiation (or Atonement and Redeemer) <u>For Our Sins</u>! Who is Seated in Heaven at the right hand of God the Father, (right now and forever) in the holy of Holies! To Intercede for <u>US</u>, to make Prayers and Intersession <u>For Us</u> to God the Father! For the Forgiveness of OUR SINS! HALLELUJAH!!! Jesus Christ came into this World <u>To Save Sinners</u> of whom I am Chief! Because Almighty God is <u>not</u> willing that <u>Any Man Should Perish</u>, But that <u>All Should come to Repentance</u>! Their Sins be Forgiven, and be <u>Washed Clean</u> through <u>FAITH</u> in Jesus Christ and his Holy Precious <u>Blood</u>! And His Great Awesome Sacrifice to God the Father, when he Died for <u>OUR</u> Sins on the Cross of Calvary! And was <u>Resurrected</u> Three Days Later! Having <u>Taken</u> the Keys of <u>Hell and Death</u> away from <u>Satan</u>!!! Jesus showed himself <u>ALIVE</u> to his disciples and over 500 brethren at one time!!! Then Jesus <u>Ascended</u> into Heaven, at the Right Hand of <u>God</u>! All Power and Authority is Given unto Jesus in Heaven and in Earth! Where <u>All His Enemies</u> Will be <u>Put Under His Feet</u>! Jesus gives us (his Disciples) Power to Tread on Serpents and Scorpions, and over all the Power of the Enemy! Because <u>Greater is He</u> (Holy Spirit) that is <u>IN YOU</u>, than He (Satan) that is in this world! Almighty God sent his Son Jesus and his Holy Spirit for <u>All of Us</u>! Because "God so Loved the World that He Gave His only Begotten Son that Whosoever "<u>Believeth in Him</u>" Should Not Perish, But Have <u>Everlasting Life</u>!" He that believeth in <u>Jesus</u> is not condemned, But He that believeth Not is condemned already, because He hath <u>Not</u> believed in the name of the <u>Only Begotten Son of God</u>! JESUS CHRIST!!! The Messiah! <u>GODS HOLY SON</u>!

Preface : A Word from the Author

Jesus said, "I Am the Light of the World : He that Followeth Me shall not walk in Darkness, but shall have the Light of Life!" I Go my way, (to the Father) and ye shall seek me, and shall Die in Your Sins! (if you Do Not believe) wither I go ye cannot come. Ye are from beneath; I Am from Above: Ye are of this World; I Am not of this World! Therefore I said unto you, that Ye shall Die in your Sins: for if Ye Do Not Believe that I Am He, (The Only Begotten SON of GOD!) YE SHALL DIE IN YOUR SINS!!! {John 8:12, 21-24} Because "Without Faith it is Impossible to Please God! For He that cometh to God Must Believe that He Is and that He is a Rewarder of Them that Diligently SEEK HIM!!!" {Hebrews 11:6} For by Grace are ye Saved through FAITH; and that Not of Yourselves: it is the Gift of God! Because "No Flesh Shall Glory IN HIS PRESENCE!!!" Almighty God sent his son Jesus, and his Holy Spirit To Save YOU; because HE LOVES YOU VERY MUCH!!! Period! GOD LOVES YOU!!! God wants you to be In Heaven with HIM! FOREVER! God wants You to Love Him, As Much as HE LOVES YOU! Do You? God said "I Am a Jealous God" and A Consuming Fire! Thou shalt Worship No other God before Me or serve Them! (Money, Fame, Possessions, Idols, False Deity) {See Exodus 20:1-5, Deuteronomy 4:24} Therefore Sanctify yourselves, and Be Ye Holy; for I AM the Lord Your God! And Ye Shall Keep My Statutes, and Do Them! I AM the Lord which Sanctify You. And Ye shall be Holy Unto ME! For I The LORD AM HOLY !!! And I have Severed You from other People that YE SHOULD BE MINE!!! Beloved, God Really Loves You. That is why He created a Way for You and I to be set Free from Sin! (The Wages of Sin is Death!) Jesus said "I AM the Way, the Truth, and the Life! No Man can come unto the Father But By ME!" {John 14:6} For there is One God, and One Mediator between God and Men, the Man Jesus Christ! {1st Timothy 2:5} God Loves You, and He Will Help You to separate Yourself from this Evil Wicked World! So that You won't be Destroyed with this Evil World on Judgment Day!!! But Be Warned! If You Refuse Almighty Gods Love and Grace and mercy, His Kindness and Longsuffering and Forgiveness toward all Sinners; and All of Mankind! If You Neglect and Ignore the Mighty Lord Jesus Great and Awesome Sacrifice for your Sins, to Set You FREE! And You Refuse His Loving Call to Repentance! But You Choose a Life of Sin and Lust and Cursing and Hatred and Evil! If You Despise Jesus Precious Blood and put him to Open Shame, by Living a Evil Wicked Life! Even though God in his Great Grace and Mercy Lovingly Sacrificed His Own Son For You To LIVE, and gave You a Lifetime to Repent!!! And be washed clean in Jesus own Blood! On Judgment Day, God will Destroy You in Hell! Do not forget Noah's Flood! God Destroys Evil! God is not only a God of Love, and Mercy!

Preface : A Word from the Author

Almighty God is also a God of <u>Holiness</u> and <u>Justice</u>, of <u>Truth</u> and <u>Righteousness</u>! Forever! The Lord, The Lord God, merciful and gracious, longsuffering and abundant in goodness and truth, keeping mercy for thousands, forgiving iniquity and transgressions and sin, and that will <u>BY NO MEANS CLEAR THE GUILTY</u>! {Exodus 34:6} God is Holy,Holy,Holy! God Judges Sin and Pride and <u>All Evil</u>! Period! Any Evil person,YOU, ME, ANYBODY! The Bible says,"God Judgeth the Righteous, and God is Angry with the Wicked every day" {Psalms 7:11}"The Fear of the Lord is to Hate Evil: Pride, and Arrogancy, and the Evil way, and the Froward Mouth Do I Hate!"{Proverbs 8:13} Also "Let <u>NO</u> Corrupt Communication Proceed <u>Out of YOUR MOUTH</u>! But that which is Good to the use of Edifying, that it may minister Grace unto the Hearers. And <u>Do Not Grieve The Holy Spirit of God</u> whereby Ye are Sealed unto the day of Redemption! Let All Bitterness, and Wrath, and Anger, and Clamor,(loud Shouting and Fighting) and Evil Speaking, be <u>Put Away From You</u>, with All Malice! And be ye kind one to another, tenderhearted, forgiving one another, even as God for Christ's sake has <u>Forgiven You</u>! {Ephesians 4:29-32} You must truly, <u>from your Heart</u>; <u>Forgive Anyone and Everyone</u> who has offended You or Wronged you in any way! So that God will Forgive <u>YOU</u> all the thousands (or Millions?) of <u>Sins YOU have committed</u> in your Lifetime! This is so Very <u>Important</u> that Jesus put it Directly into "The Lords Prayer" when his disciples asked him to teach them how to pray. " Our <u>Father</u> which art in Heaven, Hallowed be <u>Thy</u> name. <u>Thy</u> Kingdom come, <u>Thy</u> Will be done in earth, as it is in Heaven. Give us this day our daily bread. And Forgive us our debts, as **WE FORGIVE** our debtors. And lead us not into temptation, but Deliver us from evil. For <u>Thine</u> is the Kingdom, and the Power, and the Glory, for ever. Amen." For if ye forgive men their trespasses, your Heavenly Father will also forgive YOU: But if ye forgive not men their trespasses, <u>NEITHER WILL YOUR FATHER FORGIVE YOUR TRESPASSES</u>!!! {Matthew 6:9} You <u>MUST FORGIVE EVERYONE WHO HAS DONE YOU WRONG</u>! Or Your Own Sins will <u>Never Be Forgiven YOU</u>! And they will be piling up on Top of <u>Your Own Head</u> like A MOUNTAIN, Ready to <u>CRUSH YOU INTO HELL ON JUDGMENT DAY</u>!!! No Wicked Evil <u>Unforgiving</u> Person will <u>EVER BE ALLOWED INTO HEAVEN</u>! EVER! You Must Forgive Them, I don't care if they spit in your face and kick you out of their house! Forgive them anyway! Because <u>Then GOD Will Forgive YOUR SINS</u>, and <u>WASH YOU CLEAN</u>! When You Truly, Sincerely, <u>REPENT</u> from all your Sins. Please also notice that Jesus directed his prayer Directly to <u>God the Father</u>! See, <u>FIVE TIMES</u> in the Lords Prayer, Jesus directed His Prayer <u>TO GOD THE FATHER</u>!!! <u>Jesus Never Prayed to Mary</u>!

Preface : A Word from the Author

If God wanted you to pray to Mary, wouldn't Jesus have said that when he taught his Disciples HOW TO PRAY! Jesus never, ever, told Anyone to Pray to Mary! EVER! His mother is a Regular Person, Just Like Us! She needed to be Saved from her sins, and Forgiven, Just Like Us! Listen to what Jesus taught his disciples. "While he yet talked to the people, behold, his mother and brethren stood outside, desiring to speak with him. Then one said unto him, behold, thy mother and brethren are standing outside, desiring to speak with thee. But he (Jesus) answered and said unto him that told him, Who is my mother? and who are my brethren? And he stretched forth his hands toward his disciples, and said, Behold my mother and my brethren! For whosoever shall Do the Will of MY FATHER which is in Heaven, the same is my brother, and sister, and mother." {Matthew 12:46} Absolutely "No Where" in the ENTIRE BIBLE, Old or New Testament does it Ever Once say or tell us to Pray to Mary! Not One Single Time! Search The Holy Bible from cover to cover and see! The word "pray" appears in the bible 313 times, "Prayer" appears 114 times, "Prayers" appears 24 times, the name "Mary" appears 54 times. {King James Version} Not One Single Time does it ever say, or even suggest that we should Pray to Mary! Never! Praying to Mary is a False Doctrine Taught By MEN! NOT GOD! It is Not in the Bible!!! Besides, NO ONE can Hear and Answer Prayers but ALMIGHTY GOD! Period! G-O-D!!! Lets look at what the Word of God says! "For there are three that bear record In Heaven! The Father, The Word, (Jesus) and The Holy Ghost! THESE THREE ARE ONE!!!" {1 John 5:7} They are the Only Members of THE GODHEAD! Jesus said, "At that day ye shall know that I am in my Father" {John 14:20} I and my Father are ONE! {John 10:30} Jesus also said, "My Sheep Hear MY VOICE and I know them, and They Follow ME! {John 10:27} "And the Sheep Hear his voice: and He calleth his own sheep by NAME, And the sheep follow him, for they know his voice! And a stranger They Will Not Follow! But will flee from him: for they Do Not Know the voice of Strangers! {John 10:3} (A Stranger is Any Other VOICE THAN THAT OF GOD!) THE FATHER, THE SON, and THE HOLY SPIRIT! THESE THREE ARE ONE! One Mind, One Accord, and One Purpose! {To Save Your SOUL!} How can You or I Possibly hear and know Jesus Voice, unless WE PRAY TO HIM! And Study the Bible! "All power is given unto me in Heaven and Earth. Go ye therefore, and teach all nations, baptizing them in the name of the Father, the Son, and the Holy Ghost. {Matthew 28:18} The Comforter, who is the Holy Ghost, whom the Father will send in my name, He shall Teach you all things. {John 14:26} When the Spirit of Truth is come, (Holy Spirit) He will Guide You into all Truth! {John 16:13}

Preface : A Word from the Author

Almighty God the Father, <u>Himself</u> ! Revealed to Jesus disciples (all who <u>believe</u> and <u>obey</u> Jesus) that, ~ 1. Jesus is his Son! ~ 2. Jesus is the Word of God! (Holy Incarnation of God, or God in the Flesh, and part of the Godhead) ~ 3. That We should <u>Hear</u> and <u>Obey</u> **Jesus**, his beloved Son in whom He (God the Father) <u>IS WELL PLEASED</u>!!! (Because if you honor the <u>Son</u> "**Jesus**" you <u>are</u> honoring **God the Father**, <u>Who sent Him</u> to us!) "And after six days Jesus taketh Peter, James, and John his brother, and bringeth them up unto a high mountain apart, (separated from this world!) And (Jesus) was transfigured before them: and his face did shine as the sun, and his raiment was white as the light! (**God** revealed **Jesus** <u>True</u> Nature and Glory from the foundation of the world, to his disciples!) And, behold, there appeared unto them Moses and Elijah talking with him! And a bright cloud overshadowed them: and behold a voice out of the cloud, which said, <u>This is my</u> **Beloved Son**, in whom I am well pleased; **<u>HEAR YE HIM</u>!!!** And when the disciples heard it, they fell on their face, and were sore Afraid! And Jesus came and touched them, and said, Arise, and be not afraid. (Woe, unto <u>Any Person</u> who chooses to appear before <u>Almighty Holy God</u>!!! Without <u>Jesus Christ</u> as their <u>Lord</u> and <u>Savior</u>!!! Washed <u>clean</u> in **Jesus**'s <u>Holy Precious Blood</u>, and <u>Covered</u> by his <u>Grace</u>! Through <u>Faith</u> in **Jesus** and his Resurrection!) And when they had lifted up their eyes, they saw no man, save Jesus only. (Keep your eyes on Jesus only, and <u>No</u> Man!) And as they came down from the mountain, Jesus said to them, tell the vision to no man, until the son of man be risen again from the dead." {Matthew 17:1-9} In the beginning was the Word, and the Word was with God, and the <u>Word was God</u>! The same was in the beginning with God. all things were <u>made by him</u>; and without him was not anything made that was made. <u>In him was life</u>; and the life was the light of men! and the <u>Word was made Flesh</u>, and dwelt among us, (and we beheld his glory, the glory as of the only begotten of the Father!) full of **grace** and **truth**. {see John 1:1-14} For the Father judgeth no man, but he hath committed <u>all</u> judgment unto the <u>Son</u>! That all men should honor the Son, even as they honor the Father. He that honoureth not the Son, (Jesus) honoureth not the Father which hath sent him! {John 5:22} Jesus said, wait for the <u>Promise</u> of the Father. For John baptized with water; but ye shall be baptized with the **Holy Ghost**! {Acts 1:4} In whom ye also trusted, (**Jesus**) after that ye heard the word of truth, the Gospel of your Salvation: in whom also after that ye **Believed**, ye were sealed with the **Holy Spirit** of <u>Promise</u>! Which is the <u>earnest</u> of our inheritance, (or Seal of Proof!) until the <u>Redemption</u> of the purchased possession! (<u>you</u>) {Ephesians 1:13-14} "If ye love me, <u>keep my commandments</u>! And I will pray the Father, He shall give you another Comforter, that he may abide with you <u>for Ever</u>! Even the **Spirit of Truth**; whom the world cannot receive, because it neither seeth or knoweth him: but ye know him; for **He** dwelleth with you, and **He** <u>Shall be **In** You</u>! The **Holy Ghost**, whom the Father will send in my (Jesus) name, <u>he shall teach you all things</u>, and bring to your remembrance, whatsoever <u>I have said unto you</u>!{John 14:15,26) So You Pray and Worship God the Father, In and through the Holy Spirit, (who lives inside you) **He** guides you, and teaches you all about Jesus! And Jesus gives Glory and Honor to the Father!

Preface : A Word from the Author

Jesus told his Disciples,"Behold, I send the promise of my Father upon you: but tarry ye in the city of Jerusalem, until ye be endued with <u>Power from on High</u>! (**The Holy Spirit!**) Then, on the day of Pentecost, they were all with one accord in one Place. And suddenly there came a sound from Heaven as of a rushing mighty wind, and it filled all the house where they were sitting. And there appeared unto them cloven tongues like as of fire, and it sat upon each of them. And they were all filled with the Holy Ghost, and began to speak with other tongues as the Spirit gave them utterance. {Luke 24:49 & Acts 2:1} The Holy Spirit of God Filled their Hearts and Souls, and they were Born Again into The Spirit!!! And Almighty God returned to His Proper place as Lord in their Lives, for which we all were Created! Having the Divine Holy Nature of God to help and guide US! The position that mankind <u>lost</u> when Adam and Eve disobeyed God, and sinned in the Garden of Eden. The Position that The Mighty Lord <u>Jesus Reclaimed</u>, <u>FOR US</u>! When our Father God sent Jesus into this World, for this very purpose; TO DELIVER US FROM EVIL! Which is Exactly <u>What the Mighty Lord Jesus Did</u>, when He Sacrificed himself to God on the cross of Calvary! Went down into Hell, Completely Crushed and Defeated Satan, Right in front of every Demon and all the Forces of Hell! And Ripped the Keys of Hell and Death from Satan's broken battered Hands, and Rose from the Grave 3 Days Later!!! Because it was <u>Never Ever Possible</u> that Hell, or Death, or the Grave; could <u>Ever</u> hold <u>The Son of God</u>! <u>The King of Kings</u> and <u>Lord of Lords</u>! <u>The Prince of Life</u>! And Jesus did All This, While Carrying The Weight of <u>All the Worlds</u> Sins, ON HIS OWN SHOULDERS!!!!!!! JESUS is so INCREDIBLY AWESOME, Our LORD And SAVIOR Is UNSTOPPABLE! Satan found this out the <u>Hard Way</u>! Jesus took back what the lying, thieving, serpent stole when he lied to Eve in the garden! Jesus redeemed <u>All of Mankind</u> that Day on the Cross! The Greatest Words ever Spoken by any man that ever lived! <u>IT IS FINISHED!!!</u> Wherefore, as by one man (Adam) sin entered into the world, and death by sin; and so death passed upon <u>all men</u>, for that all have sinned: for if through the offence of one many be Dead! Much more the grace of God, and the gift of grace, by one man, <u>Jesus Christ</u>, hath abounded unto many. For if by one man's offence, death reigned by one; much more they which receive Gods grace and the gift or righteousness through Faith, shall have <u>Life</u> by One! "Jesus Christ" For as by one mans disobedience many were made sinners, so by the obedience of one shall many be made righteous. {Romans 5:12-19} And Though Jesus is Gods Son, yet he learned obedience by the things he suffered; and being made perfect, He became the author of Eternal Salvation unto all them that <u>Obey Him</u>! {Hebrews 5:8}

Preface : A Word from the Author

Not every one that saith unto me, Lord, Lord, shall Enter into the Kingdom of Heaven! But He that Doeth the Will of my Father which is in Heaven! {Matthew 7:21} Then said one unto him, Lord, are there few that be Saved? And he said unto them, Strive to Enter in at the Strait gate: for many, I say unto you, will Seek to Enter In, and Shall Not Be Able!!! {Luke 14:23} Therefore, brethren, we are debtors, not to the flesh to live after the flesh. (evil fleshly desires) For if ye live after the flesh, Ye Shall Die!!! (For whosoever commiteth Sin is the Servant of Sin! and the Wages of Sin is DEATH!) But if ye through the Spirit Do Mortify the deeds of the body, YE SHALL LIVE!!! For as many as are LED BY THE SPIRIT OF GOD!!!!!!! They are the Sons of God! {Romans 7:23, 8:12, & John 8:34} So I ask you, Are you Truly Born Again? Are You TRULY LED BY THE "HOLY SPIRIT OF GOD"? Do You Live a Holy Life? Before the All Seeing, All Knowing, NOTHING IS HIDDEN FROM HIS EYES; Holy, Holy, Holy, ALMIGHTY GOD!!! Everything You Do on this Earth is being recorded in Heaven above! And You will have to answer for All the deeds done in your Body, either good or Evil! And the True Motives as to why you did them! And All the Words that came Out of Your Mouth! For by thy words you will be justified, and by thy words you will be condenmed! I Want YOU To Be Ready on JUDGMENT DAY! So YOU can Enter into Heaven! And Not BURN IN HELL! FOR ALL ETERNITY!!! Heaven and Hell Are Real Places! IT'S TRUE! For we must all appear before The Judgment Seat of Christ; that every one may receive the things done in his body, according to that he hath done, whether it be good or bad. Knowing therefore the Terror of the Lord, We Persuade Men! {2 Corinthians 5:10} The hour is coming, in the which all that are in the graves shall hear Jesus' voice, and shall come forth; they that have done Good, unto the resurrection of Life! And they that have done Evil, unto the Resurrection of Damnation! {John 5:28} And I saw the dead, small and great, Stand Before God; and the books were opened: and another book was opened, which is the Book of Life: and the dead were judged out of those things which were written in the books, according To Their Works! And whosoever was not found written in the book of Life was cast into The Lake of Fire!!! And I heard a great voice out of heaven saying, Behold, the tabernacle of God is with men, and He will dwell with them, and they shall be his people, and God himself shall be with them, and be their God. And God shall wipe away all tears from their eyes; and there shall be no more death, neither sorrow, nor crying, neither shall there be any more pain: He that overcometh (sin and evil) shall inherit all things; and I will be his God, and he shall be my son. (or daughter) But the fearful, and unbelieving, and the abominable, and murderers, and whoremongers, and sorcerers, and idolaters, and All Liars, shall have their part in the Lake which Burneth with Fire and Brimstone!!! Which is the Second Death! {Revelation - 20:12, & 21:3,7-8} Jesus himself warned us saying, "Do not fear them that can only kill the body, but Fear Him which is able to Destroy both body and soul in Hell! (Almighty God!) {Matt. 10:28}

Preface : A Word from the Author

For the Wrath of God is revealed from Heaven against All ungodliness and unrighteousness of men! Who hold the truth in unrighteousness! {Romans 1:18} O'Generation of Vipers, who hath Warned you to flee from the Wrath to Come? Bring forth therefore fruits, (as concrete proof) meet for Repentance! And now also the Ax is laid unto the root of the trees: therefore every tree which does Not bring forth Good Fruit is hewn down and Cast into the Fire! I indeed baptize you with water unto repentance: but he that cometh after me, (Jesus) is mightier than I, whose shoes I am not worthy to bear: He shall baptize you with the Holy Ghost and with Fire! Whose Fan is in his hand, and He will Throughly Purge his Floor, (You!) and gather his wheat into the garner; but he will burn up the chaff (Every Evil Person) with unquenchable Fire!{Matt 3:7-12} I beseech you therefore, brethren, by the mercies of God, that ye present your bodies a living sacrifice, holy, acceptable unto God, which is your reasonable service. And be not conformed to this world: but be ye Transformed by the Renewing of your Mind, that ye may Prove what is the good, and acceptable, and Perfect will of God! {Romans 12:1} And we know that all things work together for good to them that love God! To them who are called according to his purpose. And them whom he called, God also did predestinate to Be Conformed to the Image of his Son! (Jesus) that He might be the firstborn among Many Brethren!{Romans 8:28} And ye shall know the Truth, and the Truth shall make You Free!!! "Jesus Christ" {John 8:32} Let us take a Good Hard Look at the Truth, about the Day, Jesus returns to a stunned, suprised, evil wicked World! And I saw heaven opened, and behold a white horse; and he that sat upon him is called Faithful and True, and in Righteousness He doth Judge and Make War! His eyes were as a flame of Fire, on his head were many crowns; and he had a name written, that no man knew, but He Himself. And he was clothed with a vesture dipped in blood: and his name is called The Word of God! And the armies which were in heaven followed him upon white horses, clothed in fine linen, white and clean. And out of his mouth goeth a sharp sword, that with it he should smite the nations, and he shall rule them with a rod of iron: and he treadeth the winepress of the fierceness and wrath of Almighty God! On his vesture and thigh was a name written, KING OF KINGS, AND LORD OF LORDS!!! And the kings of the earth, and the great men, and the rich men, the chief captians, and the mighty men, and every bondman, and every freeman, Hid Themselves in the dens and in the rocks of the mountains; And said to the mountains and the rocks, Fall on Us! And Hide Us! From the Face of him that Sitteth on the Throne! And from the Wrath of the LAMB!!! For The Great Day of His Wrath is Come!!! And Who Shall Be Able To Stand ??? {Revelations 6:15-17} & {Revelations 19:11-16} It is a Fearful thing to fall into the hands of The Living God!!! {Hebrews 10:31} Whoso despiseth the word shall Be Desroyed: but he that feareth the comandment shall Be Rewarded! {Proverbs 13:13} The Lord is known by the judgment which he executeth: the wicked is snared in the work of his own hands! The wicked shall be turned into Hell, and all the nations that Forget God!{Psalms 9:16-17} The Apostle Paul who was lifted to the third heaven, said, therefore knowing the Terror of the Lord We Persuade Men!

Preface : A Word from the Author

Beloved, today, right now; our Lord and Savior is in the Holy of Holies, on the Mercy Seat !!! Where the Cherubims stretch forth their wings on high, covering the mercy seat!{Exodus 25:20} Signifying Gods grace and mercy to Us, (mankind) and the covering he gave To US through his Holy Son Jesus Christ! The Lamb of God that taketh away the sin of the world! {John 1:29} So that Today, you and I can come boldly to the throne of Grace, that we may obtain mercy and find grace to help in time of need!{Hebrews 4:16} to receive mercy and forgiveness for our sins! When we truly Repent and Forsake (Stop Doing!) those Sins! Then and only Then will Jesus' Holy Precious Blood Wash you Clean! Almighty God does not cover, and will never cover ; UNREPENTED, UNFORSAKEN SIN!!! NEVER! The wages of Sin is Death!{Romans 6:23} That is why, the very First words out of Jesus own mouth! When he began to preach the gospel, after fasting 40 days and nights, being tempted of the devil. (Jesus put the devil to open shame! and Jesus returned in victory and full power of the spirit!) The very first words of the gospel, as Jesus began to preach were "Repent, for the kingdom of heaven is at hand!" {Matthew 4:17} Turn away from and stop doing SIN!!! "Be ye Holy, for I AM HOLY saith the LORD GOD!!!" If my people, which are called by my name, shall humble themselves, and PRAY, and SEEK MY FACE, and TURN FROM THEIR WICKED WAYS!!! THEN!!! (and only Then!) THEN WILL I HEAR FROM HEAVEN, AND WILL FORGIVE THEIR SINS!!! {2 Chronicles 7:14} Elect according to the foreknowledge of God the Father, through sanctification of the Spirit, unto Obedience and sprinkling of the blood of Jesus Christ! {1 Peter 1:2} Important, please notice that YOUR OBEDIENCE comes FIRST before the Sprinkling of Jesus Holy Precious Blood that Washes You Clean of Your Sins, AFTER you Repent from them! For your sanctification in the Spirit Before Almighty Holy God! That is why Jesus calls us All to Repent Today! Today is the Day of Salvation! Harden not your heart as in the provocation, in the day of temptation in the wilderness. But exhort one another daily, while it is called Today; least any of you be hardened through the deceitfulness of sin! Because today, right now, Jesus is on the mercy seat and you can find grace to help! Do not wait, your life is like a vapor that vanishes quickly away! Poof ! Tomorrow is not promised to anyone! Billions of people hope to repent Tomorrow, and Never Make It! Will you wait until your whole body and soul are completely engulfed in Brimstone & Fire, and then try to Spit on your Big Toe! It will Never Work! Today Jesus is on the mercy seat! On Judgment Day Jesus will be seated on a Throne of Justice and Judgment! Today if you repent You will receive mercy and Forgiveness! On Judgment Day, If you haven't truly Repented, been forgiven, Washed clean in Jesus Blood, and Covered by Jesus Grace! You will be Judged, and held responsible for your own works, and Pay the Price for your own Sins! Forever in Hell!!! IT IS A FEARFUL THING TO FALL INTO THE HANDS OF THE LIVING GOD! Therefore, Knowing The Terror of the Lord!!! WE PERSUADE MEN!!! I cannot possibly with mere words accurately describe, or convey to you the awesome power and holiness and purity, the incredible soul changing, pride destroying impact, it is to tremble in the presence of THE LIVING GOD!!!

Preface : A Word from the Author

Beloved, Any Unrepentant Sinner, Liar, Thief, Adulterer, Fornicator, Homosexual, Murderer, Drunkard, Abuser, Hateful, Lustful, Evil Speaking, (Cursing, Gossiping, Slanderer) Wrathful, Idolatrous, Covetous, Unforgiving, Unbelieving, Blasphemous, Atheist, God Hating, Unclean Person, and Defiler of themselves with Mankind; who Love Evil, and Hate Holiness, Truth and Light! Who Then try to (in their Unrepentant, Unclean, Unforgiven State) Kneel Before The Almighty Holy, Awesome, Sinless, All-Powerful, ONE TRUE LIVING GOD MOST HIGH!!! To kneel before **God** as a rebellious, unrepentant sinner, is **Permanent, Eternal, Damnation!** THAT WHICH ALMIGHTY GOD DESTROYS, IS TOTALLY DESTROYED FOREVER!!! ETERNALLY!!! WITHOUT REMEDY OR ESCAPE! There is NO WAY OUT OF HELL!!! EVER!!! It would be a Better Choice, to walk up to an 100 Billion Mega-Ton Atomic Bomb, and PRESS THE DETONATION BUTTON!!! But even That, (the utter obliteration of your Fleshly Body) **Would Not** Deliver You From the Hands of **ALMIGHTY HOLY GOD**!!! Beloved, There is only ONE WAY INTO HEAVEN!!! JESUS CHRIST!!! THERE IS ONLY ONE SAFE PLACE IN EXISTENCE, IN THE UNIVERSE!!! (This or any other Universe!) JESUS CHRIST!!! To Be A Living, Breathing, Born Again, Holy Spirit Filled, Member of THE BODY OF JESUS CHRIST!!! The Only Begotten Son of God!!! Is the only Safe, only Clean, only Protected, only Covered, ONLY SAFE PLACE IN THE ENTIRE UNIVERSE!!! Is Gods Son JESUS CHRIST!!! "I AM the Way, The Truth, and The Life! No Man can come unto the Father, But By ME!"{John 14:6} "I AM the resurrection, and the life; he that believeth in me, though he were dead, yet shall he Live!!!"{John 11:25} Mohammed cannot save you! Buddha cannot save you! Mary cannot save you! Jesus is the Only Way Into Heaven! Period! Jesus said,"Strive to enter into the Strait Gate""For many will seek to enter in, and shall not be Able!" Because broad is the way which leadeth to Destruction, and many people will go into it, Because Strait is the gait, and narrow is the way, which leadeth unto Life! And only a Few People will be Able to Find It!" {Luke 13:24 & Matthew 7:13-14} The Apostle Paul said, there are many runners that run in a race, but only one recieveth the Prize! So run, that ye may obtain (receive Eternal life in Heaven!) And every man that Striveth for the mastery is temperate (self controlled) in all things. Now they run to win a worthless prize; but we, Eternal life in Heaven! Therefore I Run, (with determined purpose) And so I fight, not as one that beateth the air! (For we wrestle not with flesh and blood) But I keep under my body, and bring it into subjection! And they that are Christ's (all that are part of the body of Christ) have Crucified the Flesh with the Affections and Lusts! {1 Corinthians 9:24 & Galatians 5:24} Are you Running & Fighting TO WIN This Battle For Eternal Life in Heaven? Have you Really Crucified your Flesh with all the Affections and Lusts? Are you really Striving to Enter In the Strait and Narrow Gate? Definition for Strive:(Greek root word: agon or agonize) to struggle for, or compete for a prize; to contend with an adversary; to fight fiercely and ferociously to obtain; to labor fervently for. Agonize: violent life or death struggle; to suffer pain in a massive struggle for ultimate victory!

Preface : A Word from the Author

As you look at your own life, and your own personal relationship with Almighty Holy God. (or do you even <u>have</u> a personal relationship with God ?) Do you see a purposed, focused, and determined, single minded, Violent, Fight and Struggle; Striving to <u>Overcome</u>, <u>Drive Out</u>, and <u>CRUCIFY</u> the sinful, lustful, covetous, evil desires and evil words and evil hatred that flow through your fleshly sinful body? Do you see a person who sincerely, fervently, humbly, prays Loves God, and seeks Gods face with all their Heart, Soul, Mind and Strength? Radically, Like their <u>Life</u> and <u>Soul</u> depend upon it? (And it Does!) Do you see someone who very <u>Diligently</u> studies The <u>Holy Bible</u>, (study to show thyself approved) who delights in the Law of the Lord and in his word doth he meditate <u>Day and Night</u>? Because your adversary the devil wants to drag you to <u>Hell with him</u>, and he will bury you under a mountain of <u>Lies</u> if you let him! You See, beloved, <u>Gods Holy Word</u> is the Helmet of Salvation! And <u>Knowing IT</u> will Protect your mind from all those Lies and fiery darts from the wicked One! But <u>YOU MUST</u> take <u>EVERY THOUGHT INTO CAPTIVITY</u> unto the <u>OBEDIENCE OF CHRIST</u>! Learning through much <u>Prayer</u>, <u>Bible Study</u>, and <u>Walking</u> consistently in <u>The Holy Spirit</u>! To Exercise your senses to <u>Discern</u> between <u>Good</u> and <u>Evil</u>, between <u>Darkness</u> and <u>Light</u>! Rightly dividing <u>the Word of Truth</u>! <u>CASTING DOWN</u> Evil Imaginations, and every Evil thought and Lie, that would exalt itself against the knowledge of <u>God</u>! Because The Weapons <u>of our Warfare</u> are not Carnal, But <u>Mighty Through God</u> to the <u>Pulling Down of Every Stronghold</u>! This is the Very <u>Front Line</u> in Your Fight against Evil in <u>the Battle for Your Soul</u>!!! The Thoughts and Imaginations that you think about and <u>let into your Mind and Spirit</u> every single day! This is <u>The Front Line of the Spiritual Battlefield</u> that either bind your heart and desires to evil strongholds or <u>Set You Free From Them</u>!!! {2 Corinthians 10:4 & Hebrews 5:14} That is the reason why Jesus told us to "build your treasures <u>In Heaven</u>, because where your treasure is, there will your <u>Heart Be Also</u>" {Matthew 6:20} If your treasure is in heaven, your mind will be consumed with Holy thoughts and desires! If your treasure is here on the earth, your mind will be consumed with riches, lusts possessions, partying, fame and fleshly desires! And if you constantly think about and crave these things, you will definitely <u>fall to them</u>! (whosoever committh sin is <u>the servant of sin</u>! and <u>the wages of Sin is Death</u>!) That is why <u>You Must</u> take every thought into captivity, and set no Evil thing before your eyes! So they can't ensnare your mind and soul with <u>Evil Desires</u>! The Holy Bible is your Sword in the Spirit! With it, you can cut through every Lie that binds <u>You</u>, Like a hot knife through butter! Jesus said, "you shall know the Truth, and <u>The Truth Shall Make You FREE</u>!!!" Thy word (the Holy Bible) is a lamp unto my feet, and a light unto my path! All Scripture is given by inspiration of <u>God</u>, and is profitable for doctrine, for reproof for correction, for instruction in righteousness; that the man of God may be perfect, completely equipped! To put on the whole armor of God, that ye may be able to stand against the tricks of the devil! For we <u>Do Not Wrestle</u> with flesh and blood, but against principalities and powers, against the rulers of the darkness of this world! Against spiritual wickedness in high places!

Preface : A Word from the Author

And your enemy (the devil) will seek to overwhelm and confuse you with cunning lies and deception! In a wrestling match, the two opponents look for leverage and power to try and maneuver and gain the superior position for victory! If Satan can confuse you with lies because you <u>Do Not Study and Know The Truth of God's Word</u>; (Jesus used God's word to cut Satan to shreds!) and you are weak because <u>You Do Not Pray Every Day</u>! And you <u>Do Not Seek God's Face</u> in Holy Prayer, Trusting Jesus and the Holy Spirit to Guide you and Teach you! You will unknowingly <u>Buy</u> every single lie the Devil tells you! Especially, If You are Not <u>Born Again</u>, and you do not have the <u>Holy Spirit</u> <u>Inside</u> of your Heart and Soul, <u>Guiding</u> you, <u>Teaching</u> you about <u>Jesus</u>, and <u>Protecting You</u>; with His <u>All Seeing</u>, <u>All Knowing</u>, Wisdom and Power!!! <u>THE HOLY SPIRIT IS GOD</u>! The Holy Spirit is <u>Your</u> Super-Awesome, All-Powerful, guide, Protector, and <u>UNBEATABLE</u> <u>ADVANTAGE</u> over your enemy, the Devil! If only you will <u>Accept Jesus Christ as your LORD AND SAVIOR</u>! <u>Invite The HOLY SPIRIT into Your Heart And Soul</u>! And Then <u>TRUST AND OBEY HIM</u>!!! "Draw nigh unto <u>God</u>, and <u>He Will DRAW NIGH UNTO YOU!!!</u>" {James 4:8} This the Very Reason Why You Absolutely, Positively, <u>MUST BE BORN AGAIN!!!</u> {John 3:3} The Very Instant that The Mighty Holy Spirit of God comes and Lives Inside of You, (Your heart and soul) You are Born Again <u>into</u> the Spirit of <u>Almighty Holy God</u>! And **You** are now a **Living Part** of the **Body** of <u>Jesus Christ</u>! And You are <u>Now Covered</u> and <u>Protected</u> by <u>Jesus Christ's Grace and Blood</u>! Satan now has <u>NO CLAIM OR RIGHTS ON YOU!!!</u> <u>You Are Bought and Paid for by Jesus own Precious BLOOD!!!</u> Almighty God our Father in Heaven has <u>ADOPTED YOU AS HIS OWN CHILD</u> and will toss Satan out on his Face!!! <u>ALMIGHTY GOD NOW OWNS YOU!!!</u> ("What? Know ye not that your body is the Temple of the Holy Ghost, which is <u>In You</u> ; ye are bought with a price and ye are not your own?") {1 Corinthians 6:19} You Still Have to Fight, to Overcome Your Own Sinful Flesh, and you will have to continue fighting! Because you are not wrestling with flesh and blood, but against evil spirits! And as you wrestle with your adversary the Devil, it is an ongoing struggle, until you either enter into Heaven or Jesus returns! Which ever comes first! But Now <u>The One True Living Almighty God</u>; <u>THE MOST POWERFUL BEING IN ALL OF EXISTENCE!!! GOD LIVES INSIDE OF YOU!!!</u> **Pray to Him**, <u>Trust Him</u>, <u>Believe In Him</u>, **Respect Him**, <u>Go to Him Humbly</u>, <u>confide and Rely on Him</u>, <u>Depend on Him</u>! The Holy Spirit will Strengthen you, Help you, Teach you, Guide you, Comfort you, and He Will Protect you! And for <u>Your Part</u>, if you will simply <u>Trust</u> and <u>Obey</u> what The Holy Spirit <u>Tells You To Do</u>!!! Have <u>Faith</u> in Jesus Precious Blood, His Resurrection from the Dead, His Grace and Awesome Atoning Sacrifice to God our Father <u>for your Sins</u>! You will Absolutely, Definitely make it into Heaven! Because of <u>GOD'S GRACE THROUGH JESUS, And ONLY BECAUSE OF GOD'S GRACE AND THE MIGHTY LORD JESUS!!!</u> You are Saved By **GRACE** Through **FAITH**, and <u>Not of Your Selves or Your Own Works</u>! It is the <u>Gift of God</u>! Least **ANY MAN** should Boast! Because <u>No Flesh Shall Glory in God Presence</u>! {Ephesians 2:8 & 1 Corinthians 1:29}

Preface : A Word from the Author

The Only Reason that Any Person that Ever Lived on the face of the Planet Earth, Who walks into Heavens Gates; and is found worthy to receive Eternal Life! The One and Only Reason that Any Person Enters Into Heaven, is because **JESUS CHRIST** Paid the Price for Our Sins! When He Shed His Precious **Blood** at Golgotha on The Cross of Calvary! Where Jesus Atoned for our sins, Reconciling Us to God! With His **Spotless, Blameless, Perfect, Holy Sacrifice** to Almighty God our Father in Heaven! Fulfilling and Completing All the Requirements of the Holy Law, Breaking us **Free** from the Chains and Bondage of the Laws of Sin and Death!!! When Jesus put Satan to Open Shame, He Spoiled All the Principalities and Powers of Hell!!! He Took the Keys of Hell and Death from Satan! Triumphing over Him in it!{Colossians 2:15} Vanquishing the Evil Enemy for All of Mankind! Setting all **God's Children Free Forever!!!** An Awesome Incredible Task that **NO OTHER MAN COULD EVER ACCOMPLISH!!!** The One and Only Begotten Son of God Did It! **JESUS CHRIST Said "IT IS FINISHED!"** Mighty Lord Jesus, I Love You So Much, it is a Great Joy and Pleasure to **WORSHIP YOU!!!** Beloved, the Small Minuscule amount of Trials and Temptations that We have to Face, are not even worthy to mention; next to the Massive, Awful, Painful, Trials and Temptations that our **Lord and Savior Jesus** had to Endure For Us! And He Did No Sin, neither was there any evil or Guile found (spoken) out of his Mouth! {1 Peter 2:22} Wherefore, Let us (overcome) and lay aside every sin which doth so easily beset us, and let us run with patience the Race that is set before us! Looking unto **Jesus** the author and finisher of our Faith; Who for the Joy that was set before Him (our salvation) He Endured the Cross, despising the shame, (even though he was Innocent and Sinless) and he (Jesus) is set down at the right hand of the Throne of God! {Hebrews 12:1} Beloved, we have an Advocate with the Father, Jesus Christ the Righteous, He is the propitiation for our Sins! {1 John 2:1} He was wounded for our Transgressions, and Bruised for our Iniquities, the Chastisement of our peace (Punishment for our Redemption) was upon Him; and by His stripes we are healed! {Isaiah 53:5} And our sins are Forgiven for his name's sake! {1 John 2:12} (when we repent from them!) Even though Jesus was God's only begotten Son, He learned obedience by the things which He suffered! And being made Perfect, He became the author of Eternal Salvation unto all them that **Obey Him** !!! {Hebrews 5:8} Jesus Christ himself was led by the Holy Spirit into the wilderness to be Tempted by the Devil! {Matthew 4:1} If God would allow his own son Jesus to go through all the Fiery Trials and Temptations by the Devil, will not you and I have to go through Fiery Trials and Temptations? Look what the scripture right above this says,"Jesus learned obedience and was made perfect By the things which He suffered!" Now the Lord Jesus was already perfect, and always was perfect! Being our Lord and Savior as a man, God Incarnate;(God in the Flesh) he was showing Us The Way to Eternal Life! (Jesus is the Way!) Our Precious Lord Jesus is not asking you to do or go through anything that He didn't Do or Go Through First! For Us! Gold that is put into a Fiery Furnace is not Destroyed, but Purified!!! And once all the Impurities are removed,

Preface : A Word from the Author

The Master of the Furnace (Jesus) can look at the Gold Purified in the Furnace, and see his own Reflection **In It**! An Excited New Father in the Infant ward at the hospital, will carefully look through the glass at all the newborn babies. To see which one is His Child and has his Face and Likeness! And when **The Father** sees His Child, he cannot take his eyes off of His Own Child! Our Father in Heaven loves you, and delights in you! He wants You to be In Heaven with Him! And like a Good Father, He will discipline a child He Loves! He is Fighting for **Your Soul!!!** If you spank a child that runs into the street, in front of a moving car; or a young child that is trying to stick a screwdriver into an electrical outlet! You are not spanking that child because you want to hurt them, but because You Love Them! And you want to Save them from Death!!! When Our Father God disciplines you for Sin, He is not Chastening you to hurt you; He is doing it because He Loves You! God does not correct his own children to Hurt them, But To **Save Your Soul from Destruction and Eternal Damnation in Hell Forever!!!** All who have Ears to Hear, Let Them Hear! **The Wages of Sin is Death! Permanent Absolute Destruction!** You should get on your knees, Pray to **God** and Thank Him for His Correction and Discipline! Ask **God** to "Please don't Ever Stop Correcting and Helping Me Heavenly Father! I Definitely Love and Need and **Trust in You, Almighty God**! I ask in **Jesus** name, Deliver me from Evil! Beloved, It is the terrible day that God takes his hands off of You, and He **Stops** Correcting and Disciplining You; that you are in Deep, Deep Trouble! "My son, despise not the chastening of the Lord; neither be weary of his correction: For whom the Lord loveth he correcteth; even as a father the son in whom he delighteth."{Proverbs 3:11} "My son, do not despise the chastening of the Lord, nor faint when thou are rebuked of him: For whom the Lord loveth he chasteneth, and scourgeth every son whom he receiveth. If ye endure chastening, God dealeth with **You** as with **A Son**; for what son is he whom the father chasteneth not? But if ye be without chastisement, whereof all are partakers, then are ye bastards, and not sons! Furthermore, we have had fathers of our flesh which corrected us, and we gave them reverence: shall we not much rather be in subjection unto the **Father of Spirits, and Live?** God chastises us for our own Profit! That We might be partakers of **His Holiness**! {Hebrews 12:5} Hear what Jesus himself said, "I counsel thee to buy of me, gold tried in the **Fire**, that thou mayest be rich; and white raiment, that thou mayest be clothed, and that the shame of thy nakedness do not appear; and anoint thy eyes with eyesalve, that thou mayest **See**! As many as **I Love, I Rebuke and Chasten**: therefore, be Zealous and **Repent**! Behold, I stand at the door, and knock: if any man hear my voice, and open the door, I will come in to him, and will sup with him, and he with me. To him that **Overcometh** (Sin and Evil) will I grant to sit with me in my throne, even as I also **Overcame**, and am set down with my Father in his throne! He that hath an ear, let him hear what the Spirit saith unto the churches." {Revelations 3:18} "Blessed is the man that endureth temptation: for when he is tried, he shall receive the crown of **Life**, which the Lord hath promised to them that love him! {James 1:12} The Trial of your Faith is much more Precious than Gold!{1 Peter 1:6}

Preface : A Word from the Author

All the Churches shall know that I Am He which Searcheth the Reins and Hearts! And I will give unto every one of you according to your Works! " Jesus Christ " {Revelations 2:23}
Upon the wicked he shall rain snares, fire and brimstone, and a horrible tempest!{Psalms 11:6}
Beloved, Our Mighty Lord and Savior Jesus is Loving and Wise; He knows how to deliver <u>You</u> from <u>Evil</u>! When a skilled Surgeon Operates on a Patient, He does all he can do to tenderly help and comfort the patient. But during the operation he must also take out his scalpel, and **Cut Out** the <u>Evil Cancer</u> that is <u>Going to Kill</u> You! It <u>Will</u> cause you some <u>Pain</u>! But <u>It Must Be Done</u>! **The Evil Must Be Removed!** Beloved, Please <u>Always Remember</u> our Precious Lord Jesus is not asking you to go through anything that <u>He Himself</u> didn't already <u>Go Through</u>!!! A <u>Billion</u> times worse and more Difficult! And He did it <u>FOR US!!!</u> <u>To Save</u> **Our Souls!!!** Jesus Christ, **<u>Was Already In Heaven! Living In Glory! Creator of the Universe! Part of the Godhead!</u>** But He Humbly Put Off His Awesome Power and Glory, came to Earth as a Humble Man, put on Human Flesh, "as the seed of Abraham and the son of David" Fulfilled all the Requirements of the Holy Law for God the Father! Created a Way for you and me, and **All of Mankind** to be **RECONCILED TO ALMIGHTY GOD OUR FATHER; AND GO TO HEAVEN!!!** "For ye know the grace of our Lord Jesus Christ, that, though he was rich, yet for your sakes he became poor, that ye through his poverty might be rich. (have Eternal Life!) {2 Corinthians 8:9} Who gave himself for our sins, that he might deliver us from this present evil world, according to the will of God our Father! {Galatians 1:4} **Jesus** Destroyed the Power of Hell and Death over every Man, Woman, and Child; He took the Keys of Hell and Death from Satan and Vanquished <u>Our Evil Enemy FOREVER</u>!!! **Jesus** delivered us from Evil, He set the captives Free, healed the brokenhearted, recovered sight to the blind, (we are all blind without Jesus!) and set at Liberty them that are Bruised! (by Sin) **Jesus Rose From The Grave**, Comforted and strengthened his Disciples by showing them that **He Is Alive Forevermore !!!** Then the Lord Jesus Ascended into Heaven, where he is seated at the right hand of God our Father in the Holy of Holies, where He Prays and Intercedes for us as our advocate with God the Father, To this very Day and <u>Forever</u>! In Heaven Above, where all principalities and Powers are subject unto him, and he is given all the Power and authority in Heaven and in earth! **ALL FOR US** !!! And <u>We</u> won't give up a few <u>Pitiful Sins</u>! So That **We Can Be Free!!!** Are We really that Blind and Stupid? **Heavenly Father**, Mighty **Lord Jesus**, Precious **Holy Spirit** Living Inside of Me, (these three <u>Are One</u>) I want You to know right now, that I Love You, and I need You so very, <u>Much</u>!!! It Is my <u>Greatest Joy and Delight</u> to kneel at Your Feet and **Worship You Forever!!!** You are Worthy, Worthy, Worthy, to Receive Glory and Honor and Power, Forevermore!!!
The Truth is that We are Blind, and Miserable, and Naked <u>Without You</u>!!! And all our Righteousness is as <u>Filthy Rags</u>!!! The <u>Truth</u> is that <u>I am Not Worthy to Kneel at Your Feet</u>, or even to be your <u>Doormat</u>! So I thank you for allowing me to! So I can touch your Precious Holy Feet!

Preface : A Word from the Author

O' My Father, Which art in Heaven, Almighty Lord God of Truth and Light, Love and Mercy, Holiness and Righteousness, Justice and Judgment! I Praise You with all my Heart, Soul, Mind, and Strengeth! **Eternally! Forevermore!!!** O'Lord, Thine is the <u>Greatness</u>, and the <u>Power</u>, and the <u>Glory</u>, and the <u>Victory</u>, and The Majesty: For All that is in the Heavens and in the Earth is thine; **<u>Thine is the Kingdom O'LORD, and THOU art Exalted as HEAD ABOVE ALL!!!</u>** {1 Chronicles 29:11} Lord God of Israel, there <u>Is No God Like Thee</u> in Heaven Above, or on Earth beneath, who keepest covenant and mercy with thy servants that **<u>Walk Before Thee with ALL THEIR HEART!!!</u>** Mighty **Lord Jesus**, I ask You humbly, "with All My Heart" please Pray for me; that I would be a **REAL MAN OF GOD!!!** In <u>True Holiness and Righteousness</u>, allways walking "In The Spirit" and "Overcoming <u>All</u> the Sins and Lust of the Flesh!" Please Strengthen me "**Holy Spirit**" in my inner Man, with Strength and Understanding in all Spiritual Knowledge and Wisdom; To Discern between Good and Evil, Darkness and Light, Rightly dividing the word of Truth, to know and fulfill God's Perfect Will for my Life! That the Lord **Jesus Christ** may dwell <u>In my Heart by Faith</u>, "Permanantly and Forever" and that I would be Rooted and Grounded in **Love**, and <u>be able</u> to comprehend with all Saints what is the breadth, and length, and depth, and hight; (of God) And to know the love of Christ, which passeth all knowledge, and that I might be <u>filled</u> with all the fulness of God! That I might walk worthy of the Lord, "pleasing Him" and being Fruitful in every Good work, and Increasing in all the Knowledge of God! Strengthened with all might, according to <u>His Glorious Power</u>, unto all patience and longsuffering with joyfulness; Giving thanks unto God my "Heavenly Father" who has Adopted <u>Me</u>, and allowed me to partake in the Inheritance of the Saints in Light! Who has Delivered Me from the power of darkness, and has Translated Me into the Kingdom of his dear Son; **Jesus Christ !** In whom we have Redemption through **<u>His Blood</u>**, even the Forgivness of Sins! Who is <u>the Image of The **Invisible God**</u>, the Firstborn of every creature! **O' Heavenly Father God**, Please Remove Every Evil, Wicked, <u>Pride</u> and <u>Sin</u> from <u>My Heart</u>! Please take thy **Holy Spirit** Scalpel and <u>Cut Evil Out of My Heart!!!</u> <u>Cut Out Every Single Root of Sin and Pride and Fleshly Lust!</u> **<u>Please Cut Out Anything and Everything That Is NOT LIKE YOU, O'Heavenly Father!!!</u>** Please take thy Mighty Finger O' God, and Engrave <u>your Precious Holy Hallowed NAME UPON MY HEART AND SOUL!!!</u> **PLEASE MAKE ME LIKE JESUS!!!** Please Make Me to Love <u>Holiness</u>, the way that <u>You Love Holiness</u>!!! Please Make Me to Hate <u>Every Sin and Evil</u>, the way that <u>You Hate Sin and Evil</u>!!! "Hate the Evil, and Love the Good, and Establish Judgment in the gate!-{Amos 5:15} You Promised us in the Holy Bible O'Father; "A new heart will I give you, and a new spirit will I put within you: and I will take away the stony heart, and I will give you a heart of flesh. And I will put my (Holy) spirit within you, and cause you to walk in my statues, and ye shall keep my judgments and <u>do them</u>! For <u>I Will</u> Put my law in their inward parts and write it <u>in their hearts;</u> and I will be their God! Fear not, for I am with thee, I will help and strengthen thee! I will not fail or forsake thee! _{Go See "God's New Covanant" near the back, for these Scripture Locations}

Preface - A Word from the Author

O'My Heavenly Father, Thou <u>One True Living God</u> of Truth and Holiness and Righteousness, **YOU are the GREATEST TREASURE IN ALL OF EXISTENCE!!!** The Creator, Author, and <u>Giver of ALL LIFE</u>!!! The Almighty God of <u>Truth</u> and <u>Holiness</u> that **Will Not Lie! Ever!!!** The <u>Most Powerful Being</u> in All of Existence, Yet You are <u>Humble</u> and <u>Loving</u> and <u>Merciful</u> to All who **Do** what is <u>Right</u> and <u>Good</u> and <u>Just</u> and <u>Fair</u> and <u>True</u>! To all who <u>Love Holiness</u> and <u>Hate Evil</u>! "Ye that Love the Lord, **Hate Evil**: He preserveth the souls of his saints; He delivereth them out of the hand of the Wicked" {Psalms 97:10} "Hate the Evil, and **Love the Good**, and Establish Judgment in the gate!"{Amos 5:15} To everyone who Loves Truth and Holiness, Goodness and Righteousness, Justice and Judgment, God is a Wonderful, Loving, Merciful, Gracious, Strong Tower, Fortress and Deliverer! But to all who <u>Love Evil</u> and <u>Lying</u>, <u>Stealing</u> and <u>Cursing</u>, <u>Lust</u> and <u>Evil Speaking</u>, <u>Gossip</u> and <u>Murder</u>! (with a gun or with your tongue) All who Love <u>Sin and Evil</u>, Adultery or Fornication, Homosexuality, Drunkenness, Covetousness, Greed, and <u>All UNHOLINESS</u>!!! To <u>All Who Love Evil</u> and <u>Sin</u> like their Father <u>SATAN</u>!!! **ALMIGHTY GOD IN HEAVEN ABOVE IS A HOLY TERROR AND DESTROYER !!!** "Ye do the deeds of your father! (Satan) Ye are of <u>your father the Devil</u>, and the Lusts of your father <u>Ye Will Do</u>! He was a murderer from the beginning, and abode not in the Truth, because there <u>is no Truth in him</u>! When he speaketh a Lie, he speaketh of his own: For he is a <u>Liar</u> and <u>the Father</u> of it!" {John 8:41-44} (Satan is the <u>Father</u> of every person who tells a <u>Lie</u> and speaks lies out of their mouth!) And <u>You Yourself</u> **Make Satan Your Father** by the very words that come out of **Your own Mouth**! And by <u>Stealing</u> and <u>Murdering</u>! The <u>deeds of</u> **Your Father "You" Will Do**! And If Satan is your Father, **Do Not Be Surprised** when God casts **You** into Hell, **with Him**!!! Every single time that you <u>tell a lie</u>, or <u>Steal</u>, or <u>Curse</u>, or <u>Gossip</u>, or <u>Do Any</u> **Evil Actions or Deeds**; In the Spiritual Realm <u>You</u> are putting Your Hand in <u>Almighty God's</u> Holy Face, and **YOU** are **SHOVING ALMIGHTY HOLY GOD AWAY FROM YOU!!!** By <u>Your Own Actions and Words</u> You are saying to Almighty God, You're Not <u>My Father</u>, I Do Not <u>Love</u> You God, I Do Not <u>Want</u> You God, I Do Not <u>Need You God</u>! I Choose Evil! Furthermore, Every time that <u>You</u> Lie, Steal, Curse, Gossip, Slander, and <u>Do Evil</u> Actions or Deeds; In the Spiritual Realm **You Yourself** are **Tying Your Soul To Evil Satan**, and giving **THE ENEMY OF YOUR VERY SOUL** a Big Hug and a Kiss, and saying I Love You Satan, and <u>I Choose</u> **You To Be My Father**! And Every Single Time <u>You</u> Do This, Satan stands there Laughing as he puts another Evil Hook into **Your Soul**, To **Drag You To Hell With Him**!!! Satan only gives you Death! <u>Only</u> **God can Give You Life**! When the One Drop of Life that **God gave to You**, is about to <u>Run Out</u>! What will you do? If you chose <u>Sin</u> over <u>Life in God</u>? He that committeth sin is of the devil; for the devil sinneth from the beginning! For this purpose the Son of God was manifested, that he might destroy the works of the devil! Whosoever doeth not righteousness is <u>not of God</u>, neither he that does not Love his brother! {1 John 3:8-10}

Preface - A Word from the Author

Abraham believed God, and it was accounted to him for Righteousness! {Romans 4:3} Faith in God, and because he believed what God said was true, God saw this as righteousness and Faith! Abraham loved God with all his heart, God loved Abraham and he was called the friend of God! The Apostle Paul gave everything to God, Including his Life, and he <u>Terrorized</u> Satan and every Demon in hell! Paul was a <u>Thorn</u> in Satans side, and he authored 14 of the books (or Letters) in The Holy Bible! (in the New Testament) Only Almighty God can tell how many lost souls were reached with the Gospel of Jesus Christ through the tireless efforts of this Mighty Man of God! The Apostle Paul said this,"I count all things but loss for the Excellency of the knowledge of **Jesus Christ my Lord**: for whom I have suffered the loss of all things, and do count them but Dung! That I may <u>**Win Christ**</u>! And be found <u>in him</u>, not having mine own righteousness which is of the Law, but that which is through the Faith of Christ, the righteousness which is of God by Faith: that I may know him and the power of his resurrection, and the fellowship of his suffering being made conformable unto his death!{Philippians 3:8} Jesus said,"Except your righteousness shall exceed the righteousness of the scribes and Pharisees, Ye shall in <u>no case</u> enter into the kingdom of heaven!" {Matthew 5:20} The Scribes and Pharisees sit in Moses' seat, and teach the Law; they put on fancy clothes and sit in the highest most important seats in the church, and make long prayers for pretense, but they only do it to be seen of men, and make money; they do not truly live what they Preach; or as Jesus put it, "they say, and do not do!" Jesus called them hypocrites (the word means "an actor playing a part") and Whited Sepulchres (big fancy graves) which indeed appear beautiful on the outside, but inside are full of dead mens bones and Sin! So ye outwardly appear righteousness unto men, but within ye are full of hypocrisy and iniquity! {Matthew 23: 3-28} Jesus said,"beware of wolves in sheeps clothing" Evil, Greedy, Men, (and world wide denominations!) whose true motive is to <u>use the gospel to make lots of money</u>! By preaching a Soft, Easy, Forgivness without <u>True Repentance</u>, you're fine just the way you are, your sin is O.K. with God, just put your <u>Money</u> in the offering basket and you're on your way to heaven gospel! God is too loving and kind to send evil sinners like <u>you</u> to hell. And they believe this <u>Evil Lie</u>, and they swallow it hook, line, and sinker! Because **That is What They Want To HEAR**!!! <u>They</u> **Love Their Sins**! And they have <u>No Intentions</u> of Stoping or Giving them up! They don't want to Crucify their Flesh on the Cross! They don't want to pick up their cross and Follow Jesus! They don't want to give <u>Full Control of their Life to God</u>! They don't really Love God with <u>all</u> their Heart, Mind, Soul, and Strength! Isn't Just a little bit of Sin O.K. Lord Jesus? <u>**NO**</u>! "There were false prophets among the people, and there <u>shall be false teachers among you</u>! who seceretly <u>shall bring in wrong teachings</u>, and many shall follow their deceptive ways, and through covetousness they shall with feigned words (easy preaching) <u>make merchandise of **you**</u>! <u>(**take your money**)</u>{2 Peter 2:1}"For the time will come when they <u>will not endure (hear) sound doctrine</u>! **(the Truth)** But after **their own Lust** they shall listen to false teachers, having itching ears; they shall <u>turn away their ears from the truth</u>, and shall be turned unto fables!" {2 Tim 4:3}

Preface : A Word from the Author

Jesus Christ said "Repent" turn away from ALL SIN and ALL EVIL, and Stop Doing It! THE WAGES OF SIN IS DEATH!!! Sin and Evil is a Permanent, Eternal, Un-Refundable **ONE WAY TICKET TO HELL and DEATH!!! THE LAKE OF FIRE!!! FOREVER!!!**
This is So Simple! Exactly what Part of Sin = Hell and Death is it that you don't Understand ? If someone with a gun or a knife were coming after you, you'ed run with all your Might!!! Sin and Evil are Dragging You To Hell, while you stand there Loving and Hugging and Kissing them passionately! And if someone who really loves and cares about you, tries to help, reach out and Pry those Sins Away From You! (like right Now!) You get Furious and Angry, cursing and screaming, and wanting To Fight with them! What are you Thinking? Where is your Brain? Are a few pitiful Sins worth giving up All of Eternity in Heaven with God and Jesus? Really? And Burning in Hell and the Lake of Fire with Satan, Suffering and being Tormented Forever? And the Best part is You Paid some Lying, Evil Preacher, YOUR HARD EARNED MONEY!!! (your money was his true motive) To Tell You WHAT YOU WANTED TO HEAR!!! Leaving You bound to your Sins and heading to Hell, if you don't Truly Repent! (only The Truth shall set you Free, because whosoever committeth Sin is the Servant of Sin! "Jesus") {John 8:32-34} Hear the words of the Apostle Paul, (a real man of God) "I marvel that you are so soon removed from him that called you into the grace of Christ unto Another Gospel: which is not another; but there be some that trouble you, and would Pervert the gospel of Jesus Christ! But though we, or an Angel from Heaven, preach any other Gospel unto you than that we have preached unto you, Let him be Accursed! I will say it again, **If Any Man Preach Any Other Gospel unto You**!!! **Let Him Be Accursed**!!! {Galatians 1:6} "For I know this, that after my departing, Grievous Wolves shall enter in among you, not sparing the flock! Also of your own selves shall men arise, speaking perverse things, to draw away disciples after them! Therefore watch, and remember, I did not cease to warn everyone with tears, both day and night!"{Acts 20:29} Beware of all kinds of "False Apostles, deceitful workers, transforming themselves into the apostles of Christ! And no marvel; for Satan himself is transformed into an angel of light! Therefore it is no great thing if his ministers (wolves) also be transformed as the ministers of righteousness; whose end shall be according To Their Works!{2 Corinthians 11:13} "Know this, in the last days perilous times shall come. For men shall be lovers of their own selves, covetous, boasters, proud, blasphemers, disobedient to parents, unthankful, unholy, without natural affection, false accusers, incontinent, fierce, despisers of those that are good, traitors, highminded, lovers of pleasure more than lovers of God! Having a form of godliness, but denying (to do Gods will) {2 Timothy 3:1} "Take heed that no man deceive you, many shall come in my name, saying, I am Christ; and shall deceive many!" The True gospel is this, accept Jesus Christ as your Lord and Savior, and Invite the Holy Spirit into your heart and be born again, Repent from all sin and evil, live a Holy Life, Do Gods will, love **God** above everything else! Love and treat people the way that you want to be treated! Take up the Cross and follow Jesus, Crucify your fleshly desires, when the flesh dies, **You Live!**

Preface : A Word from the Author

Do you not know, that all who were baptized into Jesus Christ were baptized unto his death? For if we have been planted together in the likeness of his death, we shall also (live) in the likeness of his Resurrection! Knowing this, that our old man is crucified with him, that the body of <u>sin</u> might be <u>destroyed</u>, that henceforth we should <u>not serve sin</u>! For he that is dead is freed from sin! Now if <u>we be dead</u> with Christ, we shall also <u>Live with him</u>; for in that he died, he died unto sin once: but in that he liveth, he liveth unto God! Likewise reckon ye also yourselves to be <u>dead unto sin</u>, but <u>Alive unto God</u> through <u>Jesus Christ our Lord</u>! Therefore, **Do Not Let Sin Reign in your Mortal body, that ye should obey it in the Lusts thereof**! Neither yield ye your members as instruments of unrighteousness unto Sin! But yield yourselves <u>unto God</u>, as those that are <u>Alive from the dead</u>! Then your members <u>will be</u> instruments of <u>Righteousness unto God</u>!(**and live forever with God**!) **For SIN SHALL NOT Have Dominion OVER YOU**!!! For ye are not under the Law but under Grace! What then? Shall we Sin because we are not under the law, but under Grace? <u>God Forbid</u>! Do you not know and understand, that to whom ye yield yourselves servants to obey, his servants ye are to <u>whom ye obey</u>; either of **Sin unto Death**, or **Obedience (to God) unto Righteousness**? For when ye were the servants of sin, ye were free from righteousness! But now being made <u>Free from Sin</u>, and become <u>Servants to God</u>, (if you truly obey him from your heart!) ye have your fruit unto Holiness, and the end <u>Everlasting Life</u>! For **the Wages of Sin is DEATH**!!! **But the Gift of God is ETERNAL LIFE through JESUS CHRIST our LORD**!!! That the righteousness of the Law might be fulfilled in us, <u>who walk not after the</u> **Flesh** <u>but after</u> **the Spirit**! For to be carnally minded is <u>Death</u>; but to be <u>Spiritually minded</u> is <u>Life and Peace</u>! So then they that that are in the Flesh <u>cannot please God</u>! But ye are not in the flesh, but in the Spirit, if (you are born again) so be that **The Spirit of God Dwell IN YOU**!!! Now if any man <u>Does Not Have The Spirit of Christ</u>, (Holy Spirit) He is none of His! (**Not Born Again!**) If the Spirit that raised up Jesus from the dead dwells in <u>You</u>, He shall also <u>quicken your mortal body</u>! Therefore, brethren, we are debtors, <u>not</u> to the Flesh! For if ye live after the flesh, <u>Ye shall die</u>! But if Ye through the Spirit <u>Do Mortify</u> the <u>deeds of the body</u>! **Ye Shall Live!** For as many as are **LED BY THE SPIRIT OF GOD!!! They! Are The Sons of GOD!!!** {See Romans Ch. 6,7,& 8} Are <u>You</u> led by the Holy Spirit every Day? Is it <u>Gods Holy Spirit</u> leading you to curse, lie, steal, gossip, slander, hate, or treat people like dirt? Is it the Holy Spirit leading you to get drunk, do drugs, lust, cheat, commit adultery, fornication, homosexuality, sex sins, watch pornography, vile filth, or party and hang out with evil devils? **No!** <u>Mortify your members which are upon the earth</u>;fornication, uncleanness, evil deeds, covetousness anger, wrath, malice, evil words out your mouth! These things bring <u>The Wrath of God upon You</u>! Whosoever doth not bear his Cross, and come after <u>Me</u>, <u>Cannot be my Disciple</u>! {Luke 14:27} Jesus said to them all, If any man will come after me, let him deny himself, and take up his cross daily, and follow me! For whosoever will save his life shall <u>lose it:</u> but whosoever will lose his life for my sake, the same shall <u>Save It</u>!{Luke 9:23} For what is a man profited, if he gain the whole world and <u>lose his own soul</u>? Or what shall a man give in exchange for his Soul?{Matthew 16:26}

Preface : A Word from the Author

In the days that we live, about 2000 years after Jesus Christ was crucified on the cross of Calvary. Most people see the cross as a beautiful piece of jewelry, that they wear around their neck. But if you could travel back in time, to Rome or Israel, some 2000 years ago, then you would see that the Cross is an Instrument the Romans used to <u>Kill Their Enemies</u>! And get rid of them <u>Forever</u>!!! When you saw a man carrying <u>A Cross</u> out of the city, you knew that, <u>That Man was a Dead Man</u>! He was <u>Going to His Grave!</u> You would Never, Ever, See Him Again! This will enlighten your Eyes, and Illuminate your Mind! When Jesus tells us to <u>Take up our Cross and Follow Him</u>! He is telling <u>You</u> to <u>Crucify the Evil Desires of your Flesh</u>! To kill all those sins and evil desires in your Flesh, and send them <u>To The Grave</u>! <u>Forever</u>! **<u>It Is Your Enemy</u>! <u>They Will Send You To Hell</u>!** You must be born again in the Spirit, into the body of Jesus Christ, and let the Holy Spirit Rise Up inside your heart and soul! Give Jesus full control of your life, to crucify your flesh and overcome the Sinful Adam-like, fallen nature, and evil desires in your fleshly body, or it will <u>Destroy You</u>!!! I am Crucified <u>with Christ</u>; but still I Live, yet not I, but Christ that <u>Lives within Me</u>! And the life which I now live in the flesh, I live by the faith of the Son of God, who loved me, and gave him self for me. I do not frustrate the grace of God: for if righteousness comes by the Law, then Christ is dead in vain!{Galatians 3:20} Ye are saved by <u>grace</u> through <u>faith</u>, and <u>not of yourselves</u> or any of <u>your own works or efforts</u>! It is <u>only</u> by the <u>Grace</u> and <u>Gift of God</u>! (Jesus Christ!) Least any man should boast!{Ephesians 2:8} Knowing that a man is not justified by the works of the law, but by his faith in Jesus Christ! For by the works of the law shall no flesh be justified! (or Saved!) Many Christians and Preachers are confused by this, or do not fully understand this point of Pauls teaching on grace. If you are only saved by grace through faith and <u>not by works</u>, why then, do we have to <u>Repent</u>, <u>Crucify our flesh</u>, <u>Overcome sin and evil desires</u> and <u>Live a Holy Life</u>? Isn't faith in Jesus All we need? <u>No</u>! Satan and every demon <u>believe</u> and <u>know</u> that Jesus is the son of God! But they are all going to burn in Hell, because they <u>Did Not Obey God</u>! Jesus said, not every one that says to me, Lord, Lord, shall enter into the kingdom of Heaven; but only they that <u>Do the will of my Father which is in Heaven</u>! {Matthew 7:21} So what happened to grace and faith? Nothing! They are still there! Lets make an illustration for better understanding. Imagine you are trapped in a prison cell, with 10 feet thick <u>stainless steel walls</u> on <u>all sides</u>! And the enemy that put you there and all his forces are standing guard outside! You are helpless with not so much as a toothpick to try and cut your way out! You are completely doomed, and could <u>never escape in a billion years</u>! Then, <u>The greatest warrior that ever lived</u>, overcomes all of the enemy forces, opens up a way into your prison cell, and says, (take up your cross and)"Follow Me" He gives you a sword and shield, a breastplate and helmet, boots, and the strength of his own <u>Spirit Inside You</u>! Then he personally guides and leads you, and helps you fight through the enemies traps and strongholds to <u>Freedom</u>! Did <u>you save yourself</u>? **<u>No</u>! <u>Jesus set You Free</u>!** You still had to fight the enemy! You still had to overcome! Only Jesus <u>set you free</u>! You are saved by grace through faith, <u>not by your own works</u>! What breaks my heart is, 93% of the world sits there in an open prison cell, <u>Racing Towards Hell</u>!

Preface : A Word from the Author

Just let that thought soak into your mind for a while. Billions upon Billions of <u>Hellbound Souls</u>, Sitting there in an **OPEN PRISON CELL !!!** Refusing to stand up and follow **Jesus** into the Light of God, and Truth, and **FREEDOM !!!** And the Reason Why they refuse to follow Jesus into God's Light? God's Light exposes Sin, and Evil, and Darkness! And **<u>they Love Their Sins</u>**! Because "Men loved darkness rather than Light, because their deeds were **evil**" and "the deeds of **<u>Your Father You will Do !!!</u>** {John 3:19 & 8:41-44} Doing God's will and living a Holy Life doesn't sound like "Freedom" to them! To them "Freedom" sounds like being chained to a drug, or chained to a bottle of Alcohol, for their Happiness! To them "Freedom" sounds like being chained to a pack of cigarettes, or chained to Sex and pornography for their <u>Happiness!</u> The only problem is when they wake up the next morning after a night of "Partying" <u>they are still unhappy</u> and need to get more Drugs, and Alcohol, and Cigarettes, and Sex, to manufacture and make up some more happiness in this so called life of "Freedom" that they are chained too! Now, "**Jesus**" Words Ring Out Loud and Clear, "Whosoever commiteth Sin, <u>Is the Servant of Sin</u>! And what most people <u>Don't Realize</u> is that Jesus words are Eternal!!! They will last <u>Forever!!!</u> If You are miserable without <u>drugs</u> now, you will be miserable without drugs <u>Forever!</u> If you are miserable without alcohol <u>now</u>, you will be miserable without alcohol <u>Forever!</u> If you are miserable without cigarettes now, you will be miserable without cigarettes <u>Forever!</u> If you Burn with Lust for <u>Sex</u> now, you will burn with lust for Sex for **All of Eternity!!!** There will be <u>No Drugs in Hell!!!</u> There will be <u>No Alcohol in Hell!!!</u> There will be <u>No Cigarettes in Hell!!!</u> And There will be <u>No Sex in Hell!!!</u> God's word says that all the souls in hell will be "vessels of wrath to fitted to Destruction" where "their worm dieth not, and the fire never shall be quenched" {Romans 9:22} & {Mark 9:43} These words out of Jesus own mouth, also destroy another one of satans lies that some churches teach about "Purgatory" (the word <u>never</u> appears, not one single time in the Holy Bible) That in purgatory you suffer for a while and then go to heaven. Jesus said that "their worm (soul) <u>Dieth Not</u>, and that <u>the Fire **Never Shall Be Quenched!**</u> Also in the parable about the "Rich man and Lazarus" the rich man burning in hell was told that there is a great gulf fixed between heaven and hell that **cannot be Passed!!!** {Luke 16:26} Go to it, and read the whole parable, the rich man in hell couldn't even get a drop of <u>Water</u> to cool his tongue! Much less a bottle of alcohol, or drugs, or cigarettes, or Sex, or <u>Any of the other Vices you will be Craving!!!</u> But That is not even the worst part! The Worst Part is that **<u>You will be separated from God!!!</u> <u>Forever!!!</u>** What you don't know or realize right now, is that even if you are living a sinful, evil life; You can still feel the presence and goodness, the love and joy, the kindness and character of Almighty God! From the drop of life that **God gave to You!** God is the author of all life, and man was created <u>in his Image!</u> The attributes of God are Love, Peace, Joy, Happiness, Kindness, Faith, gentleness, goodness, meekness, the most precious moments of your **entire Life!** You felt through the drop of God's life **He gave You!** In hell you will be **<u>Permanently Separated From God!!!</u>** No Love, No Joy, No Peace or happiness! Only Anger, Wrath, Hate, torment,& weeping!

Preface : A Word from the Author

Beloved, God has an Endless supply of Life and Living Water that **He wants to Give to YOU!!!** For centuries Man has been searching for the Fabled "Fountain of Youth!" And all along the True source of Eternal Life has been right in front of him! For him that has ears to hear, Let Him Hear! **JESUS CHRIST IS THE SOURCE OF ETERNAL LIFE !!!!!!!** Believe in Him! Obey Him! Trust Him! Follow Him! Pray to Him! Seek His Face! Learn His ways! Jesus is the only begotten Son of God! Jesus Christ is the Bread of Life!{John 6:33-51} He that believeth on me, out of his belly (soul) shall flow rivers of Living water! (the Holy Spirit) {John 7:37}"I AM the Resurrection and the Life, He that **Believeth on Me**, though he were dead, Yet **Shall He Live!!!** {John 11:25} Jesus Christ is the Messiah, The Lamb of God, Jesus Christ is the only way into Heaven!!! Period! **Jesus Christ towers over this entire Universe!!! All Power in Heaven and in Earth is Given unto JESUS CHRIST!!!** {Matthew 28:18} Even the Arch-Angels and the Seraphim, and all the Host of Heaven fall down at his feet and worship, saying with a loud voice, Worthy is the Lamb that was slain, to receive power, and riches, and wisdom, and strength, and honor, and glory, and blessing! And every creature which is in heaven, and on the earth, and under the earth, and such as are in the sea, and all that are in them, I heard saying; Blessing and Honor, and Glory and Power, be unto him that sitteth upon the throne, and unto the Lamb for Ever and Ever! And the four beast said, Amen. And the four and twenty elders fell down and worshiped him that liveth for ever and ever!" {Revelation 5:5-14} Beloved, I hope and pray, that by this point, you hear and see; and you know, and understand, that if you don't have Jesus Christ as your Lord and Savior! You don't have Eternal Life! If you are not **Born again** you are **Dead!** Jesus told one of his disciples, Follow me; but he said, "Lord, let me first go and bury my father." Jesus said unto him,"let the dead bury their dead; but go thou and preach the Kingdom of God!"{Luke 9:59} (Jesus saw those who were only living in the flesh, and not Born Again in the Spirit, as Dead!) The Apostle Paul said, "She that liveth in pleasure is dead while she liveth!" {1 Timothy 5:6} True Life, True Riches and Treasure, is to be **Born Again in the Spirit**, into the **Living Body of Jesus Christ**! And to Have your name written in Heaven, in **God's Book of Life!!!** Compared to that, everything else is worthless dung! Everything here on earth is temporary! Being born again in the spirit, into the body of Jesus Christ is **Eternal!!! Permanent!!! Forever!!!** Absolutely, Positively, Nothing, That You will ever do in your Entire Lifetime on this earth is more Important than **YOUR PERSONAL RELATIONSHIP WITH ALMIGHTY GOD!!! HIS SON JESUS CHRIST!!! AND THE HOLY SPIRIT!!! Absolutely Nothing is More Important Than That!!!** The day that your fleshly body dies, your house and car will be worthless as dust! Your gold and jewelry, your property, and all your Money will be absolutely worthless to you, as the dust to which your body will return to!!! The only thing that will matter then, is your personal relationship with God and his son Jesus Christ! Did you do God's will, repent from your sins and bring forth fruit worthy of repentance? Are you washed clean by Jesus precious blood? You will stand before God and give an account for the life you lived, and the deeds that you did here on the earth! To see if you are worthy to receive Eternal life in Heaven!

God's New Covanant

A New Heart Will I Give You, and A New Spirit Will I Put Within You! And I will take away the stony Heart out of your flesh, and I will give You A Heart of flesh! And I will Put My Spirit Within You, and Cause You to Walk in my Statues, and Ye Shall Keep My Judgments, And Do Them! For I Will Put My Law in Their Inward Parts, and Write it in Their Hearts; And I Will Be Their God, and They Shall Be My People! And they shall Teach no more Every Man his neighbor, and Every Man his Brother, Saying know the Lord. For They shall All Know Me, from the Least of Them unto the Greatest of them; Saith The Lord! For I will Forgive Their Iniquity, and I will Remember Their Sins No More! What Shall We then say to these Things? If God Be For Us, Who Can Be Against Us? Because Jesus maketh Intercession for Us, According to the Will of God! And We know that all things work togther for Good to them that Love God! To them that are called According to His Purpose! And to them He Called, He also did Predestinate to be conformed to the Image of his Son; that he might be the Firstborn among many Brethren! And whom He called, Them He also Justified; and whom He Justified, them He also Glorified! Who shall lay anything to the charge of God's Elect? Seeing It is God that Justifieth! Who Can Condemn Us! Or Who Shall separate us from the Love of Christ? Shall tribulation, or distress, or persecution, or famine, or nakedness, or peril, or sword? Nay, in all these things we are more than Conquerors through Him that Loved us! For Christ to you-ward is not weak, but is Mighty and Powerful in You! Fear not; For I am with Thee, Be not dismayed for I am thy God; I will Strengthen thee; Yea, I will help thee; Yea, I will uphold thee with the right hand of my righteousness! I will in no wise Fail Thee, Neither will I in Any wise Forsake Thee! {Heb.13:5,Isa.41:10,Jer.31:33,Ezk.36:26}

Faith and Trust in God!

Now Faith is the substance of things hoped for, the evidence of things not seen! For by it the Elders obtained a good report. Abraham <u>Believed</u> God, and it was accounted to him as Righteousness!!! Through Faith we understand that the worlds were framed by the word of God, so that things which are seen were not made by things which do appear! (or evident to the physical human eyes! God is a Spirit and Lives in the Spiritual Realm.) All things were Created by Almighty God through his Son Jesus Christ! Who is the Firstborn of every creature! In the Beginning God created the Heaven and the Earth!{Genesis 1:1} In the beginning was the Word, and the Word was with God, and the Word <u>was</u> God! The same was in the beginning with God. <u>All</u> <u>Things</u> were made by him; and without him was not anything made that was made! In him was <u>Life</u>; and the life was the Light of Men!{John 1:1} I and my Father are <u>One</u>! The very first and crucial foundation of faith and trust in God, is Belief that **Jesus Christ** is the Son of God, and that **The Holy Bible** is the **True Word of God**! Jesus Christ, Who <u>is</u> God, said that Heaven and Earth would pass away, but my <u>word</u> will <u>not</u> pass away! <u>All</u> the People who do not <u>believe</u> that the <u>Bible</u> <u>is</u> the Inspired word of God! Do not <u>know</u> **God**; or have the slightest <u>clue</u>, who **JEHOVAH** the <u>All Powerful</u> and <u>Almighty Creator</u> of the **Entire Universe Is !!!** Almighty God <u>Created</u> a Hundred Trillion Planets and Galaxies <u>across</u> the <u>Universe</u>! And <u>God</u> easily holds them <u>all</u> in place, with just the power in <u>his</u> pinky <u>Finger</u>!!! And you do <u>not</u> think that Almighty <u>God</u> is capable of making one single <u>book</u> on one small planet! <u>Please!</u> It only clearly <u>shows</u> that you <u>Do</u> <u>Not</u> Know **Who** God Is! And more Importantly, that you have <u>never</u> been in the One True Living God's, Universe shaking, soul scorching, sin destroying, unbelief destroying, all consuming Holy Fire presence! A place that can <u>only</u> be achieved through <u>Faith,</u> and <u>Trust,</u> and Prayer, Prayer, Prayer!!! Without <u>Faith</u> It is Impossible to please God, for he that cometh to God must believe that he is, (real) and that he is a rewarder of those who **Diligently Seek Him!!!** {Hebrews 11:6} "Seek Ye my Face!" Because God has made it Crystal Clear that the <u>Just</u> shall <u>Live by</u> **Faith**! {Habakkuk 2:4} All of the people who live sanctified, holy lives, separated unto God; can only achieve it through Faith and trust in God! By looking beyond the physical realm and reaching by Faith and Trust into the Spiritual Realm to see the unseen Creator that is hidden to the naked physical eye, but who Illuminates the entire Universe with his Magnificent Brilliance and Splendor to the discerning Spiritual Eyes of Faith and Trust! Those people who know that God <u>cannot</u> and will <u>never Lie</u>, and have full confidence and Faith that <u>all</u> Scripture is given by inspiration of God! And is profitable for doctrine, for reproof, for correction, for instruction in righteousness; that the man of God may be perfect, thoroughly furnished unto all good works! Because the Holy Scriptures are able to make thee wise unto salvation through **Faith** and **Trust** which is in **Jesus Christ**! {2 Timothy 3:16} So many people want to learn how to increase their faith, even Jesus disciples asked him, lord increase our faith! There's a great promise in the Bible that says, "Faith comes by hearing , and hearing the word of God!" If you want to increase your Faith, <u>Study the word of God</u>, <u>every Day</u>; spend lots of <u>Quality Time</u> alone with God in Prayer! Jesus said in his magnificent prayer to God the Father, in John Ch. 17, And this is Life Eternal, that they may <u>know thee</u> the One True Living God, and Jesus Christ, whom thou hast sent. {John 17:3}

Faith and Trust in God!

There came a man to Jesus. kneeling down to him, and saying, Lord have mercy on my son; for he is lunatick, and sore vexed! For ofttimes he falleth into the fire, and oft into the water. And I brought him to thy disciples, and they could not cure him. Then Jesus answered and said, O faithless and perverse generation, how long shall I be with you? How long shall I suffer you? Bring him hither to me. And Jesus rebuked the devil; and he departed out of him, and the child was cured from that very hour. Then came the disciples privately to Jesus, and said, Why could we not cast him out? And Jesus said unto them, because of your unbelief; for truly I say unto you, if you have faith as a grain of mustard seed; ye shall say unto this mountain, remove hence to yonder place; and it shall remove; and nothing shall be impossible to you! Howbeit this kind goeth not out but by Prayer and Fasting! {Matthew 17:14} Many people think this means, this kind of devil goeth not out but by prayer and fasting. No!!! Not at all! This kind of Unbelief goeth not out but by prayer and fasting! Real Faith will remove any mountain, or any devil in your way! But it is up to You to build up a close, real, personal relationship with Almighty God, through Prayer, Fasting, Bible study and Quality Time!!! Alone and uninterrupted with God, Jesus, and the Holy Spirit! Please also notice that in the sermon on the mountain, Jesus did not say, "If ye fast" he said "When ye fast" meaning not if you choose to fast, but that you will be fasting! Fasting not only crucifies the flesh, it opens you up to the spiritual realm; where it is possible to get closer to God and increase your faith! All of the greatest men in the Bible had personal Encounters and Personal Experiences with Almighty God! To them, it was not only faith; but they were telling us the Facts of the encounters that they personally had with God! It takes you Far beyond Faith, when you kneel and tremble in the earthshattering, terrifying, Almighty Presence, that is the **One True Living God of Creation!!!** And these encounters with God did not just accidently happen by chance, these men of God searched and cried out to, and Sought for God very carefully and very diligently! And God rewarded them for their efforts! Because our God is a Rewarder of them who very Diligently and Humbly Cry Out, and Search for, and **Obey** Him! I was so blessed, that many years ago when I was still a young man, I diligently studied and learned the teachings of Jesus Christ! And I took them to heart, and sincerely believed him for the face value of what Jesus Said! And it has saved me from much heartache and needless worrying that most of the world suffer through. Yes, I still have my fair share of trials and tribulations; but I have learned to take life's regular burdens off of my shoulders, and give them to God. And I am going to share some of those principals or teachings with you now. Jesus said, take no thought for your life, what ye shall eat, or what ye shall drink; nor yet for your body, what ye shall put on. Is not the life more than meat and the body than raiment? Behold the fowls (birds) of the air; for they sow not, neither do they reap nor gather into barns; yet your heavenly Father feedeth them. Are ye not much better than they? For which of you by taking thought can add one cubit unto his stature? {Matthew 7:25} Translation, all of the worrying and heartache that you do in your mind and soul, will not help your circumstance or situation not one little bit! our Father God has said that he will provide you with everything that you truly need! So my beloved brethren, cast down all those worrying thoughts, and Trust God to do it!

Faith and Trust in God!

Therefore take no thought, saying, What shall we eat? or, What shall we drink? or wherewithal shall we be clothed? (for after all these things do the Gentiles seek:) For your heavenly Father knoweth that ye have need of all these things. But Seek Ye First the Kingdom of God, and his righteousness; and all these things shall be added unto you! (God will take care of you, and everything that you truly need in your entire life!) Therefore take no thought for the morrow; for the morrow shall take thought for the things of itself. Sufficient unto the day is the evil thereof. {Matthew 7:31} So many people lie awake in bed at night worrying about the situations in their lives, bills, rent, food, and the like. My beloved brethren, please learn to give these types of burdens over to God, and have faith and trust that he will take care of you and your needs. Now this also requires you to use common sense, if you take the bill money and go on a frivolous shopping spree, or gambling, or partying in a bar or night club and waste your resources! Do not blame God when you find yourself in hot water at the end of the month! Or if you go out and act stupidly breaking the law, or drive carelessly, or go join a group of get rich quick schemers and find yourself in a legal mess! So many people go and do foolish, dumb, unwise things; and then find themselves on their knees trying to then ask God, Lord "How did this Happen?" If you go racing through your life, foolishly, at 100 MPH and do not take careful care and use common sense; do not be surprised when you crash and burn, or put yourself in problem after problem! A wise person will always stop and think about their actions and the likely results and consequences, and a really wise person will Pray to God for guidance and wisdom in any matter, before they do anything! "I will instruct thee and teach thee in the way which thou shalt go, I will guide thee with mine eye." "Teach me thy way O'Lord, and lead me in a plain path because of mine enemy!" {Psalm 32:8, 27:11} "Do not enter into the path of the wicked, and go not in the way of evil men!" {Proverbs 4:14} This is how you can activate your Faith in God's wisdom and Trust in God's guidance. By going to God in prayer, seeking God's face every day, depending and relying upon God for all wisdom, knowledge, and understanding! And of course God speaks to you through the Holy Bible, that is why you should be studying it every day! So that you will already have the wisdom, knowledge, understanding, and discernment to face life's problems when they happen! And of course God will allow you to go through certain trials and tribulations. "Beloved, do not think it strange concerning the firey trial which is to try you, as though some strange thing happened unto you. But rejoice, inasmuch as you are partakers of Christ's sufferings; that when his glory shall be revealed, ye may be glad also with exceeding joy!" {1 Peter 4:12} The Holy Spirit lead Jesus into the wilderness to be tempted by the devil for 40 days and nights! And if God would allow his own son to be tested, will he not allow you and me to be tested? Jesus himself, told us in Revelation "and all the churches shall know that I am he which searcheth the reins and hearts; and I will give unto every one of you according to your works!" "I counsel thee to buy of me gold Tried in the Fire, that thou mayest be rich; and white raiment that thou mayest be clothed, that the shame of thy nakedness do not appear; and anoint thine eyes with eyesalve that thou mayest see! {Revelation 2:23 & 3:18} A life that has faced no adversity or testings, will have no character or mature fruits of the Spirit! As David said, It is good for me that I have been afflicted, that I may learn thy statutes. {Psalm 119:71}

Faith and Trust in God!

Jesus himself let his disciples faith be tried, even when he was right there with them. One day Jesus was teaching the multitudes out of a boat while they were on the land right by the sea shore. And the same day when evening was come, Jesus told his disciples, let us pass over to the other side. And when they had sent the multitude away, they took Jesus, still in the same ship, to go across. Then there arose a great storm of wind, and the waves beat into the ship, so that it was now full. And Jesus was in the rear part of the ship, asleep on a pillow; and they awake him, and say unto him, Master, carest thou not that we perish? And he arose, and rebuked the wind, and said to the sea, Peace, be still. And the wind ceased, and there was a great calm. And Jesus said unto them, Why are ye so fearful? How is it that ye have no Faith? And they feared exceedingly, and said one to another, What manner of man is this, that even the wind and the sea obey him? {Mark 4:35} Brethren, do not think for one second that Jesus did not see, and know, that a storm was coming that night! But he was asleep on a Pillow! Resting comfortably in his Fathers arms, in full Faith and Trust! Jesus knew that he was destined for the Cross, it was the Fathers will! Jesus knew that his disciples must still go and preach the Gospel all over the world! So he knew that they would not perish in the boat, but that God would use that moment to Glorify his son, and test and build the disciples Faith in Jesus! Many people always remember that Jesus calmed the wind and sea in this Scripture, and well they should! But there is another important message in this story, that many people miss or pass over! The first thing Jesus asked his disciples was, Why are ye fearful? Where is your Faith? The first thing God wants you to see is, Jesus was Right There IN the Boat WITH THEM!!! Resting Comfortably!!! In full Faith and Trust that the Father would Protect and Keep Them Safe! In the Face of the Storm! If you Love and Trust God, Cast Down Every Fear! Know, Believe, and Understand that No Storm or Trial in your Life is to Great for **Almighty God** to Handle! Take your eyes off of the tiny ant hill in front of you, and look up into Heaven at **The Creator of the Entire Universe** that holds you in his All Powerful Hands! My beloved brethren, open your ears and heart, and listen very carefully to these words out of Jesus own mouth, and rejoice! "My sheep hear my voice, and I know them, and they follow Me! And I Give unto them Eternal Life! And **They Shall NEVER PERISH!!!** Let me say it again, "**NEVER PERISH!!!**" Neither shall Any Man Pluck them Out of my HAND! (no one) My Father, which gave them to me, **IS GREATER THAN ALL!!!** And No man is able to pluck them out of my Fathers Hand! I and my Father are One! {John 10:27} Hallelujah! Praise the Lord!!! Jesus Christ, (who is God! and cannot Lie!) Has promised to give all his sheep Eternal Life, and that they Shall Never Perish! And that No One can pluck them out of his or his Fathers Hand! (and God the Father is even Greater and more powerful than Jesus! That is a Mind blowing thought!) Jesus asked his disciples, Where is your faith? He was right there in the boat with them! God in the Flesh! Hurricanes, 100 foot waves, Tornadoes, and Earthquakes could have hit that boat and they would be Fine! They had seen Jesus walk on the water! But they took their eyes off of Jesus, and focused on the trial and test that they were in at that moment. Look at Jesus great promise right above this! And have Faith and Trust that God will Do what he said he will do! Lean not to your own understanding!

Faith and Trust in God!

My beloved brethren, we must always remember that Almighty God's ways are <u>far Greater</u> than our ways! And Gods Thoughts are <u>far Higher</u> than our thoughts! God is <u>not</u> a man that he should Lie!!! Or let one single untruth or falsehood cross over his Holy lips! God loves truth, holiness, judgement, and Righteousness! The words of the Lord are pure words, as silver tried in the furnace 7 times!!! And it is absolutely **<u>IMPOSSIBLE</u>** for God to Lie! God has said,"My covenant I will not break, nor will I alter the thing (words) that have gone forth out of my lips!" {Psalm 89:34} Jesus Christ said, Heaven and Earth shall pass away, but my Words shall <u>not</u> pass away! {Luke 21:33} The Entire Universe would erupt into Chaos, with planets and Galaxies colliding before Almighty God would <u>ever</u> let a lie or untruth proceed forth from his mouth! When God says something, it will stand True <u>Forever</u> and Ever! And Jesus said,"I give my sheep Eternal Life, and they shall Never Perish!" And Jesus was right there <u>in</u> the boat with his disciples, through the trial and testing of wind and waves and storm that they would have to go through! And Almighty God <u>is</u> right there <u>in</u> the boat with <u>you</u> my beloved brethren! When you are Born Again, you become the Temple of Almighty God, and the One True Living God of Truth and Holiness **Lives Inside of You!!!** Remember, Jesus Christ said, Behold, the Kingdom of God is <u>within You</u>! {Luke 17:21} The Apostle Paul said,"Know Ye Not, (do you not know and understand) that ye are the Temple of God, and that the Holy Spirit of God <u>Dwelleth in You</u>! If any man defile the Temple of God, him shall God destroy, for the temple of God is Holy, which temple ye are! {1 Corinthians 3:16} And because the Holy Spirit of God Lives <u>Inside of you</u>, he is with you at all times; to comfort and guide you, to teach and lead you unto all of God's truth and Holiness! Now this does not mean that you will not have to face trials and testings, No, on the contrary; you will have to face trials and testings! Even Jesus was led by the Holy Spirit into the wilderness to be tempted and tried by the devil! How can anyone grow up in the spirit and reach the next level of fruitfulness, until they pass the current level that they are at? Your teachers in first grade, did not send you to the second grade until you were ready. Remember God's Holy Spirit is living inside of you, there to comfort and guide you every step of the way! And Jesus has already faced every trial that we have to go through! And God will only allow it when you are ready, the Scriptures says that God will never give you more than you can handle, and will always make a way out of every temptation. And like the disciples, Jesus is right there <u>with You</u> in the boat, to face any Storm, or Trial, or Temptation You will have to endure! God has said, "Do not fear, for <u>I AM</u> with thee; be not dismayed, for I am thy God! I will strengthen thee; I will help thee; yea, I will uphold thee with the right hand of my righteousness! (Jesus is seated at God's Right hand! :) {Isaiah 41:10} God has said he will <u>Never Forsake You</u>! "For the Lord will not forsake his people for his great name's sake, because it hath pleased the lord to make you his people."{1 Samuel 12:22} And God has promised to put his Holy Spirit <u>inside</u> of you, and cause you to walk in all his statutes, and keep his judgments and <u>do</u> them!{Ezekiel 36:25-27} I will sprinkle clean water upon you, and ye shall be clean, from all your filthiness, and from all your idols, will I cleanse you! I will also give you a new heart, and a new spirit will I put <u>within</u> you! I will take away the stony heart, and give you an heart of flesh! I will put my spirit in you, and cause you to walk in my statutes & judgments and do them!

Faith and Trust in God!

So my beloved brethren, as I am writing this chapter on Faith and Trust in God, I dare not overlook the complete and utterly overwhelming importance of studying, learning, memorizing, meditating on and Knowing the Word of God! **The Holy Bible!!!** Inside and out, front to back, book by book, and chapter by chapter, Precept by Precept, Line upon line, every Jot and tittle! (dot of the I and cross of the T) **Your Soul Depends upon It!!!** The Holy Bible is the most printed and best selling book in the history of mankind, by a very, very, incredibly huge amount! My beloved brethren, you Must know the word of God, better than you know your own name and Address! Any Christian who try's to walk with God in the spirit, stand up against the spiritual forces of darkness, and enter into heaven without a complete and fully detailed intimate knowledge of the Holy Bible! Is just like a soldier in World War II trying to storm the beaches at Normandy with Nothing but his Underwear shorts on!!! How can you possibly Fight and Win the War, without Knowing the **Commander and General's BATTLEPLANS!!!** You cannot possibly Win without them! To him that has ears to hear, let him Hear, The Holy Bible is **The Voice of God!!!** Let me say it again, The Holy Bible is **The Voice of Almighty God Speaking to YOU!!!** Jesus said, my sheep Hear My Voice, and I know them, and they follow **ME!!!** And a stranger they will not follow, but will flee from him; for they know not the voice of strangers! {John 27:5 & 27:10} It is so utterly Crucial and Important to Hear and Know the Voice of Jesus Christ that every effort and constant diligence must be undertaken and strived for relentlessly!!! You absolutely **Must Must MUST KNOW JESUS VOICE!!!** And You must Know what Is Not Jesus Voice! My beloved brethren, whom I love so dearly, I stress this one point so very much, because Knowing Jesus Christ Voice is one of the most crucial Keys and Cornerstones for you to Enter into Heaven! And I am going to tell you 3 steps towards achieving this most important Goal! Number 1. **Prayer and Obedience!** Pray to God and his Son Jesus (who is God) Constantly! Every Day! When you are at work or around other people, Pray to him silently in your mind. And Tell Jesus,"Lord Jesus, I love you, and I need You! I must know you Lord; and I must know Your voice Jesus, because I need You! Without you Lord, I am blind, and miserable, and naked, and dead! I have absolutely nothing without you Lord Jesus! Please Teach me and Show me Your Voice Jesus! Please Give me Spiritual ears to Hear and Know Your Voice Jesus! And give me wisdom and true discernment to Know what Is and what Is Not your Voice Lord Jesus! I am Trusting and depending upon you God, please give me clear Understanding and Spiritual Revelation into your word and Your Voice O'God! And pray to God as much as you can, sincerely! Humbly! Love him! call to him Reach out to him! Seek God's face! Say, I must be close to you O'God, help me, Fill me with your Holy Spirit, Let not my heart be far from you, Let it not just be lip service O'God, draw me closer! In Jesus Holy name I ask and pray! And spend time in God's presence Just adoring him in silence! At first and often, God will Just bless you with his presence, nurturing you, loving you, and as you spend more time with God he will start to show you area's in your life that need to be cleaned up and sanctified, bad words, gossip, bad habits, bad attitudes, evil things on the Internet and T.V. that you should not be looking at or watching! This is where obedience comes in, will you obey God?

Faith and Trust in God!

My beloved brethren, the obedience to God that you <u>do</u> or <u>do not do</u>, will determine weather or not you grow or do not grow in maturity and holiness in the spirit! If you obey God you <u>will</u> grow in the spirit, and bring forth good mature fruits of the Holy Spirit in your life! If you do <u>not</u> obey God, you will just be a seed stuck in the mud of your sins, or a small unproductive tree that will bring forth no holy mature fruits in your life! Billions and billions of people pray to God and Jesus every day, but they never <u>obey</u> God's convictions in their heart and soul, to <u>Repent</u> from and <u>Get Out</u> of their <u>Sins</u>! And that is where billions of people are stuck at, captives, in the mire of their sins! Jesus said, who so ever commiteth sin is the servant of sin! But they cannot or <u>will</u> <u>not</u> grow in the spirit, or get any <u>closer</u> to God, until they <u>Obey</u> <u>Him</u> and actually **Do God's Will!!!** You cannot and <u>will</u> <u>not</u> move forward to step 2 in Christian maturity, until you <u>Do</u> God's will at step 1 and <u>remove</u> the sin in your life, that God has shown you! Period! The wages of sin is <u>Death</u>, death to your spiritual growth in God; and death and destruction in hell to your soul, eventually, if you do not get out of that sin! And that is why we <u>must</u> pray to God, and build a strong personal relationship with Almighty God!!! Because that is where the power to <u>overcome</u> every sin and evil desire is, <u>In God</u>! I can do <u>all</u> things through Christ which strengtheneth me! {Philippians 4:13} Being in Almighty God's actual Holy presence is a heart changing, and soul shaking experience! Like a hot furnace that burns away and destroys sin and evil desires from the inside, in your heart! God actually changes the moral and spiritual desires inside your heart! Let me give you an illustration to show you exactly what I mean. Imagine a sheriff in the old west that takes out a posse on the range to catch an outlaw bank robber! Once the sheriff hunts down the bandit and catches up to him, he takes his guns, puts the shackles on him, and hauls him back to Jail; to stand trial before the Judge! When he gets back to town, he takes the outlaw, puts him inside the steel jail cell, takes the key, and locks him in! The outlaw has been hunted down and subdued! But take a good look at the outlaw in the jail cell, look at his <u>heart</u>! He is <u>still</u> an outlaw in his heart, nothing has changed, but the fact that he was captured against his will! He is still an outlaw, and if he can escape from his jail cell tonight, he'll be right back robbing and stealing tomorrow! Many people in churches are just like that outlaw, a Sheriff named the Holy Spirit has brought them in and subdued them, but secretly, in their heart of hearts! They still yearn for, and desire, and pine away for their sins! And that is where being Born Again, and having a close Personal Relationship with God really comes in and makes all the difference! Your fleshly man and old Adam like fallen, sinful nature will <u>always</u> yearn for and desire sin! That is why Jesus said you must take up your cross every day and crucify your fleshly desires! But when you are Born Again and the Holy Spirit of God comes and lives <u>inside</u> of you, he can change your very heart and soul! And give you new holy desires, and make you hate and loath the old retched man, and sins that you used to love. "Therefore if any man be in Christ, he is a <u>new</u> creature; old things are passed away, Behold all things are become new! {2 Corinthians 5:17} But you have to truly <u>want</u> to, and ask God to change you! Once again, this is where a real, true, personal relationship with God comes in! As you get a <u>True</u> vision and knowledge of God and Jesus, you begin to see how awesome they really are! And how blind, miserable, and naked you are, and your desires turn toward God, we need God!

Faith and Trust in God!

OK, we have looked closely at step 1. In Hearing and knowing God and Jesus voice, which is this, **Prayer and Obedience**; we will now look closely at step 2. in Hearing and knowing God and Jesus voice, which is **Holy Bible Study and Your Personal Relationship with God!** Beloved brethren, many people, Christians, layman, and even pastors and preachers, Do Not have a real personal close relationship with the One True Living God, or his son Jesus Christ! Most only have a second hand knowledge of another persons supposed relationship with God. And their image, and knowledge, and Idea of God's character and personality, are forged by and come through another persons image, ideas and dealings with God! And are only taught by another person, or Church, or denominations teachings on God. Let me state this very clearly, there is, was, and will never be another source to truly learn personally about, to know, and receive a True Revelation of God, than by Almighty God Himself! No one Else! Yes god uses prophets, yes God uses pastors and preachers, yes god uses evangelist and teachers! But even the most Godly, and Holy men and women of God, who do preach the full, complete Gospel of Jesus Christ! Can only bring you cupfuls of living water, if they are truly living and walking what they preach! I am telling you to **Go To** the very **Source** of life himself **Almighty God!!!** And Dive Headlong into God's endless supply of **Living Water**! Jesus said, that He that believeth on me, as the Scripture hath said, out of his belly shall flow rivers of living water! {John 7:38} There is **No** human being in existence but **Jesus Christ** that can ever truly represent, embody, illustrate, personify, preform, produce, or show the results and life changing, soul shaking, heart rending results, that can only come from being in the actual undescribable (with puny human words) the Awesome Presence of the One True Living Almighty God of Creation! Nothing else can or will ever duplicate the Ultimate Presence of God the Father, God the Son, (Jesus Christ) and of God the Holy Spirit! The Holy Trinity! For these three are One! {1 John 5:7} Who can possibly teach you more about God than God himself? No One! Who can possibly help you more than the most powerful being in Existence? No One! Who can possibly guide you better than the all seeing, all knowing, source, author of all life, wisdom, knowledge, and Spiritual & Physical Understanding? No One! Who can possibly Strengthen you, and cause you to grow in Spirit and in Truth; than the One True Living God of Spirit and Truth! No One! God knows more about you, than you know about yourself! Almighty God sees and knows exactly what you think and feel, exactly where you are at, and exactly where you need to go, and grow in the spirit! And **You Need to Go to God!!!** You need God! And Jesus Christ is **The Only Way** to Almighty God the Father! So you need Jesus! And there is only one Rocksolid sure foundation where you must begin at, and build upon, to ensure you are on the right path (strait and narrow) to heaven, and a rock solid foundation of Truth, and of Holiness! And that is to accept Jesus Christ as your Lord and Savior, and Invite God's Holy Spirit in to your Heart and Soul, so you can be Born Again in the Spirit; into the actual body of Jesus Christ, which is the True Church; and Learn, study, memorize, and know **The Holy Bible!!!** Which is the True Word of God! Which is your sword in the spirit, to cut through all the enemy's lies! And your Helmet of Salvation to Protect your mind from all the enemy's lies and false doctrines and teachings!

Faith and Trust in God!

My brethren, Holy Bible study and our own personal relationship with God, work hand and hand together, to teach you about Almighty God the Father, his son Jesus Christ and God's Holy Spirit! We diligently study the Holy Bible, not just for book knowledge or to say that we know the Holy Scriptures better than anyone else, no. We diligently study the Holy Bible for the express purpose and motive to <u>know</u> God, and to seek God's Face, and to Hear and know God's voice; and to have a real, true, close, personal relationship, with the **One True Living God!!!** Who Inspired and wrote the Holy Bible by his powerful Holy Spirit, for that very purpose; so that we could know Him, God our Father who created us in his own image, and gave us life! The Holy Bible and Prayer, (which is the bedrock foundation of communication with God to build our relationship with him) The Bible and prayer is the place to go to learn about Jesus, the life of Jesus, the works and actions of Jesus, and Jesus own words and teachings, <u>for</u> <u>Your</u> <u>Self</u>, undiluted and unfiltered by anyone else! The Bible is the place to go, to learn about Almighty God the Father, his character, his dealings and his actions and reactions towards men individually and all of mankind! God's patience, love and forgiveness towards mankind; and God's Holiness, Righteousness, Judgement and Wrath against sin & evil! And the Holy Bible is the place to learn about the Holy Spirit of God, because the Holy Spirit never speaks about himself, the Holy Spirit always teaches you about Jesus, and always brings to your remembrance Jesus own words, and the Scriptures from the holy bible and shows you God's will for your life! The Holy Spirit will convict you in your heart and soul of <u>all</u> <u>sin</u>, and you will feel grieved in your heart, soul, and spirit, if you have any kind of real relationship with God, Jesus, or the Holy Spirit! So that when you feel that conviction in your heart, soul and spirit; that is the Holy Spirit telling you <u>don't</u> <u>do</u> <u>it</u>! You are about to sin, stop; because he is making a way out for you, obey him! Beloved brethren, the Holy Bible is the blueprint and concrete solid foundation where you must start at, and build upon, to truly hear, know, and understand Gods voice and will for your life! God, first and foremost, speaks to you <u>through</u> the **Bible**! And then God backs it up in prayer, what you have learned in the bible! God never goes against his own word, God will not tell you something contrary or that does not agree with sound doctrine, God's commandments or the teachings of Jesus! And you must use and exercise <u>Common</u> <u>Sense</u>! Some things that are sinful and evil are really obvious, and other sins you are aware of <u>in</u> your spirit, otherwise why would you even <u>be</u> questioning or looking at, or doubting doing <u>it</u>, if you haven't already been convicted of <u>it</u> in your spirit? The Bible is the most awesome book in the world, by Far; The whole world today <u>Badly</u> <u>Needs</u> the wisdom, and the knowledge and understanding, taught in the Holy Bible! Today we think we are so advanced, smart, and far ahead of the people who lived hundreds or thousands of years ago, with our computers and smart phones and I pads and communications and technologies and TV series and Internet and all the constant Entertainment! Our Brains are turning into preprogrammed **Mush!** We can't even think for ourselves anymore! We are so preoccupied and busy with our devices, and music and TV shows and entertainment, games, and foolishness that doesn't even exist in the <u>Real</u> <u>World</u> we live in! Stuff that only diverts our attention away from God, and glorifies sinful, evil things, and hatred! And the Devil's purpose for all of this stuff, to control our minds, so we never stop to hear the voice of God!

Faith and Trust in God!

Now, my brethren, we will look at some key Scriptures that give important details on how the Holy Bible, and your own personal relationship with God, must be used together, and work together; to step by step, build and grow your relationship with God, and to slowly but surely learn, perceive, hear and really get to know God's precious voice, every day for your life! So remember, my beloved brethren, if you really want to hear God's voice for the close, personal, intimate details in your life; you must start at the basic Commandments, and obey God in the first basic things that God's Holy Spirit tells you to Do! Like removing all the sins and iniquities that you already know about, that are in your life! You must do those things first, to get closer to God, You must remove any obstructions in your spiritual pipeline to God, and then you will receive a stronger flow of living water into your soul and spirit! And through it all, you must remember that we walk by Faith, not by feelings or by sight! But by Trust in God's word, because we know that what God said is the Truth! Jesus said that the heavens and the earth will pass away, but my words will not pass away! God's Word will stand forever and ever! OK, here are the key Scriptures and details on how your relationship with God, & the Holy Bible work together! Jesus said, "Search the Scriptures; for in them ye think that ye have eternal life! And ye will not come to me, that ye might have eternal life! And this is life eternal, that they might know thee the only true God, and Jesus Christ whom thou hast sent!" {John 5:39, 17:3} My beloved brethren, this is so important; people across the whole world, search the scriptures for the secrets of eternal life! The Truth is in the Scriptures, Yes, absolutely!!! But Jesus said the Life is not in the scriptures, Eternal life is in Jesus Christ! Being a living, breathing, active part of the body of Jesus Christ in the Spirit! That is why "Ye must be Born Again in the Spirit!" Jesus said that, Ye will not come to **ME**, that ye might have eternal life! And Jesus said that This is Life Eternal, that they might **KNOW THEE** the **One True Living Almighty God** and **Jesus Christ** whom thou hast sent! Translation: Your Eternal Life and the Salvation of your very Soul is **IN** your **Relationship** with **ALMIGHTY GOD**, and You Personally **Knowing God** and his son **Jesus Christ!!!** And the Holy Bible is the true word of God, that God uses to speak to you through, so that you will know the Truth; and use that truth to Build a real, true, sincere Relationship with God and Jesus Christ; who is the creator and giver of all life! And your relationship with God is where your eternal life and living water actually flow from! The Living Water and Eternal Life flow from God, through the body of Jesus Christ, to You; through God's Holy Spirit who comes and Lives inside of You, when you are Born Again in the Spirit, into the actual body of Jesus Christ! Which is the only Safe and Protected place in the Universe, from the Judgement and Wrath of God against all sin and iniquities and Evil! For the wrath of God is revealed from heaven against all ungodliness and unrighteousness of men! My Brethren, that is why we must know the Holy Scriptures, which are able to make thee wise unto salvation through **Faith** which is in Jesus Christ! All Scripture is given by inspiration of God, and is profitable for doctrine, for reproof, for correction, for instruction in righteousness! That the man of God may be perfect, thoroughly furnished unto all good works! {2 Timothy 3:15} So the Holy Bible is the Word of God, to instruct us, and to teach and correct us about all things in God, to help us to actually know God; and to build a close, personal, intimate, relationship with God and Jesus Christ!

Faith and Trust in God!

Because God, Jesus Christ, & the Holy Spirit are the only True source of eternal life in the Universe! And these three are one! {1 John 5:7} So brethren, actually knowing God, Jesus Christ, and the Holy Spirit and building your own personal, intimate, relationship with God! Is the real, true, rocksolid foundation, on which the eternal life and salvation of your very soul, rely and depend upon! So your Prayer Life, and communication with God and Jesus Christ; is the most important and crucial thing you do, that actually build and maintain your relationship with the One True Living God in Heaven! Your prayer life to God is the actual lifeline for the living water, that Jesus said would flow like a river out of our belly, (soul) and when you don't pray, or stop praying to God; you cut off the flow of God's living water into your soul! Living water that you need to maintain your spiritual life and strength in God! If you stop watering your garden, all the good fruit on the trees will shrivel up and die eventually! That is why your personal relationship with God, and your Prayer life to God are the most Important thing that you will ever do in your whole entire life! Your relationship with God is your **Life**! And without God in your life, you are **Dead**! And your Prayer Life is your lifeline to God and Jesus; so my beloved brethren, Pray, Pray, Pray, every day; Pray, Pray, Pray, night and day Pray Pray to God like your life depends upon it, because it does! And study the Holy Bible every day, the Scriptures talk about the washing of water by the word. The Apostle Paul said, "as Christ loved the church and gave himself for it; that he might sanctify and cleanse it with the washing of water by the word (of God) That he might present it to himself a glorious church, not having spot or wrinkle, or any such thing; but that it should be holy and without blemish! For we are members of his body, of his flesh, and of his bones!"{Ephesians 5:25} In Romans, Paul wrote,"I beseech you brethren, by the mercies of God, that ye present your bodies a living sacrifice, holy, acceptable unto God, which is your reasonable service. And do not be conformed to this world, but be ye transformed (by Prayer) and the renewing of your mind, (Bible Study) that ye may prove what is good, and acceptable, and the perfect will of God!{Romans 12:1} So the Bible says that studying the word of God will bring a fresh cleansing and washing to your soul and mind, and do not be conformed to this world and it's evil ways, but to present your body to God as a living sacrifice, holy, acceptable unto God; and to be Transformed (when Jesus was praying on the mount, he was transformed, and his face did shine like the sun; and his clothes were white as the light!) be transformed by the renewing of your mind, holy Bible study to wash away the worlds filth, and renew your mind with the Word of God! All the time you are doing this, you are building and strengthening your Relationship with God and Jesus! And by exercising your senses to discern between good and evil, darkness and light, and actually learning to hear and know the Precious voice of God! And when God sees that you are sincerely determined to obey him and do his will, and hear his voice, God will definitely speak to you, and you will hear God's voice, and know that it is Him speaking to You! And as you study the Holy Bible, you will learn more and more about God and Jesus! And as you exercise your senses to discern between good and evil, and darkness and light, and you grow in the spirit! You will be developing your Spiritual Ears, and strengthening your mind and spiritual understanding of God's Voice, by reason of use of those faculty's or senses, simply by using them! And ask God to give you wisdom to know his voice!

Faith and Trust in God!

My brethren, in the last few pages, we have been looking at and studying on how to Hear and Know God and Jesus Voice. Step 1. was **Prayer and Obedience**, Step 2. was **Holy Bible Study and Your Personal Relationship with God** So, we will now look at Step 3. which is **Praise and Worship** Many people do not know and understand how Important and Powerful Praise and Worship really are! All the great wise men and theologians over the centuries have pondered and contemplated, and have tried to figure out, what is the True meaning of life, and man's purpose for living and being? Is man here simply to build and invent stuff, and to be fruitful and multiply, or is there a greater and more noble purpose for mankind? The truth and the answer is in us, and all around us the whole time The very fact that mankind is looking, and searching, for a Greater meaning for his life, and the true purpose for his very being here; Shows and illuminates the Fact that there is a God sized hole in the very heart and soul of every Man! And that no other person, activity, posession, item, entertainment, or thing, can ever possibly meet or satisfy that need; than the One True Living Almighty God that Created man in his own Image! Mankind needs a Real, True, Relationship and fellowship with God! And Almighty God wants and desires a real true, relationship, and fellowship with Man! Just look back to the beginning of creation, in the Garden of Eden; God created all the animals and birds and and fish, and every creature, and insect, small and Great! But only One Single Creature did God create in His Own Image, Man! Mankind is special, we can think, and reason, and have feelings; we can love, and feel pain, and understand meaning and Joy and ecstasy and sorrow! God created all the creatures on earth for his pleasure and enjoyment of creating and giving life to other creatures. But only with Man, did God walk with, and talk with, and teach, and communicate and have fellowship with, there in the Garden of Eden! But all mankind must never forget, that Almighty God is also Deity! God is Holy, Holy, Holy! God is Jehovah! God is Alpha and Omega! God is the Creator and the Judge of All the World! Almighty God owns every soul of every man, woman, and child who ever lived, and we will All stand before God, and answer for, and give an account for the lives that we lived here on the earth; with the life that Almighty God gave to us! Almighty God is **NOT** just another man!!! And can never ever be treated, or thought of as another man! We must work out our own salvation with Fear and with Trembling before Almighty God! And the Answer to the Question of, Why we are here? and, Why did God create mankind in his own image? My beloved brethren, once again, The Mighty Lord Jesus Christ gives us the answer! "The hour cometh, and now is, when the true worshipers shall worship the Father in spirit and in truth, for **The Father Seeketh such** (and Created Mankind) **To Worship Him!!!** God is a Spirit, and they that worship him, must worship him in Spirit and in Truth!" {John 4:23} God is seeking a Holy people why love Truth and Justice, Holiness and Righteousness; to Worship him in spirit and in truth, and be his family in Heaven! And we are created to be part of the body of Christ, and walk in spirit and truth, and do good works! "For we are his workmanship, created in Christ Jesus unto good works, which God hath before ordained that we should walk in them."{Ephesians 2:10} Thou art worthy, O Lord, to receive glory and honor and power, for thou has created all things, and for thy pleasure they are and were created!{Rev.4:11}

Faith and Trust in God!

Praise ye the Lord, for his name alone is excellent; his glory is above the earth and the heavens! Let them praise the name of the Lord, for he commanded, and they were created! O' that men would praise the Lord for his goodness, and for his wonderful works to the children of men! Praise ye the Lord, blessed is the man that feareth the Lord, and delighteth greatly in his Commandments! That they might observe his statutes, and keep his laws! Praise ye the Lord! Let the sinners be consumed out of the earth, and let the wicked be no more! Bless thou the Lord, O' my soul, Praise ye the Lord! Who can utter the mighty acts of the Lord? Who can show forth all his Praise? To the end that my voice may sing praise to thee and not be silent! O'Lord my God, I will give thanks unto thee forever! The Lord is my strength and my shield, my heart trusted in him and I am helped; therefore my heart greatly rejoiceth, and with my song I will praise him! I will bless the Lord at all times, his praise will continually be in my mouth! Make a joyful noise unto the Lord, all the earth; make a loud noise, and rejoice, and sing praise! Let every thing that hath breath, Praise the Lord! Praise Ye the Lord!!! :)

{Psalms 148, 107:31, 112:1, 105:45, 104:35, 106:2, 30:12, 28:7, 34:1, 98:4, 150:6}

And in that day thou shalt say, O'Lord, I will praise thee; though thou wast angry with me, thy anger is turned away and thou comfortedst me. Behold, God is my salvation, I will trust and not be afraid; for the Lord JEHOVAH is my strength and my song; he also is become my Salvation! Therefore with joy shall ye draw water out of the wells of salvation! Praise the Lord, call upon his holy name, declare his doings among the people, make mention that his name is Exalted! Sing unto the Lord, for he hath done excellent things; this is known in all the earth! Cry out and shout, thou inhabitant of Zion! For Great is the Holy One of Israel in the midst of thee!{Isaiah Ch. 12} (we are God's temple} **~ I Am the Lord, that is my Name; and my Glory I will Not give to another, neither will I give my Praise to Graven Images! ~ "Almighty Jehovah God"** ~ {Isaiah 42:8} Jesus Christ told us that "God the Father seeketh True worshipers, to worship him in spirit and in truth!" and we are all invited to be his family in heaven! Because "God is not willing that any should perish! But that all should come to repentance!"{2 Peter 3:9} So I ask you, my beloved brethren, will you answer God our Fathers call for, "True Worshipers" who worship God in spirit and in truth? If you want to hear God's voice and do God's will, This is God's voice speaking directly to you! Jesus Christ is God in the flesh! And Jesus is personally, directly, telling you God the Fathers will! Our Father is seeking true worshipers, to worship him in spirit and in truth! So, What exactly is "True Worship" in Spirit and in Truth? So many Christians and believers, simply think that true worship is just standing up in Church on Sunday, holding up their hands, and singing praise songs and saying,"We Praise you God and we worship you!" and " We Praise your Holy Name Lord Jesus, we worship you!" And Yes, my beloved brethren, that is praise and worship! But True Praise and Worship, in Spirit, and in Truth, is also so much more than just that! True worship, in spirit and truth, is a whole complete Life; that is lived in True Holiness, and sinlessness, and obedience to God's will; Walking under complete and full control of Jesus Christ our Lord, and obedience to the Holy Spirit of God who lives inside of us! A holy life that is separated unto God, bringing forth good fruit, worthy of true repentance! Walking in the Spirit! For as many as are Led by the Spirit of God, they are the sons of God! {Romans 8:14}

Faith and Trust in God!

This I say then, Walk in the Spirit, and ye shall not fulfil the lust of the flesh! For the flesh lusteth against the Spirit, and the Spirit against the flesh, and these are contrary the one to the other; so that ye cannot do the things that ye would! (and give in to the sinful desires of your flesh!) But if ye be led of the Spirit, ye are <u>not</u> under the law! Now the works of the flesh are manifest, which are these; Adultery, fornication, uncleanness, laciviousness, Idolatry, witchcraft, hatred, variance, emulations, wrath, strife, seditions, heresies, envyings, murders, drunkenness, revellings, and such like; of the which I tell you before, (it happens) as I have also told you in times past; that they (all the people) which do such things (as these) <u>Shall</u> <u>Not</u> Inherit the kingdom of God! But the fruit of the Spirit is Love, Joy, Peace, Longsuffering, Gentleness, Goodness, Faith, Meekness, Temperance; against such (attributes, character traits, and attitudes as these) there is no Law! And they that <u>are</u> Christ's have <u>crucified</u> the flesh with the affections and lusts! If we live in the Spirit, let us also walk in the Spirit! {Galatians 5:16} But remember, my brethren, Do <u>Not</u> be deceived; God is not mocked (made fun of, ridiculed, or taken lightly) for whatsoever a man soweth, that <u>shall</u> he also reap! For he that soweth to his <u>flesh</u> shall of the flesh reap corruption; (and death) but he that soweth to the Spirit, shall of the Spirit reap life everlasting! {Galatians 6:7} Knowing this, that our old man is crucified with him; (I am crucified with Christ) that the body of sin might be <u>Destroyed</u>, that henceforth we should <u>not</u> serve sin! For he that is dead (and crucified with Christ) is freed from sin! Likewise, reckon ye also yourselves to be dead indeed unto sin, but alive unto God through Jesus Christ our Lord! Therefore <u>do</u> <u>not</u> let sin reign in your mortal body, that ye should obey it in the lust thereof. For sin <u>shall</u> <u>not</u> have dominion over you! For ye are not under the law, but under grace. What then? Shall we sin, because we are not under the law, but under grace? God forbid! Do you not know, that to whom ye yield yourselves servants to obey, his servants ye <u>are</u> to whom ye obey! Either (the servant) of sin unto <u>Death</u>, or (the servant of God) and of obedience unto righteousness! (that bringeth forth fruits unto holiness, and in the end eternal life in Christ Jesus) For the wages of sin is death, but the gift of God is eternal life through Jesus Christ our Lord! {Romans 6:6 -23} So my beloved brethren, let us take up our cross and crucify our flesh every day and follow Jesus example for our lives! let us press toward the mark of the high calling of God in Christ Jesus! Let us walk in the Spirit, and Worship God in Spirit and in Truth, To the Glory and Praise of Almighty God in the Highest! Because if we really want to worship God our Father in Spirit and Truth, and be True worshipers; we must <u>live</u> a life of Holiness and obedience to God's will, and walk in the spirit, and be led by the Holy Spirit! True worshipers do <u>not</u> live like the devil 6 days a week, and then try and come and worship God on Sunday! Every Day must be <u>lived</u> Holy before God! Because if you live a sinful, evil, wicked life of lust, hatred, and greed! "When ye spread forth your hands I will hide mine eyes from you; yea, when ye make many prayers, I will not hear; your hands are full of blood! (and iniquity) Wash you, make you clean; (repent) put away your evil doings from before mine eyes; cease to do evil! {Isaiah 1:15} Do you think that you can take a mouth that curses, and tells lies, and filthy evil statements or jokes, or gossip, or hatred about others; and then take that same mouth, and try to Worship and Praise Holy Almighty God with it? And that worship will be acceptable and pleasing to God, in spirit and truth?

Faith and Trust in God!

Do you think that you can take hands that steal, or swindle, or commit adultery and fornication, or homosexuality, make rude evil gestures, or hit and hurt others, or run schemes and crooked evil businesses, or scam operations that take advantage of simple minded easy targets; and take those same evil hands, and hold them up and worship Holy Almighty God with them? No! Do you think you can take a lustful, covetous, greedy, sin loving, evil heart; that can't wait to go out and commit more sin, lust, and evil deeds! An Evil Heart that has no intentions, or desires, to Stop Sinning or to even fight against your sinful evil ways; a selfish heart that only loves and cares about satisfying your fleshly sinful desires! Do you really think you can take a heart like that, and try to love, and to worship, and to praise our holy heavenly Father? And that it will be True Worship, in Spirit and in Truth! My beloved brethren, I am writing this, and telling you this because **I Love You**, and I want your praise and worship to God our Father to be Well Pleasing to him! Just as much as I want my own praise and worship to Almighty God to be well pleasing, and acceptable to his holy Heart! And I have to take up the Cross and Crucify my own flesh every day, and nail the sinful fleshly desires of my old Adam like fallen nature, to the cross of Jesus Christ just like you do! Because nothing else means more to me than being with God and our Lord and Savior Jesus Christ in Heaven! And seeing You in heaven one day, my beloved brethren! That is the very purpose I am pouring out my Heart and Soul to Almighty God for You! Because I Love You! And I will spare no effort on my part, and say a thousand prayers, or shed a million tears to God our Father, to see you all berthed in the Spirit into the very Body of Jesus Christ! And when you are walking in the Spirit, led by the Holy Spirit, worshiping God in Spirit and Truth, determined to do God's perfect will with all your heart and soul; and overcome all sin, and your name is written in Heaven, in Gods book of Life; because Jesus Holy precious Blood has washed you clean! And when I see you in heaven, and give you a big hug; then, I will be satisfied and happy, my beloved brethren! Know this, that when you are sincerely, and you are completely determined to live a holy sanctified life, separated unto God; and overcome every sin and worship God in spirit and truth, and you pray to and build your relationship with God every day! And you are determined to do God's will, and hear and know God and Jesus voice every day! Then, God will be determined that you do hear and know his voice, and you will hear and know his voice! And as you walk and worship in the spirit and truth, and you pray and study the Bible, and obey the Holy Spirit! You will be growing in the spirit and building your relationship with God, and learning to hear and know God's voice, and will for your life, and you will be building up your faith and trust in God! And (this is important) you must always remember, my beloved brethren, when you pray to God at the beginning, and the end of every day, and you have strived sincerely with all your heart, to enter into the strait and narrow gate that leads to life eternal! (like Jesus told us to do) And you have done the will of God, (which is our duty, and the Holy Spirit will compel us to do) and you obeyed the Holy Spirit; we must always remember that it is God who truly saved us, and that you are only saved by Grace through Faith in Jesus Christ! Not by your own works or efforts, it is the gift of God! Who accomplished and completed our salvation through Jesus Christ his only begotten Son! Not of your own doing or works lest any man should boast! Because no flesh shall glory in God's presence!

God's Love, Grace, and Mercy!

My Beloved Brethren, the very first thing I want to tell you in this Chapter, is that **Almighty God** Our Father in Heaven; Truly, Honestly, and Sincerely, **Loves You Very Much!** And that God, in his tender Love, Grace, and Mercy; with all his Heart! Wants **you to be in Heaven with Him for All of Eternity! Forever!** This is the Absolute Truth, Guaranteed; and I will Prove It To You, Totally and Completely, Directly out of the Holy Bible! Almighty God loves you, and Created You and Me, and All of Mankind for the specific purpose that We would be his Family in Heaven! To Be with Him Forever! Do Not Let the Devil tell you anything else! You know that Satan is and always will be a Liar! And that the Devil will do anything, or tell you anything (evil cunning lies) to **deceive You** and take you to Hell with Him! Do Not believe the Devil's lies, or let him **Pull You Away from God!!!** He is come only to Steal, Kill, and Destroy You! But Jesus came to **give us life**, and **Jesus has defeated Satan!** Jesus Christ put Satan and all the forces of darkness to open shame, Triumphing over them in It! Jesus Christ has Vanquished our Evil Enemy Forever, and **Destroyed the bonds of Hell and Death and the Grave!!! Jesus Saved** and Delivered All of Mankind from the powers of Darkness and Death! And our Father God is **the One** who sent Jesus here to Save Us and Deliver Us from Hell and Death! Just the Fact that God sent Jesus here to Save Us, proves that God wants Us and is willing to **Fight For Us to Keep Us!** And that is, my beloved brethren, crystal clear proof that God loves you and wants you in heaven with him! Our Father **God created you and me!** And Almighty God has already accomplished and done, everything we need to be in Heaven with Him! **Forever!!!** Because **God wants You to be**, IN HEAVEN WITH HIM!!! Jesus makes this fact, Crystal Clear in the Holy Bible! Remember Jesus parable,"A certain man made a great supper, and bade (or invited) many; and sent his servants at supper time to say to them that were bidden, **Come**; for all things are ready. (because Jesus has already Paid the Price for our sins! Now we just need to **come to him!**) And they all with one consent began to **make excuses!** (there is No Excuse that anyone with a correctly functioning Brain, could ever make, to **not** want to Enter into Heaven!) The first said unto him, I have bought a piece of ground, and I must needs go and see it; I pray you have me excused. And another said, I have bought five yoke of oxen, and I go to prove them; I pray thee have me excused. And another said, I have married a wife, and therefore I cannot come. (So you see brethren, they were All Invited, but other things on this earth were more Important to **them!**) So the servant came and showed his lord these things. Then the master of the house, being angry, said to his servant; Go out quickly into the streets and lanes of the city, and bring in hither the poor, and the maimed, and the halt, and the blind. And the servant said, Lord, it is done as thou hast commanded, and yet there is room. So the Lord said unto the servants, Go out into the highways and hedges, and "Compel them to **Come In!**" That my house may be filled. (Jesus told his disciples to Go into All the World and Preach the Gospel!) For I say unto you, That none of those men which were bidden shall taste of my supper! {Luke 14:16} How shall We Escape, **If** We Neglect so Great a **Salvation**; which at the first began to be spoken by the Lord, and was confirmed unto us by them that heard him? {Hebrews 2:3} Or remember Jesus parable, about The Lost Sheep, What man of you, having a hundred sheep, if he lose one of them, doth not leave the ninety and nine in the wilderness, and **Go After** that which is **Lost, Until He Find It?** {Luke 15:3}

God's Love, Grace, and Mercy!

And when He hath Found It! (the one lost sheep, out of the flock of an hundred!) He layeth it on his shoulders **Rejoicing!** And when he cometh home, he calleth together his friends and neighbors, saying unto them, **Rejoice with Me**; for I have Found my Sheep which was Lost! I say unto you, that likewise, there **Shall Be Joy In Heaven** over One sinner that Repenteth, more than over ninety nine just persons, which need no repentance! Either what woman having ten pieces of silver, if she lose one piece, doth not light a candle, and sweep the house, and seek diligently till she find it?(brethren that is why we need to light our candles, and let our light shine, so that lost souls can be saved!) And when she hath found it, she calleth her friends and neighbors together, saying, Rejoice with me; for I have found the piece that I had Lost! Likewise, I (Jesus) say unto you, there is **Joy** in the presence of the angels of God, over One sinner that Repenteth! So to clarify these parables taught to us by Jesus; When One Single Soul is Lost, God searches diligently to Find it, and to **Save It!** And Jesus sends his servants, and disciples, into the streets and lanes, into the highways and hedges, to Preach the Gospel unto all the World! And **Compel** them **To Come** to The Marriage Supper of the Lamb! Because the Salvation for **Your Soul** is prepared and Ready to Receive You! And Jesus Christ is **Calling You Right Now** to **Come to Him!** So that He can lay **You On His Shoulders** and **Carry You Home** (to Heaven) **Rejoicing!** And when One Sinner **Repents** and Turns from their Sins, and goes to **Jesus to Be Saved!** There is Great Joy and Rejoicing in God our Father's precious heart, and he calls the angels in heaven to Rejoice with him; over **One Sinner** that Repenteth! That is how much God our Father in Heaven **Loves You** and wants you to be with **him!** But, my beloved brethren, If that one lost sheep cares more about the things of the World; (like the men in Jesus parable!) than the **Salvation of his Soul!** And when he hears the Great Shepherd Jesus, calling Out His Name, and he runs in the other direction, (into the wilderness of sin!) and Refuses to Repent!!! **How Will He EVER BE SAVED!** The Decisions You make on this earth, Will Have Consequences on **Your Soul**, for All of Eternity! God ~ Wants ~ To ~ Save ~ You!!! But If **You Don't Go To Jesus!** You, by your Own Actions and Decisions; **Will Seal Your Own Fate!!!** Multitudes, Multitudes, in the valley of Decision! Brethren, "The Wages of Sin is Death! But the **Gift of God is Eternal Life** through **Jesus Christ** our Lord!" Don't Be Blinded by Sin! It will Destroy You! We must All take heed to God's Warnings in the Holy Bible! Let us now look at Jesus parable about "The Prodigals Son" A certain man had two sons, and the younger of them said to his Father, give me the portion of goods that falleth to me and he divided unto them his living. And not many days after the younger son gathered all together, and and took his journey into a far country. And wasted his substance with riotous living. And when he had spent all, there arose a mighty famine in that land; and he began to be in want. And he went and joined himself to a citizen of that country; and he sent him into his fields to feed the swine! And he would fain have filled his belly with the husks that the swine did eat; and no man gave unto him! Then when he came to himself, he said, How many hired servants of my father's have bread enough and to spare, and I perish with hunger! I will arise and go to my father, and will say unto him, Father, I have sinned against heaven, and before thee! And am No More Worthy to be Called Your Son; make me as one of thy hired servants! And he arose, and came to his father, But when he was yet a great way off, his father saw him,

God's Love, Grace, and Mercy!

When his Father saw him coming, he had compassion, and Ran, and Fell on his neck, and Kissed him! And the son said to him, Father, I have sinned against heaven, and in thy sight, and am no more worthy to be called thy son! But the Father said to his servants, Bring forth the best robe, and put it on him; and put a ring on his hand, and shoes on his feet! And bring hither the fatted calf, and kill it, and let us eat and be merry! For this my son was Dead, and He is Alive Again! He was lost, and now he is found! (my brethren, it is very Important for us to notice and See what Jesus said here, when the son was lost in sin, Jesus said **He was Dead!**) His physical body was alive, but his Spirit and Soul were Dead! But when He came Back to His Father! (Almighty God, The Creator and the **Giver of All Life!**) Jesus Said that **He was Alive Again!** That is Why Ye Must Be Born Again Into the Spirit! (into God the Father of Life!) The lost Son felt conviction, regret, and sorrow for his sins; and the rebellious things that he had done! Thus his sorrowful words, "I have sinned against heaven, and in thy sight; and am no longer worthy to be called thy son!" The Lord is nigh unto Them that are of a Broken Heart; and **Saveth** such as be of a **Contrite Spirit!** {Psalm 34:18} The Sacrifices of God are a broken spirit; a broken and **contrite heart**, O' God, thou **Wilt Not Despise!** {Psalm 51:17} Let us look closely at all the things that the lost son did!

1.- The lost son came to himself (to his senses and he realized his sinful ways were destroying him and that he was perishing!) When the wicked man turneth away from his wickedness that he hath committed and **Doeth** that which is Lawful and Right, he shall **Save his Soul Alive!** Because He Considereth, and turneth away from **all his transgressions** that he hath committed, **he shall surely live, he shall not die!**

2.- He humbled himself, and went to his Father! (God resist the proud, but gives grace to the **Humble!**) If my people, which are called by my name, shall humble themselves, and Pray, and Seek my Face, and **turn from their wicked ways!** Then will I hear from heaven and forgive their sins!{2 Chronicles 7:14}

3.- He confessed his sins! If we **confess our Sins**, (to God) he is faithful and just to **forgive us our sins**, and to cleanse us from All Unrighteousness! Because if we walk in the Light, as He is in the Light, we have fellowship one with another, and the **Blood of Jesus Christ cleanses us from all sin!** {1 John 1:7}

4.- He came back to his Father, and submitted himself, (under God's Covering, Guidance, and Control!) Because his own Rebellious ways had put him on the wrong path that only lead to death and destruction! He that Dwelleth in the Secret Place of the Most High shall Abide under the Shadow of the Almighty! I will say of the Lord, He is my Refuge and my Fortress, **My God**; in Him will I **Trust!** Surely he shall Deliver thee, he shall Cover thee with his feathers, and under his wings shalt thou Trust! His Truth shall **be thy Shield and Buckler!** {Psalm 92} (Ye shall know the truth, and the **Truth shall make you free!**) I will Instruct thee and teach thee in the way which thou shalt go; I will **Guide Thee with Mine Eye!!!** Thy Word is a Lamp unto my feet, and **A Light unto my Path!** Thou wilt show me the **Path to Life!!!** {Psalms 32:8, 119:105, & 16:11- John 8:32} By Mercy and Truth iniquity is purged; and by Fear of the Lord, men depart from evil! Blessed are they whose iniquities are forgiven, and whose sins are covered! Blessed is the man to whom the Lord will not impute sin! {Romans 4:7} Because the lost son felt guilt and sorrow for his sins, he returned to his Father very humbly, feeling only worthy to be a mere servant! God the Father instantly sees his broken heart and spirit, and knows his **repentance** is heartfelt and true!

God's Love, Grace, and Mercy!

When the lost son actually returned to his Father, he learned his father's True feelings! The Whole Time his fathers loving heart was yearning for his son, (who he loved dearly!) to return to him and to be at his Fathers Side! Where he belonged! We see this is true, because his father didn't stand there at the front door, scolding and reprimanding him! No! His Loving Father Ran Out the front door, raced across the yard, and Embraced him in his arms, falling on his sons neck crying, hugging, and kissing Him! Love! **True Love!** Is what awaited him Upon His Return to his **Loving Father!** His Father fully restored him, and **Covered Him Instantly!** We see this is True, because his Father immediately commanded that the Best Robe be put on him; a ring on his finger, (a sign of royalty) and shoes on his feet! (so his feet and his path were Protected and Guided! My Beloved Brethren, We Must let this message sink Deep Into our Minds, and Into our very Hearts and Souls!!! Remember, This is **Jesus Himself**, teaching us about **God our Father's** Character, Love, Compassion, **Grace and Mercy!!! Jesus is God!** He cannot Lie! And Absolutely **No One** Knows **God the Father**, better than **Jesus Christ**; **Gods Only Begotten Son!** So if there is still **any doubt in your Heart and Mind**, that Your Sin is to Great, and Your iniquity is to Terrible, for You to Ever Return to God; **YOU ARE WRONG!!! God Loves You Very Very Much!** And Almighty God is Searching and Calling for You to **Return to Him This Very Instant!** That is the Very Reason why Jesus taught us this parable, about The Prodigals Son! For him that has Ears to Hear, Let Him Hear! Almighty God is trying to Find and Save You; and Jesus Christ is the Lamb of God and the Great Shepherd that God has sent into the wilderness of sin, (this world) To Find You! And to Light your way Home, (Jesus said, I AM the Light of the World!) and to Lay You on his Shoulders and Carry **You Home!** (to Heaven!) **Rejoicing!!!** We are feeding you (teaching) directly from the Scriptures in the Holy Bible! Word for word, letter by letter, step by step, Precept upon precept, line upon line, every jot and tittle, (dot of the I, and cross of the T) Teaching you In the Spirit, and Through the Holy Spirit! (for only the **Holy Spirit can Give You Life** and True Revelations!) Feeding your spirit Real Spiritual Meat, cut up into Bite sized pieces! (and Not the Watered Down Milk Message that most of the world hears!) And the Word of God very clearly says This!!! Almighty God the Father of All Creation, sent his only begotten son **Jesus Christ** into the world to **Save You**, (we are making the word personal, and focused directly toward You!) and **Wash You Clean** from All Sin and Iniquity and **Cover You with his Grace and Love!** And to Clothe you in a **Spotless White Wedding Garment!** And to make you a True Child of God that is unashamed to speak Jesus Holy Precious Name to **All The World!!!** And to Give You a **New Heart** and a **New Spirit**; Transforming You into a **New Creature!!!** (for if any man **Be in Christ He is a New Creature**, old things are Passed Away; Behold, all things are Become New!) Recreated in the Image of him (God) that created him! Do Not Be Conformed to **this World**, but **be ye transformed** by the **Renewing of Your Mind!** Always Striving to Walk in the Spirit, and to be led by the Holy Spirit in all things! Thereby causing you to walk in God's statutes and keep his commandments and **Do Them!** So that you bring forth fruit worthy of **repentance!** (for herein is my Father glorified, that ye bear much Fruit! So shall ye Be my disciples!) And that Jesus Christ may **Live** and **Dwell in your Heart** by **Faith!** So that you can be strengthened by his Spirit in the inner man, and be filled with all the fullness of **God!**

God's Love, Grace, and Mercy!

Almighty God sent his **Holy Spirit** to the Earth, to help, strengthen, comfort, teach, and **Guide**; All who truly Believe that **Jesus Christ** died on the Cross of Calvary for their sins! And **Rose from the Grave** three days later, because it was Never Possible that death or the grave could Ever **Hold the Son of God!** The Holy Spirit will always Do what our Father God has sent him here to do! God Promised to put His Spirit "into" the Heart and Soul of Any Person who **Simply Believes in Jesus Christ through Faith!!!** And who Accept Jesus Christ as their **Lord**, and their **Savior**; Repent from all their sins, Pray to Jesus (who is God!) and ask Jesus to wash all their Sins Away with his **Holy Precious Blood!** Then Invite their Lord and Savior, Jesus Christ, to come **Live** and **Dwell** inside of their Heart and Soul **By Faith!!!** Through the Holy Spirit of God, Promised by Our Father in Heaven! God sent his Holy Spirit to come and **Breathe his Breath of Life**, into our dead souls so that we would be **Born Again into the Spirit!!!** Into the very body of Christ, and Transform Us into New Creatures, with New Hearts, New Minds, and New Desires! Transformed and Recreated into the Image and likeness of him that created Us! "**Jesus Christ!**" We know that all things work together for good to them that Love God, to them who are called according to his purpose; For all those God has called, he also did predestinate To Be Conformed to the **Image of His Son!** That he might be the Firstborn among many brethren! {Romans 8:28} And **God** has Promised in the New Covenant that "I will Put my Holy Spirit Inside of **You**, and **Cause You** to Walk in my Statutes, and Ye Shall keep my Judgments and **Do Them!!!** For I will sprinkle clean water upon you, (the Holy Spirit!) and **Ye Shall Be Clean** from All of Your Filthiness, and from all of your Idols! (sinful strongholds!) I Will Cleanse You! And I Will take away the stony (hard) heart Out of You, and I will put a New (soft tender) Heart of flesh, Inside of You! {Ezekiel 36:25} Jesus said to, wait for the Promise of the Father, for **Ye Shall Be Baptized with the HOLY GHOST!!!** And Ye Shall Receive Power, after the Holy Ghost is come Upon You! And Ye shall be witnesses for Me, unto the uttermost parts of the earth! Peter said unto them, **Repent**, and **Be Baptized** every one of you in the name of Jesus Christ, for the Remission of Sins; and Ye Shall Receive the **Gift of the Holy Ghost!** For the Promise is unto You and to your children, and to All that are afar off, even as many as the Lord our God shall call! {Acts 1:4-8, 2:38} And the Comforter, which is the Holy Ghost, who the Father will Send in my Name, **He Shall Teach You All Things!** And bring all things to your remembrance, whatsoever I (Jesus) have said unto you! And when the comforter is come, who I (Jesus) will send unto you from the Father, even the (Holy) Spirit of **Truth**, which proceedeth from the Father, **He Will Guide You into All Truth!** For He shall not speak of himself; but whatsoever he shall hear, that shall he speak! For He Shall Testify of Me! (Jesus) Because I still have many things to say unto you, but **Ye cannot bear them now!** Howbeit (the Holy Spirit) will show you things to come! And He Shall Glorify Me; (**Jesus!**) for he shall receive of mine, (God's plans and will for your life!) and **Shall show it unto You!!!** {John 14:26, 15:26, 16:12} And I will pray the Father, and he shall give you the Comforter, that **He** may abide with you **Forever!** Even the (Holy) **Spirit of Truth!!!** Whom the world cannot receive, because it cannot see him, neither know him; but **Ye know him**, for He Dwelleth with you, and **SHALL BE IN YOU!!!** And whatsoever ye shall ask in my name, **I will Do It**, that the **Father** may be Glorified in the **Son!** {John 14:13-17}

God's Love, Grace, and Mercy!

So my Beloved Brethren, All who call out for Jesus to Save them and Wash their Sins Away, with his **Holy Precious Blood!** By accepting Jesus Christ as their Lord and Savior, and Submitting their Lives under Jesus Authority and Control! Striving to Walk in the Spirit, and to be Led by the Holy Spirit, in all things! Every single day of their lives, **Obeying what the Holy Spirit of God tells them to Do!!!** Crucifying their Own Will and Fleshly Desires, nailing it to the Cross of Jesus Christ! Just Exactly like Jesus Did for Us, for **our Sins**, to **Set Us Free!!!** Even though Jesus did no sin, was not guilty, and did **Not Deserve Any Punishment!** Therefore I am Crucified with Christ, but still I Live; yet it is not I, but Christ that Lives (and rules) inside of me! And the life which I now live in the flesh, I live by the Faith of the Son of God; who loved me, and gave himself for **Me!** {Galatians 2:20} Because Jesus suffered and died on the Cross for us, while we were yet Sinners! With the hope and desire that we would simply come to Him, so that He could Save Us; and we would Receive the **Gift of the Holy Spirit**, which was promised to us by our Father God in Heaven! To All who Believe in his only begotten son, Jesus Christ! So that the **Holy Spirit of God** could come and Dwell in us, Living Inside of our very Hearts and Souls, and Rise up in our mortal bodies in his Mighty Omnipotent Power! And Transform us into the likeness of Jesus Christ! Who is the Image of the Invisible God, the Firstborn of every creature! And to Cleanse and Prepare you for the hope that is laid up for you in Heaven, that you have heard before by the word of the **Truth** of the gospel! Which is come unto you, as it is in all the world! For this cause We Do Not Cease to Pray for You, and to desire that ye might be filled with the knowledge of his will in all wisdom and Spiritual Understanding! That ye might walk worthy of the Lord, (living holy sanctified lives) unto all pleasing, being fruitful in every good work, and Increasing in the **knowledge of God!** Strengthened with all might, according to his Glorious Power, unto all patience and longsuffering with **Joyfulness!!!** Giving thanks unto the Father, (who sent Jesus to save us!) which has **made us** (eligible) to be partakers of the Inheritance of the Saints Walking in the Light! (of **God**) Who hath **Delivered Us** from the power of darkness, and hath **Translated Us Into the Kingdom of his Dear Son! JESUS CHRIST!** In whom We have Redemption through his Blood, even the **Forgiveness of Sins!** And he is the Head of the body THE CHURCH! Who is the beginning, the Firstborn from the Dead; that in all things he might have the preeminence! For it Pleased the Father that **IN HIM** all the fullness (of Heaven) should **Dwell!** And having Made Peace through **the Blood of his Cross**, by him to reconcile all things unto himself; by him, I say, whether they be things in Earth, or things in Heaven! And you, that were sometime alienated and enemies in your mind by wicked works, yet now hath **He Reconciled!** In the body of His Flesh through Death, to **Present YOU HOLY**, and **UNBLAMEABLE**, and **UNREPROVEABLE IN HIS SIGHT!** And to prepare you for the Marriage supper of the Lamb, Jesus Christ! If Ye Continue **IN THE FAITH** Grounded and Settled, and **Do Not** be moved away from the **Hope of the Gospel**, which Ye have heard, and is Preached to Every Creature which is Under Heaven! Even the Mystery which hath been hid from Ages and Generations, but is now made manifest to his saints! Who God would make known the riches of the mystery that is Christ in you, the hope of glory; who we preach, warning every man, and teaching every man in all wisdom! That we may present every man **Perfect in Christ Jesus!** {Colossians 1:5-28}

God's Love, Grace, and Mercy!

The Apostle Paul said, "We Preach **Warning Every Man**, and Teaching Every Man in All Wisdom! That we may Present every man **PERFECT IN CHRIST JESUS!**" There are No More Dire Warnings Against Sin being Preached in the Ice Cold Churches and Pulpits Today!!! There are **Very Few** Fiery, **God Consumed**, Fire Breathing Preachers, Bellowing Out the Anointed Word! That **The wages of Sin** is **DEATH and HELL and DESTRUCTION!!!** There are **almost no bold Preachers** willing to **Point OUT SIN and say "THOU ART THE MAN!!!"** Why Not? Because a Preacher that is **Living in Sin** is too **Convicted and Powerless to CRY OUT AGAINST SIN!!!** Jesus said, "out of the abundance of **the Heart the MOUTH SPEAKETH!!!** A heart that is encrusted with **Sin** is **Powerless to Speak Out Against Sin!!!** And even if he does preach against sin, his words are empty and fall dead to the ground! Because the letter killeth and the **Spirit Giveth LIFE!!!** And if the **Holy Spirit of God** is not Burning like a Fire **In His Heart**, because He is not Walking what he is Talking; and he is not living a truly holy sanctified life, Separated **Unto God!** His words are not only useless, They are **Dangerous and Deadly!** Any preacher who is blatantly living in **Sin**, is ministering **Death** to his congregation!!! Because If His heart is sinful and corrupt, then his words are sinful and corrupt, and All of the **Seeds those Words are planting into the hearers Hearts are SINFUL and CORRUPT!!!** Period! Why did the people who heard Jesus, say, "never a man spake as this man spake?" And Jesus, "speaks as **No other Man Speaks!** and that he teaches with Authority, and speaks with Power! Because his Heart and Soul were Pure and Holy, burning with the **Fire** and **Love** and **passion for God**! His one passionate desire is to **Do God the Father's Will**, Speak his Father's Word, and **to always do those things that Please the Father!!!** Plus there are many Characters in the Holy Bible who Spoke with God's Fire and Powerful Anointing! Paul, Moses, Samuel, Elijah, Daniel, Isaiah, Jeremiah, Ezekiel, David, Enoch, Elisha, John the Baptist, just to name a few! And the Scripture says, God is no respecter of persons! If you diligently and passionately **Love God**, **Do His Will**, and **Seek his Face in Prayer**, and **stand up for God** Like they did! God will do the same things for You! Remember, Jesus said, Greater things than I have done, Ye Shall Do! Paul said, knowing the Terror of the Lord, we Persuade and Warn Men! John the Baptist said, O' Generation of Vipers, who hath Warned You to flee from The Wrath to Come! Therefore, bring forth Fruit that is Worthy of Repentance! Paul said that, we preach Warning every Man that we may present him Perfect in Christ Jesus! Jesus himself said, **Be Ye Perfect as your Father in Heaven is Perfect!** The very first step in being Perfect, is having a **Heart on Fire for God** that **WANTS TO BE PERFECT!!!** And that is the Secret, not that you can't fall down, but that **You Never Ever WANT TO FALL DOWN!!!** And if you do (you will still reap what you sow) but you will **Get Right Back Up**, put it under the blood of Jesus Christ and truly and sincerely strive to **overcome all Sin**! A Heart like **That, will Get Closer and Closer to God Every Single Day!** (Draw nigh unto God and He will draw nigh unto You!) But this one thing I do, forgetting those things which are behind, and reaching forth to those things which are before, **I Press Towards the Mark of the High Calling of God in Christ Jesus!** Just Keep **Fighting for God** no matter what **sin**, or **temptation** you must face! A piece of coal under pressure, turns into a Diamond!

God's Love, Grace, and Mercy!

And the great pressure turns a worthless lump of coal, into a beautiful, valuable diamond! (do you really want to be of Great Value to **God's Kingdom**?) Then you Must Face the Pressure, and Go through the pain and fire of temptation! The Holy Spirit led Jesus into the wilderness **To Be Tempted of the Devil!** {Matthew 4:1} The night before Jesus was crucified, when he was in the garden of Gethsemane, he took Peter, John, and James with him, and he began to sorrowful and very heavy! (all the forces of Hell and darkness were assaulting him viciously, Determined to Destroy Jesus in those last few hours! Struggling to prevent Jesus from **Freeing mankind on the Cross!**) That's when Jesus told his disciples "My soul is Exceeding Sorrowful even unto death! Tarry ye here and watch with me!" The burden of all the worlds sins were weighing heavily on our Lord and Saviors Soul! My Brethren, this is the most important and Crucial hours in the history of the World! The most Powerful being in the Universe, **Almighty God!!!** Is compelling his son, the flesh and bone man, the lamb of God, **Jesus Christ** to the Cross; To **Crucify his Flesh!** And all the forces of Hell and Darkness, are **Fighting against this flesh and bone Man**, the **Mighty Lamb of God, Jesus Christ!!!** To Pull, Rip, and **Tear Him Away from Accomplishing His Goal!** And the Man Jesus Christ is the very **Soul and Point** where all this pressure is Being Applied!!! There is an old saying, "this is where the rubber meets the road!" It signifies the spot where the pressure from the two opposing forces Collide! And if that Point is not strong enough, it **will be Ripped apart and Destroyed!!!** My Beloved Brethren, Our Lord and Savior, **Jesus Christ** is **Alive and Well!!!** And He is more than able to **Carry the burden of the whole Worlds Sins on his Shoulders!!!** And Jesus Precious Blood is more than able to **Wash All our Sins Away** and **Make Us Clean and Pure Before Our Father God in Heaven!!!** That is Why, it is my Great Delight and Joy, my Desire, and Privilege; To Praise Jesus Holy Name! And that Jesus Christ, would even allow dust and dirt like me; to come and kneel at his **Holy Precious Feet!** And **To Worship Him for All of Eternity In Heaven!!!** Because I am not even worthy to be his doormat! And my brethren, if you and I truly and sincerely want to be just like Jesus; we must also **crucify our Flesh on the Cross!** And face the **Pressure** and **Go through the Fire and Pain** of **Temptation!** Because it is the very crucible where God Transforms You into the image and **likeness of Jesus Christ!** Gold that is put into the Furnace is not destroyed; it is cleansed and it is Purified! And our Father God can see his likeness In US! That night in the garden, Jesus first prayed, O' my Father, if it be possible, let this cup pass from me; nevertheless **not as I will, but as thou will!** The second and third time; O' my Father, if this cup may not pass away from me, except I drink it, **Thy Will Be Done!** God the Father himself, handed Jesus this cup of pain! Jesus confirmed this when He told Peter, put up thy sword; the cup that my Father has given me, **Shall I Not Drink It!** {John 18:11} And if we want to be Real Men and Women of God, at some point we will also have to drink Our Cup of Pain! Have you never noticed and realized, that the greatest characters in the Bible; went through the Most Pain and Suffering! And the Greatest one of all, Jesus Christ; had the most Pain and Suffering!!! Why is this? Jesus himself, gives us the answer! I counsel thee to buy of me Gold Tried in the Fire, that thou may be rich; and white raiment, that thou may be clothed, and that the shame of thy nakedness Do Not Appear; and anoint thine eyes with eyesalve, that thou may See! Therefore be zealous and **Repent!**

God's Love, Grace, and Mercy!

Blessed is the man that endureth temptation! For when **he is Tried**, he shall Receive the Crown of Life! Which the Lord hath promised to them that **Love him!** {James 1:12} My beloved brethren, do you want Your Life to Truly Glorify God, and to Shine God's Light to a lost and dying world? Do you truly want to bring forth, Good Holy Fruit, that is worthy of repentance? Do you want your life to Be Transformed and purified like gold in the fire, and your words to be pure words as silver purified in the furnace seven times? Do you want Your Character to shine God's light, like Diamonds and Precious Stones, forged in the Fire of God's Word, and Created and Tried under the Pressure of Temptation? And not to allow your Life to be nothing but wood, hay, and stubble, that will only Burn Up in **God's Holy Fire** on Judgment Day! Because no other foundation can any man lay, than the one that is laid, which is Jesus Christ! Now if any man build upon this foundation, gold, silver, precious stones, wood, hay, stubble; Every Man's work shall be made manifest! (clearly revealed) For the (judgment) day shall declare it, because it Shall Be Revealed by Fire, and the **Fire Shall Try Every Man's Work!** To See of what sort it is? And if any man's work abide which he hath built thereupon, (remain and not burn up in the fire) He shall receive a Reward! But if any man's work shall be burned, he shall suffer loss; but He Himself (his soul) shall be saved, yet so as by **fire!** If he himself is found worthy to enter into God's kingdom! {1 Corinthians 3:11} Do you Truly and Sincerely **want your life to glorify our Father God in Heaven**, and be precious and well pleasing in **God's Eyes**; and to be called great in **The Kingdom of Heaven**? Then, my beloved brethren, **You Must Do God's Will** and **You Must Keep God's Commandments!** Jesus himself said, "Whosoever shall break one of these least commandments, and shall teach men so, he shall be called the least in the kingdom of heaven; but whosoever **shall Do and Teach them**, the same shall be called great in the kingdom of heaven! You know that the princes and rulers in the world exercise dominion over the people, and they that are great exercise authority upon them! But it shall not be so among you; but who so ever will be great among you, let him be your minister; and whosoever will be chief among you, let him be your servant! Even as the son of man (Jesus) did not come to be ministered unto, but to **minister unto others**, and **To Give His Life** a ransom for many! {Matthew 5:19, 20:25} Let us look at this word [Least] and clarify it, a lot of people get confused by it. In this verse Jesus taught that whosoever shall break God's commandments, and teach other people to break God's commandments shall be called least in heaven! Obviously this is **bad**, to disobey God and to teach others to disobey God! The word Least here imply's the same evil and rebellion that Satan teaches to his evil spirits, and to the world! But there is another verse where Jesus says, "He that is Least among you all, the same shall be great!" {Luke 9:48} In this situation his disciples were reasoning among themselves, which of them should be the greatest! And Jesus perceived the thoughts of their hearts, and he could see the **pride** in their **hearts!** Brethren, **Beware of Pride!** Pride is one of the Main Characteristics and key attitude, or aspect and demeanor of **Satan himself!** Pride is the Sin that cost Satan everything, and Got him kicked out of Heaven and **Pride sent him to Hell!!!** He was not content with what he had, as an **Arch Angel!!! No!** Satan wanted to be in God's seat, Like God! But Satan learned the hard way, ages ago, that there is **Only One Living God! Almighty Jehovah God!!!** And All of Mankind will find out that **Almighty God Rules the Universe!**

God's Love, Grace, and Mercy!

Pride is a Fleshly, Carnal, Attitude and Attribute of Mankind's Evil Heart; from the Fallen, Corrupted, Adam-Like Sinful Nature, that is **Controlling Most of Mankind!** (God saw that the wickedness of man was great in the earth, and that every imagination of the thoughts of his heart was only evil continually! Genesis 6:5) And Satan uses this Pride in man's heart against him, he nurtures and he manipulates man's Prideful nature, and uses it to Destroy men and all of mankind! Pride causes discord and disagreements, and fights, and wars! Pride has caused millions and billions of murders, and killings, and deaths, over the centuries! Cain killed Abel because of the pride that burned in his heart! God accepted Abel's lamb sacrifice of offering; (and almost all things are by the law purged with blood; and without shedding of blood is no remission! Hebrews 9:22) Cain brought fruit of the ground that was not respected, and Cain was very wroth, and his countenance fell! And the Lord said unto Cain, why art thou wroth? and why is thy countenance fallen? If thou doest well, shalt thou not be accepted? (if you **Do the Right things**, you will be accepted!) And if thou doest Not well, Sin lieth at the door! And unto Thee shall Be his Desire! {Genesis 4:2} (For whosoever committeth sin is the servant of sin - Jesus) God accepted Abel's offering and this infuriated Cain! But Cain, instead of humbling himself, and going to God; and asking God how to get it Right! He got angry at Abel Instead, because he thought he was better than Abel; and who was Abel, to show him up! But Abel his brother, did not have any part in Cain's offering to God! It was only between Cain and God! But Cain's prideful heart thought he was better than Abel, and got mad at him instead! Abel was innocent in the whole matter! And when Satan saw that Cain's prideful evil heart was burning with Rage, and Hatred towards his own brother Abel! (if thou doeth not well, [think about and entertain, hateful, wrathful, murderous, **Thoughts in Your Mind**;] Sin lieth at the door!) Satan saw his opportunity to whisper into Cain's ear,"Kill Him!" And Cain, instead of "**Casting Out**" this evil thought immediately; in a moment of Fleshly Rage, Cain killed his own brother! Basically over a few pieces of **Fruit!** If only Cain would have asked Abel; Abel would have given him a lamb to offer up to God! But instead of remaining calm, using wisdom, and **praying to God for the "right" solution** to his problem. Cain yielded to his flesh, and flew off the handle with rage, and killed his innocent young brother Abel! I thank Almighty **God**, that **God Himself** took the whole situation Out of Man's Hands! Because God Provided his **Own Lamb** for all of mankind; **Jesus Christ!** The Lamb of God that taketh away the **Sin of the world!** Who did our Father's will, and sacrificed himself to **Show God Our Father's love for us!** And it goes right back to the **Heart** situation, Cain wanted to be The Greatest, The Man, First Place, the Head Honcho! Just like Jesus 12 disciples who were reasoning among themselves who was the greatest! And Jesus, perceiving the thought of their heart, set a child by him, and taught his disciples to **Humble themselves like a little child!** Because Humility is the opposite, and the destroyer of pride in your heart! A small child has No Attitude or Set Ways, he is humble, willing to learn, ready to receive, without any argument or scepticism! He is willing to serve and help others, and be the Least! Jesus told his disciples, he that is least among you all, the same shall be great! {Luke 9:48} This is the least that is good, that all should strive for, But what exactly does this Least mean? Simply this, God's servant who Has Crucified himself **for God**, and sacrificed his own dreams, plans, and life, to do God's will! He is least, God is all!

Gods Love, Grace, and Mercy!

Any man or woman, boy or girl; who willingly **Want To** sacrifice and crucify their **own will** and **plans**, their desires and life in this world! If you give up 100% of your own will and life to **God**,(like Jesus did) and actually give God 100% **Full Control** of your life in **Everything!** Then you are the least that Jesus was telling his disciples about, and then you will truly be great in the eyes and the **Kingdom of God!!!** The Very Least is when there is None of You, minute by minute, hour by hour, day by day, Every Day! And You are crucified with Christ, and Walking in the Spirit; and truly **Being Led by the Holy Spirit!** And **God is in FULL CONTROL and ALL in ALL**, Mind, Body, and Soul! This is how our Lord and Savior Jesus Christ; (our perfect example) lived his life! Jesus told us to Take Up our Cross every single day, and **Follow him!** (for whosoever will save his own life in this world will lose it, but whosoever will lose his life in this world (crucify it) for my sake and the gospel's, the same shall **Save It!** - Mark 8:35) The Christian who shines God's light to this world, and who's Christ like life and presence on this earth Destroy the very **Gate's of Hell!** (whom Jesus said the gates of hell **Shall Not Stand Against US!!!** The Church and very Body of Christ !) Is the **Christian** who willingly **want's to** hand over the reins and full control of their **Entire Lives** and goals and plans to God! For the express purpose to Do only God's will for their lives! And to work, and labor, and strive for the **Kingdom of God!** Just like Jesus did for us, to **Save our Souls!** (Jesus is not asking you to Do anything that He didn't **already do for US!**) To **Save** us! Jesus said my meat (food that feeds and nourishes me, and satisfy's my soul!) is to Do God my Father's Will, and I Do always those things that Please my Father! And **IF** You, my beloved brethren, are **truly A Living Born Again Member and Part of the Body of Christ!** Your will and Goal will be consumed with doing Almighty God our Father's **Will ~ For ~ Your ~ LIFE!!!** To repent from all sin and iniquity, and Live a sanctified Holy life; separated unto God! And striving to enter into the strait and narrow gate that leads to Life! And to bring forth fruit that is Worthy of Repentance! And then shine God's light to a **Lost and Dying World** that Jesus died to Save! And minister to them with Love, and Compassion, and patience; and actually **Show Them Jesus** by the way you Live your Life; and not just by the words that come out of your Mouth! The Apostle Paul told Timothy, the husbandman that laboreth **Must** be First partaker of the fruits!{2 Timothy 2:6} In other words how can you show and teach anybody else, how to **Bring forth holy fruit worthy of repentance**! If you yourself aren't bringing forth holy fruit worthy of repentance, and walking with God yourself! There are many people who say out of their mouth that they are christians, and go to church on sunday; but live sinful lives the other six days and twenty three hours in the week! And have absolutely No Intention to Stop Doing or even Fight against the Sin in their lives! But Jesus said to Repent, he also said; Depart from me Ye that work Iniquity! Jesus said in Revelations, To him that overcometh will I give to eat of the tree of life, which is in the midst of the paradise of God! Overcome what? **Sin and Iniquity!!!** And then when you are Obeying God, and have established a real Prayer Life, and you have Diligently Studied the Holy Bible, and have a knowledge and understanding of the whole Bible! Because God speaks through the Bible, and you'll never have a rocksolid foundation and grasp of God's Voice without a rocksolid **Prayer Life** and Understanding of the **Holy Bible!** We all must Exercise our senses to discern between good and evil, darkness and light, to **know and obey God!**

God's Love, Grace, and Mercy!

Because my beloved brethren, if You Love God as much as **God Loves You**, you will want to seek his Holy Face in Prayer Every Day! If you are **Born Again** in the Spirit into Spiritual Body of Jesus Christ, which is the Church, by the power of **God's Holy Spirit** that actually lives and dwells **Inside of You!!!** Your Hearts Desire and Wish as a child of God, will be to **Do God's Will** for Your Life, and to Be Well Pleasing in his Sight! Because the Spirit of Christ in you, will compel you to God's throne; whereby we cry **Abba Father to God**! The **Holy Spirit** will teach and guide you to love and to fellowship with God, and to **Learn** and **Do God's will** for **Your Life!** Because that is the very Purpose of being **born again**, to reconnect and establish a close **personal relationship** with the **one True Living Jehovah God**! Who Created us to be his children and family in Heaven! And restore us to the likeness and image of God our Father, who created us! Therefore my beloved brethren, your old sinful, Adam-like, evil nature, is being Crucified; and **You** are being Transformed into a **New Creature!** Created in the **Image of God!** And Almighty God Himself is delivering you from evil and corruption, from the Death and Destruction that awaits all the doers of Sin and Evil!!! And **Jesus is Saving You** from the inevitable **Wrath of God** that **Will Be Revealed on the Great and Terrible JUDGMENT DAY!!!** And this is the truest meaning of God's Love, and Grace, and Mercy, for all of mankind; that **he sent** his son Jesus to **save** and **cleanse us** from all of our sins, and God put his own Holy Spirit Inside of us, to guide us, and teach us, and comfort us, so that **God himself can deliver us from all Evil!** And the deadly path that man himself **Chose to Take**; when man, (Adam) separated **Himself from God**, who Created him and **Gave Him Life!** When **Man disobeyed** and sinned, and rebelled; choosing the path of evil, and aligning himself with Satan and Death! Even though God warned Adam, (just like he is warning you and me against sin today) that the Day you eat from the tree of The Knowledge of Good and Evil **You Shall Surely DIE!!!** (and sadly, to this very day; most of mankind chooses evil, and sin, and Death; over **God** and **Holiness** and **Life!!!**) But just like God told Elijah, I have reserved (and kept) to me, **7000 Men** who have not bowed the knee to baal! (Satan) And **Almighty God Will Always** reserve to himself, **All** of those men and women who Truly and Sincerely **cry out to God with All their Heart and Soul**, and **All their Mind and Strength!** And that is why, my beloved brethren, **I am Absolutely Positive** that neither death, nor life, nor angels, nor principalities, nor powers, nor things present, nor things to come, nor hight, nor depth, nor any other creature, shall be able to separate **us from the Love of God**, which is in **Christ Jesus our Lord!!!!!!!** Because **In Christ Jesus we are MORE THAN CONQUERORS through GOD WHO LOVES US!** Don't you realize that **the Most Powerful Being in the Whole Entire Universe Lives INSIDE of You!** That if **God is for you**, who can be against you? {Romans 8:31} **NO ONE!!!** There is Nothing or Any Being in Existence that can alter or change **God's Plan and Love for You** but **YOU!!!** You are the **Only One** that can **separate you from God! YOU!!!** My Beloved Brethren, that is why I **Implore you** to **do God's will for your life**! I will stand on the highest mountain, and exclaim to the **Entire Universe** and **All of Mankind! DO GOD'S WILL FOR YOUR LIFE TODAY!!!** My Beloved Brethren, **there will be NO second chances when you stand before God!** Either you **Did God's will**, or **You Did Not!**

God's Love, Grace, and Mercy!

If you are truly a Living Part and a Member of the **Body of Jesus Christ**, walking in the Spirit and being **Led by the Holy Spirit of God!** You will be Functioning and Working in Union with **Jesus Body!!!** Actually Knowing the will of God for your life, and **Doing IT!** Most of the people who say that they are Christians out of their mouth don't really have the slightest clue of what God's will and purpose for their **Life IS!!!** My beloved brethren, I tell you this with **Love** and **Compassion**, and **Humility**; knowing full well that I myself am only **Dust and Dirt!** But we serve the one true living **Almighty God of Creation**, who is able to take dust and dirt into his mighty hands and make it into holy living vessels for his glory! And any Christian who makes their life a sacrifice to God, and makes it his or her Mission and Goal to seek "God's Face" with much Prayer and fasting, and **OBEDIENCE TO GOD!!!** And spends Lots of quality time **alone with God** in his Holy Presence, Seeking to **Know** his **Heart and will for Their Life!** God **will show them his will!** But remember this, my beloved brethren, when you are alone with God in his Holy Presence, if there is **Unrepented** and **Unforsaken SIN in Your Life!!!** That is The Only Thing that God will even speak to you about! God's will first and foremost for your life is that you **repent** from all Sin and Iniquity; and **Be Ye HOLY for I AM HOLY!** And that your life bring forth good holy fruit **Worthy of True Repentance! FIRST!** Paul told Timothy that the laborer **must FIRST** be partaker (or bring forth holy) fruits first, before he can teach others how to do what he has already done in **His Life!** Likewise God is Not going to speak to you about anything else to do for him until you **do the first thing** that God told you to do! Be Ye Holy! And sadly, this is why most Christians never learn what God's full will for their whole life really IS! Because they never even accomplished the first thing **Jesus** told them **To Do** when he began to preach the gospel, **Repent** for the kingdom of heaven is at hand! {Matt. 4:17} For Living Water to truly flow unhindered through a conduit or pipe, any obstruction (or sin) must first **Be Removed!** Then the Living water can flow freely and powerfully to all those around it! (your family) When you bring your car to a mechanic to see why it won't run properly or even start, the first thing he is going to do is see what part is not working and not functioning as it should! And he will either fix that part or replace it! When you go to a doctor because you are sick and don't feel well or can't walk or eat or breathe properly, he will look at that corresponding part of the body that controls that function! So my beloved brethren, when God's children who are supposed to be functioning parts, and living members of the body of Christ **Don't Do What God Has Called Them To Do!!!** The body of our Lord and Savior **Jesus Christ Suffers from It!** If the hand won't bring Food to the mouth, the whole body will starve, if the feet and legs won't walk the body will not get to where it needs to go, if the eyes will not see then the whole body will fall into a ditch! And if the **Mouth will Not Speak**, the True Word of God, that Jesus **Told Us To Go** into the Whole World and Preach the Gospel of Jesus Christ! How will all the **lost souls** going to hell around you, **Be Saved! Souls that Jesus Died to SAVE!** You will instantly say that the gospel is being preached everywhere around the planet, and I will tell you that the Pharisees thought that they were Preaching the **Word of God Too!** But Jesus called them hypocrites and Whited Sepulchers, because they **appeared** to be beautiful on the outside, but on the inside they were full of sin and iniquity but Jesus said leave them alone, they have their reward! But **Go Ye and Preach The Kingdom of God!**

God's Love, Grace, and Mercy!

All True Christians who are Saved by the Precious Blood of Jesus Christ, and the Grace and Mercy of Almighty God our Father! And Are actual Living Members and Part of the **Body of Jesus Christ**, **ARE Called to Do God's Will** Here on the Earth! We are his hands and his feet, and his Representatives here on the earth, to Live and Teach and Show the **True Gospel of Jesus Christ** to a lost and dying World!!! My beloved brethren, if **You** are truly a part of the body of Christ, the **Holy Spirit** will Compel You to **Do the Will** of God our Father! Which is to **1. Live a Holy Life that is well pleasing to God our Father!** And **2. To Do the work of the body of Jesus Christ (of whom we are members of His Body,)** which is to **Go into All the World** and **Preach the TRUE Gospel of Jesus Christ!** Repent from, turn away from, and **Stop Doing All Sin and Iniquity!** Hate Sin, Fight against Sin with All your Heart, and Overcome **Sin and Iniquity in Your Life!** This is the **TRUE** Gospel of Jesus Christ!!! Not just begging people for **MONEY** and **DONATIONS** and **OFFERINGS**, and **Comforting them IN THEIR SINS**; and just letting them feel comfortable in their sinful wicked lives **FOR THEIR MONEY!!!** Because the **REAL UNDENIABLE, ROCK SOLID, ETERNAL TRUTH,** is that **THE WAGES OF SIN IS DEATH!!! FOREVER!!! PERIOD!!!** And my beloved brethren, if **THAT** is **NOT** your message to your family, your friends, your church or congregation, then you are not preaching the **True gospel of Jesus Christ!** Jesus Christ will forgive your sins when **you truly REPENT FROM THEM!!!** When Jesus saved the woman caught is adultery from being stoned to death, he said to her, woman, where are thine accusers, has no man condemned thee? She said, no man Lord, then Jesus told her, neither Do I condemn thee, **Go and SIN NO MORE!** My Beloved Brethren, in most churches and Religious Denominations, they don't **Teach the Basics of SALVATION Anymore!!!** They don't teach people **Holiness**, and **Purity**, and **Sinlessness**, and separation from **The WORLD** anymore! But Almighty **God** our Father in heaven **Commands** all of US, **BE YE HOLY!** I will say it again, **BE YE HOLY!!! FOR I - AM - HOLY!!!** Touch Not the Unclean Thing and **Then I Will Receive You!!!** Do Not be Conformed to This World! But Be YE TRANSFORMED By the **Renewing of YOUR MIND!** (Prayer, Bible Study, Obedience!!!) Today most Churches only Preach and teach Forgiveness, and offerings! And they are Destroying their Own Congregation! Who Mistakenly now believe, there is NO NEED TO REPENT!!! God will just Forgive ALL MY SINS with **NO CONSEQUENCES!!!** What a Lie from Hell!!! The Holy Bible says Plainly and Simply, **YOU WILL REAP WHAT YOU SOW!!!** (you will receive the punishment for all the **Evil Deeds** that you do in your body! And you will receive the blessings and rewards for all the Good, Holy, Righteous Deeds that you do in your Body!) Just ask any person who was there in Sodom and Gomorrah, If the wages of Sin is Death! And they will ask you, Have you ever been hit by a Piece of **Fire and Brimstone?** Raining Down from Almighty God in Heaven!!! Well, there is Plenty of It!!! Waiting in Hell, In the Lake of Fire, for Unrepentant Sinners! Who Love their sins, and have absolutely **No Intention** of repenting from, and turning Away from their sinful lifestyles! My Beloved Brethren, Our Father in Heaven Is a Merciful and Loving God who **Will Forgive Your Sins** and **Blot Out Your Trespasses,** when **You TRULY and SINCERELY R-E-P-E-N-T and TURN AWAY From THEM!**

God's Love, Grace, and Mercy!

My beloved brethren, we must <u>never forget</u> that our Father God is a <u>Holy God</u>, and the ruler and judge of the <u>whole world</u>, and the <u>Entire Universe!!!</u> To **Almighty God** <u>Alone</u> belongs the **Kingdom**, the **Power**, and the **Glory!!!** Forever and Ever and Ever Eternally! Almighty God <u>Created It</u>, He <u>Owns It</u>, and **God Will Rule Over the Entire Universe Forever!!! Period!!!** Almighty God <u>Created You and Me</u>, and **every living thing!** The plants, the trees, the animals, every human being, and every spiritual being! Almighty God Rules over <u>All the Kingdoms of Heaven and Earth</u>, of men and angels, <u>Forever!</u> God created us, and <u>we will all</u> answer to God on judgment day! Almighty God has plainly and clearly said to the to the entire human race; "Behold, **All Souls are Mine**, the soul of the father, so also the soul of the son <u>is mine!</u> The soul that sinneth, **It Shall Die!**" {Ezekiel 18:4} The Scripture also plainly says that "God judgeth the righteous, and God is angry with the wicked every day!"{Psalms 7:11} and that "The Lord is far from the wicked, but he heareth the prayer of the Righteous!" {Proverbs 15:29} My Beloved Brethren, It is my sincere hope and prayer that it is becoming **Crystal Clear** to everyone that **Sin and Evil** will **DESTROY YOU FOREVER!!!** That is why you must **Love and Cry Out** to **Jesus Christ with All your Heart and Soul**, and **Every Fiber in Your Very Being!!!** Because **Jesus Christ** is the <u>only</u> person in the Entire Universe that can **Save Your SOUL**, **Wash Your Sins AWAY** and **Make You Clean and Pure Before ALMIGHTY HOLY GOD!!!** Through <u>Faith in his Name</u>, <u>Belief that Jesus is the Messiah</u>, the only begotten <u>Son of God</u>, and <u>Trust that his Precious Holy Blood</u> that he shed when he was crucified on the cross of Calvary, will wash your <u>Sins Away!</u> And the <u>Truth</u> that **Jesus Christ Rose from the Grave** Three Days later, ascended into heaven; and is now seated at the <u>Right Hand of God</u>, and is <u>our advocate with the Father!</u> Jesus Christ the Righteous, and he is the Propitiation for our sins; and not only <u>our sins</u> but the sins of the <u>whole world!</u> {1 John 2:1} Because You are saved by <u>Grace through</u> **Faith**, and <u>Not</u> by your <u>own works</u> or puny human efforts, it is by the <u>Gift of God</u> that you are saved! Because <u>No Flesh</u> shall glory in <u>God's Presence!!!</u> {Ephesians 2:8} & {1 Corinthians 1:29} For there is **ONE GOD** and **One Mediator between God and men**, the man **Jesus Christ!!!** {1 Timothy 2:5} Jesus said,"I AM the Way, the Truth, and the Life; no man can come unto the Father **BUT BY ME!**" {John 14:6} Mohammed <u>cannot</u> save you! Buddha <u>cannot</u> save you! Mary <u>cannot</u> save you! **Jesus Christ is the One and the Only Way into Heaven!!!** You must accept Jesus Christ as your Lord and Savior, truly and sincerely Repent from all of your sins, and <u>Do</u> the will of God our Father every single day! Jesus said, not every one that saith unto me Lord, Lord, shall enter into the kingdom of heaven! But they that <u>actually</u> **Do the will** <u>of my Father which is in Heaven!</u> It is easy to <u>say you are a Christian</u> with your mouth! It is completely another thing to <u>live</u> a holy sanctified life separated unto God, to walk and talk like **Jesus** did! By taking up your cross every single day and crucifying all your fleshly lusts and desires! And Nailing your wicked sinful flesh to the cross of Jesus Christ! You must deny yourself, pick up your cross and follow Jesus, because the wages of sin is death but the gift of God is eternal life through Jesus Christ our Lord! The Apostle Paul said, I am Crucified with Christ, and still I live, yet not I but Christ that lives inside of me! And the life I now live, I live by the faith of the Son of God! (Jesus) Who Loved me, and Gave himself for me! {Galatians 2:20}

God's Love, Grace, and Mercy!

Beloved, our Father God is holy and has always destroyed sin and evil from the foundation of the world. God cast Lucifer (or Satan) and all the angels that rebelled with him out of heaven! God drove Adam and Eve out of the garden of Eden when they disobeyed and sinned! But God has created mankind to be with him in Heaven! God always had a way for mankind to be saved from the foundation of the world! God knew that Adam would fail and sin! But that did not stop God from giving Adam the chance and the opportunity and everything he needed to succeed! Beloved, Our Father God was never going to let the Sin and Failure of One Man be the destruction and downfall of all Gods children, created in his own Image! Our Father God and our Lord and Savior Jesus Christ had a Covenant made together before the very Foundation of the world! To Save All of God's children and to provide a way for all of mankind to overcome Sin and Evil and Death! And our Holy Loving Father God, and his only Begotten Son Jesus Christ; Have Created a way, and given Every Man, Woman, and Child the ability and the opportunity to make it into Heaven! Beloved, Heaven is Where God wants You to Be!!! And **Jesus Christ** is your way to Be There! For by one man sin entered into the world, and death by sin; and so death passed upon all men, for that all have sinned! (But our Father God, being just and fair and righteous!) Saw that if by the sin and disobedience of one man, death passed upon all men! So God Has decreed that by the obedience and holiness, and righteousness of **one man! Jesus Christ!** That the forgiveness of sins, and holiness, and **LIFE** may be passed upon all men! For if by one man's offence, death reigned by one; even so by the Righteousness of one man, the free gift came upon all men unto Justification of Life! For as by one man's disobedience many were made sinners; so by the obedience of one shall many be made righteous! {Romans 5:12-19} So our God sent his own son, made in the likeness of man, according to his covenant promises; the son of David, born of the seed of Abraham! Our Lord and Savior Jesus Christ, through his Holy, Spotless, Sacrifice to God on the cross of Calvary! Who being made Perfect, became the Author of Eternal Salvation unto all them that **Obey Him!** {Hebrews 5:9} Because God is **Not willing** that any man should perish! But that all men should come to repentance and **Be Saved** by the knowledge of the **Truth**, about the **Saving Grace** of our Lord and Savior, **Jesus Christ!** {2 Peter 3:9 & 1 Timothy 2:4} My beloved Brethren, hear the very words spoken by Almighty God himself, "Say unto them, As I Live Sayeth the Lord God, "I have **No Pleasure in the Death of the Wicked!**" But that the wicked turn from his way and Live!" "Turn Ye, Turn Ye from your Evil ways; for **Why will Ye Die?**" "Wash You, make you clean; put away the evil of your doings from before mine eyes! Cease to do evil! Learn to do well;" seek judgment, relieve the oppressed" come now, and let us reason together; saith the Lord. though your sins be as scarlet, they shall be as white as snow; though they be red like crimson, they shall be as wool. If ye be willing and obedient ye shall eat the good of the land! (Go to Heaven) but if ye refuse and rebel, (like Satan) then ye shall be devoured by the sword! (and face my wrath) for I the Lord have spoken it! {Ezekiel 33:11 & Isaiah 1:16-20} Beloved, we know that all things work together for good, to them that **Love God!** All that are called according to his purpose, and who God called he also did predestinate to be Conformed to the Image of his Son! That he might be the firstborn among many brethren! So God sent Jesus to save and cleanse us all from Sin, and be God's family in Heaven. The reason he created us!

God's Love, Grace, and Mercy!

So my beloved brethren, cry out to God! Go to him humbly and sincerely in prayer, ask him to forgive all your sins, and trespasses, and iniquities! Plead for the blood of Jesus Christ, God's only begotten son to cover you! <u>Believe</u> in Jesus and <u>Trust</u> that his blood <u>can</u> wash your sins away through <u>Faith</u> in his name, and Jesus Christ's Resurrection from the dead! And God's <u>Grace</u> can and <u>will</u> Cover You! Remember the thief on the cross, he cried out to Jesus on the last tick of the clock in his life, and God saved him! He was the luckiest man in the bible! By the grace of God he was crucified right next to the Savior of the World! He believed in Jesus and said, "Lord remember me when you come into your kingdom" and Jesus told him "Today you will be with me in paradise!" Only two people were there on crosses next to Jesus, the other thief railed against Jesus saying, If thou be the Christ, save thyself and us.{Luke 23:39} He'll regret what he said for all of eternity! Beloved, let us learn an important lesson from the two thieves. One believed in Jesus, and one did not! One is in paradise, the other one is not! We must cry out to Jesus in prayer for ourselves, and work out our own salvation with fear and with trembling! We will not be in the same position as that man who was crucified next to Jesus! Many people mistakenly think they can wait to be saved later, and <u>never</u> make it! <u>Today</u> is the day for your salvation! You could be gone tomorrow! Don't be dumb and let sin harden your heart! Be Smart! God is calling you today, right <u>Now</u>! Do not think that you are too bad or sinful, you are <u>not</u>! God wants to save you! God is not willing that <u>any</u> should perish, but that all should come to repentance!{2 Pet 3:9} Jesus appeared to Saul (the Apostle Paul) on the road to Damascus, even though he was persecuting Christians, throwing them in jail, and even having some killed! (he stood by and consented as they stoned Steven, a man full of the Holy Spirit, Faith and Wisdom!) But God still had mercy on him, as the Apostle Paul said, because he did it ignorantly in unbelief. {1 Tim 1:13, Acts 9:1-9} You see Paul thought he was doing the right thing in his heart, things he was taught as a Pharisee. God saw his heart and had big plans for this Pharisee named Saul! Just one real encounter with the Mighty Lord Jesus to shine God's Light in his Heart, and point him in the right direction and he became the Apostle Paul! One of the Greatest and Mightiest Men of God that ever Lived! Paul wrote 14 Epistles or letters in the New Testament of the Holy Bible! He started countless Churches all over the whole Ancient World! God worked special miracles by the hand of Paul, so that handkerchiefs brought from his body would heal the sick of their diseases or drive out evil spirits! {Acts 19:11} The Apostle Paul Terrorized the forces of darkness and was a Thorn in Satan's side! Only Almighty God can tell how many souls were reached and saved by the Gospel of Jesus Christ, through the relentless efforts and obedience to God, by the Apostle Paul! Yes, Almighty God had big plans for that Pharisee named Saul; even though he was persecuting and threatening Christians, going down that road to Damascus! So lost sinner, do you still believe you are too bad for God to reach? Just one real heart changing encounter with the Mighty Lord Jesus, and you'll find out that God has big plans for your life too! Nothing is impossible for God! "Know therefore that the Lord thy God, <u>he</u> <u>is</u> <u>God</u>! The (one True Living) <u>Faithful</u> God, which keepeth Covenant and Mercy with them that love him and keep his Commandments to a thousand generations! And repayeth them that hate him to their face, to destroy them; he will not be slack to him that hateth him, he will repay him to his face!" "Moses"{Deuteronomy 7:9} Jesus blood can wash your sin away!

God's Love, Grace, and Mercy!

So my beloved brethren, as we have seen; Almighty God is Equal, Fair and Just! Our God is a God of Love, and Grace; of Mercy, and Forgiveness! And our God is a God of Holiness, and Righteousness; of Justice, and Judgment! As it says in the Holy Scriptures, Mercy Rejoiceth against Judgment and Judgement against Mercy! You cannot have one without the other! If you <u>Do</u> that which is <u>Good</u> and <u>Right</u> and <u>True</u> and <u>Fair</u> and <u>Holy</u>, Almighty God will have mercy, and bless, and reward you! On the other hand, if you <u>do</u> that which is <u>Evil</u> and <u>Wrong</u> and <u>Wicked</u> and <u>Bad</u> and <u>Sinful</u>!!! Then the wrath and judgment of the one true Living Holy Almighty God will come down upon you on Judgment day! Because God is Fair and Equal, Holy and Balanced, God is no respecter of persons, any person; you <u>will</u> reap what you sow! You <u>will</u> receive the rewards for the deeds that you <u>Do</u> here on the Earth, with the life and the body that God gave to you! Please always remember my beloved brethren, that God sent his son Jesus to <u>save</u> you and wash you clean from all sin and iniquity! To cover you with his grace and mercy and love! And to clothe you in a spotless white wedding garment, to prepare you for the marriage supper of the Lamb in Heaven! God sent his Holy Spirit to the earth, Specifically to help you, and strengthen you, to comfort you, and teach you, and guide you! The Holy Spirit will help and guide all who simply <u>Believe</u> that Jesus is the son of God, and died for their sins, and that he was Resurrected and ascended into heaven, at the right hand of God the Father to atone for our Sins! All who call out to Jesus in prayer to save them and wash their sins away, with his Precious Holy Blood! Simply by submitting to Jesus Christ and accepting him as their Lord and Savior! Because Jesus has suffered and died on the cross for us, while we were yet sinners! With the hope that we would simply go to him, so that he could save us and bring us to Heaven for all of Eternity! And we would receive the Free Gift of the Holy Spirit, promised to us by God! According to the Covenant that God our Father, and his Son Jesus Christ made before the Foundation of the World! The Holy Spirit of God will breathe the breath of God's Life into your Soul, so that you can be Born Again in the Spirit, into the body of Jesus Christ! Which is the True Church, and the <u>only</u> safe place in the Universe, protected and covered by God's grace and mercy! Protected on the Great and Terrible Day of Judgment, from the Wrath of Almighty God against <u>all</u> Sin and Evil, all Wickedness and Iniquity! That is the reason why, my beloved brethren, I preach the full Gospel of Jesus Christ! To alert and to warn every single person on earth, of the coming Judgment Day! And to tell everyone the good news, which is what the word gospel means, good news, the good news that God's only begotten son Jesus Christ <u>can</u> and <u>will</u> **Save Your Soul!** If only you will <u>let</u> him, and cry out to him, and <u>obey</u> him! The very good news that we are <u>all</u> invited to the marriage supper of the Lamb of God, in Heaven Above! That is the message that Almighty God the Father in Heaven has sent to us! God is our Father, he created us, he loves us! God wants us to be in heaven with him for all of eternity! God personally sent his son Jesus to save us and to cleanse us from all sin and iniquity! God Personally sent his <u>own</u> Holy Spirit to <u>Live</u> inside of our heart and soul! To Comfort and Guide us, to Strengthen and Teach us, to Protect and Watch over us, to deliver us from sin and evil! So that we could have a Personal and Intimate Relationship with Almighty God our Father, Creator of the Universe, who now Lives Inside of <u>Us</u>! We are his Temple!

Holy Fire and Holy Ground!

The Lord our God is an <u>All</u> <u>Consuming</u> <u>Fire!</u> These words were first written down by Moses in the book of Deuteronomy 4:24; then repeated by the Apostle Paul in Hebrews 12:29, I added the word all. These two men certainly <u>knew</u> God better than most of the men that ever walked on the earth! The Lord God is a Holy God, and <u>any</u> person who wants to, and would try to <u>walk</u> with God, and <u>talk</u> with God, or have a <u>close</u> personal relationship with the One <u>True</u> Living Almighty Jehovah God; <u>must</u> be <u>holy</u>, and **live a Holy sanctified life**! Set apart from the world of sin, Iniquity, and all Evil! Or God will not let you get <u>close</u> to him, enter into his Holy presence, or have a close **Personal Relationship** with <u>Him</u>! Let me make this Crystal Clear, God **<u>HATES</u>** Sin, Lying, Stealing, Iniquity, Unholiness, Unrighteousness, Rebellion, and **<u>All Evil!</u>** God is angry with the wicked every day! {Psalms 7:11} And believe me, you <u>Do Not</u> want Almighty God (the most powerful being in the Entire Universe!) <u>Angry</u> at you every day! Unfortunately the sad truth is that most of the Christians, Preachers, and the people who live on the earth; <u>Do Not</u> have a real relationship, or the slightest clue, who the One <u>True</u> Living Almighty <u>God</u> of all Creation is! Their Image and Idea of <u>who</u> and what <u>God</u> is was formed by what another puny human being <u>told</u> them, not by the earth shattering, universe shaking, real <u>personal</u> <u>Presence</u> of the One True Living Jehovah God! That can <u>never</u> <u>ever</u> be accurately described, relayed to, or comprehended, by any puny human <u>words</u> in mans vocabulary! <u>Nothing</u> but Almighty <u>God's</u> <u>Real</u>, <u>True</u>, <u>Actual</u>, Universe shaking, <u>Personal</u> Holy <u>Presence</u>! Can ever give you a real <u>true</u> accurate revelation and understanding of Almighty God's Holiness, Glory, Unlimited, Endless, Infinite, Power and Might!!! The Apostle Paul was lifted up to the third heaven and saw unspeakable things that are not even allowed for man to utter! But if you read in his epistles, he doesn't talk about gold streets or solid walls of diamonds, emeralds, and precious stones! What he does say is that "It is a Fearful Thing to fall into the Hands of the **<u>Living God!!!</u>**" And "Therefore knowing the Terror of the Lord," we do our best to "Persuade men" to prepare their lives for the coming of the great and terrible, "<u>Judgment</u> <u>Day!</u>" What got burned into the Apostle Paul's heart, mind, and soul, is that "We must <u>all</u> stand before the **Judgement Seat of Christ!**" And answer to Almighty God, and give an account for <u>all</u> the things and <u>Deeds</u> that we have done in our body, with the life that <u>God</u> gave to us! And we must answer for all the <u>words</u> that came out of our mouths, be it truth or lies, Holy righteous pure words; or evil lies, curse words, hateful, slanderous, vile filth and gossip to hurt others! And we <u>will</u> answer for how we <u>treated</u> other people, and how we acted towards and treated Almighty God while we were down here on this earth! Moses spent 40 days alone with God on Mount Sinai while the Israelite people stayed at the base of the Mountain and trembled with <u>Fear</u>! They told Moses,"<u>you</u> go talk to <u>God</u> and we'll stay <u>here</u>!" You can tell us what God said! Sin will make you <u>hide</u> from God, Just like Adam hid from God the Israelites did not want to get to close to God's actual Holy presence! God's Holy presence exposes sin, all sin; that's why the <u>world</u> hates God, and hides from God to this very day! They love their <u>Sins!</u> And this is the condemnation, that light is come into the world, and men loved darkness rather than Light because their deeds were evil! For every one that doeth evil hateth the light, neither cometh to the light, lest his deeds should be reproved! {John 3:19} But Moses warned the Israelites, (and us!)

Holy Fire and Holy Ground!

Know therefore that the Lord thy God, **He is God!** (of the whole Entire Universe! And the only one in Complete and Total Command and Control, **Forever!**) He is a Faithful God, which keepeth his covenant and mercy with them that love him and keep his commandments to a thousand generations! And God repayeth them that hate him to their face, to **destroy them!** He will not be slack to him that hateth him, he will repay him to his face! {Deuteronomy 7:9} My beloved brethren, this is a serious and severe warning, Moses was an humble man; God had revealed his glory and Awesome Power to Moses. And Moses was giving the message and warning to the Israelites, and to us! Moses said, "Be sure that your Sin will find you out!" {Numbers 32:23} Translation: If you sin, and you do not keep Almighty God's Commandments, but you choose to live a life of lying, stealing, adultery, fornication homosexuality, lusting, drunkenness, greed, evil and iniquity; and rebellion like Satan! Then you are choosing to put your soul in mortal and terrible Eternal danger Forever! When you stand before God on the Great and Terrible Judgment Day! Because all of your sins and iniquities will be waiting there to Find You Out and Destroy You on Judgement Day! Unless you Truly Repent From and **STOP** Doing all those Sins and Iniquities! Because Then, when you really, truly, repent from, forsake, and stop doing all sin and iniquities; **Jesus Precious Blood** can and will, Wash You Clean! And Cover you with God's Grace, Mercy, Love and Forgiveness! But God does not, and will Not Cover up any Unrepented and Unforsaken Sin! (For him that has ears to hear, let him Hear!) My beloved brethren, we would all be wise to remember what Jesus said, "Broad and wide is the road or path that leads to **Destruction!** And many people will go and enter into that path to hell and destruction! Because very strait and narrow is the way and path that leads to life! And only a few people will be able to enter in to that strait and narrow road! For many will seek to enter into that strait and narrow path to heaven, and will not be able! My beloved brethren, I love you all so very much, and I want you to make it in to Heaven with all my heart! That is why I pray and cry out to our Holy and Mighty Father God, and carry Jesus burden and message to the whole world! And personally write and show to you, all these important parts and verses of scriptures from God's Holy Word that will Stand Forever True! So you can read and know and understand who Almighty God really is from God's own word, so that you can see and hear with your own eyes and ears, the True Gospel of Jesus Christ! And so that you can feel with your own heart, and consider and decide in your own mind, what these verses of Scripture and truth from God's Holy Bible mean to you personally! I am just your servant, bringing you a full plate of steak, (not watered down milk) for you to personally consume, receive, and grow from; and to consider, meditate on, and decide for your own selves, in your own heart, what God is personally saying to you through his Holy Bible that he inspired and gave to us all for correction and instruction in truth and righteousness. Because I know God personally, and I love God with all my heart, and it's God's will for my life to take his Holy Word and cut down and destroy all the evil lies, deceptions, and false doctrines that Satan has deceived the whole world with! And show the Real Truth of God, to make it Plain and crystal clear and easy for all to understand! It is my Job to cut down Mountains, fill in the valleys, make the crooked roads straight, and Pray down Holy Fire upon Satan's Evil head!

Holy Fire and Holy Ground!

And the Real Truth is that You Do Not want to stand before Holy Almighty God on Judgement Day, with unrepented and unforsaken sin in your life and soul! You will not be ready! Especially because Jesus sacrificed himself on the cross to set you free, make you clean and deliver you from all sin and evil! And if you just disregard and Ignore Jesus's great and awesome sacrifice to cleanse your soul and set you free from all sin and evil, and yet you still personally choose to stand before Almighty, Holy, Jehovah God of Truth and Holiness; as an evil, sinful, rebellious child of the devil! You will be rejected and destroyed, just like Satan; who did the same thing! And you will be cast into hell just like Satan! Once again let us look at and consider the words of the Mighty Lord Jesus, Who said, "Ye are of your father the devil, and the lusts of your father ye will do! He was a murderer from the beginning and abode not in the truth, because there is no Truth in him. when he speaketh a lie, he speaketh of his own; for he is a liar and the father of it! Every time that you choose sin and evil, you are choosing to make Satan your father! "The Lusts of your father ye will do" Every time that you tell lies out of your mouth, you are proving (by the very words that come out of your mouth) that Satan is your father! "for he is a liar, and the father of it!" Telling a lie, any lie is No Small Matter!!! Lies are one of the very Identifying marks and traits of Satan himself. And all Satan's children bear these marks and traits, that is how God's children, (who exercise their senses to discern between good and evil) know and identify good people, and evil people in this world! (Jesus said, "ye shall know them by their fruits") and living a sinful, evil life, and telling lies and filthy, foul curse words and gossip out of your mouth, are the clear and unmistakable marks of Satan and his children! And make no mistake, my beloved brethren, for because of these things cometh the Wrath of God down upon the children of disobedience! {Ephesians 5:6} For the wrath of God is revealed from heaven against all ungodliness and unrighteousness of men! {Romans 1:18} But to all the children of God, who Love God and keep his commandments, and put their Faith and Trust in God, all who do what is pure and Holy, good and true, Faithful and just and Righteous! They shall receive God's Grace and Love and Mercy and blessings! Blessed are the pure in heart, for they shall see God! Blessed are the merciful, for they shall receive mercy! Blessed are the meek, for they shall inherit the earth! Blessed are the peacemakers, for they shall be called the children of God! Blessed are they which do hunger and thirst after righteousness, for they shall be filled! So, Seek ye first the kingdom of God, and his righteousness, and all these things shall be added unto you! God will definitely help those who put their faith and trust in him, sincerely with all their heart and soul! Those who obey and follow Jesus and "strive to enter into the strait and narrow gate" because all things work together for good to them who love God! And if Almighty God be for you, (the most powerful being in the Entire Universe!) Who can be against you? (NO ONE!) Because God has promised, "They that wait upon the Lord, shall renew their strength! They shall run and not get weary, the shall walk and not faint! They shall rise up with wings as Eagles! For **God** himself has said, Fear thou not; for I am with thee: do not be dismayed for I am thy God; Yea, I will strengthen thee; Yea, I will help thee; Yea, I will uphold thee with the right hand of my Righteousness! {Isaiah 41:10} Be strong, I will not fail or forsake thee!!!

Holy Fire and Holy Ground!

Our God is an all Consuming Fire! And when Jesus Baptizes you with Holy Ghost Fire, you must let the Holy Spirit take full control of your entire life, if you want to be the real man (or woman) that God created you to be, from the foundation of the world! (O' how many people never reach their full potential in God!) God wants every part of your life, your heart, your soul, your mind, your time and affections! All of You! Satan can't have any part of you! Because our Father God is a Jealous God! And an **All Consuming Fire!** And when God's Holy Fire and Holy Spirit and anointing, comes and Lives and Dwells Inside of You! So does Almighty God's Awesome, Mighty Power! The Apostle Paul said, "What, know ye not, (do you not know and understand) That "Ye are the Temple of God!" and the Spirit of the Living, Almighty God **Lives and Dwells Inside of You!** {1 Corinthians 3:16} When the Master begins to forge a steel blade, and he takes the cold steel and plunges it into the red hot coals, (Holy Fire) you can instantly see the difference between the Cold Steel blade and the Red Hot Embers. But as it stays and abides in the red hot coals, (Holy Fire) of the hot furnace. (body of Christ) The Fire is transferred into the steel blade, so that after a while there is no difference between the red hot (Holy) Fire of the coals on the Altar, and the Implement put into the Fire! (You) The Red hot fire has now transferred it's (Holy) fire and heat, (and power) into the piece put into the fire (you) and they are now the same in appearance and heat! (Holiness and Purity) Now there is no difference between the two! They now burn together as One in (Holy Fire) Power and Heat! Gold put into a red hot furnace is not destroyed, but purified! And when all the impurity's come out, and are removed; the furnace Master can look into the gold and see his own Reflection in the purified Gold! A Lump of worthless coal that is put under great pressure and heat, inside of the Earth! Is Transformed into a beautiful, precious, Diamond! A Human Soul plunged into God's Holy Fire, (the body of Christ) and placed on the Altar of God! The One True Holy Anvil and Cornerstone Foundation, **Jesus Christ!** And then Pounded by (Satan) the Hammer of Fiery Trials and Temptations, it becomes a sharpened, Powerful Sword, and useful Tool in the Hands of Almighty God! Who is the Master and the very person who Forged and Created the Sword, and put it (You) into the Fire! To Create a Powerful and useful tool here on the earth, for this very purpose; to use it, to help set more of God's children free! This is why the Apostle Paul, or Elijah, or Job, or Joseph, or Moses, or Isaiah, or Jeremiah, or Daniel Never complained about the Fiery Trials and Temptations they had to go through! Because they had an understanding of this Trial by Fire process, and they were willing to suffer the Pain and Agony on the Spiritual Battlefield! To be a useful tool, and be used by Almighty God, and see more of God's Children (us and all of our Brethren) **Set Free** and make it **Into God's Holy Kingdom!** Great men of God, who unselfishly sacrificed their Lives and Body's, so that God could use them to set other Lost Souls **FREE!!!** But Now it is up to You and Me, what are **We** going to do about all the Lost Souls going to hell all around us? Nothing? Are we too busy watching T.V. or on the Internet texting or playing games, throwing party's, Barbecue cookouts? Wouldn't want to miss the big game for a single lost soul, or Bob's party is on Friday night, can't miss that! If Today's Church, we "so called" Christians, had to stand up next to the Saints and Martyrs in the bible, we would all be embarrassed!

Holy Fire and Holy Ground!

The Title to this Chapter is Holy Fire and Holy Ground, or (Hallowed) Ground! So we are going to take a look at the definition for the words "Holy" and "Hallowed" used by Jesus in the Lords prayer. ~ Holy ~ Belonging to God, Devoted to God; Under God's control and Command; Clean and Pure; Free from all Sin; Faithful, Divine, Sanctified; Blessed, Consecrated, Sacred, unblemished. ~ Hallowed ~ to make Holy, or made Holy; clean, pure, set apart unto God; clean and pure in God's eyes and sight; without spot or stain; to be accepted and allowed into God's Holy presence. When God appeared to Moses as Holy Fire in the Burning Bush, and God spoke to Moses out of the Fire; He told Moses, Draw not hither, or do not get any closer. First take thy shoes off of thy feet, for the place where you are standing is Holy Ground! Most people do not understand the significance of this act of Moses taking his shoes off! Before Moses could get any closer to God, he had to take his shoes off! Moses and all of Israel knew, and understood that this act of taking your shoes off, meant that you were giving up all of your rights, and the person that you gave the shoe to was now Master, owned full control and had all of the authority and Command over you! So Moses understood that what God was saying to him was, "Moses, before you can get any closer to me, you have to give me full control of your Life," to truly and sincerely be Led by my Holy Spirit, Follow my command and do my will in all that I tell you to say and Do! God must have full command and complete control of your whole entire life in all that you say and do, if you truly want to walk closer to him in the Spirit; and get closer to God in Spirit and Truth! **God** must have **Full** and **Complete Control!** That is why Jesus said, "I have spoken unto you only the words that my Father gave me to say, For I do nothing of myself; but as my Father hath taught me, I speak these things! And he that sent me is with me, the Father hath not left me alone; for **I Always Do those things that Please Him!**"{John 8:28} And "He that hath seen me hath seen the Father, I am in the Father and the Father in me! For the words that I speak unto you I speak not of myself; but the Father that dwelleth in me, "**He Doeth the Works!**" {John 14:9} God the Father had **Complete Control** over everything Jesus said and did! Everything! And so, my beloved brethren, If you Really and Truly want to Walk and Talk; and Live and **Pray** just like **Jesus Christ!** And get Closer to **God** in **Spirit** and in **Truth**, you must give God Complete Control over your Entire Life and everything that you Say and Do! And just like Jesus, you must Do Almighty God the Fathers Perfect Will for your Life! And then, my beloved brethren, your Life and Prayers will Terrorize the Kingdom of Darkness, and Tear Down the very Gates of Hell! And Then God will use you, to be a Thorn in Satan's side! Hallelujah!!! Also, please always remember what Jesus told us; not every one that sayeth unto me, Lord, Lord, shall enter into the kingdom of heaven, but he that **Doeth** the **Will of my Father** which is in heaven! Many will say to me in that day, Lord, Lord, have we not prophesied in thy name? and in thy name cast out devils? and in thy name done many wonderful works? And then will I profess unto them, "I never knew you; depart from me, ye that work Iniquity!" {Matthew 7:21} ~ Iniquity ~ wickedness, gross injustice; sin or evil; depravity. Jesus Christ our Lord and Savior told us, "We must actually Do God the Fathers will," if we want to "Enter into the Kingdom of Heaven!" What is God the Fathers will? "Be Ye Holy for I am Holy!"

Holy Fire and Holy Ground!

Beloved, God wants you to understand that holiness is not something that can be bought or earned by our own works, or puny efforts; holiness only comes by faith that Jesus blood cleanses us from all sin! Yes, we must Do the will of God in our Lives; Yes we must repent from and forsake all sin and Stop doing it! Yes we must crucify all our fleshly desires on the cross, take up our cross and follow our Lord Jesus Christ Every Day! We do this because we Love God, and the Holy Spirit Compels us to Repent and Forsake all sin and iniquity in our lives! And the Holy Spirit Guides us to Do God's will! But at the end of each and every day, after you have done the will of God our Father! You must say to yourself, "I am an unprofitable servant, and I have only done that which is my duty to Do!" And that only Jesus has made me clean, only Jesus has made me Holy, only Jesus precious Blood and his Awesome Sacrifice to God the Father on the Cross; has opened the Gates of Heaven to us! And it is Only because of "**Jesus Christ**" the "Mighty Lamb of God, that taketh away the Sin of the World!" That **Anyone's** name is Written in "**God's Book of Life!**" It is only because of **Jesus Christ** and his Sacrifice on the Cross, and his Resurrection from the dead; that we can have **Eternal Life** with God! You are saved by Grace through Faith and not by works, It is the Gift of God! Because "No Flesh" shall glory in **Almighty God's**, **Awesome**, **Magnificent**, **Presence**! And that Gift is **Jesus Christ!** I Love You so much Jesus! I Praise your Holy Name Forever and ever! Worthy is the Lamb that was Slain, to Receive Power and Riches, Wisdom and Strength, and Honor and Glory, and Blessings!!! You see it is only the righteousness we receive through faith in Jesus Christ that makes us Clean and Pure in God's eyes and in God's sight! Because our own righteousness is as filthy rags in God's sight. But as the Apostle Paul put it so eloquently when he said, "We do not seek the righteousness which is by the workings of the Law. Knowing that a man is not justified by the works of the law, but by the Faith of Jesus Christ! Even we, who have believed in Jesus Christ, that we might be justified by the Faith of Christ, and not by the works of the law; for by the works of the law shall No flesh (man) be Justified!{Galatians 2:16} I seek to be Found in him, not having mine own righteousness, which is of the law, but that which is through the faith of Christ, the righteousness which is of God by faith! That I may know him, and the power of his resurrection, and the fellowship of his sufferings, being made conformable unto his death! If by any means I might attain unto the resurrection of the dead!!! **I Press Towards the Mark** of the **High Calling of God in Christ Jesus!!!** {Philippians 3:9} So my beloved brethren, we must walk and live in the spirit, and be led by the Holy Spirit every day! For, "as many as are Led by the Spirit of God, they Are the Sons of God!"{Romans 8:14} And if we live in the spirit, let us also walk in the spirit! For if we walk in the spirit we shall not fulfil the lusts of the flesh! {Galatians 5:16} Because if we live and walk in the spirit, we are a living, breathing, part and member of the **Body of Christ!** Covered by God's Grace, Mercy, and Love! And there is now therefore, no condemnation to them who are in Christ Jesus, for the law of the Spirit of life in Christ Jesus hath made me free from the law of sin and death! For what the law could not do, in that it was weak through the the flesh, God sent his own son in the likeness of sinful flesh, condemned sin in the flesh! So that the righteousness of the law might be fulfilled in us! In Christ Jesus! {Romans 8:1}

Holy Fire and Holy Ground!

When God appeared to Moses on Mount Sinai, (the whole Mountain range is called Horeb, Sinai is one of the Peaks) God spoke to Moses out of the burning bush. God told Moses to remove his shoes, and give him full control of his life! Almighty God's infinite power, perception, wisdom, knowledge, understanding, and unlimited sight, is beyond the realms of Time and Space, across all of the Physical and Spiritual universe; and is Incomprehensible to man, and far beyond the reach and understanding of the puny human mind! Almighty God is Sovereign, Omnipotent, Immutable, Infinite, and Eternal!!! No One can teach or help you, to strengthen you, and Guide you in Spirit and Truth, through life or the Physical and Spiritual Universe; Better than **Almighty God**, who Created It!!! No One!!! When the One True Living Almighty Jehovah God, and Creator of the Universe! Comes to you and says, give me full control of your Life, you say **YES!!!** Yes, Yes, Yes! Thank God Moses was Intelligent enough, and Smart enough to know this! Incredibly, there are Billions and Billions of people on the earth, who say No to God and Jesus! No to God, No to Eternal Life??? **YOU BIG DUMMY!** Who? Who Else can Teach You, Guide You, or **Help You** more than **ALMIGHTY GOD!!! NO ONE!!!** Who Else can **GIVE ~ YOU ~ ETERNAL ~ LIFE??? ~ No One! ~ NO ONE!!!** Use your Brain! The Pharisees thought that Peter (a fisherman) was unlearned and ignorant, but he was smart enough to say to Jesus, "Lord, to who (else) shall we go, **Thou** hast the words of **Eternal Life!**" When God told Moses, the place where you are standing is "Holy Ground!" God was not talking about a 4 x 8 piece of Real estate or earth, on the Top of Mount Sinai! No, God is a Spirit, God Lives, and walks, and Moves In the Spiritual Realm! And all those who would Pray to, worship, or walk and talk with Almighty God must do it **In Spirit and In Truth!** Holy Ground is not a place or spot of earth or dirt location! Holy Ground is a spiritual location Inside of your heart, mind and Soul, where God teaches, guides, leads, conditions, and trains a man or woman of God, to walk in the Spirit! To be Led by the Holy Spirit to be a living, active, productive, fruitful, nourishing, and helpful part and member of the **Body of Christ** in the Spirit! Holy Ground is a place reached only through Faith and Trust in God, and true spiritual growth in the Holy Spirit; and empowered by the Holy Spirit! By holiness, prayer, and doing God's will; True repentance and forsaking of all sin, iniquity, and evil! To show your love and Obedience to God, by bringing forth good, holy, Fruits of the Spirit, worthy of real repentance! And concrete Proof of a true and sincere change in your heart and life! If any man be In Christ, he is a New Creature, old things are passed away; behold all things are become New! "Holy Ground" is a place of maturity and growth in the spirit, a Spiritual condition that a man or woman achieve in their Walk and Relationship with God! And **Holy Ground** can only be reached and achieved through the Spirit, by a Real, very close and **Personal Relationship** with **ALMIGHTY GOD, JESUS CHRIST** and **The HOLY SPIRIT!!!** (These Three are One! ~ 1 John 5:7) The Holy Trinity of the Godhead, who always walk in **One Mind**, and **One Accord!** And it's only through sincere prayer and constant communication with God! Diligent Bible study, submission and obedience, to **God** by actually doing **God's Will for Your Life!!!** Can you reach Holy Ground and Live and walk in the Spirit with God!

Holy Fire and Holy Ground!

My Beloved, your own Personal Love for, and Relationship with, Almighty God; is the one and only place where you can Find and Get the strength, to repent from and **Overcome** all the sin and iniquity in your life! And to Crucify the fleshly, carnal desires in your body, and the fallen sinful nature of your old, (Adam like) man! Jesus told us the reason, the First Commandment is; "Thou shalt love the Lord thy God with all thy heart, all thy mind, all thy soul, and all thy strength!" Because where your Treasure is, there shall your Heart be also! And when you Love our Father God in Heaven, Above all Else; any person, earthly treasure, possession, or riches; it gives you a personal reason, and a burning desire to Strive and Fight for God with all your heart, soul, mind, and strength! And when you really, truly love God; you will spend quality time alone with God! Praying to God in your prayer closet and seeking God's face, waiting upon God; and they that wait upon the Lord Shall Renew their Strength! Strength to Crucify your old man's carnal, fallen, Adam like nature; Strength to Overcome all of your sins and iniquity! Strength to Do God's will for your life! Strength to pray down **Holy Fire!** Strength to stand, walk and Live on **Holy Ground!** My beloved brethren, if you Really, Truly want to Stand, and walk and live on Holy Ground; you must Walk, and Talk, and Live a **HOLY ~ LIFE!** Because without holiness, no man shall see God, or shine God's light to the world, and make his life count for God, Jesus, or heaven! {Hebrews 12:14} You must **Live ~ A ~ Holy Life!** If you want to **Pray Down Holy Fire** and see lost Souls set Free; and Stand Up for God, and Make your Prayers Feared in Hell! **You ~ Must ~ Actually ~ LIVE ~ A ~ HOLY ~ LIFE!!!** The reason that the "so called" Church of today, is so Helpless and Powerless; is because it has **No Holiness**, **No Purity**, **No Sanctification**, **No Separation unto GOD!!!** Today's Church Lives Just like the **World!!!** There is No Difference between the Two! The People who are suppose to be God's Children, Live Just Like the Devil's kids! Lying, Stealing, Cursing, Gossiping, Greedy, Selfish, Covetous, Hateful, Unforgiving, Drunkards, doing Drugs, fighting, strife, envy, divisions, Adultery, Fornication, Homosexuality, Lust, Evil, Pride, Mean and Nasty, Backbiters, complainers, Unholy, unmerciful, unthankful, Vile Pornographic Filth, Watching all kinds of evil Junk on the Internet! And Preachers who won't Stand Up for God, and tell the True Gospel of Jesus Christ! And call Evil, **Evil!** and Sin, **Sin!** Who stand up in their Pulpits and preach soft, easy, sermons to their congregations; Preachers who don't want to step on anyone's toe's, or Ruffle any Feathers, or Hurt anyone's Poor little Feelings! But **will let their Soul's Burn in Hell!** For all of eternity! You helpless sinner, God loves and forgives you, just put your money in the plate! You don't need to **Repent** like Jesus Told you to Do **In The BIBLE!!!** Just forget about the Apostle Paul's **WARNING** about **JUDGEMENT DAY!!!** He didn't know what he was talking about, just because God had him write half of the New Testament in the Bible, doesn't mean he was right! Or John the Baptist words, "O' Generation of Vipers, who hath Warned you to flee the **Wrath** (of God) to Come!" Therefore Bring Forth Fruit (Holy Lives) Worthy of True Repentance!" For the Ax is laid unto the root of the trees, every tree that does not Bring Forth Good Fruit Shall Be Hewn Down and **Cast into the Fire!** (of Hell) Beware of **Any Preacher** who does not tell you to Repent from all Sin!

Holy Fire and Holy Ground!

My beloved brethren, there are many Preachers today, who speak well, are colorful and inspiring to watch and listen to, they tell good story's, they help the needy and feed the Poor! They teach biblical principals and truths, and all these things are fine and good! But they will <u>not</u> preach <u>hard</u> against sin or cry out against <u>all</u> sin, iniquity, evil lives, abortion, disobedience to God, or point out and put their finger on specific sins or wrong doings in their own congregations or denominations! And the reason why is because <u>if</u> they preach hard against sin and iniquity and evil, like Jesus, or Paul, or Moses, or any of God's <u>Real</u> Prophets and Servants; they will be <u>Hated</u> by the people, Just like Jesus and God's Servants were! And the Church's tithes and offerings, by it's congregation, or Television followers will plummet like a piece of fiery brimstone! And because these Preachers and Churches have put their Church under bills and financial burdens and obligations; they <u>will</u> <u>not</u> cry out, or really preach against personal sins and lifestyles! Think about what Jesus said, "The world cannot hate you, (you are of this world) but it hateth me, <u>Because I Testify of it</u> that **It's Works are EVIL!!!**" {John 7:7} "Woe unto you, when all men shall speak <u>well</u> of you! For so did their fathers to the <u>False</u> <u>Prophets!</u> And "Blessed are ye, when men shall hate you, and shall separate you from their company, and shall reproach you, and cast out your name as evil, for the son of man's sake! Rejoice ye in that day, and Leap for Joy; for, behold, Great is your reward in Heaven! Because that is exactly how their fathers Treated, and did to the <u>Real</u> Prophets of God! {Luke 6:22} And why is it like this? "Men Loved Darkness rather than Light, because their deeds, (and hearts) were Evil!" {John 3:19} God's <u>True</u> Preachers, and <u>Real Servants</u> can and <u>must</u> preach and teach <u>all</u> of God's word from the Holy Bible! Anyone who Truly Walks with God, Stands for God, and Speaks for **God**! Who is **Led** by **God's Holy Spirit**, will <u>always</u> speak and say, what the <u>Holy Spirit</u> wants them to **Say!** Regardless of the circumstances or conditions or troubles and trials they may be facing! You must remove all sin and iniquity; your heart and life must be placed upon God's Holy Altar, and the Holy Spirit be <u>allowed</u> to apply his Holy Scalpel to your <u>Heart</u> and <u>Life</u>! Let us look at the Holy Scripture to see exactly Why! {Joshua 7:1} "But the children of Israel committed a trespass (or sin) in the accursed thing, (all sin and iniquity, or evil, is accursed and hated by God!) and the <u>anger</u> of the Lord was kindled against the children of Israel! And they <u>fled</u> from before the town of Ai and were <u>defeated</u>! And Joshua rent his clothes and fell to the earth upon his face before the ark of the Lord until the evening, he and the elders of Israel, and put dust upon their heads!" And this still happens in our churches today, people committing and living in sin, who feel convicted; go to the altar, fall on their face and cry and wail; but they do not <u>remove</u> the sin, and go <u>do</u> the same <u>sin</u> tomorrow! But the Lord said unto Joshua, **Get Thee Up!** Wherefore liest thou thus upon thy face? (what are you doing?) Israel <u>has</u> <u>**sinned**</u>, and they have also transgressed my covenant which I commanded them, for they have taken the accursed thing, **(Sin)** and have also stolen and disassembled, and have put it among their <u>own stuff</u>! (allowed sin and iniquity in their lives!) Therefore they could <u>Not</u> <u>Stand</u> before their enemies, but turned their backs before their enemies, because <u>they</u> were accursed! Neither will <u>**I Be with You Any More**</u> until <u>**You Remove the Accursed thing from among You!**</u> **(Sin!)** God hates and destroys all sin and evil!

Holy Fire and Holy Ground!

God told Joshua, "Get Thee Up!" (Rise Up and Fight, and overcome the sin in your life!) Wherefore liest thou thus upon thy face? (Get up and Do something about it!) Drive all the sin out of the Camp! (your lives!) Up, sanctify the people; and say, Sanctify yourselves against tomorrow; for thus sayeth The **Lord God** of Israel, "There is an accursed thing in the midst of thee, O Israel!" (there is sin in your heart and life!) Thou cannot stand (on Holy Ground) before thine enemies, until ye Take Away the accursed thing! Neither will **I Be with You Anymore**, except ye destroy the accursed thing from among you! (and remove the sin from your life!) All the people in Churches across the world, who lay on the altar, and cry and wail to God; and know very well, exactly what their sin and trespass is! But they have No Intention of Truly Repenting from their sin, and **Obeying God!** But are perfectly content to live and stay in their backslidden, disobedient condition and sin! And laying on the altar, crying and wailing to God, just to make yourself feel better about your sinful life; when You have **No Intention** of changing, means nothing! You Just want to be comforted **in your Sins!** God's says this to you,"Get Thee Up!" wherefore liest thou thus upon thy face? Get up and Do something about it!" Remove the accursed sin and evil from your life! Get Up and Sanctify yourself, remove the evil and sin from your life and soul, you cannot stand on Holy Ground when there is an accursed thing (sin) in the midst of thee! Neither will I be with thee any more, until You Remove the accursed sin from your Life and Soul! {Joshua 7:12} Cast away from you all of your transgressions, whereby ye have transgressed; and make ye a new heart and a new spirit, for **why will Ye Die?** As I Live sayeth the **Lord God**, I have No pleasure in the death of the wicked! But that the wicked turn from his evil way and live! Turn ye, turn ye from your evil ways and live, why will ye die?{Ezekiel 18:31,33:11} For whosoever's name was not found written in **God's Book of Life** was cast into the **Lake of Fire!** {Revelations 20:15} My beloved brethren, in this late hour of sin and evil in our world, in these Last Days, there is No Time for games or foolishness in the Church, or in our individual lives! All the people and churches who carelessly, and nonchalantly, disobey God and ignore God's Holy Word and Commandments, will Not be ready to Stand before Holy, Almighty God on Judgement Day! If the Righteous scarcely be saved, where shall the ungodly and the sinner appear? {1 Peter 4:18} For behold, the Lord cometh with ten thousands of his saints to execute judgement upon all!{Jude 1:14} When the Lord Jesus shall be revealed from Heaven with his mighty Angels, in flaming fire taking vengeance on them that do not know God, and that do not obey the Gospel of our Lord Jesus Christ! Who shall be punished with everlasting destruction from the presence of the Lord, from the glory of his power! For the unrighteousness in them that perish; and because they received not the love of the Truth, that they might be Saved! And for this cause God shall send them a strong delusion, that they should believe a lie! That they all might be damned who believed not the truth, but had pleasure in unrighteousness! {2 Thessalonians 1:7, 2:10} But if, when I say to the wicked, thou shalt surely die; if he turn from his sin, and do that which is lawful and right; (if he repent) and walk in the statutes of life, without committing iniquity; he shall surely live, he shall not die. None of his sins that he has committed shall be mentioned to him, if he has done that which is right, he shall live! Ezekiel 33:14

Holy Fire and Holy Ground!

So Thou, O son of man, I have set <u>thee</u> a watchman; therefore thou shalt <u>hear</u> the word at my mouth, and <u>warn</u> them from <u>me</u>! When I say unto the wicked, O wicked man, thou shalt surely die; if thou dost <u>not</u> speak to warn the wicked from his way, that wicked man shall die in his iniquity; but his blood will I require at thine hand! Nevertheless, if thou <u>warn</u> the wicked of his way to turn from it; if he does <u>not</u> turn from his (sinful) way, he shall die in his iniquity; but thou hast delivered thy soul! Therefore, O son of man, Speak, Thus speak ye saying, If our transgressions and our sins be upon us and we pine away <u>in</u> them, (and continue to sin) how should we then live? Say unto them, As I Live, saith the **Lord God**, I have no pleasure in the death of the wicked; but that the wicked <u>turn</u> from his evil way and <u>Live</u>! Turn ye, turn ye from your evil ways; for why will ye <u>die</u>? Therefore thou son of man, say unto the children of thy people, The righteousness of the righteous, <u>shall</u> <u>not</u> deliver him in the day of his transgression! (and sin) As for the wickedness of the wicked, he shall not fall thereby in the day that he <u>turns</u> (and repents) from his wickedness; neither shall the righteous be able to live for his righteousness in the day that he sinneth! When I say to the righteous, that he shall surely live; if he trust in his <u>own</u> righteousness, (and say in his heart that my Lord delayeth his coming; and he begins to sin, be drunken) and commit iniquity, <u>all</u> his righteousness shall <u>not</u> be remembered; but for his iniquity and sin that he <u>hath</u> committed, he <u>shall</u> <u>die</u>! Again, when I say unto the wicked, thou shalt surely die; if he <u>turn</u> from his sin and <u>do</u> that which is lawful and right; If he turn and <u>walk</u> in the statutes and commandments of God, and <u>Stop</u> committing sin and iniquity, he shall surely <u>Live</u>! When the righteous turneth from his righteousness, and committeth <u>sin</u> or iniquity, he <u>shall</u> even die thereby! But if the wicked shall turn from his wickedness, and <u>Do</u> that which is lawful and right, he shall <u>live</u> thereby! **<u>I will Judge every one of you after his ways, saith the Lord God!</u>** Ezekiel 33:7 Moreover, the word of the Lord came unto me, saying, Now, thou son of man, wilt thou judge, wilt thou judge the bloody city? (and country!) Yea, thou shalt <u>shew</u> her all her abominations! Then say thou, Thus saith the Lord God, the city sheddeth blood in the midst of it, (abortion, murder) that her time may come, and maketh idols against herself to defile herself! Thou art become guilty (USA) in thy blood that thou hast shed! (70 Million **Innocent Babies Murdered!**) and hast defiled thyself in thine idols which thou has made; and thou has caused thy days to draw near, and art come even unto thy years! Therefore I have made thee a reproach unto the heathen, and a mocking to all countries! (are you listening closely United States?) Those that be near, and those that be far from thee, shall mock thee, which are infamous and much vexed! **<u>Thou hast despised mine Holy Name and things</u>** and hast profaned my sabbaths! (your Preachers Ignore my Holy Commandments, your churches are dens of <u>Sin</u> and <u>Iniquity</u>!) Thou art the land that is <u>not</u> cleansed, nor rained upon in the day of mine indignation! There is a conspiracy of her prophets in the midst thereof, like a roaring lion ravening the prey; they have devoured souls; they have taken treasure and precious things! Her priest have violated my law and have profaned mine holy things! They have <u>put no difference</u> between the <u>holy</u> and <u>profane</u>! Neither have they <u>shewed the Difference</u> between the <u>unclean and the Clean</u>, and have hid their eyes from my holy Commandments, and I am profaned among them! Ezekiel 22:1-8 24-26

Holy Fire and Holy Ground!

My beloved brethren, I love the United States and I want the best for our country! But America is a evil, wicked, cesspool of vile filth and sin! Lying, thieving, devils, committing adultery, fornication, homosexuality, covetous, hateful, cursing, gossiping, drunkards and ungodly people, are all over our country, and in our churches! Pastors and preachers who want to be Politically Correct, and will not Stand up for **God** and call sin, Sin; and evil, **Evil!** But Jesus said, "You cannot serve two masters!" Either you **Stand** for **God** 100% percent in your life, or you do not! Either your Heart and Soul Burn with **Holy Fire** for God, or it does not! Because our God is a consuming fire! Jesus said, I know thy works, that thou art neither hot or cold; I would that thou were hot or cold! So then because thou art lukewarm, I will spew thee out of my mouth! (reject you from the body of Christ!){Revelation 3:16} Because, "He that is not with me, is against me!"{Luke 11:23} All the pastors and preachers who are living sinful, ungodly and unholy lives, and preaching soft, easy, lukewarm sermons; that only teach about God's love, grace, mercy, and forgiveness; without one word about repentance, sin, or holiness and Judgement! Just to rake in lots of money, because they know, that is what "unrepentant sinners" want to hear! "Her priest and princes have violated my law, they have put no difference between the holy and the profane, neither have they shown the difference between the clean and the unclean, they are like wolves ravening the prey, to shed blood, and to destroy souls, to get dishonest gain! (money) Her prophets have deceived them with foolish Council, seeing vanity, and divining lies unto them saying, Thus saith the Lord God, when the Lord hath not spoken! {Ezekiel 22:26-28} And they have devoured souls! But when those preachers and pastors stand before **Almighty Holy Jehovah God!!!** All the **Evil Imposter's**, charlatans, thieves, and wolves in sheep's clothing; who's true motive is just to fleece God's people for money and stuff cash into their bank account; will **Severely Regret** every single **Penny** that they ever took in **God's Holy Name!!!** It is a **Fearful Thing** to fall into the hands of the **Living God!** My beloved brethren, please always remember the full, Complete Gospel Truth! Yes God gives us love, grace, mercy and forgiveness for our sins; after we truly repent from our sins and **Stop** doing them! Not Before! Again, let us look at what God's word says to each and every one of us! "If my people, which are called by my name, shall humble themselves, and Pray, and Seek my Face, and **TURN ~ FROM ~ THEIR ~ WICKED ~ WAYS!!! Then Will I Forgive their Sins!!!** {2 Chronicles 7:14} Most of the scriptures we have been studying in the last few pages say the same word, **Turn! Turn!** Turn from Sin, Turn from Evil, Turn from Iniquity! If the wicked man Turns from his evil ways, He shalt surely **Live** and not die! That is God our Fathers, Love, and Grace, and Mercy, and Forgiveness to all of us! That is why the very First Word! that came out of Jesus mouth, when he began to Preach was **"REPENT!!!"** Let us look at that very verse! "From that time Jesus began to preach, and to say, Repent, for the kingdom of Heaven is at hand!"{Matthew 4:17} Repent, hate and crucify your sins, fight against them, drive the sin out of your life, overcome all sin because sin separates **You** from **God!** The wages of Sin is death! But the Gift of God is Eternal Life through **Jesus Christ** our Lord! {Romans 6:23} Repent, Turn from all evil, and thou shalt **Live and not Die!**

Holy Fire and Holy Ground!

And I sought for a man among them, that should make up the hedge, and **Stand in the Gap** before me for the land, that I should not **Destroy It!** But I found None! (God is looking and searching for a godly man or woman, to stand up before him, and make intercession and prayers for the people; like Abraham, and Moses, and Samuel, and Daniel did!) To Intercede before Almighty God, and show God Proof that there are still good, and holy, and godly, and faithful, and righteous people, worthy of **Jesus dying** for, and God holding back his great wrath and Judgement Day to save them! God is watching us, and weighing us in the balances; we need only to look at Jerusalem, and many others in the Old Testament, to see that when evil and wickedness tipped the scale, God's wrath was released! In Noah's day; upon Sodom and Gomorrah; several times upon Jerusalem; Almighty God's rod of correction was unleashed! Judgement unto Victory, and the United States is well Overdue! When a a country, or government, or people disobey, and ignore, God's Holy Commandments and ban or forbid **God** from their system, and instead embrace sin and evil! Under the guise of political correctness, God's Judgement and Wrath will not be far behind! "The Wicked shall be turned into Hell, and all the Nations that Forget God! {Psalms 9:17} Therefore I have poured out mine indignation upon them; I have consumed them with the fire of my wrath! Their own ways, I have recompensed upon their heads, saith the Lord God! {Ezekiel 22:30} Do not be deceived, God is not mocked, you will reap Exactly what you Sow! Either Holiness and Righteousness, and Obedience to **God**, that leads to Eternal Life! Or Sin and Wickedness, and Evil rebellion, to Eternal Damnation in hell with Satan! For the Wrath of God is revealed from Heaven against all ungodliness and unrighteousness of Men! {Romans 1:18} So my beloved brethren, whom I Love so very much, what condition is your heart and soul In? Does your heart and soul burn with God's Holy Fire? Or is it encrusted with sin and evil and iniquity? Do you Love God with all your heart, and soul, and mind, and strength? Does your life and personality, deeds and actions, and **Prayer life!** Show and prove in holiness and purity, that you Do indeed Love God with all your heart? Do you really and truly have a close, and personal intimate relationship with God? Can God come to you, and speak to you at anytime? About anything in your life? And will you listen to him? God wants you to know that he loves you very much! And that He, **Almighty God!** Wants the very best for you! And God Loves You! He had me write this book just to tell you that! God really wants to have a very close and personal **Relationship with You!** And he wants the very best for you in your life, and forever! That is why he gave you the very best things he has in his Universe! His Awesome Son Jesus, to cleanse and set you free! His Holy Spirit to Guide you, teach you, comfort you, help you, Live inside of you, and lead you every step of the way! God gave you his Holy word, the Holy Bible to speak to you through, so that you can learn to hear and to know **His Voice!** And God gave you himself, so that you can personally Go to him, pray to him and seek his face, and **Personally Know God our Father!** Who created us, and gave us life! God really loves us, and wants us to be in Heaven with him, and his Magnificent Son, Jesus Christ! God wants the Best for You! But tell me, my beloved brethren; **Do you want the best for Yourself**? Why will you settle for a short evil life, here on earth? When Jesus Christ has opened heavens gates, to **God!!!**

Holy Fire and Holy Ground!

We must Strive to Enter into the strait and narrow path that leads to Life! Many people will seek to enter into Heavens Gates, and will not be able! The path to Heaven is a Life lived on **Holy Ground!** A Holy Sanctified life, separated unto God, and Close to God! **Holy Ground** is a place or life of ~

1. ~ Giving up all of your rights, and will, by humbling yourself and giving God complete control!
2. ~ Living a life of Holiness, Sinlessness and Purity; If you Love me keep my Commandments!
3. ~ Communication with God, through prayer, bible study, a close personal relationship with God; How can you Do God's perfect will for your life, if you don't know what God's perfect will is?
4. ~ Obedience to actually Do God's will for your life; "Not every one who says to me, Lord, Lord, shall enter into heaven; but they that **Do** the will of God my Father, Shall Enter into Heaven!"
5. ~ Crucifying all your sinful, carnal lusts and desires; Spiritually getting **on the cross** with Jesus! "Anyone who does not bear his cross and follow me every day, cannot be my disciple! "Jesus"
6. ~ Living and walking in the Spirit with God, always alert and sensitive to God, and being Led by the Holy Spirit; to actively work and function as a living member of the body of Christ!
7. ~ God is First and Always the greatest, and most important Love of your Life! And God does not do this for God's sake, but for **Your** sake, **God is Eternal**; God has Eternal Life Forever! God already has and owns everything! Forever! God does not need You! **YOU ~ NEED ~ GOD!!!** God Commands you to love him with all your heart, soul, mind, and strength; so that **You** will Cling to him, Pray to him, Trust in him, have Faith in him, and **Obey Him**! So that Almighty God can, love you, teach you, guide you, cleanse you, sanctify you, and give You Eternal Life!

So you see, my beloved brethren, The First and Great Commandment of God, to love God with all your heart, soul, mind, and strength; is for your benefit, so that Almighty God can be a loving Father to you, and prepare you for the real life; Eternal Life with God in heaven, Forever! And it is that life eternal life, that our enemy Satan desperately wants to steal from you and drag you to hell with him! So our enemy Satan manipulates our flesh, and the carnal desires of the flesh, to pull you away from God! And that is why God sent Jesus to **Save us**, and **Cleanse us**, and **Free us**, and show us how to Crucify all our fleshly sins and desires! On the Cross! Jesus is not asking you or me, to do anything, that he did not already do or go through on the cross, for us, First! **Jesus Christ** is Awesome, **Jesus** is Magnificent! Just take up your cross and follow him every day, and you will see for yourself! The Mighty Lamb of God that takes away the sin of the World! Jesus Christ took the keys of Hell and Death away from Satan, triumphing over him in it, and putting Satan to open shame! Jesus Christ vanquished our evil enemy forever! Now we just have to believe in Jesus, trust and obey him, and live and walk in Jesus Victory, by living and walking in the spirit as part of the Body of Christ! You see, my beloved brethren, when God looks at any person who is a living, active part, of the body of Christ, God sees his son Jesus Christ, of whom we are an actual living part and member of his body! That is why Jesus said, **"You"** must be **Born Again in the Spirit** or you cannot See or Enter into the Kingdom of **God!** {John 3:7} God is a Spirit, the Kingdom of God is a Spiritual place, and we must be born again into the spiritual body of Jesus Christ, the only spiritual path or doorway into Heaven!

Holy Fire and Holy Ground!

When God appeared to Moses in the midst of the burning bush on Mount Sinai, and said, "I am the God of thy father, the God of Abraham, Isaac, and Jacob!" God had already been working on, and refining Moses heart, soul, mind and spirit for many years. All through Egypt, and in the desert, to bring him to a place where he would totally and completely Trust God and not himself! When God told Moses to take his shoes off, (and give up all his rights, which is what the act of taking his shoes off really meant) because the place he was standing is Holy Ground! It was not a location of earth or dirt he was physically standing on, but it was a place Moses had reached in the spirit, through prayer, obedience, humility, suffering, Fiery Trials and Tribulation! To bring his heart, soul, mind, and spirit to a location, and condition, Close to God! (Remember Moses could not get any closer to God until he gave up his own rights, and submitted to God's complete control, authority, and will for his life!) Where he would be willing, prepared, and ready, to walk, talk, and live; Closer to God in the Spirit! (unfortunately human beings are stiff necked and stubborn, self willed, and self centered; and must be broken, "like a wild horse" before they come to the "end of their rope, or self" and Finally Realize that **GOD MUST BE IN TOTAL AND COMPLETE CONTROL!**) If you really want to make it into heaven, and survive the **Spiritual Battle**, on a **Spiritual Battlefield**, against a **Spiritual Enemy** that you cannot beat alone! **"ALMIGHTY GOD" Is The TRUE MASTER and UNSTOPPABLE POWER in the UNIVERSE! GOD WILL RULE FOREVER!** And Jesus is the only way to God! And being a living, Holy Spirit filled member, and part of the body of Christ puts you inside of **God**! And **God** inside of you! You are God's Temple! Jesus said, "I and my Father are One!" {John 10:30} So "Put on the Armor of God," he "God" is your Armor! And live and walk in the spirit, and "abide" inside the body of Christ! Jesus said to "Abide in me, for you can do nothing without me!" So, my beloved brethren, abide in Jesus Christ, because Jesus Christ is One with God, Jesus Christ is God, And Jesus has already defeated Satan! So when you are in Christ, in God, on the Spiritual battlefield; God will smash your enemy Satan, to **Smithereens!** When you live and walk in the spirit, and abide in Christ! {John 15:4} And as ye have received and learned Christ Jesus the Lord, so walk ye in him; to be strengthened with might by his spirit in the inner man! That Christ might dwell in your heart by faith; that ye, being rooted and grounded in love; may be able to comprehend with all saints, what is the breadth, and length, and depth, and height, of God's mighty power and deliverance for you! And to know the love of Christ, which passeth knowledge, that ye might be filled with all the fullness of God! When ye put off and crucify the sinful fallen nature of the old man, which is corrupt according to the deceitful lusts! And be renewed in the spirit of your mind, when ye put on the new man; which after God is created in righteousness and true holiness! And renewed in knowledge after the Image of the one who created you, **God!** Do not be conformed to this world, but be ye transformed by the renewing of your Mind! (**Study your Bible!**) That ye may prove what is good and acceptable, and the perfect will of God! Draw nigh unto God, and He will draw nigh unto you! And learn to live and walk in the spirit with God, to give God full control of your life and get closer to God in spirit and in truth! Strive to enter into the strait and narrow path, and get your life on Holy Ground, Close to God!

Holy Fire and Holy Ground!

Moses was now in a place to lay down his own will, plans, and goals, give up his own rights; and go on to accomplish God's will and goals for his life. (to lead God's children out of slavery and bondage, and guide them to the promised land!) By willingly submitting, and giving God complete control and authority of his life, and obeying God; Moses became one of the greatest men of God who ever lived! And one of the greatest men who ever lived on the earth, Moses wrote the first five books in the Holy Bible! The greatest, most read, most studied, most printed, most copied, Book ever written in history! Needless to say, Moses made the Right Choice when he took his shoes off; and **Gave Almighty God Complete Control** over his entire Life! Because Moses, and Elijah, were the two men that appeared on the Mount of Transfiguration; and spoke to Jesus about his death and crucifixion which he would accomplish at Jerusalem!{Luke 9:30} And Moses was the only one that God allowed to come up to him on the top of Mount Sinai for 40 days; and put him on a rock, (Jesus) covered him with his hand, and God caused his Glory and Power to pass close by to Moses; Proclaiming the Name of the Lord! (Jesus Christ) The Lord spake unto Moses face to face, as a man speaks to his friend! {Exodus 33:11} And Moses has been living in Heaven, enjoying Eternal Life, in **Almighty God's Holy Presence** for around 3,500 human years now! It's obvious that Moses made the Right Choice by **Obeying God!!!** And my beloved brethren, that is exactly what **Almighty God** wants from you and me! To give God full and Complete Control of your whole Entire Life! Most Preachers don't tell you that, when they ask, or invite you, to accept Jesus Christ as your Lord and Savior! But that is Exactly what it means! You are Giving Up all of your rights, and authority over your life! And you are stepping down off of the Throne of your own heart and life; and You are willingly putting **Jesus Christ** as Lord and King upon the Throne of your own heart, soul, mind, and spirit! And you are willingly giving Jesus Christ **Full** and **Complete Control** of your whole **Entire Life!** And You (in the spirit) are nailing yourself to the cross of Jesus Christ! And Crucifying your own life, to do the perfect will of God instead! This is exactly what the Apostle Paul meant, when he said, "I am Crucified with Christ, but Still I Live!" And I know, my beloved brethren, that those words, and that information, just cut into the Heart and Soul of many readers, but that is OK, we must let God's word Cut into our Heart, and his Holy Fire, burn into our soul to cleanse us, and purify us, and prepare us to **Stand** before the **Judgement Seat** of **Christ!** The word of God is Quick and Powerful, and Sharper than any Two Edged Sword, and is able to pierce even to the dividing asunder of the Soul and Spirit, and the joints and marrow, and is a discerner of the thoughts and intents of the Heart! {Hebrews 4:12} It can be painful when the Holy Spirit cuts away sin and evil out of your life! I know my brethren, I have been on the cutting end of the Holy Spirits Scalpel many times! But that's OK, our flesh has to be crucified, and must die; if you want to Live, and have Eternal Life in Heaven! I Thank the Holy Spirit, and beg him to Never Stop cutting away and Removing all Sin and Evil! And I pray to God every day, and ask in Jesus Holy precious name, for God to put me into the Furnace of his Holy Ghost Fire; and Burn away any part of me that is not like **God my Father!!!** I will suffer any Pain, and Go Through any Fire!!! Nothing in this Universe, or in Existence, will keep me from being Just like my Lord and Savior **Jesus Christ!!!**

Holy Fire and Holy Ground!

Therefore, my holy brethren, partakers of the heavenly calling, consider the Apostle and Great High Priest of our profession, Jesus Christ! Who was made of the seed of David according to the flesh; and declared to be the **Son of God** with power, according to the spirit of holiness by his resurrection from the dead! By whom we have received Grace and Apostleship, for Obedience to the Faith among all nations for his name. Who was faithful to him (God) who appointed him, as Moses was also faithful in all his house. For this man (**Jesus Christ!**) was counted worthy of much more glory than Moses! Inasmuch as he who hath builded the house, hath more honor than the house. Every house is builded by some man; but he that built all things is God! And Moses truly was faithful in all his house, as a servant, for a testimony of those things which were to be spoken after! But Christ as a son over his own house; whose house we are, (as part of his body) if we hold fast the confidence and the rejoicing of the hope, firm unto the End! (Fight the good fight of Faith; and press towards the mark of the High calling of God in Christ Jesus!) Wherefore as the Holy Ghost saith, To day if ye will hear (and obey) his voice, Harden not your Hearts, as in the provocation, in the day of temptation in the wilderness! When your fathers tempted me, proved me, and saw my works forty years! Wherefore I was grieved with that generation, and said, They do always err in their heart; and they have not known my ways! So I sware in my wrath, they shall not enter into my rest! {Hebrews 3:1 & Romans 1:3} Beloved, we must keep our eyes and hearts on Jesus Christ, and remain steadfast and obedient unto the end! Jesus has passed into the heavens, he is our High Priest and advocate with God! we cannot let our hearts be hardened through the deceitfulness of sin, or riches, and the lusts and cares of this world! Jesus is our treasure and reward, and Eternal life with God in heaven is worth more than all of the gold and riches of a million planet earths! So let us learn (from the Holy Spirit) all of God's ways, and be obedient to God's holy precious voice! Let us not grieve the Holy Spirit of God! (by whom we are Kept by the power of God, through Faith, unto salvation and the redemption of our souls!) As our fathers grieved the Holy Spirit, and would not learn, and obey God our Father's Holy Ways! Wherefore they kindled God's wrath and anger against them, and their carcasses fell in the wilderness of sin! For the wrath of God commeth down upon the children of disobedience, and God is angry with the wicked every day! {Colossians 3:6 & Psalm 7:11} But we have Received Grace and Apostleship, for obedience to the faith among all nations for his name; because our sins are forgiven for his name's sake! (Jesus Christ) For we have not an great high priest, which cannot be touched with the feeling of our infirmities; but was in all points tempted like as we are, yet without sin! Therefore let us come boldly unto the throne of Grace, that we may obtain mercy, and find grace to help in the time of need! {Hebrews 4:15} So, Repent from all of your sins, in truth and sincerity, from your heart; and **Stop Doing Them!** Then Go boldly to God's throne of Grace, with full confidence and **Faith**, that **Jesus Precious Holy blood** will Wash all of your old, **Repented and Forsaken Sins Away!!!** And Mortify your members which are here upon the earth; adultery, fornication, homosexuality, drunkenness, covetousness; also put off all of these; anger, wrath, malice, blasphemy, filthy communication out of your mouth, do not lie one to another! Be ye not partakers with them, and let it not once be named among you, as becometh saints!

Holy Fire and Holy Ground!

For ye were sometimes darkness, but now are ye light in the Lord; walk as the children of the Light! Because the fruit of the Spirit is in all goodness and righteousness and Truth! Proving what is acceptable unto the Lord. And have no fellowship with the unfruitful works of darkness, but rather reprove them! For it is a shame to even speak of the things which are done by them in secret! But all things evil are reproved, and are revealed by the Light, for whatsoever exposes sin and evil, is God's Light! Wherefore he saith, Awake thou that sleepest, and arise from the dead, and Christ shall give you life! Awake, to all who can hear my voice and read this book; Awake and Arise into God's glorious Light and Eternal Life! Climb up out of your grave of sin and death! **Get Thee Up!!!** Why liest thou in a grave of Sin and Eternal Death? Awake and arise, and Christ shall give thee Life! Jesus has Risen from the Grave, and conquered **Hell and Death!** Neither is there salvation in **ANY OTHER NAME** whereby a man can be Saved! Get Thee Up! Accept Jesus Christ as your Lord and Savior! And Do God's will, Sanctify and Cleanse your heart and soul by repenting from all sin and evil! Let Jesus's Precious, Holy, Blood wash all of your sins away, by Faith and Belief in his name and Resurrection! So that God's grace, mercy, and love, can cover and protect your soul, from hell and death, through the Power of the Holy Spirit! Go to God in Prayer! Get on your knees and Cry out to God, and seek his Holy Face! Humble yourself before Almighty God, and say, Heavenly Father, I sacrifice my Life, Heart, and Soul upon your Holy Altar; I accept your son Jesus Christ as my Lord and Savior, I Invite You, "Mighty Holy Spirit," into my Heart and Soul, Forevermore! Save me Heavenly Father! I Trust in you O' God, Deliver me from Evil! Teach me how to Live and Walk in the Spirit, and to be led by your Holy Spirit; in spirit and in Truth! Give me spiritual Ears to Hear and Know **YOUR VOICE!!!** Because I Must know **Your Holy Voice O' God!** (**STUDY YOUR BIBLE!!!**) If I am to walk, and Talk, and Live with you **In The Spirit!** Give me spiritual wisdom, knowledge, and understanding, Teach me how to exercise my spiritual senses to discern between good and evil; darkness and light! Rightly dividing the word of truth, put forth in your holy word, The Holy Bible! For Jesus has said that,"Heaven and Earth shall pass away, but my words shall not pass away!" God's Holy Word **Shall Stand Forever!** And that not one jot or one tittle, (dot of the i or cross of the T) shall pass from the law, but all shall be Fulfilled!" And what saith the law, that shall be fulfilled? "We have an advocate with the Father, Jesus Christ the Righteous, and He is the propitiation for our sins; and not only our sins, but the sins of the entire world! Because God so loved the world, that he gave his only begotten son, that whosoever **Believeth in Him** should not perish, but have **Eternal life!** According as he has chosen us in him, (part of his body) before the foundation of the world, that we should be Holy and without blame before him in love! God predestinated us unto the adoption of children by Jesus Christ to himself! To the praise of the glory of his grace, wherein he hath made us accepted in the beloved! In whom we have **Redemption through His Blood**, the **Forgiveness of Sins**, according to the riches of his grace! And we are his witnesses to these things; and so also is the Holy Ghost, whom God has given to them that obey him! I will call upon the Lord and shall be saved from my enemies! Did you know that death was your enemy? "The last enemy that shall be destroyed is death!" {1 Corinthians 15:26}

Holy Fire and Holy Ground!

The Prophet Elijah told King Ahab, send word, and gather unto me all of Israel unto Mount Carmel, and also bring the 450 prophets of Baal and 400 prophets of the groves which eat at Jezebel's table. So Ahab sent unto all the children of Israel, and gathered the prophets together at Mount Carmel. And Elijah came unto all the people, and said, How long halt ye between two opinions? (how long will ye claim to be a Christian but cling to this world, and still love the world and its sins and desires in your heart?) If the Lord be your God, then follow him; but if Baal then follow him! and the people did not answer him a word! (it is easy to sit silently in church, but another thing to stand up for God speaking out against sin and evil to the world!) Then Elijah said unto the people, I, I only, remain a Prophet of the Lord! But Baal's prophets are 450 men! Let them therefore, give us two bullocks; and choose one bullock for themselves, and cut it in pieces, and lay it on the wood, but put no fire under it! And I will dress the other bullock, and lay it on the wood, and put no fire under it! Then; call ye on the name of your gods, and "I will call on the name of the Lord" (**Jesus Christ!**) and the God that answereth by **Fire**, let him be **God!** And all the people answered and said, It is well spoken. (have you called out to God very diligently and Faithfully, refusing to stop until God puts his "**HOLY SPIRIT**" and "**FIRE**" into your **Heart** and **Soul!!!** Until **You** are **Born Again into the Spirit!!!**) And Elijah said unto the prophets of Baal, Choose you one bullock for yourselves, and dress it first; for ye are many; and call on the name of your gods, but put no fire under it. And they took the bullock and dressed it, and called on the name of Baal from morning, even until noon, saying, O' Baal, hear us. But there was no voice, nor any that answered. And they leaped upon the altar which was made. And it came to pass at noon, that Elijah mocked them, and said, Cry aloud; for he is a god; either he is talking, or he is pursuing, or he is on a journey, or peradventure he sleepeth, and must be awaked. And they cried aloud, and cut themselves after their manner, with knives and lancets, till the blood gushed out upon them! (the gods of sin and iniquity in this world, only take your life and blood; but they cannot and will not give you any real eternal life!) And it came to pass, when midday was past, and they prophesied until the time of the offering of the evening sacrifice, that there was neither voice, nor any to answer, nor any that regarded. (after putting all of your efforts into a life of sin and iniquity, in the end; your life will have nothing to show but sorrow and regret, and death!) And Elijah said unto all the people, Come near unto me. And all of the people came near unto him. And Elijah repaired the altar of the Lord that was broken down. (God really loves and cares about you, and wants you to come to to him, so that he can help you! and show you how to repair and fix, your broken down sinful life and relationship with him; and give you **Real Eternal Life!**) And Elijah took twelve stones, according to the number of the tribes of the sons of Jacob, to whom the word of the Lord came, saying, Israel shall be thy name! And with the stones he built an altar in the name of the Lord! And he dug a trench around the altar, as great as would contain two measures of seed.(we must let God dig deep into our lives to build a sure rocksolid foundation that will stand forever! and there is only one rocksolid foundation and cornerstone that will **Stand Forever**, that foundation is **Jesus Christ!**) And Elijah put the wood in order, (we must put our lives in order) cut the bullock into pieces, (cut the sin out of your life and burn it on the altar to God!)

Holy Fire and Holy Ground!

And Elijah took the cut up pieces of bullock and laid them upon the wood, on the altar he had built; and said, fill four barrels with water, and pour it on the burnt sacrifice, and on the wood. And he said, Do it the second time. And they did it the second time. And he said Do it the third time. And they did it the third time. And the water ran round about the altar; and he also filled the trench with water. And it came to pass at the time of the offering of the evening sacrifice, that Elijah the Prophet came near, and said, **Lord God** of Abraham, Isaac, and Israel; let it be known this day that thou art **God** in Israel, and that I am thy servant, and that I have done all these things at thy word! Hear me O' Lord, hear me, that this people may know that thou art **The Lord God**! And that thou hast turned their heart's back again. Then **The Fire of the Lord Fell**, and consumed the burnt sacrifice, and the wood, and all the stones, and the dust, and licked up the water that was in the trench! (and if you turn your Heart back to God, repent from your sins, and offer your life upon God's altar! Almighty God's **Holy Ghost Fire** will consume you, burn all your sins away, and prepare you to stand before God on **Judgement day**!) "For our God is a Consuming Fire!"{Hebrews 12:29} And "I beseech you therefore, brethren, by the mercies of God, that ye present your bodies a **Living Sacrifice**, holy, acceptable, unto **God**! Which is your reasonable service!"{Romans 12:1}"For I indeed baptize you with water unto repentance; but he (Jesus) shall baptize **You** with the **Holy Ghost**, and with **Fire!**"{Matthew 3:11} "For we - must - all appear before the **Judgement Seat of Christ**; that Every One may Receive for the things done in his body, according to what he hath done, weather it be good or bad. Therefore, knowing the **Terror** of the **Lord**, we persuade men!"{2 Corinthians 5:10} So repent ye, and be converted, that your sins may be blotted out, when the times of refreshing shall come from the presence of the Lord; For God shall send Jesus Christ, which before was preached unto you! (and all the world!) {Acts 3:19} Behold, the Lord cometh with ten thousands of his saints, to execute Judgment upon all! For now is the axe is laid unto the root of the trees, and every (person) that does not bring forth Good Fruit, (holy lives) worthy of true repentance, shall be hewn down and **Cast into the Fire!** Where there shall be weeping and gnashing of teeth! For whosoever's name was not found written in **God's Book of Life**, was cast into **The Lake of Fire!** Because the wages of Sin is Death, but the gift of God is Eternal Life through our Lord and Savior, Jesus Christ! And when Elijah had called down the Fire of God upon the altar, and the Fire of God had consumed everything! When all the people saw it, they fell on their faces and said The Lord, he is God; the Lord he is God! (and if You pray down God's **Holy Ghost Fire** into Your heart, and soul, and life! Do God's will and let "our God, who is a consuming fire" consume You! All the people around you will see "by the way you live your life" that; the Lord he is God, the Lord he is God!) Because you never have to advertise a fire, it always burns brightly in the darkness! And Elijah said unto the people, Take the prophets of Baal; let not one of them escape! And they took them, and Elijah brought them down to the brook Kishon, and slew them there! {1 Kings 18:19-40} Destroy all the sin and iniquity in your Life! Slay them, Crucify them and Overcome them! Let not one of them Escape! Jesus said, to him that overcometh will I give to eat of the tree of life, in the paradise of God! And his name shall be written in the Book of Life, and I will confess his name before my Father God!

The Basic Rules to Live by Every Day!

1. Thou Shalt Love the Lord thy God with all thy heart, soul, mind & strength!
2. Thou Shalt Love thy Neighbor as Much as You Love Yourself!
3. Thou Shalt have No other gods before me, the Lord God is a Jealous God!
4. Do Not make or have any graven images or idols, to worship or serve them!
5. Do Not Take the Name of God in Vain, in Any Way at All!
6. Remember the Sabbath Day, to keep it Holy! A Day Set apart for God!
7. Honor Thy Father and Mother, that you may live long upon the Earth!
8. Thou Shalt Not Lie, tell untruths, or bear false witness about thy neighbor!
9. Thou Shalt Not Steal, or Take Anything That Does Not Belong To You!
10. Thou Shalt Not Commit Adultery or Fornication, or any other sexual sins!
11. Thou Shalt Not Covet Any of Thy Neighbors Stuff, Money, or Property!
12. Let No Corrupt Communication or Evil Words Come Out of Your Mouth!
13. Study To Be Quiet, and Not Quick to Speak or spew out rash, harsh words!
14. Live a Holy, Pure, Sanctified Life, Separated Unto Almighty God!
15. Have an Established Prayer Life, Talking to, and Obeying God Every Day!
16. Study the Holy Bible, Memorize and Meditate on the Scriptures every day!
17. Worship Almighty God and Jesus, in the Spirit, and in Truth, Every Day!
18. Walk in the Spirit, Be Sensitive to the Holy Spirit! Be Alert at All Times!
19. Take Every Single thought in your mind into captivity, to the obedience of Jesus Christ! Casting out imaginations, and any evil thing, that exalteth itself against the Knowledge of God! Cast Down Any Hateful, Sinful Thoughts!
20. Do Not be unequally yoked together with unbelievers; what fellowship hath righteousness with unrighteousness? And what communion hath Light with darkness? For ye are the Temple of the Living God; for God hath said, I will dwell and walk in them; and I will be their God and they shall be my people. Wherefore come out from among them, and be ye seperate, saith the Lord! Do not touch the unclean thing, and I will recieve you and be a Father to you!
21. Do Not Put anything evil in front of your eyes, or listen to evil stuff in ears!
22. Bring Forth Good Holy Fruits of the Spirit in your Life! Love, Peace, Joy, Longsuffering, Gentleness, Meekness, Faith, Goodness, and Temperance!

The Basic Foundation of God

Almighty God, in his all-seeing and all-knowing wisdom, has created a **Basic Foundation** for his children to follow and Live By! The **Holy Bible** is the word of God and is profitable for doctrine, for reproof, for correction, for instruction in righteousness. That the man of God may be perfect, thoroughly furnished unto all good works.{2 Timothy 3:16} Now there are around 783,137 words in the Bible (old and new Testament) and the chance that every man, or group, or denomination, or church would agree on every single one of these 783,137 words is 0.0% !!! Seeing that "Every man does that which is right in his own eyes! But the Lord pondereth (or examines) the hearts!" (your true motives) {Proverbs 21:2} But we must all "Do that which is right in the Eyes of the **Lord thy God!**" {Deuteronomy 13:18} Because We will all kneel at the Judgment seat of Christ! To answer for, and give an account of All the deeds done in the body! {2 Corinthians 5:10} And every Word that comes out of our mouth!{Matthew 12:34-37} Our Father God in Heaven, knows that mankind is stiff necked, (hard headed) and has evil hearts! (men loved darkness rather than light, because their deeds were evil! John 3:19) Therefore, God gave us a **Basic Foundation** to stand upon; for every true child of God! Who sincerely, **loves God**, and **wants to do his will!** That is why, before God had Moses write the first 5 Books of the Holy Bible! (Genesis, Exodus, Leviticus, Numbers, and Deuteronomy) God personally took his own Finger and wrote **The Ten Commandments** in Stone, and gave them to Moses for all the people to **Do** and **Obey!** To make **God's will** perfectly crystal clear, for all the people to easily understand and obey without excuse! So that the simplicity of the Gospel is not too difficult for anyone, but easy for all to understand! To avoid profane and vain babblings, that the Apostle Paul said were dissensions, debates, and endless genealogies, that only minister questions rather than godly edifying, which is in faith! That if any man teach otherwise, and does not consent to wholesome words, even the words of our Lord Jesus Christ, and to the doctrine which is according to godliness! He is proud, knowing nothing, but doting about questions and strife of words, that only cause envy, strife, railings, evil surmisings, perverse disputings of men of corrupt minds, and destitute of the Truth! Supposing that gain is godliness: to avoid and stay away from these people! {1 Timothy 1:4 & 6:3-5} And avoid all these debates, disagreements, and questions, that only bring about heated arguments, and fights, that only destroy the peace and tranquility, and does not promote the peace and godly edification in the spirit of **Love and Unity!** God Almighty and his only begotten son Jesus Christ, taught a **Basic Foundation** for all mankind to stand upon, and live their lives by these basic rules! Now, let me be crystal clear at this point, This **Does Not** mean that you are to ignore or disregard the rest of the **Holy Bible!** All Scripture is given by inspiration of God, Jesus said,"Do not think that I have come to destroy the law, I came not to destroy the law, but to fulfill the law! For every jot and tittle (dot of the I, and cross of the T) shall in **No** wise pass from the law, but it all shall be fulfilled! Heaven and earth shall pass away, but my words shall not pass away!{Matt. 5:17,24:35} But this **Basic Foundation** are pillars for you to live your life by from day to day, so that you can keep yourself on the strait and narrow path that leads to Life! Simply by **Staying in the Basics!**

The Basics to Live by every Day

One day a man asked Jesus, "Which is the first (or Greatest) Commandment of All?" (From God) And Jesus answered him, and said, Hear, O Israel; (and all God's Children) The Lord our God is one Lord: **And Thou Shalt Love the Lord thy God with All thy Heart, and with All thy Soul, and with all thy Mind, and with all thy Strength! This is the first and great Commandment!** And the second is like unto it, namely this, **Thou Shalt Love thy neighbor as thyself**!!! There is **No** other Commandments Greater than these! On these two Commandments hang all the Law and the prophets! {Matthew 22:37 & Mark 12:29} The **Most Important thing** that **You will ever Do, in Your Entire Lifetime**, is **TO LOVE GOD!!!** God is your Life! God is your Provider! God is your Protector! God is Your Future! Jehovah God the Father is EVERYTHING YOU NEED!!! **WITHOUT GOD YOU ARE DEAD!** If You Don't Have JESUS, **YOU DON'T HAVE GOD! YOU MUST LOVE GOD above ANYTHING and EVERYTHING ELSE IN YOUR LIFE!!!** Every Treasure in this world is Worthless Dung, next to your Relationship with God and Jesus!!! Everything in this world is **Temporary!** God and His son Jesus Christ, are **Permanent! Eternal!** Almighty God is the **All Powerful Eternal Spirit! He is the One True Living God Most High! God is Life!!!** God has Endless Life within himself, Forever! He doesn't need us! **We Need Him! GOD LOVES US!** He wants us to be in Heaven with Him Forever! That is Why He Created Us! When you love God with all your Heart, it pleases God; but it doesn't benefit God, it benefits You! God calls us to offer up ourselves as a living sacrifice, Holy, acceptable unto God; with our Love, our Praise, and our Worship! So that we could have God's life in us! God already has Everything! He Created it All Through his only begotten son **Jesus Christ**! All things were Made by Him, and without him was not anything made that was made! In him was Life, and the life was the Light of men! {John 1:3} Jesus created you, me, and All the World Around You! **The Entire Universe!!!** Without Him was not Anything made that was made! And Almighty God can Do it all over again, a billion times if He wants To! Almighty God has the Power and the Authority to **Do Anything!!!** Because **ALMIGHTY GOD IS THE POWER AND THE AUTHORITY!!! Forever and Ever!** God has already said in The Holy Bible, That He is going to create a new heavens and a new earth! {Isaiah 65:17 & 2 Peter 3:13} And I am going to be in heaven, worshiping God and Jesus Forever! And **You can be there too!** Accept **Jesus Christ** as your Lord and Savior, Repent from every sin, let Jesus Precious Blood Wash You Clean, and live a Holy Life; **YOU MUST DO GODS WILL!** (Be Ye Holy, for **I Am Holy!**) And Your Name will be Written in **God's Book of Life! Forever!!!** But The Soul that Sinneth, **IT SHALL DIE!!!** {Ezekiel 18:4-32} It is so Easy to See that when You Love God with all of your Heart, all of your Soul, all of your Mind, and all of your Strength! It is You that receives all his blessings, his grace, his mercy, his forgiveness, his love, and his Life! It is You that gets Washed Clean from All Sin and Evil, and All Unrighteousness!!! It is You that gets Reconciled to Almighty God!!! It is You that gets a Holy, Right Relationship with Our Father God and Eternal Life! Why would you not, Love God with all your heart, soul, mind, and strength?

The Basics to Live by every Day

The second part of the two Commandments, on which Jesus said all the Law and Prophets hang, (and are founded on and depend upon) is <u>Thou shalt Love thy neighbor as thyself</u> ! You must love and treat <u>Your Neighbor</u>, exactly the same way that you love and treat <u>Yourself</u> ! You must show the same care and compassion to your neighbor as you would to yourself, your mother or father, your wife or husband, or your son, daughter, brother, sister, or other family members! Jesus said, Do unto others as you want done unto <u>You</u>! (treat and respect people the same way that you want to be treated and respected)"Therefore all things whatsoever ye would that men should <u>Do to You</u>, <u>Do Ye</u> even so <u>to them</u>: for this is the Law and the Prophets." For what measure ye mete, it shall be measured to you again! {Matthew 7:2 & 7:12} (Almighty God in Heaven is <u>Going to treat you Exactly the same way</u> that **YOU TREAT OTHERS!**) If <u>You</u> are Loving, kind, compassionate, gentle, forgiving, and merciful to <u>other People!</u> God will be Loving, kind, compassionate, gentle, forgiving, and **Merciful To YOU!** But! **IF YOU ARE** Evil, Mean, nasty, cruel, hateful, hurtful, brutal, unmerciful, uncompassionate, unforgiving; inflicting pain and terror and torture on others! And you lash out at them with evil, mean, hurtful words; or spread gossip, slander, degrading, foul terrible words to hurt or insult them to others! Or if you physically hurt, punch, hit or kick, spit on, slap, deprive of food, clothing, shelter; or steal their money or belongings and treat them like dirt! When <u>you</u> stand before <u>the Judgment Seat</u> of Christ, **The One True Living ALMIGHTY GOD!** (and **YOU WILL** <u>kneel</u> at Jesus Feet!) Almighty God in Heaven above, **The Most POWERFUL BEING IN ALL OF EXISTENCE! AWESOME ALMIGHTY GOD** <u>Is going to treat You</u>, and **DO UNTO YOU! EXACTLY AND PRECISELY WHAT YOU DID UNTO OTHERS!!!** Do unto others what **YOU WANT DONE TO YOU!** For what measure ye mete, **IT SHALL BE MEASURED TO YOU AGAIN!!!** It is a Fearful Thing to Fall into the hands of the **LIVING GOD!!!** Therefore Knowing **The Terror of the Lord**, We Persuade and **WARN MEN** of the **COMING JUDGMENT!!!** John the Baptist said, "O' Generation of Vipers, Who hath warned you to flee from <u>the wrath to come</u>? Therefore, <u>Bring forth fruit</u> worthy of repentance!"{Luke 3:7} (live a holy life as solid <u>proof</u> of <u>True Repentance</u> and your <u>turning away from all Evil</u>!) Paul said, Do Not Be Deceived, <u>God is not mocked</u>, whatsoever a <u>man soweth</u>, that <u>Shall He Reap!</u>{Gal 6:7} Jesus himself said, "God the Father hath given me the authority to Execute the Judgment, and the hour is coming, when all who are in the graves (every person who ever lived) shall hear my voice, And shall come forth; they that have done <u>Good</u> unto the resurrection of <u>Life!</u> And they that have done <u>Evil</u>, unto the resurrection of <u>Damnation!</u>"{John 5:27} Every single thing that <u>You</u> do to all of your neighbors (the other men and women on the earth) shall be **DONE TO YOU!** Unless You <u>Truly Repent and Turn from All Your Wicked Ways</u>, Ask All the people you have done wrong to <u>forgive you!</u> Go make restitution for the wrongs you did, apologize, return stolen money or things! Then get down on your knees (if you are physically able to) and <u>Humbly go to God in Prayer</u> and <u>Sincerely ask God to Forgive All Your Sins</u>, and to <u>Wash You Clean in Jesus Holy Blood!</u> If you truly repent, humbly and sincerely. God will forgive your sins, and give you eternal life in heaven!

The Basics to Live by every Day

Not only did Jesus teach us to "Love your neighbor," Jesus took it one step further and also said to "Love your enemies." In the Sermon on the Mountain, (think about that, listening to **God Himself** preach the Message! Awesome! Well, you can hear it too, it's in Matthew Chapters 5,6 &7) In the Sermon on the Mountain, Jesus said, "Ye have heard that it hath been said, Thou shalt love thy neighbor, and hate thine enemy. But I say unto you, Love your enemies, bless them that curse you, do good to them that hate you, and pray for them which despitefully use you, and persecute you! So That ye may be the children of your Father (God) which is in heaven! For he maketh his sun to rise on the evil, and on the good, and sendeth rain on the just and the unjust. For if ye (only) love them which love you, what reward have ye? Do not even the publicans the same? {Matthew 5:43} Jesus not only taught this, he also did the same thing for us, when he gave his life on the cross, and Died for Us! To Wash us clean from Sin, while we were still sinners, and thus rebels and enemies of a Holy God! Because "He that is not with me is against me!""Jesus Christ" {Matthew 12:30} And rebellion is (just as bad) as the sin of witchcraft, and stubbornness is as iniquity and idolatry! Because thou hast rejected The Word of the Lord, He hath also Rejected thee! {1 Samuel 15:23} Jesus truly Loved Us, and shed his precious blood to set us free from hell, and death and sin; even though we were rebellious sinners, and disobedient to a Holy Loving God. Who Created Us and gave us Life, a Universe with a sun and stars, and a beautiful Earth to live on, with food and water, and everything we needed! Almighty God gave you one drop of Life, His Life! God created us, (mankind) In His Image! What are You doing with that one drop of life that God gave you? What are you doing with the mind and body and soul, created in Gods own image, that He gave to you? Do you Love and thank God every day for it? Do you Love and Worship and obey Almighty God, the Father of all Life? Or have you rebelled against the very One who gave you Life? Do you live a Holy life, and walk close to God, and serve the mighty Lord Jesus? Whose blood can wash you clean from all iniquity and sin, because Jesus Christ is the **One** and **Only way** to get into **Heaven!** Or have You chose to serve sin, and evil Satan, the Very Enemy of your Soul! Who truly is **Your Worst and Most Deadly Enemy**, Who accuses You to God! Satan tells God that You deserve to Burn in Hell with Him for All of Eternity! And Satan fights against You Day and Night, he never sleeps, Determined to Drag YOU TO HELL WITH HIM!!! Let me ask you an Important question Does your life, and the Deeds that YOU DO and the words that COME OUT OF YOUR MOUTH PROVE THAT SATAN IS RIGHT? That Satan Is Your Father, and you deserve to Burn in Hell? Remember, Jesus said," The Deeds of Your Father YE WILL DO!!! {John 8:41-44} Do you do holy, godly, deeds of Truth and Love in your life, like our Holy Father God, who art in Heaven? Or do You Do Evil, hateful, sinful deeds like lying, stealing, lusting, hurting, gossiping, swearing, slander, with evil, vile, filthy words flying out of your mouth, just like YOUR FATHER SATAN? And the Lusts of Your Father Ye Will Do! Remeber, Jesus said,"Whosoever committeth Sin, IS THE SERVANT OF SIN!"{John 8:34} And that THE WAGES OF SIN IS DEATH! (and HELL!) But **The GIFT of GOD is Eternal LIFE through JESUS CHRIST our LORD!**{Romans 6:23}

The Basics to Live by every Day

One day, when the drop of life that God gave to you, is about to run out! What will you Do ??? If You have been Living an Evil, Sinful Life, serving Satan! And **Not Serving Almighty God!!! And his Awesome Holy Son, JESUS CHRIST!!!** Who is the **Only One** that can Wash Your Sins Away, and Make You Clean, when you stand before Almighty, Holy God, on Judgment Day!!! For there is only **One God**, and **One** mediator between God and men, the man **JESUS CHRIST!** {1 Timothy 2:5} Because when that drop of Life Runs Out, that lying thief Satan, Does Not Have Any Life to Give You! Satan only wants to **Drag You to Hell with Him! ONLY GOD and his Holy Son JESUS CHRIST!!! CAN GIVE YOU ETERNAL LIFE!!!** O-N-L-Y G-O-D !!!!!!! That is why the First and Great Commandment is "Thou shall Love the Lord thy God, with all thy Heart, and all thy Soul, and all thy Mind, and all thy Strength!" Not for God's sake, for Your Sake! You are the one who benefits from Loving God, and Walking with God, and Praying to God, and **Obeying Almighty God!!! YOU!!!** You - You - You!!! **GOD IS LIFE!** Your Life! Forever! Without **Almighty God,** YOU ARE DEAD!!! FOREVER! ETERNALLY! PERMANENTLY!!! God Commanded us to Love him with all our Heart, Soul, Mind, and Strength; so that He could put His Life and Holy Spirit into Our Soul! And Deliver us from Evil! So that God's Holy Spirit can guide us, and teach us, and comfort us, and cleanse us, and prepare us for the marriage supper of the Lamb of God, (Jesus Christ) and Eternal Life in Heaven! That is God's Purpose and design when He created You, (and all of mankind) from the Foundation of the World! So That You, can be in Heaven with Him for all Eternity! Why would you Not Want That??? Why would You not Fight for That? And Strive for That with all your might, and all your strength, and every single cell and atom that is in your entire being? Jesus told us to,"Strive to enter in at the strait gate, for I say unto you, that many will seek to enter in, and will not be able!" Because wide is the gait, and broad is the way, that leadeth to destruction! And there will be many (people) which go into It! Because strait is the gate, and narrow is the way that leads to Life, and only a Few (people) will Be Able to Find It!!! {Luke 13:24 & Matthew 7:13} The Apostle Paul said, that there are many runners that run in a race but only one wins the prize! So run in this race, (for eternal life) so that You may Win the Prize! Please always remember, my beloved brethren, that Moses led Hundreds of Thousands of Israelites, out of Egypt, in the Exodus to the Promised Land! But that only two of them, Two, (2) !!! (of the grown adults) Joshua and Caleb! Crossed the Jordan and entered into Canaan! (The Promised Land!) Beloved, I am not telling you this to scare you, but to warn you, **Because I Love You,** and **I Want YOU to Make it into Heaven!!!** Because half-hearted, flimsy, Luke-warm, casual, careless, nonchalant, ho-hum, well I-go-to-church every Sunday, Christians!!! **WILL NOT MAKE IT INTO HEAVEN!!!** Just ask the 99.9 % of the Israelites who left Egypt! **YOU ARE IN A FIGHT FOR YOUR SOUL!!! You had better Fight, and Scratch, and Claw, and Study Your Bible, and PRAY, PRAY, PRAY, Night and Day, and Pray Your Way to the Very THRONE OF ALMIGHTY GOD!!! GRAB HOLD of the HORNS on the ALTAR!!! GET A SOLID UNSHAKEABLE GRIP ON JESUS CHRIST!!! AND NEVER LET GO!!!**

The Basics to Live by every Day

You absolutely positively must put everything else in your life behind you, set your sights on God! And his only begotten Son, **Jesus Christ**! Get Yourself a **Holy Bible** if you don't have one. (King James Version) Begin to Read and study it every day! Start with the New Testament if you are not familiar with the bible. Read Matthew, Mark, Luke, and John first, and study the life of Jesus! Let every single word Jesus said, go deep into your heart and soul and mind! Take each verse, one by one, and carefully think about and meditate on what the Lord is saying to you, for your life! Go to Jesus humbly, like a little child, open to hear what he has to say, without any preconceived notions. Devour every word like an infant on his mothers breast, hungry to grow, and humble to receive it, like a blank page without any writing on it, ready to receive the truth for the first time, in full faith! Knowing that Every Word in it Is True, Because God Cannot Lie, it is Impossible for God to LIE! {Hebrews 6:18} And The **Holy Bible is The Word of God!** Always put your full **Faith in God! And Trust Him Totally and Completely!** Because without **Faith** it is impossible to please God! For he that commeth to God must BELIEVE that He Is, and that he is a Rewarder of Them That (very) **DILIGENTLY SEEK HIM!!!** {Hebrews 11:6} You **Must Diligently Pray, Seek God**, and **Talk to Jesus** in Holy Prayer, EVERY SINGLE DAY!!! Night and day! Faithfully and Fervently, like a Heat Seeking Missile, refusing to take your eyes off your target, (Jesus) until you reach God! Worship God (in the Spirit and in Truth) communicate with God, Love God, and fellowship with God, Every Single Solitary Day!!! That is **The Only Way** You are Ever Going to build a Close, Personal, Meaningful, Holy, Intimate Relationship, with **The One True Living Holy God!!!** Only by constant bible study and much sincere, compassionate, heartfelt, Diligent Prayer! Will You ever Learn to Know and Recognize, **JESUS AWESOME PRECIOUS VOICE!!!** Above All Others! Jesus said, "my sheep **Hear My Voice**, and **I Know Them**, and **They Follow Me!!!** {John 10:27} And a stranger they will not follow, but will flee away from him, for they do not know the voice of strangers! {John 10:5} Respectfully and humbly, go to **Almighty God,** the most Powerful Being in the Entire Universe! In prayer, and ask God to be merciful to me a sinner, Please forgive me all my sins, my trespasses, and my iniquities, and Wash Me Clean in thy Holy son Jesus precious blood! And clothe me in a spotless white wedding garment, and make me unashamed to speak thy Holy Precious name! Take Jesus blood and apply it to the doorpost of my heart, and soul, and spirit and my very Life and being! Please make me Just like Jesus, to walk like Jesus, and talk like Jesus, and act like Jesus, to Pray like Jesus Prays, and to bring forth good Holy fruits in my life, like Jesus! (Herein is my Father Glorified, that ye bear much fruit, so shall ye be my disciples!) {John 15:8} And **Live a Holy Life that is well Pleasing to God Like Jesus!** The **only way** to accomplish this is to be **Born Again in the Spirit**, by excepting **Jesus Christ** as your Lord and Savior! Inviting the **Holy Spirit** to come into your heart and soul, and take full control of your life and cleanse you from every sin and evil! By **Walking in the Spirit**, and by **obeying what Jesus Tells you to do!!!** Christianity is not a church building, or a group of people, an idea, a way of thinking, a theology or a philosophy! Christianity is **A Personal, Intimate Relationship with God Living Inside of You!**

The Basics to Live by every Day

The Only way You are ever going to have a Close, Personal, Intimate, Relationship with **God the Father**, his son **Jesus Christ**, and the **Holy Spirit**; (these three are One!) {1 John 5:7} Is Only by spending a lot of Time alone with God in Prayer, Uninterrupted in a Quiet, Silent, room or space! The Lord Jesus, spent a lot of time praying to God the Father, even whole nights praying to God! And **Jesus Was God**, so what do you think you and I are going to have to do, to learn to hear Gods Voice! Only by diligently **Praying and Studying the Holy Bible**, will you ever learn what IS and what **IS NOT Jesus Voice!** "My sheep **Hear** and **Know** My Voice!" If it Does Not line up to what **The Holy Bible** says, **It Is Not God!** That is why You Must know the bible, to cast down evil lies! When you go to God in prayer, say "Jesus" I must know your Voice! (Jesus Is God) Please give me Spiritual Ears to **Hear YOUR Voice**, a mind to understand, and a heart that will receive and **Obey!** By Praying Humbly and Respectfully to **Almighty God**, work out your salvation with Fear and Trembling! {Phili. 2:12} (always remember, God has the awesome power to Save or Destroy you!) Jesus himself said, "I will forewarn you Who You Should Fear, Fear Him, (**Almighty God!**) that has the **Power to Destroy**, and cast both **Body and Soul into HELL!!!** Yea, I say unto You, **FEAR HIM!**" {Matthew 10:28 & Luke 12:5} The fear of the Lord is the beginning of knowledge! Behold, the eye of the Lord is upon them that fear him, and upon them that hope in his mercy. The secret of the Lord is with them that fear him, and he will show them his covenant. Let all the Earth fear the Lord, let all the inhabitants of the world stand in Awe of Him! {Psalms 3:8, 3:18 & 25:14} &{Proverbs 1:7} The Apostle Paul, who was caught up to the third heaven into paradise, and saw and heard unspeakable words that are not lawful for a man to utter said, it is a **Fearful** thing to Fall into the Hands of **The Living God!** & Therefore, knowing the **Terror of the Lord**, we persuade men! {Hebrews 10:31 & 2 Corinthians 5:11} (and warn them of the coming **Judgment Day!!!**)
By Diligently Praying to God, studying **The Holy Bible**, Truly Repenting from each and every sin, Sincerely from **Your Heart!** By Living a Holy Life and Obeying what Jesus Tells You To Do!!! **Be Ye Holy!** You will steadily, Draw nigh unto **God**, and he will draw nigh unto **You!**{James 4:8} To draw closer to God, you must except Jesus Christ as your lord and Savior! Believe in your heart by faith, that he died on the cross for your sins! For "If thou shalt confess with thy mouth the Lord Jesus and shalt believe in thine heart, that God hath raised him from the dead, thou shalt be saved!" {Romans 10:9} Invite the **Holy Spirit** to come and Live in Your Heart Forever, to fill you with the Holy Spirit and to be **Born Again** into the Spirit! Ask the Holy Spirit to Guide and Teach you how to Live and Walk in the Spirit; to cleanse you from every sin and evil! **The Holy Spirit is God! Living Inside of You!** The Apostle Paul said, know ye not that Ye are the temple of God, and that The Spirit of God dwelleth In You! Jesus,"when he had offered up prayers and supplications with strong crying and tears unto him that was able to save him from death, was heard in that he feared! Though he were a son, yet he learned obedience by the things which he suffered! And being made perfect, he became the author of **Eternal Salvation** unto all them that **Obey Him!**" {Hebrews 5:7}

The Basics to Live by every Day

For every True Christian, who is striving to Walk with God, and wants our Heavenly Father to be Well Pleased and Glorified by them and their Life! (For herein is my Father glorified, that ye bear much fruit so shall ye be my disciples! John 15:8) **Obeying God is Absolutely Crucial!** The main Difference between the people who **Go To Heaven**, and the people who **Do not make it in!** Is that they have Faith in **Jesus Christ,** that he is **God's Son!** That God raised him from the dead, and we have redemption through his **Blood** that cleanses us from all sin! They are **Born again** in the Spirit, they now Live and walk in the spirit, and are **Led by the Holy Spirit** to **Do God the Fathers Will!** Jesus told us directly,"Not every one that saith unto me, Lord, Lord, shall enter into the kingdom of Heaven! But he that **DOETH THE WILL OF MY FATHER WHICH IS IN HEAVEN!!!** Not, he that Hopeth to go to heaven! Not, he that prayeth to go to heaven! Not, he that readeth his bible to go to heaven! Not, he that goeth to church every Sunday, to go to heaven! Not, he that standeth in the pulpit and preacheth, Jesus, Jesus, to go to heaven! **BUT HE!!!** > **THAT DOETH!!!** < **THE WILL OF MY FATHER!!! ~ HE SHALL ENTER INTO HEAVEN!!!** {Matt. 7:21} Doeth is an **Action** Word! It Requires YOU ~TO ~DO ~IT!!! Not, think about it! Not, hope it will get done by someone else! Not, contemplate doing it! The Main difference between the people who **Go To Heaven**, and the people who **Do Not Make it in!** The people in heaven obeyed God, and actually, physically, **Did God The Fathers Will, For ~Their ~Lives!** Lucifer and one third of the angels, that were already in Heaven! Rebelled, and Did Not Obey Almighty God, and were cast out of Heaven! And now Fearfully Dread the coming **Judgment Day!** When **Almighty God** is going to cast them all into **the lake of fire**, prepared for the devil and his angels! {Matt.25:41,Rev 20:10} Almighty God is the same, Yesterday, Today, and Forever, God Does Not Change! What do you think God will Do to you and me, if we also rebel, and Do Not Do God's Will in **Our Lives???** Jesus said, "Many will say to me in that day, Lord, Lord, have we not prophesied in thy name? and in thy name have cast out devils? and in thy name done many wonderful works? And then I will profess to them **I Never Knew You!** Depart from me, **Ye That Work Iniquity!** (Live sinful lives) The Soul that sinneth, it shall Die! {Ezekiel 18:4} Beloved, Almighty God is a Holy, Holy, Holy, God of Truth, and Justice, and Righteousness! And He is also a God of **Love**, and **Compassion,** and **FORGIVENESS!!!** God Loves Each and Every One of Us!!! That is Why God sent his only begotten son **Jesus Christ** to call us all to to repentance! To forgive all our sins and wash us clean! So that We can **Be With God For All Eternity in Heaven!!!** That is the very reason why God has Created You and Me! "For God so loved the world, that he gave his only begotten son, that whosoever believeth in him, Should Not Perish, but Have **Everlasting Life!!!** For God Is Not Willing for **Any Man to Perish**, but that **ALL** should come to Repentance! And the knowledge of the **Saving Grace** of our Lord and Savior, **Jesus Christ!** Beloved, **GOD LOVES YOU**, and he is longing to **Forgive your sins**, and **Set You Free of Hell and Death!** I don't care how bad a sinner you think You Are! **Please Go To Him!** Repent! Pray to God for forgiveness! That is Gods will for your life!

The Basics to Live by every Day

Because if **You Do God The Fathers Will**, by **Truly Repenting** from **All Sin and Iniquity** and **Evil Deeds** that **You Are Doing in Your Life! And STOP Doing Them**, **Striving** to **Overcome Every Sin!** Determine in your mind, to **Truthfully** and 1000% **SINCERELY from your HEART To Fight with all Your HEART, all Your SOUL, all Your MIND, and All Your STRENGTH!** To **Live a HOLY, Godly, Clean, Pure and Sanctified LIFE**, that is **Separated UNTO GOD!!!** And to **Sincerely** with **All Your Heart, Soul and Very Being! FIGHT TO DRIVE OUT AND OVERCOME EVERY SINGLE SIN, TRESPASS**, and **EVERY INIQUITY IN YOUR LIFE!** Then **Almighty God** will see and know that **You Really Mean BUSINESS**, from **Your HEART!** Because it's not the claims said out of your mouth, but the **True Motives** and **Desires** of your very **Heart** and **Being**, that Almighty God Sees and Rewards or Judges You For! It is **Your Heart** and **Your True Motives and Desires That God Sees as PERFECT or EVIL!!! YOUR HEART!!!** This People draweth nigh unto me with their Mouth, and honoureth me with their their Lips, But **THEIR HEART IS FAR** (Away!) **FROM ME!!!** {Matthew 15:8} And "If my people, which are called by my name, shall humble themselves, and **Pray**, and **Turn from their WICKED WAYS! (Stop Sinning!) Then!** (and only then!) **Then will I hear from HEAVEN**, and Forgive their Sin! {2 Chronicles 7:14} God knows You better than you know yourself ! **BELIEVE IT! IT'S TRUE!** God knows Exactly how many hairs are on your head! Do You? **No!** God knew everything about you, when you were still in your Mothers Womb! God knows Why you Do, the things that you Do, Better than You Do! Almighty God knows the very day, hour, minute and second, that your body is going to Die! **Almighty God** knows and sees Everything! **You Cannot Fool HIM! Trust Me!** The **Only Thing that You or I Can Do**, is Go to God, and **Pray to Him HUMBLY!!!** And say, O' Heavenly Father, Almighty God who art in Heaven, **You** are **The Most Powerful Being in the UNIVERSE!!!** And I am only Dust and Dirt! **PLEASE BE MERCIFUL TO ME A SINNER!!! PLEASE FORGIVE ALL MY SINS, TRESSPASSES, AND INIQUITIES O' FATHER GOD Please Forgive Me**, and **HELP ME**, and Deliver Me from Evil! O'God I am helpless without you and your Holy Son Jesus Christ! Please Forgive me for all of my sins, and wash me clean in Jesus Holy Precious Blood! That Jesus shed for me, when he sacrificed himself, and died on the cross of Calvery! To Atone for all of my sins, and wash me clean, to reconsile me to you! **God My Father who art in Heaven! O'God, I accept Jesus Christ as my Lord and Savior!** Father, Please put your precious **Holy Spirit** inside my Heart and Soul, cause me to be **Born Again in the Spirit!** O' Mighty **Holy Spirit of God**, I invite You into my Heart and Soul! Please come and Live inside of Me forever! Please help me, and comfort me, and guide me, and teach me, and cleanse me from every Sin and Evil, Pride and wickedness! Purify my Heart and Soul, and make me Holy & Pure and prepair me for **The Marrage Supper of the Lamb! O'Heavenly Father**, Almighty Jevovah God of Holiness, Truth and Light! **I Surrender** my Heart and Soul, my Spirit and very Being into your hands, and lay then upon your altar! I seek the righteousness that is by Faith in **Jesus Christ!**

The Basics to Live by every Day

O' Heavenly Father, Mighty Lord Jesus, Precious Holy Spirit Living Inside of Me! I (*Your Name*) **I AM TRUSTING AND DEPENDING ON YOU!!! ALMIGHTY JEHOVAH GOD!!!!!!!** There is **No One Greater** that I can Pray to than **YOU!!!** There is **Absolutely No One HIGHER, MIGHTIER,** or **MORE POWERFUL** than **YOU!!!** In All of **Existence** in the **Entire Universe!** The **One True LIVING GOD of ALL CREATION!!!** The **Eternal, Holy, Everlasting Spirit!!!** In Whom **THERE IS NO EQUAL,** Forever and Ever and Ever! The God of Abraham, Isaac, and Jacob! The Great **I AM That I AM**, that called unto Moses out of the burning bush! {Exodus 3:4} The God, Our Father who art in Heaven, of our Lord and Savior **Jesus Christ!** Who Died on the Cross of Calvary, and Offered Up Himself to God, as a Spotless, Perfect, Holy Sacrifice to God! To Atone for All Our Sins, and reconcile us to God, by his precious, Holy Blood that cleanses us from **ALL SIN!!!** {Hebrews 7:27 & 1 John 1:7} The Mighty Lamb of God which taketh away the Sin of the World! {John 1:29} To Almighty God in Heaven, to whom belongeth the Kingdom, the Power, and the Glory, Forever and ever! Heavenly Father, I have no confidence in the Flesh! But I have all confidence, and Faith, and **Trust in YOU!!!** Because **Nothing is Impossible for YOU!!! NOTHING!!!** {Philippians 3:3 & Luke 1:37} And You, **Father God**, have promised us in your Wonderful, Awesome, Holy word; **(The Holy Bible)** that **YOU YOURSELF** would take the hard Heart of stone, out of US! And that **YOU** would give us a heart of flesh, and that **YOU, Heavenly Father God,** would **Put Your Holy Spirit Inside of US!** And that **YOU** would cause us to walk in All your Statutes and **DO THEM!!!** That **YOU** would put your laws into our minds, and write them upon our hearts! O' Heavenly Father, **You** said, "I will be to them a God, and they shall be to me a people: for I will be merciful to their unrighteousness, and their sins and their iniquities will I remember no more, and I will save you from all your uncleanness, for my own Holy Names sake!" {Ezekiel 36:26 & Hebrews 8:10} Beloved, **ALMIGHTY GOD** himself promised us, and said, "Fear Thou Not, for **I AM** with Thee, be not dismayed; for **I AM THY GOD! I Will Strengthen Thee!** Yea, **I Will Help Thee! I Will Uphold Thee with the right hand of my Righteousness!** Be strong and of good courage, Do Not Fear, nor be afraid of them! (Evil) For the Lord thy God, **He** it is, that doth go **with Thee! He Will Not Fail Thee, Nor Forsake Thee!** {Isa 41:10, Dt 31:6} No Weapon formed against thee will prosper! And No man can pluck thee out of my hand! For if Almighty God be for you! Who can be against you? Because Jesus maketh intersession for us! According to the will of God! For **You Are Kept by the Power of GOD!** Through Faith, unto Salvation! (you are saved by Grace through Faith, and not by works, it is the **gift of God!** least any man should boast!) Beloved, If Almighty **Jehovah God** of all creation; The All Powerful authority and Judge of All the World! Has Washed you clean in his own son Jesus' precious Holy Blood, and has Pardoned and Forgiven you of all trespasses and sin! Because of **Jesus Christ** spotless, blameless, sacrifice, on the cross of Calvary! And **Jesus** holy precious **Blood** that cleanseth us of All Sin! {1 John 1:7} If **GOD** has saved you, who can overturn **God's** decision? **NO ONE!!!!!!!**

The Basics to Live by every Day

This then is the message we have heard of him, and declare unto you. That God is Light, and in him is no darkness at all! If we say that we have fellowship with him, (God) and we walk in darkness, we lie, and do not the truth! But if we walk in the light, as he is in the light, we have fellowship one with another, and the blood of Jesus Christ his son, cleanseth us from all sin! If we say that we have no sin, we deceive ourselves, and the truth is not in us. If we confess our sins, he is faithful and just to forgive us our sins, and to cleanse us from all un righteousness. If we say that we have not sinned we make him a liar, and his word is not in us. My little children, I write these things unto you, that ye sin not! And if any man sin, we have an advocate with the Father, **Jesus Christ** the Righteous! And he is the propitiation for our sins; and only for ours, but also for the sins of the whole world! And hereby we do know that we know him, if we keep his Commandments! He that saith, I know him, and keepeth not his commandments, is a liar, and the truth is not in him! But whoever keepeth his word, in him verily is the love of God perfected; hereby do we know that we are in him. He that saith he abideth in him, (Jesus) ought himself also to walk, even as He (Jesus) walked! {1 John 1:5} This awesome Scripture shows us that our Father God truly, loves us, and wants to forgive our sins! But what most people don't see, is that this Scripture exposes our heart, and our true motives! Many people read this Scripture and see it as a license and excuse to just go out and sin! They mistakenly seam to think that God doesn't care if they sin, and will just forgive sin without any consequences! They couldn't be more wrong! God's word also says,"Do not be deceived, God is not mocked! (not to be played with) Whatsoever You Sow, that will you also Reap! {Galatians 6:7} (either Holiness unto life, or Sin unto Death!) The Holy Bible says,"The word of God is quick and powerful, sharper than any two edged sword, even piercing and dividing between the soul and spirit, and is a discerner of the **thoughts and intents of the Heart**! {Hebrews 4:12} In other words, if when you read, "if we say that we have no sin, we lie, and the truth is not in us" and you think to yourself, "great" I'll just continue to tell lies, get drunk, do drugs, steal, commit adultery, fornication, homosexuality, murder and all the sins that I love to do, and God will just forgive them, You are only deceiving Yourself!!! Because the word of God is exposing the motives and intents of Your Evil Heart! You want to Sin! And you completely missed what the word of God really said,"If we walk in the Light, as he (Jesus) is **In the Light**, then the blood of Jesus cleanses us of all sin! If you have ever walked into a kitchen infested with roaches, and you turn on the Light switch, all the roaches scatter and hide in the dark hidden corners, they don't want to be exposed to the Light! Sinners who do not truly come to God or his Holy son Jesus, because they know he will expose their sins, and tell them to repent and **Stop Doing Them**! Are just like those scattering roaches, they have no Intention of Giving up their Sins! And this reveals the true motive of their heart! They don't love God, so they run from him, they love their sins! Lets make an illustration for understanding, Imagine a man walking up a steep mountain trail, he slips on some gravel and is sliding towards a deadly 500 foot drop! he is scratching and claw-ing at every root and shrub he can grab! Look in his heart, he does **not want to Fall!** God sees your Heart! Every True Christian who walks in the light, fights hard against sin! He does not want to fall!

The Basics to Live by every Day

And this is what our father God in Heaven Sees! A Pure Sincere Heart, that is very **Diligently** and **Fervently** Crying out and seeking for him in **FAITH!** Strong Faith and Trust and Belief in **God** and his only begotten son **Jesus Christ**! A person that **WANTS** to walk in **True Holiness** and **True Righteousness**, and Live a **Holy Life** that is well Pleasing to **God** our Father in Heaven! Beloved, this can only be done by **FAITH** and **BELIEF** in our **Lord** and **Savior, Jesus Christ!!!** Because you are only saved by **Grace** through **Faith**, and **NOT** by any **works or deeds** or physical actions or accomplishments you could ever do in your body! It is the **Gift of God!** {Ephesians 2:8} Knowing that a man is not justified by the works of the law, but by the **Faith of Jesus Christ**, even we have **Believed** in **Jesus Christ**! That we might be justified by the **Faith in Christ**, and **not** by the works of the law: for by the works of the law shall no flesh be justified! (or saved) But if, while we seek to be justified by Christ, we ourselves also are found sinners, is therefore then Christ the minister of Sin? God Forbid! {Galatians 2:16} What then? Shall we sin, because we are not under the law, but under grace? God forbid! Do you not know and understand, that to whom ye yield your self servants to obey, his servant ye are to whom ye obey! Either (the servant) of **Sin unto Death**, or (the servant of God and Jesus) and obedience unto **Righteousness and Life!** {Romans 6:15} For as (God) the Father raiseth up the dead, and quickeneth them; even so the Son (**Jesus**) quickens whom he will! For the Father judgeth no man, but hath **Committed all Judgment unto the Son!** That all men should honor the son! Truly I say unto you, he that heareth my word, and **Believeth** on (God) that sent me, hath Everlasting Life, and shall not come into condemnation; but is passed from Death unto Life! Truly, I say unto you the hour is coming, and now is, when the dead shall hear the voice of the Son of God: (**Jesus**) and they that hear shall Live! For as the Father hath life in himself; so hath he given to the son to have life in himself. And (God) hath given him Authority to Execute The Judgment, because he is the son of man! (God in the Flesh) Marvel not at this, for the hour is coming, when all who are in the graves, (every person who ever lived) shall **Hear Jesus Voice**, and shall **come forth**! They that have done **Good**, unto the Resurrection of **Life!** And they that done **Evil**, unto the Resurrection of **Damnation!** {John 5:21-29} Beloved, God the Father, has given his only begotten son, **Jesus Christ,** power over all flesh, that he should give **Eternal Life** to all who confess with their mouth, **Faith** in the Lord Jesus, and **Believe** in their heart that God has raised him from the dead! For with the heart, man believeth unto righteousness; and with the mouth confession is made unto Salvation! For the Scripture saith, Whosoever believeth on him shall not be ashamed, and that Jesus Christ is the author of Eternal Salvation unto all who **obey him!** {Heb 5:9} And this is life eternal, that they might know thee, the the only True God, and **Jesus Christ** who thou hast sent! Beloved, pray to God every morning and thank him for allowing you to live another day! Ask God to wash you clean in Jesus Precious Blood, to lead and guide you by the **Holy Spirit**! To cause you to walk in True Holiness and Righteousness, to take every thought into captivity unto the obedience of Jesus Christ! To put a bridle on your tongue, so that no corrupt communication can proceed out of your mouth! And always remember that you are only saved by your Faith in Jesus! Not by works!

The Basics to Live by every Day!

The Power of Life and Death are in the **Tongue!** He that speaketh Lies shall Perish! {Proverbs 18:21 & 19:9} **NO LIAR** shall **enter** into God's Kingdom in Heaven! "And there shall No Wise enter into it (Heaven) any thing that **Defileth**,(their mouth or body) or worketh **Abominations**, (Homosexuals, Adulterers and Fornicators) or **Maketh a LIE!**" (Tells Lies out of their Mouth!) {Revelation 21:27} For without (all those who are kept **Out of HEAVEN**!) are dogs, and sorcerers, and whoremongers, and idolaters, and whosoever loveth and maketh A LIE! (**ALL LIARS!**) {Revelations 22:15} My beloved brethren, telling a Lie **Is No Small Matter!!!** Telling **Lies** will Absolutely, Definitely, **SEND YOU TO HELL!!! FOREVER!!!** Telling **Lies** and **Murder** are The Key Defining Traits, and The Key Identifying Marks of **SATAN HIMSELF!!!** Listen to these very words, out of **Jesus** own mouth! Jesus said,"Ye are of your father the devil, and the lusts (or actions and deeds) of your Father **Ye will do!** He was a murderer from the beginning, and abode not in the Truth, because there **Is No Truth In Him!** When he speaketh a Lie, he speaketh of his own; for He is a Liar, and the **FATHER OF IT!!!**" Many people mistakenly think that this means Satan is the author of every Lie. **NO!!!** What Jesus is saying here, is that Satan tells Lies; and that **All Satan's Children Tell Lies!!!** Just Like **Their Father Satan!!!** For **He is a Liar, AND THE FATHER OF IT!!!** If You tell Lies **Out of Your Mouth, You Yourself, MAKE SATAN YOUR FATHER!!!** By the very Words, and **LIES** that **You Choose to Speak, Out of Your own Mouth!** Satan does not control Your Tongue! **YOU CONTROL YOUR TONGUE!!!** And if You Choose to **Tell Lies** just like your father Satan! **Do Not Be Surprised, When You Find Yourself Burning in Hell! Just like Your Father Satan!!! Almighty Holy Jehovah GOD's Children, DO NOT TELL LIES!!!** Jesus Christ Holy Servants and disciples, who are led by **The Holy Spirit!** Do Not Tell Lies! Because they know that this is the very Identifying Mark of **Satan Himself** and **all of Satan's Children!** All of **God's Children** have Repented from Lying and **STOPPED TELLING ANY LIES OUT OF THEIR MOUTH!** Period! Because **The Holy Bible** plainly says,"Let No Corrupt Communication proceed Out of Your Mouth, but that which is Good (and Holy) to the use of edifying, that it may minister grace unto the hearers. And Do Not Grieve (with lies and evil words) the **Holy Spirit of God**,(that lives inside you) for by him are ye sealed, (as proof of your adoption by our Father God into Heaven!) unto the day of your Redemption! Let all bitterness, and wrath, and anger, and clamor (loud shouting and fighting), and evil speaking (gossip, slander, filthy words and jokes) be put away from you, with all malice!" (Evil intent in your Heart!) {Ephesians 4:29} "O' generation of vipers, how can ye being evil, speak good things? For out of the abundance of the **heart** the **mouth speaketh**! A Good man with a Good Holy Heart speaks forth good things! And an evil man with an **Evil Heart** speaks forth evil things! But I say unto you, that every idle word that men shall speak, they shall give account thereof in the day of **Judgment!** For by Your words you will be justified, and by Your words **Ye shall be Condemned!** "**Jesus Christ**" {Matthew 12:34} "Whosoever keepeth his mouth and his tongue, keepeth **His Soul** from troubles and **Hellfire!**"{Proverbs 21:23} Be wise and control your tongue from speaking Evil!

The Basics to Live by every Day!

The Tongue is a little member, and boasteth great things. Behold, how a great forest can be set on fire with just a small spark! Even so the Tongue is a fire, a world of iniquity (and sin); so is the Tongue among our members, that it defileth the whole body! It setteth on Fire the course of (a man's) nature; and it is **set on Fire of Hell!** Every kind of beast, and bird, and serpent, and things in the sea, have all been tamed by mankind! But the Tongue can no man tame; it is an unruly evil, full of Deadly Poison! (but **God** can tame it! For those who yield their tongue to the control of the **Holy Spirit!**) Therewith (our tongue) we praise and bless God the Father, and with the same tongue we curse men, who are made in the image of God. Out of the Same Mouth proceeds blessings and cursing! My brethren, these things aught not to be so! {James 3:5} In other words, do you think that you can curse, and lie, and gossip, and slander, and speak Evil words of hatred towards men? And then use **that same** Evil vile Tongue, and try to worship and praise a **Holy**, **Pure**, **Sinless**, **ALMIGHTY GOD IN HEAVEN!** And it will be accepted and pleasing to **Holy Almighty God**? **NO!** When ye spread forth your hands, I will hide mine eyes from you; yea, when ye make many prayers, I will not hear; your hands are full of blood! Wash you, make you **clean!** Put away the evil of your doings from before mine eyes; cease to do Evil! Learn to well; (good and Holy) seek judgment, relieve the oppressed, judge the fatherless, plead for the widow. Cleanse your hands ye sinners! Purify your hearts, (and tongues) all ye double minded! Draw nigh unto God, and he will draw nigh unto you! Come now, and let us reason together, saith the Lord! Though your sins be as scarlet, they shall be as white as snow; though they be red like crimson, they shall be as wool. If ye be willing and obedient, ye shall eat the good of the land! (enter into Heaven!) But if ye refuse and rebel (like Satan), ye shall be devoured with the sword (and be cast into Hell!) For the mouth of the Lord hath spoken it! {Isaiah 1:15 & James 4:8} Proverbs 18:21 says, "The Power of Death and Life are in the Tongue!" Your tongue, my tongue! Death, not only to You, but to all those around you! Your children, your family, your wife or husband, your mother or father, your brothers and sisters, your friends! Your evil words can not only destroy **You**, they can and will influence and Destroy all those around You! **Your Loved Ones!** Paul said,"Do not be deceived, evil communications corrupt good manners! Awake to righteousness and sin not! {1 Corinthians 15:33} Are you personally filling your children and family's hearts and souls with **evil**, that will send them to **Hell!** Remember, Jesus said,"you shall give an account (and answer) for **Every Word** you speak, on **Judgment Day!**" If you are the "Head" of your home, and **You teach them Evil!** What will **You** Say when you kneel before Holy Almighty GOD! But beloved, the Power of Life is also in your Tongue! Behold,"a wholesome Tongue is a tree of **Life!**" The words of the Lord are pure words, as silver tried in the furnace, purified seven times!"{Proverbs 15:4 & Psalms 12:6} Scripture says,"Let your words be good to the use of edifying that it may minister **Grace** unto the hearers! Also, with the heart, man believeth (in **Jesus Christ**) unto righteousness, and with the mouth confession is made unto salvation. Eyewitnesses testified that Jesus, "spake as no other man" and all bear witness to the gracious words that proceeded out of his mouth! Even Jesus testified,"the Lord hath anointed me to preach the gospel to the poor, deliverance to the captives, recover sight to the blind! **Holy Pure Words Give Life**!!!

The Basics to Live by every Day!

John the Baptist, used his words to preach life! Jesus said he was a burning and a shining Light! The Apostle Paul used his words to Preach the Gospel of Jesus Christ! God used that Awesome, Tireless Man of God, to reach most of the known World! By foot, or horse, or sailing ship! With his spoken, Passionate Words and handwritten Letters! No phones, no cars, no trains or planes, No Internet, texts or tweets, no skyping, no Mega-Churches or 100,00 seat stadiums! Through wild forest, and Jungles, and raging Seas, in the Dark-Ages, whipped, stoned, and chained in prison cells, hated in every single country! In perils from wild animals, barbarians, and his own country-men! Satan trying to kill him! And The Apostle Paul turned the known world, upside down on it's head, in his day, for Jesus Christ! But we Christians today, start to get restless and agitated, staring at our watches, if our pastor starts to get long-winded, 45 minutes into his Lukewarm, Watered-down milk sermon! Sitting on our soft cushioned pews, in our Air conditioned, stained-glass Churches! While Most of the World races to **Hell!!!** The same world, that our Lord and Savior, **Jesus Christ**, Died to Save! And told Us to go into **all the World** and **Preach the Gospel**! We Christians today- God help us! If we had to stand up next to the Apostle Paul, on Judgment Day! We would want to crawl under a rock and hide, as The Lord told us "Thou wicked and slothful servant"{Matthew 25:26} And I tell you that, with a broken heart and tears! It gives me No Joy! Satan's children will strap a bomb to their chest, and blow themselves to smithereens in a crowd, and send themselves straight to hell for Satan! Believing his evil lie about 70 virgins, that appeal to their lusting, sinful, flesh! While God's children, who Hear the Truth, can't be bothered with Lost-Souls! They are far to busy with their Barbecue Cookouts, favorite TV shows, worldly possessions, favorite sports team, computer-games and internet searches! And if for some reason they do think about God, Their Favorite TV Preacher is sure if they just buy his new book on "Thinking Positive" and plant an $100 to $1000 dollar seed in his false gospel ministry. That God will definitely multiply it 100x fold, and bless them with the new house or car that they've always wanted! While Jesus looks down from heaven with tears running down his face, burdened for all the lost souls going to hell, with only a **Few Real** men and women of **GOD** to help him to carry the real spiritual burden for a Lost and Dying World! Heavenly Father **Please Help Us ! We Really Truly Need YOU at This Crucial Point in Time!!! More Than Any Other Time!!! In The World's History!!! HEAVENLY JEHOVAH FATHER GOD!!! WE ~ NEED ~YOU!!!** You Promised in Your Word that when the enemy comes in like a flood! That **You, Heavenly Father**, Would Lift Up A Standard Against It ! **We Need You Now!!!** My beloved Brethren, how can we use our words to minister Life and Grace, with **The Gospel of Jesus Christ** to a Lost and Dying World, if we never OPEN OUR MOUTH and TELL THEM ??? The TRUE GOSPEL!!! NOT BEG THEM FOR MONEY!!! When all those **Charlatans**, and **Thieves**, and **Wolves in Sheep's Clothing**, and **Angel's of Light**!!! Who's True Motive is to **Get Rich using The Gospel**, and **Stuff Your Cash into Their Pockets!** By preaching a soft, easy Gospel, with **No True Repentance from Sin! Stand Before Almighty God!!! God** is going to stuff them into the deepest parts of **Hell Forever!** Because they lied to God's children and helped Satan send Lost souls to Hell! For their own greed! Precious Souls that Jesus died to save!

The Basics to Live by every Day!

Jesus Christ preached **Repent**, for the Kingdom of Heaven is at hand! (**Get Out of Your Sins!** Turn away from and **Stop Doing Them!** Wash You, Make You Clean! Cleanse your hands ye sinners! and Purify your Hearts ye double minded! **Be Ye Holy!** Because Now is your chance to **Go To Heaven!**) Multitudes, Multitudes, In the vally of decision! Because the day of the Lord is near! **Judgment Day!** Alas, for the day of the Lord cometh, for it is nigh at hand! And as a Destruction from the Almighty shall it come! Blow Ye the Trumpet in Zion, and sound an alarm in my Holy Mountain! Let all the inhabitants of the Land (and Earth) Tremble! And the Lord shall utter his voice before his army; for he (**Jesus**) is strong that executeth his word! Because the day of the Lord very Great and Terrible day, and who can abide it? The sun shall be turned into darkness, and the moon into blood, before the great and terrible day of the Lord come! The Lord shall roar out of Zion, and The Almighty **God** of Heaven shall utter his voice from Jerusalem, and the heavens and the earth shall shake! But the Lord (**Jesus**) will be the hope of his people, and the strength of all God's Holy children!{see Joel Ch.1,2,3} For the **Lord Jesus** shall be revealed from Heaven with his Mighty Angels, in Flaming Fire, taking vengeance on them that Do Not know God! And **Do Not Obey** The gospel of our Lord **Jesus Christ**! Who shall be punished with **Everlasting Destruction** from the presence of the Lord, and from the glory of his power! Because they (ignored Jesus) and did not receive the Love of the **Truth** that they might be **Saved!** {2 Thessalonians 1:7 & 2:10}(Please **Go and Read it** for yourself) So shall ye know that **I AM The LORD your GOD** dwelling in Zion, my Holy Mountain! For it is written, **As I Live**, Saith the **Lord God Almighty**, that **Every Knee shall Bow to Me**, in Heaven and in Earth, and that **Every Tongue shall Confess to God**, (every single creature that **Almighty God** has created!) that **JESUS CHRIST is LORD!!!** To the Glory of GOD the FATHER!!! For **We shall all stand** at the **Judgment Seat of Jesus Christ!** And Every One of Us **Shall Give** an account of himself to **God!** {Romans 14:10 & Phillipians 2:11} "One day there were some people that came and told Jesus, about certain Galilean's, who Pilate had killed and mixed their blood in with the sacrifice. Jesus, answering said unto them,"Suppose ye that these Galilean's were sinners above all the Galilean's, because they suffered such things? I tell you nay, but, except ye repent, ye shall all likewise perish! Or the eighteen upon whom, the tower of Siloam fell, and it slew them; think ye that they were sinners above all men that dwelt in Jerusalem? I tell you, nay, but except ye repent, ye shall all likewise perish!" He (Jesus) also spake this parable;"A certain man had a fig tree planted in his vineyard, and he came and sought fruit thereon, and found none! Then he said unto the dresser of the vineyard, Behold, these three years I come seeking fruit on this fig tree, and find none, cut it down! Why cumbereth it the ground? and he answering said unto him, Lord, let it alone this year also, till I dig about it, and dung it! And if it bear **Fruit**, well; and **if not**, then after that, thou shalt **cut it down!** {Luke 13:1-9} O' generation of Vipers, who hath warned you to flee from the wrath to come? Bring forth **Fruit**, worthy of **Repentance!** For the ax is laid unto the root of the trees! {Luke 3:8} **"Every tree that does not bring forth good fruit is Hewn Down and Cast into the Fire!"** "A good tree brings forth **good fruit**, but an evil tree brings forth **evil fruit**, therefore by their **Fruits**, "**Ye shall know them!**" "**Jesus Christ**" {Matthew 7:17}

The Basics to Live by every Day!

Are the Fruits of your Life, (your words, lifestyle, activity, goals, attitudes, demeanor towards others, and accomplishments) glorifying God? Does <u>Your Life</u> bring forth holiness, purity, righteousness, and **God's Truth**? And shine God's Holy Light to men, your neighbors, and the world around you? If the local News station did a segment on you, and your life; Questioning your Family, Friends, Neighbors Co-workers, or casual acquaintances. Would they say that you were kind, patient, loving, thoughtful, compassionate, easy to get along with, caring, mild mannered, well spoken, helping others through all of life's trials and tribulations? Treating all the people around you, the same way that <u>You Yourself</u> would want to be treated. Or would all the people who are around you on a daily basis, for hours, or days, or months, or years; who <u>Truly know You</u>, and your daily character, lifestyle, words that come out of your mouth, your <u>true demeanor</u> and attitude towards other people! (family, co-workers, boss, or strangers) Would they say that when the camera's off, and your pastor's not looking, that you are an rude, mean, nasty, uncompassionate, uncaring, gossiping behind their back, hateful, slandering, filthy speaking, cursing, blame casting, mocking, unforgiving, obnoxious, evil, threatening, bullying, bad mannered, ill-tempered, punching, lying, thief, and murderer, <u>like your evil father Satan</u>! How do you truly <u>Live Your Life</u>? What if the local News caster asked to bring the camera <u>into Your House</u>, and film <u>Inside</u> and <u>Show to the world</u> your daily Life? And also <u>Look</u> and <u>See</u> what is really on Your own personal Home <u>Computer</u> or <u>Smart Phone</u>! Would <u>Fear grip your Soul</u> as your mind raced ahead of all the stuff you'ed have to run into your house and <u>Hide from the camera's</u> un-blinking, fact proving, all seeing **Eye!** Would you have to quickly run in ahead of the camera's, saying, Just give me a couple of minuets to straighten up the place, so you could go in and hide the alcohol bottles, full or empty, (now a days, most drunkards wouldn't even <u>care</u>) or go hide your drugs, (either illegal, or prescription bottles just laying around) or hide your filthy books or pornographic dvds, (again, now-a-days most people are so evil, that they wouldn't even care who saw it!) or stolen items your friend, or neighbor, co-worker, or <u>the Police</u> are looking <u>For!</u> Would you run and delete Evil, vile, Pornographic filth, or illegal child porn, or incriminating evidence of theft, fraud, scams, hustles, shakedowns, intimidations adulteries, unfaithfulness, illegal relationships and business practices, extortions, pimping, prostitution gambling, swindles, or a mountain of other illegal activities that I don't have enough time or paper to cover it all; would you have to run inside and delete the files? Supposed law-biding citizens or quote un-quote, good Christians, or even pastors and preachers, if you ask them if they want you to install an awesome Bible-study hardware, or Godly Holy Books hardware, on their computer or smart phone, you will get a quick, No! Please understand, <u>I Love Everyone!</u> And <u>I Want to See</u> as many people on **The Planet Earth**, as Possible, **Make It INTO HEAVEN!!!** But to Me, anyone who truly loves God, with all their heart, and soul, and mind, and strength! Would <u>take</u> and <u>use</u> **Any Tool or Help** available that Truly and Honestly <u>Teaches You</u> **The Holy Bible**, and Opens up God's Holy Word to You, and helps to stoke and ignite God's Holy Fire in <u>Your Soul!</u> If you truly Love and Want to **Be Like Jesus!** You will Study God's Holy Word, Day and Night! And you will Pray constantly to <u>God</u>, night and day to completely **Fill You** with **the Holy Spirit**, and to **Totally Consume Your Heart** with **Holy Fire!!!**

The Basics to Live by every Day!

If You want to **Be Like Jesus**, You have to **Strive** to be Like Jesus! Some Christians might ask, "Do I need to be like Jesus? To Live, and walk, and talk, and Pray, and to **Obey God the Father** like Jesus? **YES!!!** The Word Christian means, "To Be Christ-Like!" God told all of Mankind, "Be Ye Holy, for "**I Am Holy!**" **Jesus Christ** is the "Absolute Pinnacle" of what **Holiness Is!** Almighty God's plan for all of mankind, from the Foundation of the World, is for us to be part of the body of Christ! For all of God's children to be washed clean in Jesus precious blood, and covered by God's Grace through Faith! The "High Calling of God" to all of us "is to be in Christ Jesus!" {Phili. 3:14, 4:13} Now you may ask, "Can I really be like Jesus? "I Can Do all things through Christ Jesus who strengthens Me," and that "We are more than Conquerors through Christ our Lord!" Because with God "nothing is Impossible!" Jesus also told us, "greater things than I do, you shall Do!" {John 14:12} And we know that all things work together for good to them that love God, to them who are called according to his purpose! And those who God called he also did predestinate **To Be CONFORMED to the IMAGE OF HIS SON! (Jesus Christ)** That he might be the Firstborn among many brethren! And those whom God called, he also Justified! And whom he Justified, them he also Glorified! What shall we then say to these things? If **God** Be For Us, (Forgiving and Covering Us) **Who Can Be Against US!** {Romans 8:28-31, 8:37} **NOBODY!!! ALMIGHTY GOD is the MOST POWERFUL BEING in ALL of EXISTENCE!!! God's Decision is Final!!! & FOREVER!!!** Because Jesus Christ is seated at the Right hand of God, right now, in the Holy of Holies, Praying and Making Intercession For Us, **To God!** All according to **The Will of God!** That Is **God's Plan for us**! **And For You!** From The Foundation of the World!!! Because God is not willing that ANY should perish, but God's will is to have all men to be Saved, and to come unto the knowledge of the Truth! {2 Peter 3:9, 1 Timothy 2:4} The Truth that their Sin's will be Forgiven if they Truly Repent from them and Turn from their Wicked Ways! Accept **Jesus Christ** as their Lord and Savior, and Obey the Gospel! Having their Souls washed clean by Jesus Precious, Holy Blood; by obedience to the Faith through the Saving Grace of our Lord and Savior Jesus Christ! And be adopted by our Father God in Heaven, and have your name written into God's **Book of Life!!!** And **No One But YOU** can Stop it, Not Satan, No Demon, No Evil Spirit! **NO ONE BUT YOU!!!** If you **Choose** to jump out of Almighty God's hand, and Ignore God's plan for you to be washed clean by Jesus blood, forgiven from Every Sin, and covered by God's Grace, and **Go To Heaven Forever!** That is God's will and desire, for your life and soul, but unless **You Do God's will**, according to Jesus, (Who is God's only begotten Son, and God in the Flesh, and the one man who knows more about God the Father and Heaven above, than **any other person that ever lived on the face of the planet earth**) According to **Jesus**, unless you **DO GOD the FATHER'S WILL**, **You will Not Enter into Heaven!** "Not every one that saith unto me, Lord, Lord, shall Enter into The Kingdom of Heaven; but He that **doeth the will of my Father which is in Heaven!**" {Matthew 7:21} Almighty God's will is for you to Go to Heaven, and he made a way for all of us to Enter in, **Jesus Christ** his Son! Jesus opened up the way. Now You must do God's will! God has done everything to save you! What are You going to Do?

The Basics to Live by every Day!

How do we, Do God's Will? 1. Love the Lord thy God with all your Heart, Soul, Mind, and Strength! 2. Love thy neighbor as thyself. Do unto others as you want done unto you, treat people how you want to be treated by them! 3. Be Ye Holy, because God is Holy! Don't Lie, steal, curse, commit Adultery, or Fornication, or Homosexuality, or Sexual Sins! Don't Murder, or get Drunk, Do Drugs, Covet other people's stuff, do witchcraft or black magic or contact evil spirits! Don't extort, cheat or rip people off. Don't gossip, slander, speak evil curse words out your mouth, say foul things about others. Don't make Rude evil gestures with your hands or body! Don't Watch Evil, Cursing, Hateful, Violent T.V. Shows, or Evil Pornographic Filth! Don't Put Anything Evil in front of your Eyes! If Jesus wouldn't watch it, You don't watch It! Fight hard to Drive out every Sin and evil Lust in your Body! Crucify your Flesh, kill the old sinful nature in your body! "That ye put off, (crucify and overcome) the old man, which is corrupt according to the deceitful lusts; and be renewed in the spirit of your mind! And put "ye"on the new man, which is created after God in righteousness and true Holiness, and is renewed in knowledge after the image of him that created you!" {Ephesians 4:22, Colossians 3:10} "Do not be conformed to this world, but be ye transformed by the renewing of your mind, (study your bible!) that ye may prove what is the good, and acceptable, and perfect, will of God! {Romans 12:2} Therefore if any man be in Christ, he is a new creature, old things are passed away, (crucified) Behold all things are become new! {2 Corinthians 5:17} There's a good lesson for our struggle in the Old Testament, that we can all learn from. When God had Moses lead Israel out of Egypt to Mount Sinai, and into the wilderness. God was watching the children of Israel, and testing them to see what they would do! Would they resort to their old ways, always relying on themselves to make their way. Trying to fend for themselves, and make their own way through the wilderness of sin. Trying to fight their enemies in their own strength and cunning, which had gotten them into bondage and slavery in the first place! Or would they Trust in God and rely upon Him to guide them, and teach them, and lead them! As a pillar of a cloud by day, and a pillar of fire by night, God lead the children of Israel! When he stayed, they stayed! When God moved, they moved! All the while Moses was communicating with God every day, going and Praying to God in the Tabernacle! Seeking God's face for instruction and direction! Do you do that? Trust God for everything! Seek his face in prayer, for instruction and direction, for everything in your Life? Not making a single move, unless you know that God is going with You! If You learn to Do this every day in **Your Life!** You will will avoid a lifetime of mistakes, heartache's and Troubles! And Sin's that will **Send You to Hell!** The Children of Israel didn't know it, but God was preparing them, to Cross the Jordan and Enter into the Promised Land! "God is come to Prove You, that His Fear may be before your faces, that Ye Sin Not! "Moses" {Exodus 20:20} In the same way, God is working to save and to prepare **Your Soul** to enter into Heaven! God told the children of Israel to fight with and destroy, and to drive out, the old inhabitants of the land! Do not make peace with them! Do Not learn and accept any of their ways! Likewise, when you accept Jesus Christ as your Lord and Savior, and you are Born Again! The Holy Spirit will guide and teach you to fight against, drive out, overcome, crucify, kill and destroy the old man! the old sinful, evil nature. And be a new Christ like man, created in God's Image!

The Basics to Live by every Day!

If You Truly want to Do God's Will, you must crucify your flesh (your old evil, lustful Sin nature) and Overcome the sinful, rebellious, evil desire's that will destroy you, and send You to an Eternal Hell! And Jesus said to them all, if any man will come after Me; let him deny himself, and take up his cross every day, and Follow Me! (into Heaven!) And whosoever doth not bear his cross, and come after me, cannot be my disciple! {Luke 9:23 & 14:27} Some Christians might even ask,"Why should I Crucify my fleshly desires, deny myself, and overcome sin and evil, to follow Jesus? God's word tell's us why! "Behold, The Lord cometh with ten thousands of his saints, to execute judgment upon all, (mankind) and to convince all that are ungodly among them of all their ungodly deeds which they have ungodly committed, and of all their hard speeches which ungodly sinners have spoken against him!{Jude 1:14} He that hath an ear, let him hear what the Spirit (of the living God) saith unto the churches, to him that Overcometh, **1.** will I give to eat of The Tree of Life, which is in the midst of the Paradise of God! These things saith the First and the Last, which was dead, and is Alive! He that Overcometh **2.** shall Not be hurt of the Second Death! These things saith He which hath the Sharp two Edged Sword! To him that Overcometh **3.** will I give to eat of the hidden manna, and will give him a white stone, and in the stone a new name written, which no man knoweth saving he that receiveth it. These things saith the Son of God, who hath his Eyes like a Flame of Fire! He that Overcometh **4.** and keepeth my works unto the end, to him will I give power (to rule) over the nations; and I will give him the Morning Star! These things saith He that hath the Seven Spirits of God, and the Seven Stars! He that Overcometh **5.** The same Shall be Clothed in White Raiment, and I will not blot out his name out of the Book of Life! But I will confess his name before my Father, and before his angels! These things saith he that is Holy He that is True, He that hath the Key of David! Him that Overcometh **6.** I will make a Pillar in the Temple of my God! And He shall go no more out, and I will write upon him the Name of my God! And the name of the city of my God, which is the new Jerusalem! Which cometh down out of Heaven from my God, and I will write upon him my new Name! These things saith the Amen, the Faithful and True witness, the Beginning of the Creation of God! To him that Overcometh **7.** will I Grant to sit with Me in my Throne, even as **I Also Overcame!!!** And I am set down with my Father in his Throne! He that **hath an ear to hear**, **let him hear** what the Spirit (of the Living God) saith unto the churches! {Revelation Chapters 1, 2,& 3}(you really need to go and read them!) For whatsoever is Born of God overcometh the world, and this is the Victory that overcometh the world! Even our **Faith!** Who is He that overcometh the world, but **He - That - Believeth** that **Jesus is the Son of God!!!** {1 John 5:4-5} I have spoken these words to you, that in me ye might have peace; in the world ye will have tribulation but be of good cheer, I have overcome the world! "Jesus"{John 16:33} "Ye are of God, little children, and have overcome them, because greater is he that is in You, (Holy Spirit) than he that is in the world "He that Overcometh **Shall Inherit All Things!** And **I will Be His God, and He Shall Be My Son!!!**" Now is come salvation and strength, and the kingdom of our God, and the power of his Christ! for the Devil, which accused our brethren before our God, day and night, is Cast Down! And they **Overcame** him by **The Blood of the Lamb**, and by **The Word** of their **Testimony!** {Revelation 12:11 & 21:7}

The Basics to Live by Every Day!

A new commandment I give unto you, that ye <u>love</u> one another; <u>as I</u> have loved you, that ye also love one another. (with the same compassion and forgiveness as Jesus! For) By <u>this</u> shall <u>all</u> men know that ye <u>are</u> my disciples, <u>if</u> ye have <u>Love</u> one to another! {John 13:34} Love and Peace and Kindness, with <u>real care</u> and <u>concern</u> for others, are the <u>True Attributes</u> and <u>actions</u> of any <u>Real</u> man or woman of <u>God</u>! That <u>walk</u> in the Holy Spirit and bring forth <u>mature</u>, godly <u>fruits</u> in their <u>lives</u>! God the Father has commanded us to "Love thy neighbor" as much as you love yourself! Not just by words, but by <u>Deeds</u> and <u>Actions</u>! Let us look at what Jesus taught on this very subject. One day a lawyer stood up and tempted Jesus, saying, Master, what shall I do to inherit eternal life? Jesus said to him, What is written in the law? How readest thou? And the lawyer said, "Thou shall love the Lord thy God with all thy heart, and with all thy soul, and with all thy strength, and with all thy mind; and thy neighbor as thy self." And Jesus said, Thou hast answered right; Do this, and thou shalt live! But he, willing to justify himself, said unto Jesus, And who is my neighbor? And Jesus answered him saying, A certain man went down from Jerusalem to Jericho, and fell among thieves, who stripped him of his clothes, and wounded him, and departed, leaving him half dead. And by chance there came down a priest that way; and when he saw him, he passed by on the other side. And likewise a Levite, when he was at the place, came and looked on him, and passed by on the other side. (both the Priest and the Levite) But a certain Samaritan, (who had no dealings with the Jews from Jerusalem!) as he journeyed, came where he was; and when he saw him, he had compassion on him. and went to him, and bound up his wounds pouring in oil and wine, and set him on his own beast, brought him to an inn, and took care of him. Then in the morning when he departed, he took out two pence, and gave them to the host, and said to him, Take care of him; and whatsoever thou spendest more, when I come again, I will repay thee. Which now of these three, thinkest thou, was neighbor unto him that fell among the thieves? And he said, He that shewed mercy on him. Then said Jesus to him, Go, and do thou likewise. {Luke 10:25} There is a wonderful chapter on Love, written by the Apostle Paul, {1 Corinthians 13} We will now study this chapter closely! First, here is Websters definition for; Charity - Love, Kindness, disposition to think and act loving and kindly to others, alms giving. Some bibles use the word Love, other bibles use the word Charity. In our study, I will use the word Love. ~ Though I speak with the tongues of men and of angels, and have not love, I am become as a sounding brass or a tinkling cymbal. (I'm just making noise) And though I have the gift of prophecy, and understand all mysteries, and knowledge; and though I have all faith, so that I could remove mountains, and I have not Love, <u>I am nothing</u>! And though I bestow all my goods to feed the poor, and though I give my body to be burned, and have not <u>Love</u>! It Profits me <u>Nothing</u>! Love suffers long and is Kind! Love does not envy! Love does not vaunt itself, is not puffed up! Love does not behave itself unseemly! Love seeketh not her own! Love is not easily provoked! Love thinketh no evil! Love rejoices not in iniquity, but rejoices in the truth! Love beareth all things; believeth all things, hopeth all things, endureth all things! Love <u>never</u> <u>Fails</u>! This is a perfect look at Jesus! Jesus suffers long, and is kind! Jesus does not envy! Jesus does not vaunt him self, and is not puffed up! Jesus does not behave himself unseemly! Jesus seeketh not his own! Jesus is not easily provoked! Jesus thinketh no evil! Jesus rejoice not in iniquity, Jesus rejoices in the truth!

The Basics to Live by Every Day!

Jesus beareth all things! Jesus believeth all things! (meaning he believes for the good, that people can and will change if they'll simply come to him and <u>Trust</u> him!) Jesus hopeth all things! Jesus endureth all things! Jesus never fails! Jesus is Wonderful, and Magnificent, and Awesome! Jesus is the Easily the Greatest Man or Human being who <u>Ever Lived</u>! Now, my beloved brethren, we'll turn the Holy Scripture on ourselves like a Mirror and put <u>our</u> name in it! I will simply write I for all of us, for this application! (don't just gloss over it, or race through it; slowly apply each one carefully and honestly to your <u>life</u> and your <u>attitudes</u>! I suffer long! (with people) I am Kind! (to people) I do not envy! I do not vaunt myself! I am not puffed up! I do not behave myself unseemly! I seek not my own! I am not easily provoked! I think no evil! (of people) I do not rejoice in iniquity or sin! I rejoice in the Truth! I beareth all things! (trials and sufferings, or hostile attitudes) I believeth all things! (meaning that you hope and think the best of other people, and don't automatically assume the worst or bad of them!) :) (this does <u>not</u> mean that you just believe every thing you hear, of all the millions of lies going around in this evil world! that's the reason why we are studying the basics!) I hopeth all things! (hope in God) I endureth all things! (be patient, slow to speak, slow to wrath!) I never faileth! (you <u>can</u> truly do this, if you learn to walk in the spirit, and be lead by the Holy Spirit every day! It takes time and growth & <u>Obedience to God</u>!) One hour at a time, one day at a time, one week at a time, one month at a time! One of the greatest things I have <u>ever</u> learned from the Holy Spirit is to <u>Study to be Quiet</u>! Keep <u>full control</u> of your <u>mind</u>, body and <u>mouth</u>! {1 Thessalonians 4:11} Do not be quick to speak or fly off of the handle! And <u>Don't</u> put yourself in a place full of people that Do! (God will help you at work!) I'm talking about bars, and clubs, and hostile places that are dangerous or just sinful to go to! What fellow ship hath Darkness with Light, or the children of God with the children of the devil?{2 Corinth. 6:14} Use wisdom, <u>think</u> and be <u>aware</u> of <u>what</u> you are doing! At <u>all</u> Times! The Apostle Paul said, "I keep under my body, and bring it into subjection;" lest that by any means, when I have preached to others, I myself should be a castaway!{1 Corinthians 9:27} My beloved brethren, there are no easy shortcuts there is no bed of roses, or fluffy marshmallow paths! You are going to have to <u>strive</u>, and to <u>fight</u> to <u>enter</u> into that <u>narrow</u> path that <u>leads</u> to Heaven, just like Jesus said! You <u>are</u> going to have to <u>take</u> up your <u>cross</u>, and **Crucify** your fleshly <u>sinful</u> <u>desires</u> every day! And Follow Jesus every day, Just like our Lord and Savior did! And told us to do, and Paul had to do, and Peter had to do, and I have to do, and <u>You</u> have to do! And we <u>All</u> have to <u>Do</u>! But you know what, The Scripture says that, "all the sufferings of this present time are not worthy to be compared to the glory which shall be revealed in us!{Romans 8:18} And that was written by the Apostle Paul, who knows a lot about it; because one day God lifted Paul to the Third Heaven, and he saw unspeakable things in heaven that it is not even allowed to mention! So the translation is that once you step into Heaven, it is so wonderful and awe inspiring and magnificent! That your memories of your small amount of suffering here on the earth, won't even be worthy to mention, or on your mind at all! Jesus called it Paradise! All of the Saints of of the Ages are there, all God's Angels will be there; The Tree of Life is there! And the Crystal Clear Living Water that Sparkles like Diamonds, and Constantly Flows from the Throne of God is There! Water so beautifully clear it's breathtaking! Best of all, God, and Jesus, and the Holy Spirit are There!

The Basics to Live by Every Day!

Of course the Holy Spirit is here on the earth with us right now! He lives inside of every single truly Born Again believer! That is born again into the Spirit of God, and is a Living Breathing part of the Body of Jesus Christ! Which is the True Church, in the Spirit, for we are seated in heavenly places <u>in</u> Christ Jesus! For behold, the Kingdom of God is <u>within</u> you!{Luke 17:21} Lord Jesus said that the Holy Spirit would live inside of us! "I will Pray the Father, and he shall give you another Comforter, that he may abide with you forever! Even the (Holy) Spirit of truth; whom the world cannot receive, because it seeth him not, neither knoweth him: but ye know him; for he dwelleth with you, and shall be <u>in you</u>! The Comforter, which is the Holy Ghost, whom the father will send in my name, he shall **Teach You** all things, and bring all things to your remembrance, whatsoever I have said unto you! When he, the (Holy) Spirit of Truth is come, he will **Guide You** into all truth! {John 14:16, 14:26 & 16:13} The Apostle Paul said,"Know ye not (do you not know and understand) that ye are the temple of God! And that <u>the Spirit of **God dwells In You**</u>! If any man defile the temple of God, him shall God destroy; for the temple of God is Holy, which temple <u>You are</u>! {1 Corinthians 3:16} There, my beloved brethren are 5 different verses out of the Holy Bible, (4 out of Jesus own mouth) that <u>tell you</u> that <u>God's</u> <u>Holy</u> <u>Spirit</u> lives **Inside of You**! If you are truly Born Again into the Spirit of God! God is a <u>Spirit</u> and they that worship him must worship him in Spirit, and in Truth! The Father seeketh for true worshippers to worship him!{John 4:23} And if you are not yet born again, Pray to God, Cry out to Jesus Christ! Ask Jesus to wash all your sins away with his precious Holy Blood, that you believe he is the son of God who died on the cross for your sins! And that he was resurrected on the third day and ascended into heaven at the right hand of God, and is our Great High Priest in the Holy of Holies! Jesus is our advocate with God the Father, to intercede and atone for our sins! Because that is exactly who and what Jesus Christ <u>Is</u>! Accept him as your Lord and Savior today, and give your life to him! Invite God's Holy Spirit to come and Live in your Heart and Soul Forever, and He <u>will</u> come and live <u>inside</u> you too; as you have just seen by the Holy Scriptures above! It is all <u>True</u> because God cannot lie, it is <u>impossible</u> for God to lie! {Hebrews 6:18} The whole Universe would disintegrate into chaos and all the planets would fly off into space, before the Creator of the Universe would ever let a lie or untruth come out of his Holy mouth and Lips! Almighty God has clearly stated that,"I will not break my Covenant, nor alter the thing (or words) that have gone out of my lips! {Psalm 89:34} So yes, my beloved brethren, the Holy Spirit can and <u>will</u> come and <u>Live Inside</u> of You! If you repent from your sins, Believe in Jesus Christ, and accept him as your Lord and Savior; in truth and sincerity! Invite God's Holy Spirit into your heart and soul by Faith in God and his Holy Son, and you <u>will</u> be <u>Born Again</u> into the Spirit, and become a Living member of the body of Jesus Christ! And the Holy Spirit of the One True Living God <u>will</u> come dwell and live in <u>You</u> making you the Temple of God! Where by we cry Abba Father, adopted into Gods family, and now covered by God's grace, mercy and Love! Therefore now, there is no condemnation to them which are <u>in</u> Christ Jesus, who <u>do</u> <u>not</u> walk after the flesh, but after the Spirit! For the law of the Spirit of life in Christ Jesus hath made me <u>free</u> from the law of sin and death! {Romans 8:1} And the life I now live, I live by the <u>Faith</u> of the Son of God!!!

The Basics to Live by Every Day!

Beware of False Prophets, which come to you in sheep's clothing, but inwardly they are ravening wolves! For such are false apostles, deceitful workers, transforming themselves into the apostles of Christ! And no marvel, for Satan himself is transformed into an angel of light! Therefore it is no great thing if his ministers also be transformed as the ministers or righteousness; whose end shall be according to their works!{2 Corinthians 11:13} And there were false prophets also among the people, even as there shall be false teachers among you! Who privily (secretly) shall bring in damnable heresies, (wrong evil teachings, and doctrines of devils, supposing that gain is godliness, we brought nothing in to this world, and it is certain that we can take nothing out) even denying the Lord that bought them, and bringing upon themselves swift destruction! And many shall follow their pernicious ways; (with trickery, salesmanship, and smooth teachings of easy forgiveness, without true heart rending and soul searching Repentance!) by reason of whom the way of truth shall be evil spoken of. And through covetousness, they shall with feigned words (fast smooth talking) make merchandise of you! (take all your Money!) whose judgment is on the way, and their damnation comes quickly! {2 Peter 2:1- 3} For the time will come when they will not endure sound doctrine, (or humble themselves under God's word and authority) but after their own lust shall heep to themselves teachers, having itching ears! (they will flock to preachers and teachers who cater to their own lusts and sinful desires, and tell them exactly what they want to hear!) And they shall turn away their ears from the truth, and shall be turned unto fables! {2 Timothy 4:3} My Beloved brethren, this is the same reaction and pattern that all of sinful mankind has displayed for thousands of years! (for men loved darkness rather than light!) This is a rebellious people, lying children, children that will not hear the law of the Lord! Which say to the seers, see not; they told the prophet Isaiah, Do not preach unto us right things, (the true word of God) preach unto us smooth things, prophesy deceits!" {Isaiah 30:10} The Holy Spirit warned the Apostle Paul, that in latter times, some people (even believers) would rebel against the True Gospel of Jesus Christ! Rejecting God's control and authority over their lives! (Rebellion is as the sin of witchcraft!) Now the Spirit speaketh expressly, that in latter times some shall depart from the faith, giving heed to seducing spirits, and doctrines of devils! Speaking lies in hypocrisy; having their conscience seared with a hot iron! {1 Timothy 4:1} (becoming numb, with callous, hardened hearts; not caring one bit about their sinful lives, or disobedience to God!) Paul warned in his letter to Timothy, know this; that in the last days perilous times shall come! For men shall be lovers of their own selves, covetous, boasters, proud, blasphemers, disobedient to parents, (and to the laws of God and man!) unthankful, unholy, without natural affection, trucebreakers, false accusers, incontinent, fierce, despisers of those that are good! (does this sound like, to you, some groups in America today, and around the world?) Traitors, heady, highminded, lovers of pleasures more than lovers of God! having a form of godliness but denying the power (control and authority of God) from such turn away! (avoid!) {2 Timothy 3:1} So, my beloved brethren, how can we know and avoid these false preachers and prophets; and wolves in sheep's clothing? Jesus gave us the answer,"You shall know them by their fruits!" (Holy Lives!!!) Every good tree brings forth good fruit, but a corrupt tree brings forth evil fruit!{Matthew 7:15} Does the Pastor and the church live holy, sanctified lives? Or is there sin in the camp, carnality and strife?

The Basics to Live by Every Day!

Brethren, it's easy to act holy and pious for one hour or so in the Church building. But walking in the Spirit with God, Living a Holy, Sanctified Life, Separated unto God, Praying to, communicating with, and Obeying God, and the Holy Spirit; every day ~ 24\7 is completely another matter entirely! Now my beloved brethren, please do not get me wrong, or misunderstand me. I am Not telling you to go to Church, and just start judging the pastor and the congregation; searching and looking for something to find wrong! And say ah ha, I caught ya. No, do not do that! Judge not, that ye be not Judged for what measure ye meet it shall be measured to you again! I am telling you to be just as sweet and loving, as kind and caring as Jesus Is! And Not Judgmental. It is before God that any person stands, and before God that any person falls! Not us! For who art thou to Judge another mans servant? So you don't do or say anything wrong! But Do be alert and aware of your surroundings, and always be sensitive to the Holy Spirit at all Times! Jesus Christ did not warn us to "Beware of wolves in sheep's clothing" for Nothing! Jesus said it in his main teaching, in "the Sermon on the Mountain!" So we must take heed to Jesus warning! My beloved brethren, every single believer has to make sure for themselves, that they are doing God's will! And Living Holy Lives, avoiding all Sin and Iniquity! Praying and Studying God's word, the Holy Bible for themselves! To make sure that they personally know God and the Truth for themselves! So that they are not being taught false doctrines, or lies and deceptions! By false ministers or preachers, and wolves in sheep's clothing! That Paul, and Peter, and our Lord and Savior Jesus Christ Warned Us to Beware of, and Watch Out For! We must strive to enter into the Kingdom of Heaven, because many people will try to enter in, but will not be able! Because broad is the path that leads to destruction, and many people will enter into that path! Because narrow is the way that leads to Life! And only a few people will be able to find it! "Jesus Christ" {Matthew 7:14} For many are called, but few are chosen! And Jesus said we shall know them by their fruits. Do men gather grapes of thorns or figs of thistles? Even so every good tree brings forth good fruit;(a holy life) but a corrupt (or bad) tree brings forth evil Fruit. (a sinful, evil life!) A good tree cannot bring forth evil fruit, neither can a corrupt tree bring forth good fruit. Every tree that does not bring forth good fruit is hewn down, and cast into the fire! Wherefore by their fruits you shall know them!{Matt. 7:15} Now the Fruits of the (Holy) Spirit are these: Love, Joy, Peace, Longsuffering, Gentleness, Goodness, Faith, Meekness, Temperance: against a life with such fruits as these there is no law!{Galatians 5:22} Now the works of the flesh (evil fruit) are these: Adultery, Fornication, Uncleanness, Lasciviousness, Idolatry, Witchcraft, Hatred, Variance, Emulations, Wrath, Strife, Seditions, Heresies, Envyings, Murders, Drunkenness, Revelings, and things like these: which I tell you now! As I have also told you in the past, that the people which Do such things as these, Shall Not Inherit the Kingdom of God! {Galatians 5:19} Know ye not that the unrighteous Shall Not inherit the kingdom of God! Do not be deceived: neither Fornicators, nor Idolaters, nor Adulterers, nor Effeminate - (Homosexuals) not abusers of themselves with mankind! Not Thieves, nor Covetous, Not Drunkards, nor Revilers, nor Extortioners! None of these shall Inherit the Kingdom of God! These are the Evil fruits that Jesus said would be Hewn Down and Cast into the Fire! For an Indepth look, see fruits and works near the back.

Spiritual Warfare

The First and Most Important Rule of Spiritual Warfare is that You Must Be Born Again by The Holy Spirit of Almighty God in Heaven! Born into the body of Jesus Christ through the Holy Spirit, by Faith in The Lamb of God! - Jesus - His Crucifixion on the Cross of Calvary! And His Resurrection from the Dead, Three Days Later! To Reclaim Us, and Reconcile Us to God by his own Blood! By Jesus' Spotless, Blameless, Sacrifice to Almighty God, to Atone for OUR SINS! It is Absolutely Impossible for Any Person who is <u>Not</u> in the Spirit, to see or <u>Enter</u> into The Kingdom of God! To Worship God in the Spirit, or to Fight a Spiritual Enemy on a Spiritual Battlefield; from Your Fleshly Body! It's Impossible! Flesh and Blood <u>Cannot</u> Inherit the Kingdom of God! It is a Spiritual Place! Furthermore, We Do Not Wrestle against Flesh and Blood, but against Principalities and Powers, against the Rulers of the Darkness of this World, against Spiritual Wickedness in High Places! Wherefore take unto You the <u>Whole Armor of God</u>!!! That Ye may be able to withstand against the Wiles and Tricks of the Devil! In these Evil Days! For though we walk in the Flesh, we do not War after the Flesh! For the Weapons of our Warfare are not Carnal, But Mighty through <u>God</u> to the pulling down of Strongholds! Casting Down Imaginations and every high thing that Exalteth Itself against The Knowledge of God! And Bringing into Captivity <u>Every Thought</u> to the Obedience of Christ! Be Strong in the Lord, and in the Power <u>His</u> Might, having your loins girt about with the <u>Truth</u>, having on the Breastplate of righteousness; your feet shod with the gospel of Peace! Above all, taking the Shield of Faith, so ye shall be able to quench all the fiery darts of the Wicked! And take the Helmet of Salvation, and the Sword of the Spirit, which is the Word of God! Praying Always with all Prayer and Supplication in the Spirit! Prayer is <u>Your Lifeline</u>!

Holiness, Prayer, and Spiritual Warfare!

If you are a true child of God, and servant of Jesus Christ; Holiness (living a Holy Sanctified life, truly separated unto God) and Prayer (constant communication and fellowship with God the Father, the Son and the Holy Spirit) and Holy Bible study (the washing and cleansing process of the word of God to transform, renew, and protect your mind!) are absolutely Key and necessary cornerstones of victorious Spiritual Warfare! If you are falling into sin and temptations, you can look back into your life, and the three main root causes are: you have been neglecting 1.- Prayer and not diligently praying and seeking God! (with uninterrupted, heartfelt, quality time!) 2.- Diligently reading, studying, thinking about and meditating on the word of God! (they that wait upon the Lord shall renew their strength! Isaiah 40:31) 3.- You have let the world and fleshly desires get into your heart and steal your affections! God is not the First and foremost love and desire of your heart! If you are spending more time with unbelievers or ungodly evil people, (God will protect you at work) I'm talking about bars, clubs, or ungodly parties! (what fellowship hath darkness with Light? or the sons of God with the children of the devil?) Or you spend hours of your free time, in front of an evil T.V. watching lust filled, gossiping, filth, or listening to worldly foul music that glorify sex and greed! If all of this evil stuff is getting into your heart, mind, and soul, you will never be able to overcome your body's fleshly desires and the old Adam like, sinful nature! Do not be deceived, Evil communications will corrupt good manners! {1 Corinthians 15:33} Be not conformed to this world, but be ye transformed by the renewing of your Mind! {Romans 12:2} Your Mind is the very Front line of the spiritual battlefield, in the fight for Your Soul! When an evil thought or desire first enters into your mind, (Paul called them fiery darts of the wicked) if you cast it out of your mind immediately! It is easier to dispell and overcome, than if you sit there and entertain it and think about it until it gets into your heart and soul. Once it drops into your spirit and gets it's hooks into you, and it starts to inflame your flesh, it will be much more difficult to fight off and overcome! That is why you must "Cast down (evil) imaginations, and every high thing that exalteth itself against the knowledge of God, and bring every thought into captivity to the obedience of Christ! Pulling down every stronghold of evil desire, in your heart and mind, that war against the Soul! {2 Corinthians 10:4} For though we walk in the flesh, we do not war after the flesh! For the weapons of our warfare are not carnal, but mighty through God to the pulling down of those strongholds! Because we do not wrestle against flesh and blood, but against principalities, against powers, against the rulers of the darkness of this world, against spiritual wickedness in high places! {Ephesians 6:10-18} If you let your mind sit, and entertain, and dwell on lustful sexual thoughts or desires until your flesh becomes aroused, you've already allowed a breach in the front lines and lost the first part of the battle! Jesus said that whosoever look's at a woman to lust after her, hath committed adultery with her already in his heart! {Matt. 5:28} The thoughts of the wicked are an abomination to the Lord! The sacrifice of the wicked is abomination how much more, when he bringeth it with a wicked mind!{Proverbs 15:26, 21:27} And not just lustful thoughts; hateful, wrathful, vicious thoughts; covetous, greedy, complaining, bickering, rebellious and violent murderous thoughts! Jesus said, out of the hearts of men, proceed evil thoughts, adulteries and fornications, murders, thefts, covetousness, wickedness, deceit, lasciviousness, an evil eye, blasphemy, pride, lies, foolishness! All these things come from within (the heart) and defile the man! {Mark 7:21}

Holiness, Prayer, and Spiritual Warfare!

The Apostle said, "Pray without ceasing" keep your mind on the Lord. This doesn't mean to speak out loud all day, or talk in tongues for all the world to hear; but pray, and talk to the Lord privately in your heart and mind. A mind that is already engaged in communication with God, is harder to inject with an evil thought or suggestion by anyone, spirit or person! The Bible says, "Be careful for nothing; but in every thing by prayer and supplication with thanksgiving, let your request be made known unto God. And the peace of God, which passeth all understanding, <u>shall keep your hearts and minds</u> through (our Lord) Christ Jesus! Finally, brethren, whatsoever things are true and honest, whatsoever things are just and pure, whatsoever things are lovely and of good report;(spiritual Psalms or hymns and melodies) if there be any virtue, and if there be any praise, think on these things. {Philippians 4:6-8} I can do all things through <u>Christ</u> which strengthens me! Be strong in the Lord, and in the power of his might! Put on <u>the whole armor of God</u>, that ye may be able to stand against the wiles and tricks of the Devil! Be sober, be vigilant; (alert and aware of what is going on around you!) because your adversary the devil, as a roaring lion, walketh about, seeking whom he may devour! Therefore, you <u>must</u> submit yourself unto <u>God</u>! Resist the devil, and he will flee from you! Draw nigh unto God, and **<u>God</u>** <u>will draw nigh unto **You**</u>! Cleanse your hands, ye sinners; and purify your hearts, ye double minded! {1 Peter 5:8 & James 5:7} Walk Holy before God, and keep in constant communication with him through Prayer and supplication! Brethren, the effectual fervent <u>Prayer</u> of a righteous man availeth <u>much</u>; because the eyes of the <u>Lord</u> are over the <u>Righteous</u>, and his ears are open unto their prayers! But the face of the Lord is against them that <u>do evil</u>! {James 5:16, 1 Peter 3:12} My beloved, <u>Your</u> personal relationship with the **One True Living Almighty Jehovah God**, is <u>the most Important Thing</u> that <u>**You will ever do**</u> in your whole <u>entire</u> existence!!! Because if <u>Almighty God</u> is <u>For You</u>, who can prevail against you? **<u>No One!</u> <u>NO!!! ONE!!!</u>** That which **Almighty God** saves, is **<u>Saved Forever!!!</u>** And that which **Almighty God** destroys, is **<u>Destroyed Forever!!!</u>** If **<u>You</u>** are Really a <u>True Child of God</u>, and a <u>Holy Spirit Filled</u>, **Born Again**, <u>Sanctified Believer</u>, that is a <u>Living Breathing Part of **The Body of Christ!**</u> Walking in the <u>Spirit</u>, through <u>Faith</u> and <u>Obedience</u> to our Lord and Savior **Jesus Christ!!!** Covered by his <u>**Grace**</u> and **Blood** through adoption by our Father God, whereby we cry **<u>Abba Father</u>**, and you are sealed by the **Holy Spirit** of promise, who is the proof of our Inheritance until the day of redemption! **<u>No One</u>** can <u>ever</u> take you <u>out</u> of **<u>Almighty God's Awesome Hands!!!</u>** Only You!!! Can destroy <u>Yourself!!!</u> By Jumping out of God's Hands, and Will, and <u>Eternal plan for your Soul!</u> By <u>Sin</u> and <u>Rebellion!!!</u> But if you <u>Love</u> and <u>Obey</u> **God**, his son **Jesus**, and the **Holy Spirit**! (these three are <u>One</u>! - 1 John 5:7) <u>No Weapon formed against **You**</u> can ever prosper!{Isaiah 54:17} Here are the words spoken by Jesus, My sheep hear <u>my voice</u>, and <u>I know them</u>, and <u>they follow me</u>! And I give unto them <u>eternal life</u>; and they <u>shall never perish</u>, neither shall any man pluck them <u>out of my hand</u>! My Father, which gave them to me, is <u>Greater than All</u>! And **No Man** is able to pluck them **Out of my Father's Hand!!!** (No One) **<u>I and my Father are One!!!</u>** "Jesus Christ" {John 10:28} We have an inheritance incorruptible, and undefiled, and that fadeth not away, reserved in heaven for you! Who **<u>are kept by the power of GOD</u>** through **Faith** unto **Salvation**, ready to be revealed in the last time! {1 Peter 1:4} **"Hallelujah!!!!!!!"**

Holiness, Prayer, and Spiritual Warfare!

Praise the Mighty Lord Jesus!!! This is one of my favorite verses in the whole Bible! **We Are Kept! BY THE POWER OF GOD!!!** The Most Powerful Being in the Whole Entire Universe!!! In All of Existence!!! **Not** by my own puny, pitiful, helpless efforts, of earthly, filthy rags; of Flesh and Dust! But **I AM SAVED BY GRACE**, through **FAITH**, and **NOT by my OWN WORKS**, or puny efforts! It is **The Gift of Almighty GOD** that I am Saved and washed clean by **JESUS Holy Precious Blood!** Because No Flesh shall glory in **God's Holy Awesome Presence!!!** (Least of all me!) That is why, as I read the Scripture, Joy and Praise, burst through my heart and soul and spirit! Listen again carefully, as I quote it closely, and personally. **I AM KEPT** (ME!) **BY THE POWER OF ALMIGHTY GOD** (the **One True Living God** of all Creation, The All Powerful **Father in Heaven** of Truth and Light!) And I AM KEPT by MY FATHER GOD through **FAITH** (in his **Son Jesus**) unto **Salvation!!!** The Salvation of your very Soul! To a place Reserved in Heaven for You! That fadeth Not Away! Beloved, It is YOUR **FAITH IN GOD**, and God's Holy Son **JESUS**, and **JESUS'S RESURRECTION** from the Dead! **THAT LEAD TO YOUR SALVATION!** Nothing Else But **YOUR FAITH!!!** Remember what Jesus told Jarius, a ruler of the synagogue, the man whose daughter was sick, and after he spoke to Jesus about her, the servants came and told the man,"do not trouble the Master any further, because the child is dead" Jesus immediately told the man, **"DO NOT FEAR, ONLY BELIEVE !!!** And she shall be made whole!" The same principal holds true for us today! No matter what problem is facing you, in your life, **Always Trust in God!!!** Take your eyes off of the tiny ant hill that is facing you, and Look at the **Almighty Jehovah God** that **Towers over the Whole Universe!!!** Our Faith in God, will cover us with his Grace! Not only for our short lifespan here on earth, but for All of Eternity! So many people, when they die, they think, That's It! Beloved, we will all die in this fleshly body. Flesh is dust, and will only last for a short time! But your Soul is Eternal, Your Soul will Last for all of Eternity!!! If you will study the **Holy Bible**, You will Learn the Truth! That it is appointed for each man once to die, and then he must face the Judgment Seat of Jesus Christ! To answer for all the deeds that we did in our bodies, and the words spoken out of our mouth! We will all die once! But the Children of God, who have been **Born Again**, into **The Body of Jesus Christ!** All those, whose names are written into **The Book of Life**, will not take part in the second death, or be cast into the **Lake of Fire!** {Rev 20:14} Your short lifespan on this earth is only temporary! Your Personal Relationship with God and Jesus is Much More Important than **ANYTHING ~ ELSE!!!** Your house will be a pile of rubble one day! Your car or truck will be in a junk yard, or crushed, recycled metal! Your gold or Jewelry will be in some body else's hands or pockets! Your body will be in a box in the ground, or cremated ashes! But, **You - MUST - And WILL STAND BEFORE THE JUDGMENT SEAT OF ALMIGHTY GOD!** We All Must stand at the Judgment Seat of Jesus Christ!!! {2 Corinthians 5:10} You, Me, Everyone!!! **THERE ARE NO EXCEPTIONS!!!** When You kneel at the feet of Holy Holy Holy Almighty God! And **The Truth** is staring you in the face, will you cry,"what have I done?" Why I did focus my whole Life here on the Earth; and neglect, ignore, and miss out on Heaven for all of Eternity? "How shall we escape, if we neglect so **Great a Salvation**; which was spoken by the Lord Jesus!" {Hebrews 2:1- 3}

Holiness, Prayer, and Spiritual Warfare!

How will you escape the wrath of God, if you just basically spit in Jesus face, and callously ignore his Great and Awesome Sacrifice to **Save Your Soul**! And just throw Jesus in the garbage can, and ignore his pain and suffering on the Cross of Calvary, where he shed his precious blood to set **YOU FREE!!!** By your own actions you are saying,"I couldn't care less about what Jesus did to save me!" I don't care about God or Jesus, or spending all of Eternity **In Heaven with them!** Why would I want to go to Heaven with God who Gave Me Life, and have peace, and joy, and happiness, for all of **ETERNITY?** When I can lie, cheat, steal, get drunk, do drugs, watch lots of evil vile filth, on the internet and T.V. Commit adultery, fornication, and homosexuality, hate, cuss, and fight with all the drunken devils that I really enjoy screaming at, and fighting with; for the 50 or so, short years, I might live on this earth! Why would I want to enjoy All of Eternity with God, when I can Burn in Hell with my enemy Satan, and be tormented forever, in the **Lake of Fire**, Instead? Maybe a better question would be, "Have you Pickled your brain with alcohol or drugs," if that is your choice? The Apostle Paul, Gave us all a very grave and serious warning in Hebrews, he wrote, "Therefore leaving the principles of the doctrine of Christ, let us go on to perfection; not laying again the foundation of repentance from dead works, and of faith towards God. Of the doctrine of baptisms, laying on of hands, resurrection of the dead, and of Eternal Judgment. And this will we do, If God Permit! For it is impossible for those who were once enlightened, and have tasted of the heavenly gift, and were made partakers of the Holy Ghost. And have tasted the good word of God, and the powers of the world to come. If they shall fall away, to renew them again unto repentance; seeing they crucify to themselves the son of God afresh, and put him to an open shame! For the earth which drinketh in the rain that cometh oft upon it, and bringeth forth herbs meet for them by whom it is dressed, receiveth blessing from God. But that which beareth thorns and briars is rejected, and is nigh unto cursing; whose end is to be burned! But my beloved, we are persuaded better things of you, and things that accompany salvation, thus we speak. For God is not unrighteous to forget your work and labor of love, which ye have shewed towards his name, in that ye have (loved) and do minister to the saints.{Hebrews 6:1-10} Also in the 1st chapter of Proverbs shows us the true rewards of Loving God, and the Dangers of ignoring God! Here are some choice verses, To know wisdom and instruction; to perceive the words of understanding; to receive the instruction of wisdom, justice, judgement, and equity; To give knowledge and discretion. A wise man will hear, and will increase learning; and a man of understanding shall attain unto wise councils. The fear of the Lord is the beginning of knowledge: but fools despise wisdom and instruction; How long, ye simple ones, will ye love simplicity? and the scorners delight in their scorning, and fools hate knowledge? Turn you at my reproof; so I will pour out my spirit unto you, I will make my words known unto you. Because I have called, and ye refused me; I have stretched out my hand and no man regarded. But ye have set at nought all my council, and would none of my reproof. I will also laugh at your calamity; I will mock when your fear cometh as desolation, and your destruction cometh as a whirlwind; when distress and anguish come upon you. Then shall they call upon me, but I will not answer; they shall seek me, but they shall not find me! Because they hated knowledge, and they did not choose the **Fear of the Lord!** They choose to ignore God and would not hear his warnings, so now they will reap what they sowed!!!

Holiness, Prayer, and Spiritual Warfare!

So, as much as (the Fire of God) is in me! I am ready to preach the Gospel to all of the world! Because I am <u>not ashamed</u> of the Gospel of Jesus Christ; for it is the <u>Power of God unto Salvation</u> to every one that <u>Believeth</u>! For therein is the righteousness of God revealed from faith to faith; as it is written, The <u>Just shall **Live by Faith**</u>! And it <u>must</u> be clearly understood, that it is **Only "By Your Faith" in Jesus Christ**, the "only begotten <u>Son of God</u>!" His <u>Sacrifice on the Cross as a sin offering and atonement</u>, to **Almighty God the Father**, for all of mankind's sins! And <u>Jesus Resurrection from the Dead</u> on the Third Day! It is <u>only by</u> **FAITH IN JESUS ~ THAT YOU ARE SAVED!!!** Because you are saved <u>By **Grace** through **Faith**</u> and <u>Not by Works</u>; least any man should boast! You <u>cannot</u>, <u>did not</u>, and will never be able <u>to save yourself!</u> **IT IS THE GIFT OF GOD!!** Least <u>any man should boast</u>, because **No Flesh will Ever glory in Almighty God's ~ Holy ~Awesome ~ Omnipotent ~ Presence !!!!!!!** Believe it! The Puny Human mind, can't even comprehend the all seeing, all knowing, all powerful, <u>Universe Creating Presence ~ That is</u> **The One True Living Jehovah GOD MOST HIGH!!!** Period! The Holiness, Purity, and Omnipotent Power of Almighty God, is <u>Far Beyond the mental faculties</u> and <u>human cognizance</u> of the tiny speck of dust that is man! **God** walks in area's and realms of Holiness and purity that can <u>only be comprehended through the **Holy Spirit**</u>! And the <u>Mind Expanding</u>, <u>Truth Revealing Revelation</u>, that can <u>only</u> be found in the undescribable, pride destroying, and soul changing presence; of the **One True Living Jehovah God Most High!!!** "For as the heavens are higher than the earth, so are my ways higher than your ways and my thoughts higher than your thoughts"{Isaiah 55:9} So that your faith should not stand in the wisdom of men, but in the power of God! Howbeit, we speak wisdom among them that are perfect; yet not the wisdom of the this world, nor of the princes of this world, that come to naught! But we speak the wisdom of God in a mystery, even the hidden wisdom, which God ordained before the world! For as it is written, "Eye hath not seen, nor ear heard, neither have entered into the heart of man, the things which God hath prepared for <u>them that Love him</u>! But God hath revealed them unto us by his <u>Spirit</u>; for the Spirit searcheth all things, yea, the deep things of God! Even so, no man can know the things of God, but by the Spirit of God! We have not received the spirit of the world, but the Holy Spirit of God; (when you are born again) that we might know the things that are freely given to us by God! Which things we also speak of, not in the words which man's wisdom teacheth, but which the Holy Ghost teacheth; comparing spiritual things with spiritual. But the natural man does not receive the things of the spirit of God; for they are foolishness unto him! Neither can he know them, because they are spiritually discerned. But he that is spiritual judgeth all things, yet he himself is judged of no man. For who hath known the mind of the lord, that he may instruct him? But we have the mind of Christ! {1 Corinthians 2:5-16} Wherefore, let this mind be in you, that was also in Christ Jesus; who made himself of no reputation, and took upon him the form of a servant! Our Lord Jesus humbled himself, and became obedient unto death; even the death of the cross! And when he had offered up prayers and supplications with strong crying and tears unto him that was able to save him from death; and was heard in that he feared! God's son learned obedience by the things which he suffered! Being made perfect, he became the author of Eternal Salvation unto all them that obey him!

Holiness, Prayer, and Spiritual Warfare!

Beloved, the first steps in obeying Jesus, is to Truly Believe and acknowledge that **Jesus is God** in the Flesh! Accept **Jesus Christ** as your Lord, (the only one in command and control) and your Savior! The only one who saved you, paid the price for your sins, (he was wounded for our transgressions and bruised for our iniquities, and by his stripes we are healed) washed you clean with his Precious, Holy, Blood; clothed us in a spotless white wedding garment, and made us accepted into the Holy Family of our Father God in Heaven! Invite the Holy Spirit into your heart and soul forever, and ask him to take full and complete control of your life! Especially the area's that you find difficult to give up control of, and can't relinquish on your own accord! (If you truly and sincerely mean it, he will do it!) Then obey him when he tells you how, and what, to do! Crucify your fleshly desires, by denying yourself, pick up your cross every day and follow Jesus! Live a Holy, Godly Life; by drawing nigh unto God, (and God will draw nigh unto you!) Walk with God, by establishing a daily, truly, heartfelt and sincere (diligent) **Prayer Life**; To form a close, Personal Relationship with our **Father God**, his son **Jesus Christ**, and the **Holy Spirit**! (these 3 are one, and the only members of the Godhead!) Ask and ye shall receive, seek and ye shall find, knock and it shall be opened unto you! "Jesus Christ" Establish a daily habit of Bible study, for the daily washing and cleansing of your soul and the renewing of your Mind! (This is done by daily **Prayer** and **Bible Study**!) As Jesus said, "Ye shall know the Truth, and the Truth shall **MAKE YOU FREE!!!** This is absolutely Crucial for your **Spiritual Life** and Successful, Victorious **Spiritual Warfare!!!** Your **Prayer Life** is like the oxygen your spirit needs to breathe to **Live**, and is only found through Prayer, Communication, and Fellowship with **God**! And Studying **The Holy Bible** very diligently, by memorizing, contemplating, and thinking about Scripture verses;(and then applying them to your life!) is the Food and nourishment **Your Spirit Needs TO LIVE!!!** (not to mention that The Holy Bible is **Your Sword in the Spirit** to fight off your enemy, and **The Helmet of Salvation** to Protect your Mind from all the Devils Lies, that he will definitely throw at you constantly! (Lies are one of Satan's Main Weapons to confuse, weaken, and discourage You!) But if You Know and Study the Holy Scripture Diligently, Every Day; You will recognize the lies, and cast them out of your Mind Like Jesus did! And you won't get confused or disoriented, they will be deflected off of your helmet of Salvation, and bounce off of your Shield if Faith! (in God's Holy Word) A Soldier that doesn't know when, where, or how to Fight, and charges in the Wrong Direction; is not only useless, but dangerous! And a Dead Soldier can't do anything at all! Brethren, If you don't give your spirit Life giving Oxygen it needs through **Prayer to God!!!** And you don't Feed your Spirit the Food and nutrients it Needs, by **Studying The Holy Bible**, the soul cleansing washing of the word, and the renewing of your mind!!! Beloved, If You Starve Your Spiritual Man of Life Giving **Prayer** and **Bible Study**, it will **Get Weak** and **Eventually Die!!!** A Weakened Spirit can't Fight off the Enemy's attack's of Sin and Temptation! And a Dead Spirit can't Fight off Anything at All! Much less wield the sword of the Spirit, Pray Down Holy Fire, Scatter the Enemy, Set the Captives Free, and Tear Down the **Gates of Hell!** Which Jesus said, "would **Not Prevail Against Us!!!**" It was King Solomon that said, "A Living Dog is Better than A Dead Lion!" So Pray to God, and Study the Bible, and the gates of hell will not prevail against You!

Holiness, Prayer, and Spiritual Warfare!

Beloved, at this point I want to talk to you about a subject that most Preachers never talk about! But it is a most important issue, (and absolutely necessary) if you want to walk in True Holiness with God! Jesus taught us directly on this subject, and I've mentioned verses already. But now, we'll look deeply into the subject, and I'll show you some scripture that most Preachers will never dare to touch or cover! But I Fear God to much, to not teach and cover every word and Precept of the Full Gospel of God! And that is the subject we will study, **The Fear of God**! Proverbs says that the fear of God is the beginning of wisdom, knowledge and understanding! But fools despise wisdom and instruction! {Prov. 1:7, 9:10} Jesus taught us, "Do not fear them which kill the body, but are not able to kill the soul; but "**Fear Him**" which is able to **Kill both Body and SOUL in HELL!!!** (Yea, I say unto you, **Fear Almighty God!**) {Matthew 10:28 & Luke 12:5} The Apostle Paul said, "always obeying (God), to work out your own Salvation with Fear and Trembling!" {Philippians 2:12} & "Let us cleanse ourselves from all filthiness of the flesh and spirit, Perfecting Holiness in the **Fear of God!** {2 Corinthians 7:1} Now, let me also say clearly, "**God Loves You ~ and ~God is Love!**" God created you to be his child in heaven forever **With Him!!!** For God so loved the world that he gave us his only begotten son, Jesus Christ; so that whosoever would Believe in him should not perish but have Everlasting Life! {John 3:16} God created a way (one way), for every person on earth to go to heaven! That Way is **Jesus Christ**! (Jesus is God) I Am the Way, the Truth, and the Life; No man cometh unto the Father (God) **But by Me!** {John 14:6} There is No other Way in existence, to get into Heaven! God made a way for us, because He Loves us! The Big Problem is **Man Doesn't Love God!!!** "Men loved darkness rather than light, because their Deeds (and Hearts) were Evil! {John 3:19} That is the Problem, in the hearts of Men, Men love Evil!!! Men love wickedness and Sin, Lying, Stealing, Cussing, Drunkenness, Murder, Adultery, Fornication, Homosexuality, Gossip, Blasphemy, Rape, Hatred, Fighting, Rebellion, Wars, **Mankind Loves Evil!!!** Here's a Memo and a Clue to the Whole Entire World! **ALMIGHTY GOD DESTROYS ALL EVIL! Period!** Will you Not Fear **Almighty Jehovah God!** God, can and will, **Cast You into Hell Forever!** You Cannot Fight God! You have a better chance, to Jump onto the Sun, and **Put it Out with Spit!!!** Than to try to Fight and Resist, the One True Living God! "Hear now this, O foolish people, and with out understanding; which have eyes, and see not; which have ears, and hear not; **FEAR YE NOT ME!** Saith, **The Lord God!!!** Will ye not tremble at my Presence?" {Jeremiah 5:21} Will ye not heed MY Warning? "Behold, All Souls are Mine! The soul of the father, so also the soul of the son is Mine! The Soul that Sinneth, **It Shall Die!!!**" {Ezekiel 18:4} For if God spared not the angels that sinned, which kept not their first estate, but left their own habitation; and cast them down to hell, and delivered them in everlasting chains under darkness, to be reserved unto the great judgment day!-2 Peter 2:4, Jude 1:6 And Destroyed Sodom and Gomorrah, and the cities around them who gave themselves to fornication, going after strange flesh, (homosexuality) and are set forth as an example,(of what God will do to evil) Suffering the Vengance of Eternal Fire! As I live, sayeth the Lord God, I have no pleasure in the death of the wicked; but that he turn from his evil way and live; turn ye from your evil ways, for why will ye die? Cast away from you all of your sins, make you a new heart and spirit, for why will ye die?{Ez.33}

Holiness, Prayer, and Spiritual Warfare!

Wash you, make you clean; put away the evil of your doings from before mine eyes, cease to do evil! Learn to do good, seek judgment, relieve the oppressed, help the fatherless, and plead for the widow. Come now, and let us reason together, saith the Lord; although your sins be as scarlet, they shall be as white as snow; though they be as crimson, they shall be as wool. If ye be willing and obedient, ye shall eat the good of the land! But if ye refuse and rebel; Ye shall be devoured with the sword; (destroyed) for the mouth of the Lord hath spoken it! {Isaiah 2:16} God wants and desires for You to go to him in Prayer, and Repent from your sins, transgressions, and iniquities; so **He can Forgive You** and **Wash You Clean** in Jesus holy, precious, Blood! Jesus said, if there is one sheep that is lost, will you not go in the wilderness and search for it? And when he hath found it, he will lay it on his shoulders rejoicing. Even so, there is more Joy in Heaven, when one lost soul repents, and is found and saved! Than over 99 souls who were not lost, and needed no repentance. Translation,God really, truly wants to save you; and deliver you from Evil, Hell, and Destruction! In another parable, Jesus told about a woman who lost a piece of silver, and she searched diligently with a candle, and swept the house until she found it! And she called her friends and neighbors together, saying, rejoice with me, for I found the piece that was lost! Likewise I say unto you, there is joy in the presence of the angels of God over one sinner that repenteth! {Luke 15:4-10} Beloved, God, Really wants to save You! But if the sheep that is lost in the wilderness, runs away, when he hears the shepherd calling for him, how will he ever be saved? If he keeps running away from the one who can save him,(Jesus) He will be lost forever! In Jesus's parable about the prodigals son,{Luke 15:11-32} the rebellious son had to come to his senses, and realize that he was the one that was perishing! (and heading towards hell} When he said to himself, all my Fathers servants have food, (and every thing they really need) while I starve and hunger (for spiritual food and true peace) out in the wilderness of sin!(headed towards hell) Then, when he finally (turned the switch in his brain to the **ON** position) and went to his Father God, his Father ran out to to embrace him, and fell into his arms with tears! He found out his Father Loved Him, and wanted him there All The Time! Sadly, the world is full of people who refuse to believe, People who love sin and evil, People who will not humble themselves and Go sincerely to God in Prayer, and **LET JESUS SAVE THEIR SOULS!** The Apostle Paul told Timothy, the Holy Spirit speaketh expressly; in the last times, some shall depart from the Faith, giving heed to evil seducing spirits, and doctrines of devils! Speaking lies in hypocrisy; having their conscience seared with a hot iron!(being so evil that their sins no longer bother or convict them, but they now sin joyfully and willingly! Without one single twinge of remorse or discomfort in their hellbound evil souls!) {1 Timothy 4:1} Know this also, that in the Last Days perilous times shall come! For men shall be lovers of their own selves, covetous, boasters, proud, blasphemers,disobedient to parents, unthankful, unholy; without natural affection, trucebreakers, falce accusers, incontinent (or never satisified with what they have), fierce, despisers of those that are good; traitors, highminded,(full of pride) and lovers of pleasures more than **Lovers of God**!{2 Timothy 3:1} Ye sinful nation, a people laden with iniquity, a seed of evildoers, who've forsaken the lord and provoked almighty God to anger! People whose understanding is darkened, being alienated from the life of God, through the ignorance that is in them, because of the blindness of their heart! Who have given themselves over to their sins!

Holiness, Prayer, and Spiritual Warfare!

For the Wrath of God is revealed from heaven, against all ungodliness and all unrighteousness of men! Who hold the truth in unrighteousness! Because that which may be known of God is manifest in them; for God hath shewed it unto them! (you were born with a good conscience that you severed and burned through with the hot iron of sin) For the invisible things of him (God) from the creation of the world are clearly seen, being understood by the things that are made, even his Eternal Power and Godhead!!! So that they (mankind) are without excuse, because that when they knew God, they did not glorify him **as God!** Neither were they thankful (to the very God who gave them life and understanding); but men became vain in their imaginations, and their foolish heart was darkened! (when you choose sin and evil not only does your Heart become darkened; that darkness Blinds Your Eyes, and Deafens Your Ears, so that you cannot See the light, or Hear the Truth! (Prayer and True Repentance are the only remedy) (The wages of Sin is Death! Now and Forever!) Professing themselves to be wise, they **became fools!** And (man in his darkened mind) changed the glory of **the Uncorruptible God**, into an image made like to corruptible man or animals! (and worshiped them instead) Wherefore God also gave them up to uncleanness through the lusts of their own hearts, to dishonour their own bodies between themselves! Man, who changed the Truth of God into a lie, and worshiped the creature (themselves) more than the Creator, (Almighty God) who is blessed forever! Amen! For this cause God gave them up (and turned them over) unto **Vile Affections**! (if you choose sin over God, he will let you have your hearts desire; and you will make yourself a slave to that sin!) (For whosoever committeth sin is the servant of sin!) And being given over to those vile affections, even the women did change the natural use of their body unto that which is against nature! (Lesbians) And likewise also the men, leaving the natural use of the woman, burned with lust one towards another; Men with Men! (homosexual gays) working that which is unseemly, and receiving in themselves that recompense of their error which was meet.'well deserved' (it is an evil vile, filthy-abomination, to take the precious seed, made in the likeness and image of God! and given only to mankind, to destroy it in human excrement! And I absolutely guarantee you, that you will **severely regret it**, when you stand before **Almighty God**!) And even as they did not like to retain God in their knowledge, God gave them over to a reprobate mind! (cast off and rejected by God) To do those things which are not convenient; being filled with all unrighteousness, fornication, wickedness, covetousness, maliciousness; full of envy, murder, debate, deceit, malignity; whisperers, backbiters, Haters of God, despiteful, proud, boasters, inventors of Evil things, disobedient to parents; without understanding, covenant breakers, without natural affection, implacable, unmerciful! Who knowing the Judgment of God, that they which commit such things are **worthy of Death**! They not only continue to do the same things; but they have pleasure in those (sinful, evil deeds and lifestyles) as they do them! {Romans 1:18-32}"Ye are of your father the devil, and the lusts of your father ye will do!"{John 8:44} Do not be deceived, **God is not mocked**;(scoffed, ridiculed, or to be toyed with, God will destroy you) For whatsoever a man soweth, (the deeds that you do) that shall he also **Reap**! (you will receive the reward or punishment, for those deeds) For he that soweth to his flesh, shall of the flesh reap corruption; but he that soweth to the Spirit! Shall of the Spirit (of God), **Reap Everlasting Life!!!** {Galatians 6:7}

Holiness, Prayer, and Spiritual Warfare!

Who knoweth the power of thine anger? Even according to thine **fear**, so is thy **wrath**!{Psalms 90:11} One thing needs to be made crystal clear! From the foundation of the world, Almighty God has always Destroyed Evil; and those evil men, or evil spirits, who hated, rebelled and fought against him! Those who **refuse** to accept the Permanent, Infinite, Unchanging, Eternal Fact, that **Almighty God**,"is", was, and always **will be**, in complete command and control of the Entire Universe; Are Eternally Doomed! God made it, God owns it, and God controls it! Period! Almighty God made you, God owns you, and God control's what will happen to you, even if you don't believe it, you are just going to find out the hard way! Just as the **Mighty Lord Jesus** said, "Thine is the Kingdom, and the Power, and the Glory!" Forever and Ever! What kingdom, All kingdoms, in heaven and earth, of men and angels! What power, All Power! What glory, All Glory! This Fact **will never Change!!!** And if You choose to do Evil and fight against Holy Almighty God, You Will Lose! Always remember, my dearly beloved, the fact that **Almighty God has always saved** those who love and obey him! Who do what is good, right, fair, just, true, holy, kind, peaceful, loving and merciful, godly and righteous! **God Loves and Protects** his own Children! And they will Live with him Forever in Heaven! But, if you offend one of these little ones that believe in me;(God's children) "it were better for him that a millstone were hanged about his neck, and that he were drowned in the depths of the sea! So to all those who offend, and hurt God's children; He cast upon them the fierceness of his anger, wrath, indignation, and trouble; by sending Evil Angels among them! He made a way for his anger; he spared not their soul from death, but gave their life over to the pestilence! And Smote all the Firstborn in Egypt, of their chief strength. But God made **his own** people to go forth like sheep, and Guided them in the wilderness like a flock! (my sheep hear my voice I know them, and they Follow me!"Jesus Christ") And He Led Them on safely, so that they feared not! And He brought them to the border of his sanctuary, which His Right Hand, (**Jesus**) had Purchased! (for ye are bought with a price: therefore glorify God in your body, and in your spirit, which are God's) {Psalms 78:49 & 1 Corinthians 6:20} "The mercy of the Lord is from everlasting to everlasting, Upon them that **Fear Him**, and his righteousness unto children's children; to such as keep his Covenant, and to those that Remember **His Commandments** to **Do Them**! The Lord hath prepared his Throne in the Heavens; and his Kingdom Ruleth over All! For as the heaven is high above the earth, so great is his mercy towards them that fear him!{Psalms 103:11-19} our Father God has mercy on and helps all who love and fear Him! What exactly does it mean, to Fear the Lord? The Fear of the Lord is **to Hate Evil**!, and pride, and arrogance, and the evil way! (lying, stealing, murdering, malice, Adultery, Fornication, Homosexuality, and all Sin!) and the Froward mouth do I Hate! {Proverbs 8:13} Gossip, Slander, Lies, cursing, wickedness, insulting, defaming others, blasphemy, filthy jokes, evil speaking, hatred, greed! The Fear of the Lord is to Depart from Evil! I want to clarify this one point, God's purpose, when he tells you to fear him; is not to make you scared of him! God wants you to love him! (the 1st command) The reason God wants you to Fear Him, is so that you **Will Not Do** or commit **Evil Deeds** that will get you **Destroyed on Judgment Day!!!** Because God Loves You! Therefore, the **Fear of the Lord** is for **Your Eternal Well Being** and **Your Salvation!** The Fear of the Lord is Life and Health to your Soul!

Holiness, Prayer, and Spiritual Warfare!

The things that You do and the Life that you Live here on this earth, will result in one, of the only two options. You will either draw closer to God, or get farther away from God! (Draw nigh unto God, and he will draw nigh unto you) You will either get hotter and more on fire for God, or your heart will get colder and more callous and hardened toward God, and the things of God! There is no middle ground! Jesus said,"He that is not with me is against me, and he that gathereth not with me, scattereth abroad." {Matt. 12:30} Many people think that they can be neutral, but if you Stand There and watch a house burn, and **Do Nothing**, you are guilty of doing nothing to help a burning soul! (to him that knoweth to do good, and he does not do it, it is sin! James 4:17) Jesus said, in Revelations,"I know thy works, that thou are neither hot or cold, I would that thou wert hot or cold. so then because you are lukewarm, and neither hot or cold, I will spue thee out of my mouth! (reject you) {Rev.3:15} I ask you this question, if you were adrift on the ocean and could see land, why would you not "immediately" start paddling or swimming towards Salvation? If you were caught in a forest fire, and could feel the heat, you would run for your Life towards Safety! So, Why aren't You Running towards **Jesus at Full Speed?** Why aren't You crying out to God in Prayer "every single day"? **Only Jesus Christ Can Save Your Soul!** My Dearly beloved, **the Fire's of Hell** await Sinful Wicked Souls! Believe It, **It is Absolutely TRUE!** Jesus Warned Us out of his own mouth,"If thine eye, hand, or foot, offend thee; **Remove it from thee!** It is better for thee to Enter into the Kingdom of God, with one eye, one hand, or one foot; than having two, and be **Cast into Hell Fire!!!** (that shall never be quenched) {Mark 9:43-47} My beloved, **Jesus** is telling you that **hell** is actually a **real place**, and he is stressing how important IT IS TO REMOVE every single besetting sin from your life and lifestyle! And anything that would keep you out of God's Kingdom! Would you trade your life on earth, for a single grain of sand? Or your whole entire family for a penny? Then why would you give up something so precious as **Eternal life in Heaven with God** For Almost **Nothing**??? (a few pitiful sins!) I'll even give you the answer and tell you why! You don't **Really Believe** (in your heart of hearts) **That It's TRUE!** Most people go to church,"just incase" there is a "God" or "a Heaven", Just to be safe; but they don't really"**Live their Life**" like **There is a God!!!** That is the True Root of the problem, **You** can't Tremble with Godly Fear and Reverence to Almighty God; who You are not **Absolutely Positive Really Exist!!!** And you can't find out that **Almighty God DOES EXIST** without the Faith to Believe It's TRUE! And the courage, strength, and sheer Audacity to Go to God in Prayer and fasting; go boldly to the throne of Grace!{Hebrews 4:16} and **Lay Hold of the Horns on God's Altar** and Tell God, **I Refuse To "LET GO" and "I WILL NOT GO AWAY" "UNTIL YOU REVEAL YOURSELF TO ME**, and "**SHOW ME YOUR AWESOME GLORY!**" That is where I (your humble servant) come in, to Testify **The TRUTH of What God has shown me!** God took me **into Heaven** one night after Prayer! I didn't know what was about to happen, I was just Praying and Worshiping God like I always Do! Because I love him, The next thing I realize is that I'm standing in Heaven! Looking into, and actually touching the Crystal Clear Living Water that sparkles like diamonds, flowing from the Throne of God! And many other things, it was the most **Awesome Experience** in my entire Life! And I am Telling You and Guarantee that **God and Heaven Are Real!**

Holiness, Prayer, and Spiritual Warfare!

Now, dearly beloved, we are going to look at the Fatal, and Deadly consequences of Not Fearing the **Lord God Almighty!** And the Terrible, Eternal Consequences of making Almighty God your Enemy! Because many people don't really, diligently, study the bible; or have a real personal relationship with God! Their understanding and perception of God, is based on second hand precepts of men, taught by lukewarm, blind preachers, desiring to be teachers of the law; understanding neither what they say, nor whereof they affirm. Which have swerved off course, and turned away from the Truth to vain jangling! {1 Tim. 1:6, Isaiah 29:13} (if the blind lead the blind, they shall both fall into the ditch! "Jesus Christ") Ye blind guides, which strain at a gnat, (tiny insect) and swallow a camel! Woe unto you, scribes and Pharisees, hypocrites! For ye pay tithes, but have omitted the weightier (more important) matters of the Law; **Judgment**, **Mercy**, and **Faith!** These Ye ought to **Have Done** also! **"Jesus"** {Matthew 23:23} Beloved, You absolutely **MUST** have **YOUR OWN PERSONAL RELATIONSHIP WITH GOD!!!** There is **No Substitute** that can **Ever Replace God in Your Life! Without GOD YOU ARE DEAD!** Even the most Godly Preacher or Pastor, that teaches 100% percent of the **Holy Bible** truth, can **never Replace God in your life! NO ONE** can ever influence, change, cleanse your soul or Guide Your Life like the **HOLY SPIRIT** can! No one can open up your mind to the Scriptures and give you revelations out of the **Bible**, like the Holy Spirit! No one can make God as Real to you as the Holy Spirit, because **the Holy Spirit IS GOD!** A **Living Member of the GODHEAD**, and part of **the HOLY TRINITY!** God the Father, God the Son, (Jesus Christ) and God the Holy Spirit! (these three are One! 1 John 5:7) Do ye not know and understand that **You are the Temple of God**, and that the **Spirit of God dwelleth IN YOU**? And if **Any Man** defile **The Temple of God, God shall Destroy him**! {1 Corinthians 3:16} Only by being in the Actual Presence of the One True Living God; can enlighten, and reveal to you the Earthshaking, and Pride Destroying, Awesome Power of God! That can transfer the True Fear of God into **Your Soul**, that helps to anchor you to the rock solid foundation,(**Jesus**) and to sustain Your Soul! That is the only possible way that you can,"as ye receive Christ Jesus, walk ye in him" because he lives **Inside You**! Without the Fear of God, you are actually blind to the Wrath of God, because your mind and soul cannot perceive (or truly understand the danger) if you are Spiritually Dead! (not Born Again) There's a Fearful example in the old Testament, of how evil and wickedness can make you completely dumb and blind to the **Wrath and Judgment** of **Almighty God** against Your Soul! There was a very wicked King named Ahab, who married a very wicked woman named Jezebel! (her wickedness was so legendary that to this day, evil women are called "Jezebel") "In the 38th year of King Asa's reign over Judah; King Ahab the son of Omri, began his reign over Israel. And King Ahab reigned over Israel in Samaria 22 years. And King Ahab did more evil in the sight of the Lord (God) than all the kings which were before him! Not only did King Ahab continue to walk in (keep doing) the sins of King Jeroboam, King Ahab took as his wife, Jezebel; the daughter of Eth'baal, the King of the Zidonians, and went and served Baal, and **worshipped him!** And he reared up an altar for Baal in the house of Baal, which he had built in Samaria. And Ahab made a grove;(a place to worship Baal) and Ahab did more to provoke the Lord God of Israel to anger than all the Kings of Israel that were before him! {1 Kings 16:29-33}

Holiness, Prayer, and Spiritual Warfare!

Now there was a certain man named Naboth the Jezreelite, (a good man) who had a vineyard in Jezreel that was right by the palace of King Ahab. And Ahab spake unto Naboth, saying, give me thy vineyard that I may have it for a garden of herbs, because it is near to my house; and I will give you for it a even better vineyard. Or if it seem good to thee, I will give thee the worth of it in money. And Naboth said to Ahab, The <u>Lord Forbid</u> it me, that I should give the inheritance of my fathers unto thee. (The Devil wants to <u>take</u> our inheritance in heaven, that is given to us by our Heavenly Father God; so the evil one will always <u>lie</u>, and say <u>he</u> will give you something <u>better</u>; do <u>not</u> believe him, all Satan can give you is <u>Death</u>!) And Ahab came into his house heavy and displeased, because of the words that Naboth had spoken unto <u>him</u>; for he had said , I <u>will not</u> give thee the inheritance of my fathers. So he laid down on his bed, and turned away his face, and would eat no bread. But Jezebel his wife came to him, and said unto him, Why is thy spirit so sad, that thou eatest no bread? And he told her, because I spake to Naboth about his vineyard; and he refused to trade it, or sell it to me. And Jezebel his wife said unto him, Dost thou now govern the kingdom of Israel? Arise, and eat bread, and let thine heart be merry. I will give thee the vineyard of Naboth the Jezreelite! (an evil, wicked person, will always lie, steal and kill, to get what they want; with <u>no care</u> or <u>concern</u> for <u>who</u> they hurt!) So she wrote letters in Ahab's name, and sealed them with his seal, and sent the letters unto the elders and nobles that were in his city dwelling with Naboth. (and God <u>will hold them just as guilty</u> as Ahab and Jezebel, for the evil they do) And she wrote in the letters, saying, Proclaim a fast, and set Naboth on high among the people; and set two men, sons of belial, (evil liars) before him, to bear witness against him! (to frame Naboth) Saying, Thou didst blaspheme God and the king. And then carry him out, and stone him, that he may die! And the men, the elders, and the nobles of the city, did as Jezebel told them in the letters!(some nobles huh) They proclaimed a fast, and set Naboth on high among the people. And there came in two (evil) men, children of belial, and sat before him; and the evil men lied to all the people, saying they heard Naboth blaspheme God and the king! Then they carried Naboth out of the city, and stoned him with stones, so that he died! Then they sent to Jezebel, saying, Naboth is stoned, and is dead. And when Jezebel heard that Naboth was stoned, and was dead; She said to Ahab, arise, and take possession of the vineyard of Naboth, which he refused to give thee! For Naboth is not alive, but dead! Then, when Ahab heard that Naboth was dead, Ahab went down to the vineyard of Naboth to take possession of it! And the word of the Lord came to Elijah the Tishbite, (God's Prophet) saying; Arise, go down to meet Ahab king of Israel, which is in samaria. Behold he is in the vineyard of Naboth, whither he is gone down to possess it. And thou shalt speak unto him, saying, "Thus sayeth the Lord God, Hast thou killed, and also taken possession?" Thou shalt also tell him, saying, "Thus sayeth the Lord," "In the place where dogs licked the blood of Naboth, shall dogs lick thy blood, even thine!" And Ahab said to Elijah, Hast thou found me, O' mine enemy? And he answered, I have found thee; because thou has sold thyself to <u>Do Evil</u> in the the sight of the Lord! Behold, I will bring evil upon thee, and will take away thy posterity, and will <u>cut off</u> from Ahab, him that pisseth against the wall, (male descendants) that are still left here in Israel! And I will destroy thine house, like I did to the houses of Jeroboam, and Baasha;(the kings before thee) for the provocation wherewith thou hast provoked me to anger, and made Israel to sin! {1 Kings - 21}

Holiness, Prayer, and Spiritual Warfare!

The Lord also spake against Jezebel, saying, The dogs shall <u>Eat</u> Jezebel's (body) by the wall of Jezreel! Him that dieth of Ahab's (descendants) in the city, the dogs shall eat; and him that dieth in the field, the birds of the air shall eat! (if you <u>do evil</u> to others, God <u>will</u> return that same evil upon your <u>own head</u>!) And there were none like unto Ahab, which did sell himself to Do Wickedness in the sight of the Lord, whom Jezebel his wife stirred up! (or incited) {1 Kings 21:23} So Ahab and Jezebel conspired to, and killed Naboth, so Ahab could steal his vineyard! And God sent the Prophet Elijah there to meet Ahab, in Naboth's vineyard; to pronounce judgment on <u>Ahab, Jezebel</u>, and Ahab's <u>family</u> for <u>all</u> the evil Ahab and Jezebel had done! That not only would the dogs lick up Ahab's blood, in the same spot where they had licked up Naboth's blood! The dogs would also <u>eat Jezebel's body</u> in the same town, <u>and</u> all Ahab's male descendants body's, would be eaten in the city, or in the field! (<u>You Will Reap What You Sow</u>!) And there also was war, for three years, between King Ahab of Israel and Syria. And in the third year, Jehoshaphat the King of Judah (of the other 2 tribes, Judah and Benjamin) came to speak with Ahab. And the king of Israel (Ahab) said to his servants, ye know that Ramoth in Gil'ead is ours; (our lands) but we <u>do</u> nothing to take it out of the hands of the king of Syria! So Ahab, said unto Jehoshaphat, will thou go with me to battle at Ramoth Gil'ead? And Jehoshaphat said to Ahab, I am with you, and all my people and horses are with you. And King Jehoshaphat said to King Ahab, Enquire, I pray thee, at the word of the Lord to day. (It was the custom of kings to seek out God's advice from the prophets, before going to war) Then the king of Israel (Ahab) gathered 400 prophets together, and said unto them, shall I go to battle against Ramoth Gil'ead; or shall I forbear? (not) And they said, go up, for the Lord shall deliver it into the hand of the king! And Jehoshaphat asked, is there not <u>another</u> "Prophet of the Lord" besides these, that we may <u>Enquire of Him?</u> (did he sense that something was wrong with <u>these</u> 400!) And Ahab told him, There is yet <u>one man</u>, Mica'iah the son of Imlah, by whom we may inquire of the Lord! But <u>I Hate Him</u>, (he never <u>tells me</u> what my sinful flesh <u>wants to hear</u>!) for he doth not prophesy good concerning me, but evil! And Ahab called an officer and said, Hasten, and bring Mica'iah the son Imlah. So both kings sat on their thrones, in their robes, by the entrance of the gate of Samaria. And all the Prophets prophesied before them. And Zedekiah, made him horns of iron and said, "Thus saith the Lord, With these shalt thou push the Syrians, untill thou have consumed them!" And all the prophets said, Go up to Ramoth Gil'ead and prosper, for the lord shall deliver it into the kings hand! And the officer that went to get Mica'iah, said to him; Behold now, the words of the prophets declare good unto the king with one mouth! Let <u>thy word</u>, be like the word of all of them, and speak that which is good! (The devil dosen't want you to <u>Rock</u> the apple cart, so he will threaten <u>You</u>, "don't take the Holy Godly road, and <u>warn people of their sins</u>! take the <u>Smooth Easy Road</u>, and say everythings O.K. so you don't have to suffer the pains of trials and tribulations," and I can <u>Lead</u> them to <u>Hell</u> without any problem's) But Mica'iah said, As the <u>Lord liveth</u>, what **the Lord** says to me, **THAT IS WHAT I WILL SPEAK!** So he came to the king, and Ahab said unto him; Mica'iah, shall we go to Ramoth Gil'ead to battle, or shall we forbear? And he answered him, Go, and prosper; for the Lord shall deliver it into the hands of the king! (but he was mocking all of the other prophets) Then Ahab said to him, how many times shall I adjure thee that thou tell me nothing but that which is true in the name of the Lord? {1 Kings Ch. 22}

Holiness, Prayer, and Spiritual Warfare!

Then Mica'iah, the true prophet of the Lord, told King Ahab and King Jehoshaphat, (in the presence of the 400 false Prophets) the true word of the Lord! And he said, I saw all Israel scattered upon the hills, as sheep that have no shepherd: and the Lord said, these have no master; let them return every man to his house in peace. (go home, do not go to war) He told King Ahab exactly what to do, but King Ahab did not listen! And the King of Israel (Ahab) said to King Jehoshaphat, did I not tell you that he would not prophesy good concerning me, but evil? Then Mica'iah, (the true prophet) said, hear thou therefore the word of the Lord! I saw the Lord sitting on his throne, and all the host of heaven standing by him, on his right hand and on his left. And the Lord said, Who shall persuade Ahab, that he may go up and fall (be killed!) at Ra'moth-gilead? And one said on this manner, and another said on that manner. And there came forth a spirit, and stood before the Lord. and said, I will persuade him! And the Lord said unto him, Wherewith? And he said, I will go forth, and I will be a lying spirit in the mouth of all his prophets! And he said, Thou shalt persuade him, and prevail also; go forth and do so! Now therefore, behold, the Lord has put a lying spirit in the mouth of all these thy prophets, and the Lord has spoken evil concerning thee! {1 Kings 22:17-23} King Ahab had **Chosen** to **Do Evil** in the sight of the Lord! He did not **fear God** or the consequences for his **evil sins** and **evil deeds**! He knew that killing Naboth and stealing his vineyard **was wrong**! But his covetous, evil heart, wanted that vineyard! So Ahab and his wicked wife Jezebel, plotted and killed Naboth, and stole his land! Now **God** is going to **kill them**! And cast them into hell! You will **reap what you sow**! Do unto others what **you want done unto you**! Two Holy Men of **God**, (Elijah and Mica'iah) men that King Ahab knew were Men of God! Both told King Ahab that **God was going to destroy him for his Evil sins and deeds!!!** But Sin and Evil had hardened his wicked heart, blinded his eyes, and deafened his ears! When you choose sin and evil, and Ignore Almighty God's commandments to **be Holy**, and to do what is good and right and just and true! God will turn you over to that sin and evil, because **that is what YOU WANTED!!!** Jesus said that, "Whosoever committeth Sin is The Servant of Sin!" And King Ahab was so deceived and blinded by his sins, that he could not hear the truth; even though he was told twice, directly to his face! By Two Powerful Men of **God!** And we can look at the Scriptures in the **Holy Bible**, that tells us exactly why! He was deceived by the unrighteousness that is in them that perish, because they **Did Not Receive** the love of **The Truth**, so that they might be saved! And even as they did not like (or want) to retain God in their knowledge! And for this cause God shall send them strong delusion, that they should believe a lie! That they all might be damned, who did not believe the truth, but had pleasure in unrighteousness! (Sin and Evil!) So God gave them over to a reprobate mind! {2 Thessalonians 2:10 & Romans 2:28} Let this be a very Serious Warning to you and me, and All of Mankind! Almighty God means exactly **what he says,** when he tells us that **The Wages of Sin is Death!** "Fear Ye Not **Me?** saith **The Lord!**" Will ye not tremble in **My Presence?** Behold, **All Souls are Mine!** The Soul that sinneth, it **Shall Die!** {Jeremiah 5:22, Ezekiel 18:4} King Ahab and Jezebel chose Sin and Evil, over God and Holiness!!! And it cost them their souls! Likewise, if you and I choose Sin and Evil, over God and Holiness, it **will** cost us **our Souls!** God says to All "Be Ye Holy, for I am Holy" Repent and live, for why will Ye Die?

Holiness, Prayer, and Spiritual Warfare!

Almighty God has always Rejected Sin from the very Foundation of the world! When Lucifer and one third of the angels rebelled, God cast them **Out of Heaven!** When Adam and Eve **sinned**, God drove them out of the Garden of Eden! (Where the **Tree of Life** was! And they had access to it! God clearly told Adam that he could eat freely from any tree in the garden, but not from the tree of the Knowledge of Good and Evil!- Genesis 2:15) God Destroyed Sodom and Gomorrah with Fire and Brimstone in One Day, for their evil, lustful sins, and Homosexuality! "**God Destroyed The Whole World**" with a Great Flood in Noah's day, because of the great sin and evil that mankind was committing on the earth, and only saved - **Eight!** - (8) human souls, (because Noah was a righteous man) to replenish the earth! Almighty God has made it clear, **All** throughout History; (just Read the **Holy Bible**!) that when Israel and mankind Obeyed God, kept his Commandments, and **Did** that which was Good, Right, Just, True, and **Holy!!!** God blessed them, helped them, protected them, delivered them from evil, and gave them **Life!** But when they disobeyed God, (and rebelled like Satan) and lived Sinful, Evil, Wicked Lives!!! (Lying, Stealing, Cursing, Adultery, Fornication, Homosexuality, Murder, Hatred, Drunkenness, Lust, Rioting, and Rebellion!) **ALMIGHTY GOD DESTROYED THEM!!!** God has clearly shown all throughout History, God does not tolerate or put up with Sin and Evil! **Almighty God Destroys It!!!** God means what he says Forever! **The Wages of Sin is DEATH!** But the Gift of God is Eternal Life, through **JESUS CHRIST our LORD and SAVIOR!!!** There is a Passage of Scriptures written in the Old Testament, in the book of Ezekiel; that almost **No** Pastor or Minister would dare to Preach on, or teach you about! But I Fear God too much to **Not** show it to **You**, because **I Love You**, and I want you to make it **Into Heaven!** And I Don't want **Anyone's Blood on my Hands** when I stand before **God!** Because I failed to Preach to you, the **Full Gospel Truth** with **Holy Ghost Fire!** You absolutely must have a clear, true, understanding of the **Holy Awesome Almighty God**, that We All Must Answer To and Give an Account of our Lives For, **ON THE GREAT AND TERRIBLE JUDGMENT DAY!!!** The following Scripture is directly out of **The Holy Bible**, in the Book of Ezekiel, Chapters 7 - 9; it is the Revelation's and Vision's that God showed to the Prophet Ezekiel (One of the Major Prophets) in the very city of Jerusalem! "The word of the Lord came to me, saying, Thou son of man, thus saith the Lord God unto the land of Israel; an end, the end is come upon the four corners of the land! Now is the end come upon thee, and I will send mine anger upon thee, and will Judge thee according to thy ways, and will recompense upon thee all thine abominations! And mine eye shall not spare thee, neither will I have pity! But I will recompense thy ways upon thee, and thine abominations shall be in the mist of thee; and ye shall know that **I AM The LORD!** Thus saith the Lord God, an evil, an only evil, behold, is come! An end is come, the end is come, it watcheth for thee; behold, it is come! Now I will shortly pour out my fury upon thee, and accomplish mine anger upon thee! And I will judge thee according to thy ways, and will recompense thee for all thine abominations! And mine eye shall not spare, neither will I have pity! I will recompense thee according to thy ways and thine abominations, that are in the midst of thee; and ye shall know that I AM the Lord that smiteth! Behold the day, it is come, morning has gone forth; the rod has blossomed, pride has budded, violence is risen up into a rod of wickedness!

Holiness, Prayer, and Spiritual Warfare!

None of them shall remain of their multitude, nor any of theirs; neither shall there be wailing for them. For my <u>Wrath</u> is upon all the multitude thereof, the vision is touching the whole multitude, which shall not return; neither shall any strengthen himself in the iniquity of his life. They have blown the trumpet, even to make all ready; but <u>none</u> goeth to the battle! For my <u>wrath</u> is upon all the multitude thereof! The sword is without, and the pestilence and the famine within; he that is in the field shall die with the sword, and he that is in the city, famine and pestilence shall devour him! All hands shall be feeble, and all knees shall be weak as water; every one of them mourning for <u>his</u> (sins) and iniquities! They shall also gird themselves with sackcloth, and horror shall cover them; shame and baldness shall be upon all their faces and heads! They shall cast their silver in the streets, their gold shall be removed their silver and their gold shall <u>not</u> be able to deliver them in the day of <u>the Wrath of the Lord!</u> They shall not satisfy their souls, neither fill their bowels; because it is the stumbling block of their iniquity! My face will I also turn from them, and they shall pollute my secret place! (the Holy Temple!) For the robbers shall enter into it and defile it! Make a chain, for the land <u>is full of bloody crimes,</u> and the city is <u>full of Violence!</u> (does this sound like a country you know, and <u>live</u> in?) Destruction cometh, and they shall seek peace, and <u>there shall be none!</u> Mischief shall come upon mischief, and rumor shall be upon rumor; <u>Then</u> shall they <u>seek</u> a vision of the Prophet! But the law shall perish from the priest, (evil wicked ministers begging for money, and comforting people <u>in their sins,</u> with an ice cold, phony soul destroying, marshmallow <u>Gospel!</u>) and council from the ancients! (deceived, confused, rulers and greedy leaders, who destroy and <u>loot</u> the very country and people they are <u>sworn</u> to protect and guide) I will do unto them after their ways, and according to their deserts (or deeds) **Will I Judge Them**!!! And then they shall <u>know</u> that <u>I AM THE LORD!</u> And it came to pass as I sat in mine house, and the elders of Judah sat before me, that the hand of the Lord God fell there upon me. Then I beheld, and lo, a likeness as the appearance of Fire! And the appearance of his loins downward was as fire; and from his loins upward, the appearance and brightness, was as the color of amber. And he put forth the form of an hand, and took me by a lock of mine head; and the spirit lifted me up between the earth and the heaven, and brought me in the visions of God to Jerusalem! (The hand of God, picked up the Prophet Ezekiel, and brings him to four different locations in the city; and shows him the sins and iniquities, that the priest, elders, and people commit there!) 1. at the entrance of the north gate of the altar was an idolatrous image of jealously (probably of some pagan god or beast) where the common people went in and out to offer sacrifices on the altar. 2. at the door of the court, inside a hole in the wall; was an door. God told him to go in and see the wicked abominations that they do here! So I went in and saw; and behold every form of creeping thing and abominable beast, and all the idols of the house of Israel, portrayed upon the wall round about. And there stood 70 men of the rulers of Israel, with Jaazaniah the son of Shaphan, all with censers in their hand; offering up a thick cloud of incense <u>to all the Idols!</u> 3. at the door of the gate of the Lords house, behold, there sat women weeping for Tammuz! (who was the Accadian sun-god) 4. in the <u>inner court of the Lords House</u>, at the door of <u>the Temple of the Lord,</u> between <u>the porch and the altar,</u> were 25 men facing away from the temple, (with their backs to God!) facing towards the east, (they were to always pray towards God!) but instead they worshiped the sun!

Holiness, Prayer and Spiritual Warfare!

Then God said unto me, has thou seen this, O son of man? Is it a light thing to the house of Judah, that they commit the abominations which they commit here! (in the inner court of God's Temple!) For they have filled the land with violence, and have returned to provoke me to anger! And, lo, they put the branch to their nose. (turn their nose up to God and disrespect him, in God's Temple!) Therefore will I also deal in fury; mine eye shall shall not spare, neither will I have pity! And though they cry in mine ears with a loud voice, yet will I not hear them! Then I heard with my ears, him say with a loud voice, Cause them that have charge over the city to draw near, even every man with his destroying weapon in his hand! And behold, six men came from the way of the higher gate, which lieth toward the north; and every man a slaughter weapon in his hand! And one man among them was clothed with linen, with a writer's inkhorn by his side; and they went in, and stood beside the brazen altar. And the Glory of the God of Israel was gone up from the cherub, whereupon he was, to the threshold of the house. And he called to the man clothed with linen, which had the writers inkhorn by his side. And the Lord said unto him, Go through the midst of the city, through the midst of Jerusalem; and set a mark upon the foreheads of the men that sigh and that cry, for all the abominations that are done in the midst of it! And to the others he said in mine hearing, Go ye after him through the city, and smite! Let not your eye spare, neither have ye pity! Slay utterly old and young, both maids and little children, and women; but come not near any man upon whom is the mark! And begin at my Sanctuary! Then they began at the ancient men (rulers and leaders) which were before the house! And he said unto them, Defile the house, and fill the courts with the slain; Go ye forth! And they went forth, and slew in the city! And it came to pass, while they were slaying them, and I was left, that I fell upon my face and cried, and said, Ah Lord God! wilt thou destroy all the residue of Israel in thy pouring out of thy fury upon Jerusalem? Then he said unto me, The iniquity of the house of Israel and Judah is exceeding great, the land is full of blood, and the city full of perverseness! For they say, the Lord hath forsaken the earth, and the Lord seeth not! And as for me also, mine eye shall not spare, neither will I have pity; but **I will** recompense their way upon their head! And behold, the man clothed with linen, which had the inkhorn by his side; reported the matter, saying, I have done as thou hast commanded me!{Ezekiel Chapter 9} My beloved brethren, this is one of the most humbling and terrifying chapters in the whole bible! Our Father God in Heaven, means exactly what he says, when he tells us, **Be Ye Holy**, for **I AM HOLY!!!** Do not be deceived by Sin, or the weakness and frailty of the flesh, or the puny limitations of the human mind! Almighty God in heaven destroys evil and sin! **All Evil** and **All Sin!** For "Thou art of purer eyes than to behold evil, and canst not look on iniquity!" {Habakkuk 1:13} This is why Jesus came to save us, and to wash us clean in his own precious blood, He said Repent, for the kingdom of heaven is at hand! Because God destroys All evil, sin, and iniquity! Period! Evil men, evil women, evil children, all Evil! Do not be deceived by the weakness of your flesh, or the frailty and darkness of your human mind! Right now, we see through a (shaded) glass, darkly; but on that day (Judgment day) face to face, it all will be revealed! When we look at a man, woman or child; our puny mind and limited understanding; is but a speck of dust limited by time and human frailty! Almighty God see's and knows all, right now! When we see a man, woman or child, we see nothing; hours and days, viewed through sinful flesh!

Holiness, Prayer, and Spiritual Warfare!

When Almighty God in Heaven looks at <u>any person</u>, man, woman, or child; **God Sees All!!!** All their <u>Heart</u>, all their <u>Soul</u>, all their <u>Mind</u>, all their <u>true motives</u>, and all of their <u>whole entire lives!</u> **<u>Instantly</u>!** From their <u>first</u> breath at birth, to their <u>last</u> breath at death! From the very <u>second</u> they were conceived in their mothers womb, <u>God</u> knew every single thing about them! Every single word or deed that they would <u>ever</u> **Do or Say** in their <u>Whole Entire Lives</u>; is **Already Known** and <u>seen</u>, and <u>perceived</u> by the **One True Living Jehovah God of All Creation!** The <u>Alpha</u> and <u>Omega!</u> (the beginning and ending!) Now, <u>we</u> see through a glass darkly, but <u>on</u> that day, Face to Face; we shall know as **We Are Known!** That is why Almighty God in heaven, the ruler of the <u>Entire Universe</u>, can judge mankind <u>at any time!</u> And God knows every single thing about **You!** "<u>Before I formed thee</u> in the belly **I knew Thee**, (even) <u>before</u> thou camest forth out of the <u>womb!</u>"{Jeremiah 1:5} **GOD IS NOT BOUND** by the limitations of <u>the Fabric of Time</u>, or <u>Distance</u>, <u>Across the Universe!!!</u> Like **Man Is**! Man is created from the dust! **<u>Almighty God is Eternal and Endless!</u>** Almighty God has **LIFE within HIMSELF! FOREVER!!!** God knows <u>No Boundary's</u>, <u>No Perimeters</u>, <u>No Limitations</u> of <u>His will</u>, his capabilities or his creative **POWERS!** Absolutely <u>Nothing</u> is <u>Impossible</u> for **GOD!** Then, you might ask, why does God try the <u>hearts</u> and reins (or desires) of men? (And all the churches shall know that <u>I Am He</u> which **searcheth** the reins and hearts; (of men) and I <u>will</u> give unto **every one of You** according **TO YOUR WORKS!**) "Jesus Christ" {Revelation 2:23} God does it <u>for our sakes</u>, to **save** our souls!!! To give <u>us</u> a chance to feel <u>convicted</u> in our hearts and souls, and consciences for our <u>sins</u> and <u>iniquities</u>! So that **We** would <u>Repent</u> and **Turn to God**, and walk in his Holy Light! So that his only begotten son "**Jesus Christ's**" precious <u>blood</u>, can and will **wash us clean from our Sins**! And <u>cover us</u> with God's grace and mercy, **when we Repent** and **Turn from our Wicked Ways!** So that <u>we can be in Heaven with God!</u> That is God's <u>will</u> from the foundation of the world, and <u>why God created us!</u> **To be with him in Heaven!!!** God's Kingdom in Heaven, and God's rule over the <u>Entire Universe</u>, over the kingdoms of Heaven and Earth, of Men and Angels, is already **Guaranteed Forever!!!** There is **No One in Existence** that can <u>ever</u> overrule **Almighty God**, or **Ever Challenge God's Authority! No One!** Always remember what Jesus said, "Thine is the Kingdom, and the Power, and the Glory! "<u>Forever and Ever!!!</u>" This is <u>God's Holy Word</u>, and it will <u>stand</u> forever! There are some confused and deceived people, who may believe Satan's lies! That the Devil would <u>try</u> to challenge **GOD** for control of the universe! It is a **EVIL LIE!** Let us look at <u>the Truth</u> in God's Holy Bible! Jesus said, I beheld Satan as lightning <u>fall from Heaven!</u> {Luke 10:18} Lightning is quick and instant, it is <u>over</u> in a second! ~ For if God spared not the angels that sinned, but <u>cast them down to hell</u>, and delivered them into <u>chains of darkness</u>, to be reserved unto <u>Judgment</u>! {2 Peter 2:4}~ Now is come salvation, and strength, and the kingdom of our God, and the Power of his Christ! For the accuser of our brethren is **Cast Down!** {Revelation 12:10}~ And having spoiled (and defeated) principalities and powers, he (Jesus) made a <u>show of them openly</u>, **Triumphing Over Them** in it!{Colossians 2:15} And the devil that deceived them was <u>cast</u> into the <u>lake of fire</u> and brimstone, and shall be <u>Tormented</u> day and night <u>Forever</u>! {Revelation 20:10} Even here on the earth, Satan could **not** lay one finger on Job (or on anyone else) without **God's** permission! {Job 1:10-12}

Holiness, Prayer, and Spiritual Warfare!

Satan's Rebellion and Futile Attempt, with one third of the now fallen angels, to try and take over Almighty God's Throne and Authority in Heaven; Failed Pitifully and Miserably! Jesus said that, He beheld (watched) Satan Fall as lightning from Heaven! Jesus only had to watch as Satan's rebellion crumbled, and Satan was defeated and **Cast Out of Heaven!** If we look closely at the Holy Scriptures, we will see that Lucifer, (the devil or satan) who was once one of God's arch-angels; we will see that it was another arch-angel, the Arch-angel Michael, and his angels! (the angels that God assigned to fight by Michael's side!) That Defeated and Cast Out Satan and his angels! Almighty God didn't even have to stain his Holy hands on that evil lying murderer! Another arch-angel was more powerful than Satan, and he defeated and threw the devil and his rebellion out of Heaven! But know this, if Almighty God had taken even one step towards Entering the Fight, Satan and all the evil spirits, would **Have Fled** in **Complete Terror!!!** All **Almighty God** would have to Do, is Speak One Word; and the whole evil rebellious fraction, would have been **Utterly Annihilated** and instantly smashed into **Eternal Hell!!!** But Almighty God is not finished with Satan and the evil spirits just yet. Although most people don't know or realize it; God uses Satan like a puppet, or a tool, to accomplish God's will and Eternal Plan for mankind, here on the earth! Blessed is the man that endureth temptation, for when he is **tried**, He shall receive a crown of Life! Jesus said, I counsel thee to buy of me, gold tried in the fire, (the fire of temptation) that thou mayest be rich; and white raiment that thou mayest be clothed, so that the shame of thy nakedness do not appear; and anoint thine eyes with eyesalve, (the Holy Spirit, worship, prayers and Scriptures) that thou mayest See! {Revelation 3:18} And here is all the Fact proving Scripture for what you have just read! "How art thou fallen from heaven, O' Lucifer, son of the morning! How art thou cut down to the ground! which didst weaken the nations! For thou hast said in thine heart, I will ascend into heaven, I will exalt my throne above the stars of God: I will also sit upon the mount of the congregation. I will ascend above the heights of the clouds; I will be like the most high. Yet thou shalt **be brought Down to Hell!** To the sides of the Pit! They that see thee shall narrowly look upon thee, and consider thee, saying, "Is this the man that made the earth to tremble, that did shake kingdoms?" {Isaiah 14:12} "And there was war in heaven: Michael and his angels fought against the dragon; and the dragon and his angels fought, but prevailed not; neither was their place found any more in heaven! And the great dragon **was cast out**, that old serpent, called the Devil, and Satan, which deceiveth the whole world: he was cast out into the earth, and his angels were cast out with him! {Revelation 12:7} So you see, my beloved brethren, Satan was cast out of Heaven, and his angels were cast out with him! And their place was no longer found in heaven, but they were all cast out into the earth! And even here on the earth Satan still has to answer to Almighty God and Jesus Christ! Remember, Satan had to ask God's permission, before he could even touch or go after Job; and remember when Jesus commanded the legion of evil spirits to go out of the man who came out of the tombs! When Jesus cast them out of the man, the evil spirits had to ask for Jesus permission before they could even go into a herd of swine. {Job 1 & Mark 5} Almighty God has, and always will have, **Full Control** over the **Entire Universe!!!** Thine, O'Lord, is the greatness, power, glory, and the victory; all that is in Heaven and Earth is **Thine!**

Holiness, Prayer, and Spiritual Warfare!

Beloved, the Holy Scriptures make it so Crystal Clear, that our **Holy Father God in Heaven**, the only **One True Living Jehovah God** of all Creation! That God is the most powerful being in all Existence! That Almighty God, and God Alone, Will Rule over the **Entire Universe Forever!!!** "**Hallelujah!!!**" The only real fight, is not over control of the universe; but over the souls of men! And even this battle has **already been Won**, by our Lord and Savior, **Jesus Christ!** When he personally **Paid the Price** for our sins, with his own precious blood; that can **Cleanse your soul from Sin!!!** (Behold, the Lamb of God that taketh away the sin of the world!) When he sacrificed himself to Our Father God, on the Cross of Calvary! With **Jesus** Spotless, Sinless, Perfect, Holy, Blameless, Offering to Almighty God! And his Resurrection on the third day, and his ascension into Heaven, at the right hand of God! Where Jesus Christ is our Great High Priest in the Holy of Holies! When Jesus said, "It is Finished" up on the cross, the path was opened up for the souls of men,"any- man, woman, or child" to Enter into Heaven! The Battle for the souls of mankind was **Won!** The Scripture says that Jesus defeated Satan and all the powers of darkness; "putting them to Open Shame, Triumphing over them in it!" {Colossians 2:15} The truth is that there was never ever **Any Chance**, that Satan and the principalities of darkness; could ever defeat, the Mighty, Awesome, Magnificent, Unstoppable, Precious, Lamb of God, **Jesus Christ!** **JESUS IS GOD!!! IN THE FLESH!!! CREATOR OF THE UNIVERSE!!!** Let it be proclaimed from the Highest Mountaintop to the lowest valley, that **Jesus Christ is Lord**; and to make all men see what is the fellowship of the mystery, which from the beginning of the world hath been hidden in **God, Who Created All Things By Jesus Christ!** {Ephesians 3:9} Who being the brightness of God's glory, and the express image of his (God's) person, and upholding all things by the word of his power, when he had by himself **Purged our sins**, sat down on the right hand of the Majesty on high! {Hebrews 1:3} Beloved, our precious Lord Jesus Christ was wounded for our transgressions, he was bruised for our iniquities, and by his stripes **we are healed!** Because your sins are forgiven you for his name's sake, and the blood of Jesus Christ cleanses us from all sin! (when you truly, sincerely, repent from **all Sin!**) Neither is there salvation in any other; for there is **No Other Name** under Heaven given among men, whereby we must be saved! See:{Acts 4:12, 1 John 1:7& 2:12, and Isaiah 53:5} Therefore, my dearly beloved, Cast Away from you all your transgressions, whereby ye have transgressed; and make you a new heart and a new spirit, for why will ye die? (because if any man be in Christ, he is a new creature) old things are passed away, (and crucified) behold all things are become new! (recreated in the image of him, **Jesus Christ**, that created him!) Be not conformed to this world, but be ye transformed by the renewing of your mind! That ye may prove what is the good and acceptable, **Perfect Will of God!!!** Repent ye therefore, and be converted, that your sins may be blotted out when the times of refreshing shall come from the presence of the Lord. {Ezek. 18:31, 2 Corin. 5:17, Romans 12:2, Acts 3:19} And I will cleanse them from all their iniquity, whereby they have sinned against me; and I will pardon all their iniquities, whereby they have sinned, and transgressed against me! For I will be merciful to their unrighteousness, and their sins and iniquities will I remember no more! I will raise a King, to execute justice and judgement in the earth; and his name (Jesus) shall be called "The Lord our Righteousness!"

Holiness, Prayer, and Spiritual Warfare!

Beloved, Almighty God and his only begotten son Jesus Christ, have already accomplished everything that You and I Needed; and have already opened up a way! (**Jesus is the Way!**) For All of Mankind to be forgiven, and washed clean of all sin and iniquity; be saved, be **Born Again**, and Live in Heaven with our Father God, for All of Eternity, Forever! When **JESUS CHRIST** said,"**IT IS FINISHED!!!**" The battle for the souls of man was Won, the way was Opened Up, the victory secured; our evil enemy Satan was vanquished, and Forever Defeated!!! By the Mighty Lamb of God, **Our Lord and Savior JESUS CHRIST!!!** Jesus has the keys of Hell and Death! Jesus is the Only One, who was worthy to take the Book out of **God the Father's** right hand, to Look upon it, and break loose the seven seals on the Book! In all of the heavens, and in earth, and under the earth, **no one** was found worthy but **Jesus!** {Revelation 5:1-7} Jesus said, "I Am the Way, the Truth, and the Life, no man can come unto (God) the Father, **But By Me!**" {John 14:6} The Battle for the souls of All Mankind is **Already Won!!!** The victory by God over evil, is **already secured!** So what's the Problem? "**MANKIND is the Problem!**" The problem is **the evil heart of MAN!** That men loved darkness rather than light, because their deeds were evil!{John 3:19}"And God saw that the wickedness of man was **great** in the earth, and that every imagination of the thoughts of his heart was only Evil continually!"{Genesis 6:5} "For out of the heart proceeds evil thoughts, murders, adulteries, fornications, thefts, lies, blasphemies; these Defile a Man! Jesus said,"Ye Will Not Come to **Me**, that **Ye might Have LIFE!!!**" and "**I Am the Bread of Life!!!**" Because, **If We WALK~IN~THE~LIGHT**, as **HE~IS~IN~THE~LIGHT!!!** and we have fellowship one with another! (then and only then!) The Blood of God's Son Jesus, **Cleanses US from All Sin!!!** {John 5:40, 6:35-51 & 1 John 1:7} (When We Walk in the Light with God, In Spirit and In Truth!!!) You see, my dearly beloved, when you walk in the light; and you have fellowship with God and Jesus, in Spirit and in Truth! Almighty God's Holy Light, exposes all Sin, all Evil and all Darkness!!! Period! So that when You or I, or any person, (man, woman, or child) begins to obey Jesus, (our Lord) and to Walk with God in the Light! (in Spirit and in Truth) God's Light, step by step, precept by precept, line upon line; God's light will begin to expose sin and evil, and all darkness!(this is the very cleansing and purifying process that the Holy Spirit uses to **Remove sin and evil** from your heart and soul; and Jesus blood, and God's grace, cover you while you are obeying God through it!) Now, therefore, there is **No** condemnation to them who are **In** Christ Jesus, who Do Not walk after the flesh, (obeying the fleshly Lusts and desires!) but who walk after the Spirit! (for as many as are Led by the Spirit of God,"they" are **the sons of God!**) {Romans 8:1-14} If you are **Led** by, and **obey** the Holy Spirit, you will have to Repent from All sin and forsake it; **Fight** against that sin and **Overcome it!!!** Fight the good fight of Faith, lay hold on Eternal Life; whereunto thou art called!{1 Timothy 6:12}And continue to walk with God in the Light! Put ye on the Lord Jesus Christ, (as you learn Christ Jesus, walk ye in him) and **Do Not** make provision for the flesh, to fulfil the lust thereof! Or your sins will make you hide from God! (like Adam and Eve did in the garden of Eden!) Only to have those sins exposed on Judgment Day!!! Every one that does evil, hate's the light, neither cometh to the light, lest his deeds should be reproved! But he that doeth truth cometh to the light, so his deeds are clearly, evidently, made in God! John 3:20

Holiness, Prayer, and Spiritual Warfare!

Jesus clearly said,"Everyone that doeth evil (and live sinful, lustful, thieving, evil speaking, rebellious, wicked lives!) Hateth the Light! neither Cometh to the Light, lest his (evil) deeds should be reproved!" (and be exposed to him by **God's Holy Light**, that he lives a sinful, wicked life, of rebellion, and evil thoughts and deeds, that **are not in God's will!** And unless he repents, changes his sinful lifestyle, and brings forth holy fruit in his life, that are worthy of true repentance! His deeds and sinful, evil lifestyle, will be rebuked and rejected, by **Holy Holy God Almighty!** Just like Cain, who slew his brother was!) Jesus also clearly said, "But He that Doeth the **Truth**,"(who truly **Loves God!** With all his heart, soul, mind, and strength! And **Wants To Walk~with~God~in~the~Light! NO** Matter What The Cost IS!) That person will **RUN~TO GOD!!!** Kneel humbly at Jesus Feet, deny all his fleshly desires and lusts, and **Lay His Life and His Will on God's Holy Altar! Forever!!!** Take Up His Cross Every Day, and **Crucify All His Evil, Fleshly, Lusts and Desires, ON~THE~ CROSS!** And **FOLLOW JESUS!!!** By coming to the Light, and Walking in the Light; following Jesus example, when he gave up his own will, and did God the Father's will! By living a holy, sinless, submissive life, to God the Father! "And this is the condemnation, (or reason that mankind is guilty!) because Light is come into the world, and men loved darkness rather than Light, because **Their Deeds were Evil!** For every one that doeth evil **Hateth the Light**, neither Cometh to the Light, lest his deeds should Be Reproved! But He that doeth **Truth**, cometh **to the light**, that his deeds may be made manifest, (clearly and evidently proven!) that they are wrought in God!" (a life Forged in Holy Ghost Fire, and Purified by Jesus Blood!){John 3:19} John the Baptist said,"And now the ax is laid unto the root of the trees; therefore every tree which does not **Bring Forth Good Fruit** (a Holy Sanctified Life) is Hewn Down and **Cast into the Fire**!(of Hell) I indeed baptize you with water unto repentance; but he that cometh after me (Jesus) is mightier than I, whose shoes I am not worthy to bear! (carry for him) He shall Baptize You with **The Holy Ghost**, and with **Fire!** Whose fan is in his (Jesus) hand, and he will thoroughly **Purge his Floor**, (anyone who is a living member of the body of Christ!) and gather his wheat (God's children) into the garner; (Heaven!) But He will burn up the chaff (all the men whose lives and deeds brought forth evil fruit and sin!) with unquenchable fire!" (you can go through Holy Ghost Fire now, or burn in Hell Fire for Eternity!) "Let this **mind** be in you, which was also in Christ Jesus; who, being in the form of God, (**Jesus is God** and part of the Holy Trinity, and Godhead!!!) But he made Himself of no reputation, and took upon him the form of a **Servant**, and was made in the likeness of men! And being found in the fashion as a Man, He Humbled Himself, and became **Obedient unto Death**, even the **Death of the Cross!!!** Wherefore God also Hath Highly Exalted Him, and given him a name which is Above Every Name!!! That at the Name of "**Jesus**" every Knee Should Bow, of things in heaven, and things in earth, and thing under the Earth! And that Every Tongue Should Confess, that **"JESUS CHRIST IS LORD!!!"** To the glory of **God the Father!** {Matthew 4:10, Philippians 2:5} For all who live according to the flesh, do **mind** the things of the flesh; but they that live after the Spirit do **mind** the things of the Spirit! For to be carnally minded is death, but to be spiritually minded is life and peace! If ye live after the flesh, ye shall die!!! But if ye through the Spirit, do mortify the deeds of the body, **YE SHALL LIVE!!!** {Romans 8:5-14}

Holiness, Prayer, and Spiritual Warfare!

For as many as **Are Led by the Spirit of God!!!** "**THEY!**" They are the sons of God! {Romans 8:14} Not every one that saith unto me,"Lord, Lord," shall Enter into the Kingdom of Heaven! But "**He That Doeth**" (actually Do, Complete, and Preform) and "**Do the WILL of my FATHER IN HEAVEN!!!**" **They Shall Enter into The Kingdom of Heaven!!!** "Jesus Christ" {Matthew 7:21} So, my Brethren, The Word of God tells Us To: 1.- Put on the Mind of Christ! (Let this mind be in you that was also in Christ Jesus; Be not conformed to this world, but Be Ye Transformed by the Renewing of your **Mind!**) 2.- Walk in the Spirit, Not in the flesh! Being **Led** by, and **Obeying, The Holy Spirit of God!!!** (walk in the Spirit and ye shall not fulfill the lusts of the flesh! For the flesh lusteth against the Spirit, and the Spirit (fighteth) against the flesh! And these are contrary the one to the other, so that ye cannot do the things (of the old mans Adam like, sinful nature) that ye would! Crucify the old sinful nature and deny yourself, take up your cross and follow Jesus! Because "if any man be in Christ, he is a **New Creature** the old things (fleshly man) are passed away, (and crucified) Behold, all things are become new!" And Re-created in the Image of him (Jesus) that Created Him! Because "If Ye Be Led" by the **Holy Spirit** (and obey what He tells you to Do!) Then, **Ye Are NOT Under the LAW!** {Galatians 5:16-18} There is therefore now no condemnation to them which are in Christ Jesus, who Do Not walk after the Flesh, but (who walk) after the Spirit! Because the Law of the Spirit of life in Christ Jesus has made me free from the Law of Sin and Death! {Romans 8:1} Stand fast in the liberty where Christ has made us free! You are washed clean by Jesus precious blood, and covered by God's Grace through **FAITH in Jesus!** And not by any works or puny physical human effort, that you or I could ever do in our fleshly bodies! You are saved by Grace through Faith, and not by works, it is the Gift of God! (through his Son Jesus) Lest any man should boast, because no flesh shall glory in Almighty God's Holy, Awesome, Presence! {Ephesians 2:8, 1 Corinthians 1:29} And as a Living Member and an actual part of the Body of Jesus Christ! You are now In the Spirit, (Heaven is within You!) and your mind must be focused on God and heavenly things, not on earthly things! (Jesus said, build your treasures in heaven, and not on the earth; because where your Treasure is, that is where your Heart "and mind" will Also Be!) For to be carnally (or fleshly) minded is death; but to be spiritually minded is Life and Peace! Because the carnal mind is at enmity (or fights) against God! For it is not subject to the law of God, neither indeed can it be! So then, they that are in the flesh, **Cannot Please God!** But ye are not in the flesh, but in the Spirit, if so be that the **Spirit of God** dwell in you! (and you are truly **Born Again!**) Now if any man have not the Spirit of Christ, he is none of his! (so Pray to God to **Fill You with His Holy Spirit!**) {Romans 8:5-9} 3.- Do God's Will for Your Life! Not think about it, Not contemplate doing it, Not hope someone else does it for You! **YOU MUST DO ~ GOD'S ~WILL!!!** According to Jesus Christ, **WHO IS GOD!!!** The Main Difference between the people who Actually Make it **INTO HEAVEN**, and the people who **DO~NOT~MAKE~IT~INTO~HEAVEN!!!** "**IS**" That the people in Heaven "Truly~and~Sincerely" **Obeyed God and DID~GOD~THE~FATHER'S~WILL!!! For Their Lives!!!** "Not every one that saith unto me,"Lord, Lord" shall Enter into the kingdom of heaven, but "**he that doeth the will**" of my **Father which is in Heaven!**" Jesus is the author of eternal salvation unto all who obey him!{Heb 5:9}

Holiness, Prayer, and Spiritual Warfare!

My beloved brethren, this is exactly and precisely why, **ye must be born again** into the Spirit of God! Jesus answered and said unto him, Verily, (or truly) I say unto thee, Except a man be born again, He cannot see the kingdom of God! Except a man be born of water, (baptized) and of the Spirit, he cannot Enter into the kingdom of God! That which is born of the flesh is flesh; and that which is born of the Spirit is spirit! Marvel not that I said unto thee, "Ye must be born again!" The wind bloweth where it listeth, (wheresoever the Spirit chooses to go!) and thou hearest the sound thereof, but canst not tell whence it cometh, and whither it goeth: so is every one that is born (again) of the Spirit! {John 3:3-8} Because, if the Spirit of him (God) that raised up Jesus from the dead Dwell In You, he that raised up Christ from the dead shall also Quicken your mortal bodies by his (Holy) Spirit that **Dwelleth in You!** {Romans 8:11} The Holy Spirit will Rise Up In You, in his Mighty Power, **(the Holy Spirit is God!)** and Quicken you, and give you the strength, and the will, and the fight, and Power to **Do God's Will!** The Holy Spirit will Rise Up in you, and **Cause You** to Fight the Good Fight of Faith, and **Overcome** every sin, temptation and evil desire, in your heart and carnal, fleshly body! If you truly and sincerely **Want Him To Do It!!! With All Your Heart, Soul, Mind, and Strength!!! The Holy Spirit Can** and **Will Do It**, Because Absolutely **NOTHING IS IMPOSSIBLE FOR GOD!!! NOTHING!!!** And The Holy Spirit is **God**, Living Inside of **You! You Are God's Temple!** (dwelling place) The Apostle Paul said,"Know ye not (do you not know and understand) that **Ye are the Temple of God!!!** And that The Spirit of God Dwelleth in You? {1 Corinthians 3:16, Luke 1:37} This is God's Promise and **New Covenant** with Jesus and his seed! (us) And It Is Impossible for **God to Lie!**{Hebrews 6:18} And we will now Show you the Scriptures that **Prove**, this **Is The Truth**, Promised to Us by Our Holy Father God, Who~Can~Not~Lie! Ever! The secret of the Lord is with them that Fear Him, and he will Show them His Covenant! {Psalms 25:14} The Old Covenant served as our teacher and schoolmaster, to Show Us that we are sinful and weak; (for all have sinned and fallen short of the Glory of God) and that **We~Can~Not~Save~Ourselves!** No matter how good our intentions were, or how hard we tried and struggled in our own strength and might! We Needed a Savior! **Jesus Christ!!!** And God used the Old Testament, under the Old Covenant; to teach and to show all of mankind, that we could not save **Ourselves! Ever!** Almighty God Knew It! And Now We Know It! We are weak, helpless, sinful, wretched, pitiful, Dried Up Dead Bones! We Needed Holy, Awesome, Powerful, **Almighty God** to Put His Mighty Holy Spirit Inside of Us! And Rise Up in His **Omnipotent Power**, inside our mortal, weak, fleshly bodies, and actually **Do~The~Job~For~Us! When We Surrender Our Will To God!!!** And Jesus is the mediator of the new covenant with God, that was foreordained before the foundation of the world! Between God the Father and Jesus, that he would lay down his glory, come to earth, and be born as a man, of the seed of Abraham; as a humble servant to Do God's will! And be obedient unto Death, even the Death of the Cross, and shed his own blood as a Perfect offering to God for Our Sins! Fulfilling his part of the new covenant with God; by his spotless, blameless, Sacrifice of his own body on the Cross! Blotting out the handwriting of ordinances that was against us, which was contrary to us, and took it out the way, **Nailing it to his Cross!** {Colossians 2:14} Jesus completed the new covenant!

Holiness, Prayer, and Spiritual Warfare!

So then, my beloved brethren, We Do Not seek the righteousness which is by the Law! Because by the deeds of the law there shall no flesh (man) be justified in God's sight, for by the law is the knowledge of sin!{Romans 3:20} But the just shall live by faith! (in Jesus Christ, and fight the good fight of faith) And be found in him, (part of the body of Christ) not having mine own righteousness, which is of the law, but that (righteousness) which is through the Faith of Christ, the Righteousness which is of God by Faith! That I may know him, and the power of his resurrection, and the fellowship of his sufferings, being made conformable unto his Death! If by **any means** I might **attain** unto the Resurrection of the dead!{Philippians 3:9} Even as Abraham believed God and it was accounted to him for righteousness! Know ye therefore that they which are of Faith, the same are the children of Abraham. The Scripture, foreseeing that God would justify the heathen through faith. Preached before the gospel unto Abraham saying, "In thee shall all nations be blessed!" So then they which be of Faith, are blessed with faithful Abraham! For as many as are under the works of the law, are under the curse; for it is written, Cursed is every one that continueth not in all things which are written in the book of the law to do them! But that no man is justified by the Law in the sight of God, it is evident; for "The just shall live by Faith!" And the Law is Not of Faith; but, the man that doeth them shall live in them. Christ hath redeemed us from the curse of the Law; so that the blessing of Abraham might come on the Gentiles through Jesus Christ! That we might receive the Promise of the (Holy) Spirit through **Faith**! Now to Abraham and his seed were the Promises made. He saith not, and to seeds, as of many; but as of one, and to thy seed which is Christ! (and all who are Born Again into the body of **Jesus Christ**, who is the seed! Receive God's Promise of the Holy Spirit through Faith!) But if the inheritance be of the law, it is no more of promise; but God gave it to Abraham (and his seed) by Promise! Wherefore then serveth the Law? It was added because of Transgressions, till the Seed (Christ) should come, to whom the Promise was made; and it was ordained by angels in the hand of a mediator. (for there is one God, and one mediator between God and Men, the man Jesus Christ! - 1 Timothy 2:5) Is the law then against the promises of God? God forbid; for if there had been a law given which could have given Life, verily righteousness should have been by the Law! But the Scripture hath concluded All Under Sin! That the Promise of Faith in Jesus Christ, might be given to Them that Believe! (in Him!) But before faith came, we were kept under the law, shut up unto the faith which should afterwards be revealed. Wherefore the law was our schoolmaster, (to teach us that We Could Not Save ourselves!) and bring us unto Christ, so that we might **Be Justified By FAITH!!!** But after that Faith is come, we are no longer under a schoolmaster! {Galatians 3} My brethren, all of our own righteousness is nothing but Filthy Rags in God's Sight! But We are Saved by **Grace** through **Faith** in the mighty Lamb of God! **JESUS CHRIST!** Through Faith that clothes and covers us with the Righteousness of Jesus Christ, the only begotten Son of God! And when Almighty God our Father in Heaven, looks at any person who is a **Born Again Living Member** of **The Body of Christ**; He **Sees** the **Blood**, and **the Righteousness** of His Own Son, Jesus Christ!!! **Hallelujah!!!** Heavenly Father, I **Thank You** so very much for your son Jesus, and your Holy Spirit! I know that all of this was done by your own hand and design, from the very Foundation of the World!

Holiness, Prayer, and Spiritual Warfare!

We will now look closely at the Holy Scriptures which reveal, God the Father's promises, and His Part to Fulfill, of the New Covenant with his Holy Son Jesus Christ, that they made before the Foundation of the world! (a covenant is an agreement or a contract, and the new covenant between God the Father, and God the Son, Jesus Christ; is Completely Guaranteed!!!) Because it is Absolutely Impossible for Almighty God to Lie! **Ever!!!** God is Forever Bound To His Word, and Must Keep His Promises!!! **Forever!!!** The Secret of the Lord is with them that Fear Him and He will show them his Covenant! My Covenant **will I not break**, nor alter the thing that has gone out of my lips! {Psalm 25:14, 89:34} Behold, the days come when I will make a New Covenant with the house of Israel, and the house of Judah. (the Spiritual seed of Abraham, born of the promise, not of the flesh!) Know ye therefore that they which are of **Faith**, (all that Believe in Jesus Christ) are the children of Abraham! {Galatians 3:7} For he is not a Jew which is one outwardly, by circumcision of the cutting of the flesh; but he is a Jew which is inwardly, and his circumcision is that of the **Heart**, in the **Spirit!** {Romans 2:28} In that he saith,"A New Covenant," he hath made the first old, which decayeth and is ready to vanish away! But now hath He (Jesus) obtained a more excellent ministry; and how also, He is the mediator of a Better Covenant, which is established upon better Promises! For if the first covenant had been faultless, then should no place have been sought for the second! This is the "New Covenant" that I (God) will make! My Beloved Brethren, these are **the Key Promises!** I will sprinkle clean water upon you, and ye shall Be Clean; from all your filthiness, and from all your idols, will I cleanse you! (Jesus said, **living water** "the Holy Spirit" shall flow out of your belly!) A **New Heart** also Will I Give You, and a **New Spirit** Will I Put Within You! And I Will Take Away the Stony (Hard) Heart Out of Your Flesh! And I Will Give You A Heart of Flesh! (a soft tender, loving heart) And **I will put my (Holy) Spirit within You**, and **Cause You to Walk in my Statutes**, and **Ye Shall Keep my Judgments and "DO ~THEM!!!"** And Ye shall be my People, and I will be your God! I will also Save You from All your Uncleanness! I will put my laws into their mind, and write them in their hearts; and I will be to them a God, and they shall be to me a people! For I Will Be Merciful to their Unrighteousness, and their Sins and Iniquities will I Remember No More! {Hebrews 8:6-13 & Ezekiel 36:25-29} Fear thou not, for I AM with Thee! Be not dismayed, for **I AM THY GOD!!!** I will Strengthen Thee; yea, I will Help Thee; yea, **I Will uphold thee** with the **Right Hand** of my **Righteousness!** {Isaiah 41:10} We have a Great High Priest, **Jesus the Son of God!** That has ascended into the Heavens, who is Seated at the **Right Hand of God**, at the Throne of the Majesty of **Almighty God on High!** {Hebrews 4:14, 8:1} And it is **JESUS** that maketh Intercession for US, according to the Will of God! What shall we then say to these things? For if **God** Be For Us, **who** can be against Us? (or overturn God's Ruling?) **NO ONE!!!** Because it is God that Justifieth! Who can condemn us? Who shall separate us from the Love of Christ? Shall tribulation, or distress, or persecution, or famine, or nakedness, or peril, or sword? Nay, in all these things we are more than conquerors! I can do all things through Christ Jesus who strengthens me! {Romans 8:31-38} Be Strong and of Good Courage, fear not, or be afraid of them; for the Lord thy God, He it is that doth Go with Thee! **He Will Not Fail Thee, Nor Will He Forsake Thee!** {Hebrews 13:5 & Deutero. 31:6}

Holiness, Prayer, and Spiritual Warfare!

I will sing of the mercies of the Lord for ever; with my mouth I will make known thy faithfulness to all generations! For I have said, Mercy shall be built up forever; thy faithfulness shalt thou establish in the very Heavens! I have made a covenant with my chosen; thy seed will I Establish Forever, and build up thy throne to all generations! God is greatly to be feared in the assembly of the saints, and to be had in reverence of all them that are about him! Justice and Judgment are the habitation of thy throne; Mercy and truth shall go before thy face! In (Jesus) name shall we rejoice all the day, and in thy righteousness shall we be Exalted! For Thou (Lord Jesus) art the Glory of their strength, and in thy favor, our horn shall be exalted! For the Lord (Jesus) is our Defense; and the Holy One of Israel is our King! I have laid help upon One that is Mighty; I have Exalted One chosen out of the people. With whom my hand shall be established; mine arm also shall strengthen him. I will beat down his foes before his face, and plague them that hate him! But my faithfulness and mercy shall be with him; and in my name shall his horn be exalted! He shall cry unto me, thou art my Father, my God, and the rock of my salvation! Also I will make him my Firstborn, higher than the kings of the earth! My Mercy will I keep for him forever more, and my covenant shall stand fast with him! His seed also will I make to Endure Forever, and his throne as the days of Heaven! If his children forsake my Law, and walk not in my Judgments; if they break my statutes, and keep not my Commandments! Then will I visit their transgressions with the rod, and their iniquity with stripes! Nevertheless my Loving kindness will I not utterly take from him, nor suffer my Faithfulness to Fail! My Covenant Will I Not Break, nor Alter the thing that is gone out of my lips! Once have I sworn by my Holiness that I will not lie unto David; his seed (Jesus) shall Endure Forever, and His Throne as the sun before me! It Shall Be Established as the moon, and as a Faithful witness in Heaven! {Psalm 89:1-37} Almighty God has Forever established his son **Jesus Christ** as the Savior of the World! He is the King of Kings and the Lord of Lords! And there will be no end to Jesus Rule over all of the Kingdoms of Heaven and Earth, of Men and Angels! **Almighty God the Father** of all creation hath Highly Exalted Him, and given him a name which is above every name! That at the name of **Jesus**, every knee should bow, of things in heaven, things in earth, and things under the earth! And that Every Tongue should confess, that **Jesus Christ is Lord!** To the Glory of **God the Father!!!** {Philippians 2:9} All Power in Heaven and Earth is given unto Jesus Christ! For the Father Judgeth no man, but hath committed **All Judgment unto the Son!** {Matthew 28:18, John 5:22} For God sent not his Son into the world to condemn the world; but that the world through him might be **Saved!!!** He that believeth on him is not condemned; but he that believeth not is **Condemned Already** because he hath **not believed** on the **Only Begotten SON OF GOD!!!** ~ **JESUS CHRIST!!!** ~ **THE MESSIAH!!!** He that believeth on the son hath everlasting life and he that believeth not the son shall not see life; but the Wrath of God abideth on him! {John 3} For we must all appear before the Judgment Seat of Christ, that Every One of us shall give an account of himself **to God!** And Receive the reward or punishment, for the deeds and things, that they have Done in their Body; during their lifetime here on the earth! All According to what he hath done, weather it be Good or Bad! {2 Corinthians 5:10, Romans 14:12, 1:18} For the Wrath of God is revealed from Heaven, Against All Ungodliness and Unrighteousness of Men!

Holiness, Prayer, and Spiritual Warfare!

The Soul that sinneth, it shall Die! For the wages of Sin is Death, but the Gift of God is **Eternal Life!** Through Jesus Christ our Lord! The righteousness of the Righteous shall be upon him, and the wickedness of the Wicked shall be upon him! But if the wicked will turn from all his sins that he hath committed, and keep all my statutes and do that which is lawful and right, he shall surely live, he shall not die! All his transgressions that he hath committed, they shall not be mentioned unto Him! In his righteousness that he hath done, He shall live! Have I any pleasure at all that the wicked should die? Saith, The Lord God! And not that he should return from his (evil) ways and live? But when the Righteous (man) turneth away from his righteousness, and committeth iniquity, and doeth according to all the abominations that the wicked man doeth, Shall He Live? All his righteousness that he hath done, Shall Not Be Mentioned! In his trespass that he hath trespassed, and in his sin that he hath sinned, In Them Shall He Die! Yet ye say, The way of the Lord is not equal! **Hear Now**, O' house of Israel; (and **All the People of the Earth!!!**) Is Not My Way Equal? Are Not Your Ways Unequal? When a righteous man turneth away from his righteousness, and committeth Iniquity, and Dieth In Them! For his iniquity that he hath done **He Shall Die!** Again, when the wicked man "Turneth Away" From His Wickedness that He hath committed, and **Doeth** that which is Lawful and Right, **"HE SHALL SAVE HIS SOUL ALIVE!!!"** Because he considereth, and Turneth Away from All His Transgressions that he hath committed, **"He" shall surely live! He Shall Not Die!** {Ezekiel 18:20-30} Are not the ways of the Lord, fair and Equal? O' Ye People and Inhabitants of the Earth? I will show mercy to the merciful; I will forgive all the sins and iniquities, of any man that **Repenteth**; and Turneth Away from **Evil**, and all Sin, and **Iniquity!!!** And any man who **Doeth** that which is Good, and Right, Just and True, and **HOLY!** On this man will I have compassion, who walketh in the Light with Mine Only Begotten Son, **Jesus Christ!** Those who Believe and trust in Jesus Blood to wash them clean from sin, and surrender their will; and submit their Lives to **Jesus'** Lordship and Authority! I will put my **Holy Spirit Inside them**, and wash them clean, and clothe them in a spotless White Wedding Garment; prepared for the Marriage Supper of the Lamb! On Those who Truly and Sincerely "**Do God's Will**," and are Actual Living Members, of the **Body** of **Jesus Christ!!!** Who **Walk in the Spirit**, and **Are Led by the Holy Spirit!** Who Take Up their Cross every single day, deny themselves, Crucify All their Fleshly Desires, and **Follow Jesus!** Faithfully and sincerely, step by step, precept upon precept, line upon line. All those who Bring Forth Fruit worthy of Repentance, and are Transformed into the Image of Jesus Christ! And who remember, Humbly, every step of the way, through it all; that You are only **Saved by Grace**, through **FAITH in Jesus Christ!!!** And NOT By Your Own Works, or Puny Human Efforts! It is the **Gift of God!!!** Jesus Christ Saved You and Paid the price for Your Sins! He is the **Only One** who **Reconciled You To God!!!** And made you clean and Holy Before God The Father; so that You can **Enter into Heaven!** These are the People whose Names are Written In Heaven, in **God's Book of Life!!!** But all the men and women who Rebel and Choose to Live Evil Wicked Sinful Lives, lying, and stealing, and murdering like their Rebellious father **Satan!** Those who Refuse to Turn from their Evil Ways, and Have Absolutely No Intentions of **obeying God!** Those who Refuse to Repent from their Sins and Iniquities will face the **Wrath of God!**

Holiness, Prayer, and Spiritual Warfare!

Therefore, (this is how) I will judge you, Every One According to His Ways (and deeds that he doeth) saith, **the Lord God!** Repent, and turn yourselves from all your transgressions; so iniquity **Shall Not Be Your Ruin! Cast Away from You ALL Your Transgressions!!!** Whereby Ye have Transgressed; and make you a **New Heart** and a **New Spirit!!!** For Why will Ye Die? For I have no pleasure in the Death of him that dieth, (in his sins and iniquities) Therefore O thou son of man, thus speak ye, saying, If our transgressions and our sins be upon us, and we pine away in them, how should **We Then Live**? Say unto them,"As I live, saith the Lord God, I Have No Pleasure In the Death of the Wicked, but that the wicked turn from his evil way and **live**! Turn ye, turn ye from your evil ways; for why will ye **Die**? Wherefore turn yourselves, and Live Ye! {Ezekiel 18:30, 33:10} My Beloved Brethren, This is where the New Covenant, and God's Promises come In! When the law was our schoolmaster, we learned that by the Letter of the Law, We Could Not make ourselves a new heart or a new spirit! Because the letter Killeth but **the Spirit giveth life!** {2 Corin. 3:6} Beloved, only by being **Born Again** into the Spirit by **Faith in Jesus**, can the Holy Spirit of God actually Enter into your Heart and Soul; and by His Mighty Transforming Power, give to you a New Heart and a New Spirit and change you, step by step, into the Image of Jesus Christ! The Apostle Paul said to "put on Christ, and as ye learn Christ, walk ye in him!" Remember brethren, that when Faith is Come "We Are No Longer Under the Law" you must Activate, and Actively Use Your Faith! And Sincerely Believe and Stand Upon God's Holy Word and Promises! That **Almighty God** "Will Do" Exactly what he said he would do! Come boldly to the throne of Grace and stand upon God's promises! Abraham Believed God and it was accounted to him as righteousness! {Romans 4:3, Hebrews 4:16} You Have To Actively Speak To the Holy Spirit, and Stand Upon God's Promises! God showed the Prophet Ezekiel how to activate his faith and speak to the Holy Spirit in the Vally of dry bones! God was showing Ezekiel the New Covenant that would come forth through Faith in Jesus! When Jesus Christ "the Messiah" was Born! {Ezekiel Chapter 37} The hand of the Lord was upon me, and he carried me out in the Spirit of the Lord, (ye must be born again into the spirit) and set me down in the mist of the valley which was full of dry bones. And He said unto me, son of man, can these bones live? And I answered, O Lord God, thou knowest! Again he said unto me, Prophesy upon these bones, and say unto them, O ye dry bones, Hear the word of the Lord! Thus saith the Lord God unto these bones; I will cause **Breath** to **Enter Into You** and **Ye Shall Live!** (remember when Jesus breathed upon his disciples and said, receive ye the Holy Ghost?) And I will lay sinews upon you, and will bring up flesh upon you, and cover you with skin, and put breath in you, and ye shall live; and **Ye Shall Know** that **I AM the LORD!** So I prophesied as I Was Commanded; and as I prophesied there was a noise, and behold a shaking, and the bones came together, bone to bone. And when I beheld, lo, the sinews and the flesh came up upon them, and the skin covered them above; but there was no breath **In Them!** Then he said unto me, **Prophesy unto the Wind!** (remember when Jesus told Nicodemus, "**the Wind Bloweth where it listeth**,"-wheresoever the spirit wants to go- and thou hearest the sound thereof, but can not tell whence it cometh, or wither it goeth, so is every one that is **born of the spirit**) And say to the wind, Come from the four winds, O breath, breathe upon these slain that they may **live**!

Holiness, Prayer, and Spiritual Warfare!

So God commanded Ezekiel the Prophet to Speak to the Wind and say, "Come from the four winds," O' Breath, (of life) and breathe upon these slain, that they may Live! (in the original Hebrew, the word "wind" is Ruah: [roo'-akh] which translates to Spirit, or Wind of the spirit! or Breath of life!, the same word used by Jesus in John 3, Ezekiel, and the Book of Acts, on the day of Pentecost! Rushing Wind!) So what Jesus is saying, is that "the wind" (Holy Spirit) bloweth wheresoever it listeth, (the Spirit of **GOD** goes Wherever it wants to Go!) and thou hearest the sound thereof, but canst not tell whence it cometh, or wither it goeth. (you can hear the wind blowing, but you can't actually see the wind itself, but you can see it's effects on the trees, and the leaves, on the dust, and such!) So is Everyone that is born (again) of the (Holy) Spirit! (physical human fleshly eyes, can't see into the spiritual realm, or see the Holy Spirit entering into a person, but you can see the effects of the Holy Spirit on the persons life) And this is Confirmed and proven True in the Book of Acts, on the day of Pentecost! When Jesus told his Disciples, to tarry ye in Jerusalem and wait for the Promise of the Father! Which ye have heard of me, for John truly baptized with water; but Ye shall be baptized with the **Holy Ghost**; and endued with Power from on High, (from Heaven!) not many days hence! {Luke 24:49, Acts 1:4} And when the day of Pentecost was fully come, they were all with one accord in one place! (they were All in agreement with Peace and Unity in the Spirit!) And suddenly there came a sound from Heaven as of a Rushing Mighty "**Wind**" and it filled the house where they were sitting. And there appeared unto them cloven tongues like as of Fire, and it sat upon each of them! And they were All Filled with the "**Holy Ghost**" and began to Speak with other Tongues, as the (Holy) Spirit gave them utterance! {Acts 2:1-4} So the "Wind" of the "Spirit of Life" Breathed upon the Apostles, and they were "**Born Again**" into the Spirit and were filled with the "Holy Ghost" by the "Spirit of God" that was Promised by the Father, through Faith in Jesus Christ! And The Apostles are Now Sanctified Holy Temples, or Tabernacles, (the Holy Dwelling Place) of **Almighty God!!!** (And filled with the Transforming Power of God!) The Power to give them New Hearts, New Holy Desires, New Minds, (let this mind be in you that was also in Christ Jesus) New Lives, and make them New Creatures! (if any man be In Christ he is a New Creature!) The same Powerful Holy Spirit of God, that Raised Jesus from the Dead; is now Living and Breathing Life into Born Again believers who walk with God in spirit and truth! And God was showing His Promised "New Covenant" Power to the Prophet Ezekiel 597 years before Jesus was Born! And we will examine even further into the promises God Revealed to Ezekiel Now! {37:10} So I (Ezekiel) Prophesied as he (God) commanded me, and the breath came into them, and they stood up upon their feet, an exceeding Great Army! Then he said unto me, son of man, these bones are the whole (spiritual) house of Israel! (spiritual children born of the Promise by Faith, not born of the fleshly bondwoman, but of the free!) Therefore prophesy and say unto them, thus saith the Lord God; behold, O my people, I will open your graves, and cause you to come up out of your graves, and bring you into the land of Israel! (Heaven!) And Ye Shall Know that **I AM the Lord**, when I have opened your graves, O my people, and brought you Up Out of Your Graves! And shall Put My Spirit In You, and **Ye Shall Live**, and I shall place you in your own land; then shall ye know that I the Lord have spoken it, and preformed it, saith **The Lord!**

Holiness, Prayer, and Spiritual Warfare!

And so, beloved brethren, just as God commanded Ezekiel to "Speak and Prophesy to the Holy Spirit!" (to prophesy means - to speak by Divine Inspiration of God!) And say, "Thus saith the Lord God," O' Breath of Life, (Holy Spirit) come and Breathe your Breath of Life "Into" these dead, dry, bones, and **Make Them Live!!!** We must also Speak to the Holy Spirit through Faith and Belief in Jesus Christ, and Full Confidence in God's Promises! (the One True Living God that **CANNOT LIE**!) Promises in the Holy Bible, that God Promised to us! Brethren, Pray and ask God to Fill You with the Holy Spirit! (pray humbly with godly fear and reverence) Then say,"Thus saith the Lord God, O Holy Spirit, Come and Breathe your Breath of Life **Into ME!!!** So that **I AM BORN AGAIN**, and **Make ME LIVE!!!**" (remember what Jesus said, "If ye then, being evil, know how to give good gifts unto your children?, how much more will Your Heavenly Father give the **Holy Spirit** to **THEM THAT "ASK HIM"** !!! Ask and **Ye Shall Receive**, Seek and **Ye Shall Find**, Knock and **It Shall Be Opened Unto You!!!**) {Luke 11:9-13} Say, Holy Spirit, You are the Executive, and the Executor of God's Will, here on the Earth! You are Spirit of God In Me, whose task it is to carry out God's Promises, and to Fulfill God's Oath to Me, Promised in **the New Covenant** by God the Father! "My Covenant will I Not Break, nor alter the thing that is gone out of my Lips!" Holy Spirit, I fully surrender control of my Life "**To You!**" (for as many as are led by the Spirit of God, they are the sons of God!) Come and breathe your **Breath of Life** into **Me**; and **Do in my Life**, what **God** the Father has sent you here to do! Holy Spirit, I invite You to come and Live inside my very Heart and Soul, **Forever!** Guide me, Teach me, Help me, Give Me Eyes to See God's will for my life! Give me Ears to **Hear God's Voice!** Give me a Mind that will Perceive and Understand and Retain what God is saying to ME! And most of All, Holy Spirit, "**GIVE ME A NEW HEART, That will "RECEIVE" and Always "DO GOD'S WILL" For My LIFE!!!** Because that is exactly what God the Father Promised he would do in the new covenant!"A New Heart will **I Give You**, and a New Spirit will **I Put Within You**, and **I will take away** the stony heart out of your flesh, and give you a heart of flesh!" And **I Will Put My Spirit Within You**, and **CAUSE YOU** to **Walk in my Statutes**, and **Ye Shall Keep My Judgments and DO THEM!!! I Will Put My Law** in their inward parts, and write it in their Hearts; and I will be their God, and they shall be my people! My Beloved, please take heed to this warning! You Must Also **Do Your Part** in the new covenant! To always seek Gods face in prayer, and to study and meditate on the Holy Bible every day! To Sincerely and Truthfully, Strive To Do God's Will, with all your Heart, Soul, Mind, and Strength! Just like Jesus Christ, your Lord and Savior, **Told You To Do! DO NOT Play Games with ALMIGHTY GOD!!! YOU WILL BE DESTROYED!!!** It is a Fearful Thing to Fall into the Hands of **The Living God!!!** Do Not Ever, "IF YOU" **Fall into SIN**, then Try to Say, that God did not keep his promise! The Holy Spirit will **ALWAYS**, Make a Way Out of Every Sin and Temptation that YOU WILL EVER FACE! Then It is Up to YOU, **TO TAKE THAT WAY OUT!!!** It is one thing if you are truly and sincerely Fighting against, and striving to overcome every sin! With **All Your Heart!!!** It is completely another thing if You Want to Sin, and Plan on Sinning in Your Heart! God Sees IT! You cannot deceive God!

Holiness, Prayer, and Spiritual Warfare!

There hath no temptation taken you, but such as is common to man; but God is Faithful, who will not suffer you to be tempted above that ye are able! But will with the Temptation, **Also Make A Way To Escape**, that ye may be able to bear it! {1 Corinthians 10:13} Beloved, think it not strange concerning the fiery trial which is to try you, as though some strange thing happened unto you; but rejoice, in as much as ye are partakers of Christ's sufferings! That when his glory shall be revealed, ye may be glad also with exceeding joy! Because the trial of your Faith, is much more precious than gold that perishes, though it Be Tried with Fire, might be found unto praise and honor and glory at the appearing of Jesus Christ! {1 Peter 1:7, 4:12} Blessed is the man that endureth temptation; for when he is Tried, He shall **Receive the Crown of LIFE!!!** Which the Lord has promised to them that love him! Let No man say when he is tempted, I am Tempted of God; for **God cannot be tempted with Evil**, neither tempteth he any man! But every man is tempted, when he is drawn away **of his own lust**, and enticed! Then when Lust hath conceived, it brings forth sin, and sin when it is finished, **Brings Forth Death!** {James 1:13} So you see, my beloved brethren, **God does Not Tempt Any Man!** We are all tempted by the lust that is in Our Own Flesh, and Our Evil Hearts, by the Adam-like sinful nature that is in corrupted mankind! From Eating from the Tree of the Knowledge of Good and Evil! That is why God told Adam Not To Eat from IT! For in the Day You Eat from It, **Thou Shalt Surely DIE!!!** {Genesis 2:17} **God Always Speaks THE TRUTH!!!** That is Why We Must BELIEVE and OBEY GOD!!! Or, It Will Be Us, my beloved brethren, **That Shalt Surely DIE!!!** I beseech you as strangers and pilgrims, (God's children who have New Holy Hearts!) Abstain from Fleshly Lusts that **War Against the Soul!** This I say then, walk in the Spirit, and ye shall not fulfil the lusts of the flesh! For the Flesh Lusteth against the Spirit, and the Spirit against the Flesh! And these are contrary the one to the other, so that Ye Cannot Do The (sinful, lustful, fleshly, carnal desires, and other evil) Things that Ye would! (You Must Crucify Your Flesh, and sincerely **Obey the Holy Spirit with All Your Heart!**) {Galatians 5:16} For if ye (do) live after the flesh, (and give in to your body's sinful desires) **Ye Shall Die!** But if ye through the Spirit do mortify the deeds of the flesh, **YE SHALL LIVE!!!** For as many (people who) **ARE LED BY THE HOLY SPIRIT!** (who walk with, and talk with, and obey the Holy Spirit!) **"And Do God's Will!!!"** **"They who are led by the Holy Spirit of Almighty God!!!"** They Are The Sons (and Daughters) of GOD! {Romans 8:13} (not the disobedient and rebellious people!) So how can you be led by the Holy Spirit? **If you do not PRAY TO GOD!** and **DILIGENTLY STUDY THE HOLY BIBLE!** Which is Your Blueprint, and The One and Only **GUARANTEED TRUE WAY TO DEFINITELY "HEAR" and "KNOW THE VOICE OF GOD!!!"** And how can you be Led by the Holy Spirit, If You Don't Talk to, and **Listen to**, and communicate with, and **Obey the Holy Spirit?** How? If you don't actually **do those things** that are Necessary to **Hear God's Voice**, and Essential to **be Led by the Holy Spirit?** My beloved brethren, if you want to Hear God's Holy Precious Voice, and be led by God's Holy Spirit, You Must Diligently Study the Holy Bible, and Pray to God Diligently every single Day! **Faithfully!!!** Jesus Christ Is God! And He Prayed to and Communicated with God the Father Constantly! And Jesus was with God the Father and the Holy Spirit since the Beginning of Creation! So You and I Must Pray!

~ The Fruits of the Holy Spirit ~

The character and personality, the attributes and attitudes, the nature and qualities of temperament, the conduct, behavior, actions and disposition of a True Christian being lead by the Holy Spirit; to bring forth true, mature fruits of the Holy Spirit, by walking and staying in the Spirit consistently, to Faithfully bring forth and show the True Nature and Character of Jesus and Almighty God!

{Matthew 7:16-20} - KJV

"Ye shall know them by their Fruits, every good tree bringeth forth good Fruit; but a corrupt tree bringeth forth evil Fruit! A good tree cannot bring forth evil Fruit, neither can a corrupt tree bring forth good Fruit! Every tree that does not bring forth good Fruit is hewn down and cast into the Fire! Wherefore by their Fruits Ye Shall Know Them!" - "Jesus Christ"

1. LOVE - To adore, cherish, desire to be with, delight in, hold dear, take pleasure in, with strong feeling of affection and tender, deep, heart felt care and concern for; another person, people or group with close relationships and ties. -ex. Love for God, love for Jesus, love for the Holy Spirit. Love for Husband, Wife, Children, Family or Friends.
2. JOY - Intense happiness, feelings of utopia or ecstasy, gleeful exuberance, pleasure, delight, bliss, elation, gladness, jubilation, extreme contentment and satisfaction with life.
3. PEACE - Tranquility, serenity, freedom from hostility, contentment, happiness, peacefulness, enjoyment of life, absence of strife or stress, void of anger or hatred.
4. LONGSUFFERING - Patient, uncomplaining, thick-skinned, not easily angered, bearing trials without murmuring, the quality of patiently enduring hardships and hostile attitudes.
5. GENTLENESS - Tender, soft loving disposition, kindly, temperate, courteous, gentle, tame, considerate, well mannered, mild, quiet, not rough or severe.
6. GOODNESS - Doing that which is right and pure, proper, virtuous, excellent, straightforward and true, lawful and correct, not evil, not lying or stealing, void of deception.
7. FAITH - a strong belief and trust in that which is unseen and invisible to the naked eye; belief without firm proof, unwavering trust, belief and trust in a supreme being; a strong trust and belief in Almighty God and Jesus Christ; trust in the Scriptures of The Holy Bible.
8. MEEKNESS - Humble, submissive, not arrogant, not proud or boastful, a person that does not have an over-inflated ego or a superior opinion of ones own-self or intelligence, or a superior opinion of ones own beauty, human worth or qualities above others.
9. TEMPERANCE - Self-control, careful, restraint, alert, cautious, mindful, prudent, awareness, not quick to speak or blurt out anything in haste, not quick to act rashly or fly off the handle over small petty matters and foolishness; moderation in food and drink.

The Fruits or the Spirit are These - LOVE, JOY, PEACE, LONGSUFFERING, GENTLENESS, GOODNESS, FAITH, MEEKNESS, TEMPERANCE: Against qualities such as these, THERE IS NO LAW! And they that are Christ's Have Crucified the Flesh with it's affections and lusts! If we live in the spirit, let us also walk in Spirit! "the Apostle Paul" {Galatians 5:22-25} KJV

~ The Works and Sins of the Flesh! ~

The actual physical actions and practices of sins committed and done in the flesh, or sins done in the body, by unsaved, unrepentant, fallen men and women; in their fleshly, unclean, unsaved, fallen state, completely separated from the love and grace of almighty God and his holy Son Jesus Christ! People who in this unsaved, unrepentant, sinful, fallen condition can never under any circumstance ENTER INTO HEAVEN! Because, "Verily Verily, (Truly, Truly) I Say unto You, Except a Man be BORN AGAIN HE CANNOT!!! SEE or ENTER INTO the KINGDOM of GOD!!! {John 3:3-5} not maybe! not possibly! not rarely! He Cannot! Jesus said,"Unless a man (or woman) be Born Again He CANNOT ENTER INTO THE KINGDOM OF GOD! So Pray to God! Become Born Again! REPENT FROM YOUR SINS!!! ALL OF THEM!!! Because "The wages of Sin is Death! Accept Jesus Christ into your Life as your Lord and Savior! Invite The Holy Spirit into your HEART!!! So that the Holy Spirit can Come in and Guide You, Teach You, and Strengthen You, with Holy Ghost Fire! Because if you give the Holy Spirit Full Control of your Life. And obey what He tells you to Do! The Holy Spirit will Destroy all of the works and Sins of the Flesh! This is Exactly what Jesus and the Holy Spirit came to Earth to Do! This is the very Act and Essence of what it truly means to be Born Again! To let Almighty Gods Holy Spirit Live and Rise Up Inside of YOU! And Beat Down Satan and every evil spirit fighting against You! (For we wrestle not with flesh and blood, but against evil spirits) And to Destroy all the works and Sins of the Flesh! So what are these "Works and Sins of the Flesh?" We will now take the word of God, "The Holy Bible" and take a close, personal, in-depth, look at "The Works (or Sins) of the Flesh!!!

{Galatians 5:16-21} KJV

This I say then, walk in the spirit, and ye shall not fulfil the lust of the flesh. For the flesh lusteth against the spirit, and the spirit against the flesh: and these are contrary the one to the other: so that ye cannot do the things that ye would. (do not give in to the sins that your flesh desires and craves) But if ye be led by the spirit, ye are not under the law. Now the works of the flesh are manifest, which are these; ADULTERY, FORNICATION, UNCLEANNESS, LASCIVIOUSNESS, IDOLATRY, WITCHCRAFT, HATRED, VARIANCE, EMULATIONS, WRATH, STRIFE, SEDITIONS, HERESIES, ENVYINGS, MURDERS, DRUNKENNESS, REVELLINGS, and such like: of the which I tell you, (now) as I have also told you in times past, that they (any person) which Do such things (as these) SHALL NOT INHERIT THE KINGDOM OF GOD!!!

{1 Corinthians 6:9-10} KJV

Know ye not, (do you not know and understand!) That the unrighteous SHALL NOT inherit the Kingdom of God? Do not be Deceived! neither FORNICATORS, nor IDOLATERS, nor ADULTERERS, nor EFFEMINATE (Homosexuals - Gays and Lesbians), nor ABUSERS of THEMSELVES with MANKIND, nor THIEVES, nor COVETOUS, nor DRUNKARDS, nor REVILERS, nor EXTORTIONERS, (The unrighteous SHALL NOT) Inherit the kingdom of God! "Do not be Deceived! God is not mocked! For whatsoever a man soweth, that shall he also Reap!!! (You Will Receive the Reward or Punishment for the things you do in your body!) {Galatians 6:7}

~ The Works and Sins of the Flesh ~

Know ye not that ye are the temple of God, and that the Spirit of God dwelleth in you? (if you are really, truly, Born again in the Spirit) If any man defile the temple of God, him shall God Destroy! Because the temple of God is Holy! And You are Gods temple! {1 Corinthians 3:16-17}

"I say unto you my friends, do not be not afraid of them that kill the body, and after that have no more that they can do. But I will forewarn you who you should fear! Fear him, which after he hath killed, hath power to cast you into Hell! (ALMIGHTY GOD!) Yea, I say unto you, FEAR HIM!!!"
  "Jesus Christ" {Luke 12:4-5}

Sanctify yourselves therefore, and be ye holy; for I AM the Lord your God! And ye shall keep my statutes, and Do Them! I AM the Lord which sanctify you. And ye shall be holy unto me: for I the Lord am Holy! And I have severed you from other people that ye should be mine! {Lev.20:7-8,26}

"The hour is coming, when all who are in the graves (Every Person that ever Lived!) shall hear his Voice, (Jesus Christ) and shall come forth; they that have done good, unto the resurrection of Life! And they that have done Evil, unto the Resurrection of Damnation!!!" "Jesus Christ" {John 5:28}

Not every one that sayeth unto me "Lord, Lord" shall enter into the kingdom of heaven, but he that Does the Will of my Father which is in Heaven!!! "Jesus Christ" {Matthew 7:21}

Strive to Enter in at the Strait Gate! For many, "I say unto you" will seek to enter in, and Shall not Be Able!!! "Jesus Christ"-{Luke 13:24}, "And there shall no wise enter into it (Heaven) anything that defileth, neither whatsoever worketh abomination, or maketh a Lie; but they that are written in The Lambs Book of Life!!!" -{Revelation 21:27}, "And Whosoever was not found written in the Book of Life was cast into the Lake of Fire!!!" -{Revelation 20:15}, "He that Overcometh shall Inherit all things; and I will be his God, and he shall be my Son!!! But the Fearful (Fearful from the root Greek word, *Deilos* - dread, timid or faithless), and Unbelieving, and the Abominable, and Murderers, and Whoremongers, and Sorcerers, and Idolaters, and All Liars, shall have their part in the Lake which Burneth with Fire and Brimstone!!! Which is the Second Death! {Revelation 21:7}

{ THE TEN COMMANDMENTS } - {Exodus - 20:1-17}

1. - I AM the Lord thy God! Thou Shall have No other gods Before Me!
2. - Thou Shalt Not Make unto Thee any Graven Images, or bow down to them and serve them!
3. - Thou Shalt Not Take the Name of the Lord thy God in Vain!
4. - Remember the Sabbath Day to Keep it Holy!
5. - Honor thy Father and thy Mother, that thy Days may be Long Upon the Land!
6. - Thou Shalt Not Kill!
7. - Thou Shalt Not Commit Adultery!
8. - Thou Shalt Not Steal!
9. - Thou Shalt Not Bear False Witness (Tell Lies) Against thy Neighbor!
10. - Thou Shalt Not Covet thy Neighbors Wife, or House, or Animals, or His Possessions!

Thou Shalt Love the Lord thy God with all thy Heart, and with all thy Soul, and with all thy Mind! This is the First and Great Commandment! And, Thou shalt Love thy Neighbor as thyself. "Jesus"

~ The Works or Sins of the Flesh ~

Now we are going to closely Examine, Inspect and Define the Works or Sins of the Flesh!
These are the actual physical <u>actions</u> or <u>deeds</u> of men that <u>Shall</u> <u>Not</u> <u>Inherit</u> the <u>Kingdom</u> <u>of</u> <u>God</u>!!!

1. ADULTERY - The Act of unfaithfulness by having sexual intercourse or any sexual encounter with <u>any</u> <u>Person</u> other than your <u>lawful</u> and <u>legal</u> Husband or Wife Alone!

2. FORNICATION - The Act of having sexual intercourse or any sexual encounter by any single, <u>unmarried</u> man and woman, who are not <u>Lawfully</u> and <u>Legally</u> married to each other!

3. MURDER - To Kill and End, Extinguish and Destroy another Human Beings Life, unlawfully; that is not in <u>True</u> Self-defense, or <u>Lawful</u> Correctional Punishment by Lawful Judicial Authority's; for Evil deeds, actions or atrocities committed by the Executed Individual!

4. STEALING or THEFT - The Act of taking something belonging to another person without their permission; the taking of unattended property or theft by breaking into their house or storage, or theft by taking something either by Intimidation or Force, by Trickery or Craftiness and Guile, or the taking of money or belongings by Brain-washing, Fair-speech, or Heresies; from simple-minded people or Individuals. It's <u>ALL</u> <u>STEALING</u>!!!

5. LYING or LIARS - To speak and tell an untruthful or false statement out of your mouth, meant to deceive or mislead; to bear false witness or say any untruthful words; to declare false Information out of your mouth or by Document, to create a false Representation or false Impression meant to deceive; To <u>Tell</u> <u>Lies</u> out of your Mouth!!!
P. S.- There is <u>No</u> such Thing as <u>A</u> <u>LITTLE</u> <u>WHITE</u> <u>LIE</u>!!! A <u>Lie</u> is a <u>Lie</u>! <u>Period</u>! And <u>ALL</u> Lies are <u>Evil</u> and will send you to <u>Hell</u>!!!

6. EFFEMINATE or HOMOSEXUALITY - The Act of two Individuals of the same sex or gender having a Perverted and Immoral sexual encounter; (one man lying sexually with another man) or (one woman lying sexually with another woman); People Immorally Living and Indulging in the Gay or Lesbian Lifestyle. It is an <u>Abomination</u>!!! "If A man lie with another man, as He Lieth with a woman, both of them have committed an abomination! They shall surely be <u>Put</u> <u>to</u> <u>Death</u>; And their own blood shall be upon them!!!" - {Leviticus 20:13}; Remember, The cities of Sodom and Gomorrah, (for which this Vile Act of Sodomy was named!) were Both <u>Destroyed</u> <u>by</u> <u>God</u> in one Day!!! Also " For this cause, God gave them up to unto <u>Vile</u> <u>Affections,</u> For even their Women did change their natural use into that which is <u>Against</u> <u>Nature</u>!!! And likewise also the Men, leaving the natural use of a Woman, Burned in their Lust one toward another; <u>Men</u> with <u>Men</u> !!!" - {Romans 1:26-27}

7. DRUNKARDS or DRUNKENNESS - Any Person who is affected by Alcoholic drink to the point of Impairment; one who is Legally or noticeably overcome by Alcohol; any person who Indulges in Alcoholic Drink for the purpose of becoming "buzzed " or "Intoxicated."

~ The Works or Sins of the Flesh ~

8. **UNCLEANNESS** - Immorally impure, Indecency, Vile Perverted sexual acts on ones own self, or against children, or mentally challenged Individuals; or even perverted sexual acts by Married men and women; watching Pornography, looking at vile evil books, Exposing yourself to others, vile filthy evil words of cursing, gossip, slander, evil jokes; Rude evil gestures towards another person with your hand or other body part; Inappropriately touching or groping another person; entertaining all types of impure and unholy thoughts and Desires, that lead to outward sins of the Flesh and all types of vile Debauchery and Filthy depravity, evil suggestions to encourage sin in others, corrupting innocent children. (uncleanness is NOT some poor, homeless person, in dirty clothes, who needs a bath!)

9. **IDOLATRY** - Any Person or object you Love, Worship, desire, cherish, or delight in more than Almighty God and his Holy son Jesus Christ; The worship of false gods or Idols; The worship or Praying to of any statue, creature, animal, sun, moon, star, constellation, false Deity, Mohammed, Buddha, Mary, Peter, or any other saint, Angel, or man made Idol; The Love of any Person, object, game, posession, thing (money, television, sports, fame); Anything that would try to take the place of, surpass and supplant ALMIGHTY GOD!!! As YOUR FIRST and GREATEST LOVE upon the throne of YOUR HEART !!!

10. **COVETOUSNESS** - Greed, selfishness, desire of possessions and earthly things, riches, gold jewels, houses, boats, cars, planes, lands, power and influence, fame, to be seen of men! Covetousness also includes desiring other peoples wives, husbands, girlfriend, boyfriend. Anything that is not yours, but you deeply desire in your heart, to have it!

11. **HATRED** - To dislike someone or something intensely, with cruelty in your heart; Illtempered, To hate someone because of the color of their skin, race, religion, beliefs, job-position, financial status, fame, disposition, group of friends, housing location near your home, or just because they are walking down the street in the wrong color clothing! (how ridicules)

12. **WITCHCRAFT** - Conjuring or communicating with Evil spirits, black magic, spell casting, voodoo, seances, incantations, divinations, enchantments, occultism, sorcery, black arts, ouji-board, crystal balls, psalm-reading, star-reading, witches, wizards, warlocks, shamans mages, sorcerers, enchantresses, magicians, soothsayers divining by evil spirits or demons; or just con-artists playing on gullible peoples fears, superstitions or curiosities.

13. **EXTORTIONERS** or Swindlers and Cheats - To obtain something by threats of violence or exposure, craftiness and trickery; to set up someone by a scam, or incriminating photos, falsified data or perjured individuals; Thievery by manipulation, rigged games, pyramid schemes; usually "set up" by the scammed persons own greed or covetousness for a quick buck or other property. Instead of legally earning them by lawful and legal means.

14. **LASCIVIOUSNESS** - Lewdness, promiscuous behavior, indecency, lustful thoughts and dalliances arousing evil sexual desires, perverted immoral sexual acts and encounters; unlawful sexual partners or sexual activities for money, possessions or other considerations

~ The Works or Sins of the Flesh ~

15. **WRATH** - Violent rage, fury, anger, bitterness, indignation, resentment, displeasure or hatred of a certain individual or group of people leading to a desire of revenge or punishment.

16. **STRIFE** - Conflict, discord, angry contentions and unrest, leading to dissensions, debates, divisions, rivalry and ultimately a rebellion or separation.

17. **SEDITIONS** - Resistance or action against true lawful authority, who are upholding that which is right and true and just; Rebellion; refusal to obey Gods commandments and laws.

18. **HERESIES** - opinions contrary to true biblical teachings established and set forth in The Holy Bible; rejection of an accepted or established concept or belief; evil teachings.

19. **ENVYINGS** - bitter longing or resentment aroused by jealousy of a person or group, that are sufficiently desirable enough to provoke to envy, to take ones place or position.

20. **REVILERS** - to speak harshly against someone; to reproach or berate verbally; to criticize and verbally abuse those who stand up for the truth of Gods laws and commandments.

21. **VARIANCE** - to move back and forth in opinion, to change or vary, to do something contrary to the ordinance or commandments established by God in the Holy Bible.

22. **EMULATIONS** - to strive to equal or surpass someone or something out of jealousy, rivalry or resentment; a competitive spirit longing to be the greatest or most important.

23. **PRIDE** - (Self-esteem, haughtiness with destain for others) too high an opinion of ones self, to consider yourself superior or more intelligent and better than others; to look down on someone else or others with destain or contempt, feeling that they are beneith you in diginity, intelligence, human quality or physical beauty; preformance, self-worth, or accomplishments, mentally, physically or money-tarrily; (amount you have in the bank) "The Fear of the Lord is to hate evil, pride, arrogance; the evil way and a froward (vile, boastful) mouth do I hate."-{Proverbs 8:13} "God resists the proud but gives grace to the humble" <{James 4:6} /   \/-{Luke 18:9-14} "And Jesus spake this parable unto certain people which trusted in themselves that they were righteous, and despised others: Two men went up into the temple to pray; the one a pharisee, and the other a publican. The pharisee stood and prayed thus with himself, God, I thank thee, that I am not as other men are, extortioners, unjust, adulterers, or even as this publican. I fast twice in the week, I give tithes of all that I possess. And the publican, standing afar off, would not so much as lift up his eyes unto heaven, but smote upon his breast, saying, God be merciful to me a sinner. I tell you, this man went down to his house justified rather than the other: For every one that exalteth himself shall be abased; and he that humbleth himself shall be exalted."

24. **SURFEITING or GLUTTONY** - to overeat food or drink (eat and drink too much) beyond the small amount that the human body truly needs and is really nessary for you to live day by day; to overindulge in food and drink; "Take heed to yourselves, least at any time your hearts be overcharged with surfeiting and drunkenness, and cares of this life; and so that day (the day of Jesus return and judgment) come upon you unawares. For as a snare (or trap) shall that day come on all them that dwell upon the face of the whole Earth! "Jesus Christ " - {Luke 21:34}

The Sin of Pride

PRIDE - This Sin is the sin that will send more people to Hell than any other sin. Period! **Pride**!!! A prideful heart says to it's self "I will do whatever I want to do!" I will do whatever my evil sinful flesh desires! And absolutely "NO ONE" is going to tell ME what "I" CAN and CANNOT DO!!! Not even "ALMIGHTY GOD" is going to tell me, what I can and Cannot do! HOW DECEIVED! HOW BLIND can you possibly BE!!! The outlaw is very bold until his eyes actually set sight on the Guillotine or the Hangman noose! When the Executioner pushes his prideful head down on the chopping block and lines up the cold steel blade on his scrawny little neck; then this bold Rebel's spine turns to JELLY! Only then does he realize what an ignorant moronically bad choice the head he is about to lose has made! Hell is Eternal and PERMANENT!!! THERE IS NO WAY OUT!!! EVER!!! The very Instant you are cast into the LAKE OF FIRE!!! Doomed to burn in Hell for ALL OF ETERNITY!!! Only then will your Brain truly realize what an Incredibly BAD choice YOU have made! For the sake of a few Pitiful Sins! For a handful of very limited days, during your short, brief, lifespan here on the earth! YOU gave up all of Eternity in Heaven for Nothing!!! Why do you think deathbed confessions are so common? Because the sinner finally realizes that the short sinful life they chose is now **over**! So now they are trying to throw the heavy chunks of hellbound sin out of their sinking ship! Something they should have been doing 30 or 40 years ago Imagine a man starving to death, clinging on to deaths doorstep, with a day or maybe two days to live. He reaches into his pocket and finds a kernel of corn! He digs a small hole in the dirt, puts in the kernel of corn, spits on it, and then covers it up. Hoping to grow enough food to live! But it's too Late! The Summer is over! The Harvest has ended! And He is NOT SAVED!!! **Not Saved!** Today is the day of Salvation! NOT TOMORROW!!! T-O-D-A-Y!!! Think about this Fact, your Entire Lifetime is not even equal to one tiny speck of sand in the Realm of Eternity! And all of the sand, in all the deserts, and all the beaches, and all the oceans, on the entire planet earth, compared to all of Eternity, **Will NOT Equal One Hour of Time** when measured next to "**ETERNITY!!!**" And You are going to choose one tiny microscopic minuscule speck of Life, for Sin? And Rebel Against the Living God who Gave that Life To You! And "**GIVE UP ALL OF ETERNITY!!!**" And **Eternal Life in Heaven**? So Vast that the human mind cannot comprehend it! **For What?** A Few Pitiful Sins! Is there one single braincell in your whole entire brain, that tells you this is the Right Choice? The Smart Choice? The Devil will lie to you, and tell you that, "You are living life Your Way! You are Living life as you see fit!" What Satan is not telling you is that this "Rebel" Road, leads straight to Hell! And there's No Way Out! And once the devil gets you there in hell with him, he is going to laugh in your face, and point his finger up towards heaven and say,"Look, Look up at Heaven, and See what I stole from **You!!!**" You gave up eternal life in heaven, forever! For Beer, Drugs and Sex! Ha Ha Ha! You Lose dummy!" Now you'll burn in hell forever with me! **I won't suffer alone in Hell Forever!** You'll be right here with with me!" Satan is your **Enemy!!!** Beloved brethren, take all the Pride and Rebellion Out of your heart; and stuff it into Satan's lying mouth, and send it to hell with him! Humble yourself, and Do God's will! Jesus died to Save You!

Introduction to: "Be Ye Perfect"

As I am Praying Tonight, I feel it is very important to write an Introduction to this Message. As this may be one of the most important Messages from <u>God</u> I have ever written. So please read it <u>carefully</u> and <u>prayerfully</u>, and then read it again. It comes directly from <u>God</u> Almighty as taught to me by his Holy Spirit! And I do not say that lightly, I Fear God Greatly; seeing as the fear of the lord is the beginning of wisdom. It is my sincere Prayer, that the Holy Spirit will Open up your <u>Heart</u> and <u>Mind</u> and <u>Ears</u>, to these words of <u>truth</u> from God's Holy Bible. As taught to us by his son, Our Lord and Savior Jesus Christ; the Messiah and God's Great High Priest! Most of the Scripture from which this message is taught, is printed out on the next page. But let me first say that I AM NOTHING BUT DUST! An <u>Earthen</u> <u>Vessel</u> for the Master Lord Jesus to use! DUST! I stand behind the Cross of Jesus Christ to deliver this Message to You. But this Dust Loves You very Much! I don't want your money! I don't want your earthly things! I don't want your praise or Admiration! I Love You and I want <u>You</u> to be in Heaven with my Lord and Savior Jesus Christ!!! And OUR FATHER GOD in HEAVEN!!! It is only because I Love Your Soul, That I deliver this message to you. Love suffereth long and is kind, love envieth not; Love vaunteth not itself, Love is not puffed up. Love does not behave it's self unseemly, Love seeketh not her own, Love is not easily provoked, Love Thinketh no Evil; Love rejoiceth not in iniquity, but Love rejoiceth in Truth; Love beareth all things, Love believeth all things, Love hopeth all things, Love endureth all things. Love never faileth: but whether there be prophecies, they shall fail; whether there be tongues they shall cease; whether there be knowledge it shall vanish away. For we know in part and we prophesy in part; but when that which is perfect is come, then that which is in part shall be done away. When I was a child, I spake as a child, I understood as a child, I thought as a child; But when I became a Man, I put away childish things. So Please take this message For what it is! A Message Directly from Almighty God, through some one who <u>Loves</u> You; and wants <u>You</u> to make it into Heaven! Jesus Christ's servant,

Don Diaz

Holy Bible Scriptures for "Be Ye Perfect"

"Be Ye therefore Perfect, Even as your Father which is in Heaven is Perfect." {Matthew 5:48}

The Parable of the Tares

Another parable put he forth unto them, saying, The kingdom of heaven is likened unto a man which sowed good seed in his field: But while men slept, his enemy came and sowed tares among the wheat, and went his way. But when the blade was sprung up, and brought forth fruit, then appeared the tares also. So the servants of the householder came and said unto him, sir, didst not thou sow good seed in thy field? From whence then hath it tares? He said unto them, An enemy hath done this. The servants said unto him, wilt thou then that we go and gather them up? But he said, nay; lest while ye gather up the tares, ye root up also the wheat with them. Let both grow together until the harvest: and in the time of harvest I will say to the reapers, gather ye together first the tares, and bind them in bundles to burn them: but gather the wheat into my barn. {Matt 13: 24-30}

The Parable of the Wise man and the Foolish man

Therefore whosoever heareth these sayings of mine, and doeth them, I will liken him unto a Wise man, which built his house upon a Rock: And the rain descended, and the floods came, and the winds blew, and beat upon that house; and it fell not: for it was founded upon a Rock. And every one that heareth these sayings of mine, and doeth them not, shall be likened unto a Foolish man, which built his house upon the sand: And the rain descended, and the floods came, and the winds blew, and beat upon that house; and it fell: and great was the fall of it. And it came to pass, when Jesus had ended these sayings, the people were astonished at his doctrine: For he taught them as one having authority, and not as the scribes. {Matthew 7:23-29}

But the Lord said unto Samuel, Look not on his countenance, or on the height of his stature; because I have refused him: for the Lord seeth not as man seeth; for man looketh on the outward appearance, but the Lord looketh on the HEART. {1 Samuel 16:7}

Let your HEART therefore be Perfect with the Lord our God, to walk in his statutes, and to keep his commandments. {1 Kings 8:61}

For the Word of God is quick, and powerful, and sharper than any two edged sword, piercing even to the dividing asunder of soul and spirit, and of the joints and marrow, and is a discerner of the thoughts and intents of the HEART! Neither is there any creature that is not manifest in His Sight! But ALL THINGS are NAKED and OPENED unto the EYES of HIM ~ {Almighty God} ~ with whom we have to Do!
{Hebrews 4:12-13}

That ye may stand PERFECT and COMPLETE in all the will of God. {Colossians 4:12}

Solomon my son, know thou the God of thy father, and serve him with a PERFECT HEART and a WILLING MIND: for the Lord SEARCHETH ALL HEARTS, and understandeth ALL IMAGINATIONS of the THOUGHTS OF THE HEART: If thou seek him, he will be found of thee; but if thou forsake him, He will cast thee off Forever! "King David" {1 Chronicles 28:9}

"Be Ye Perfect"

Do you remember the parable that Jesus taught, about the man who sowed good seed in his field; But in the night, an enemy came and sowed tares among the wheat; and went his way? In this message, I am going to illuminate that parable. So that it will be easier for our minds to better understand the deep truths hidden in this simple parable that our awesome Lord and Savior, Jesus taught to us.

(And Expose some of Satan's lies for an extra bonus!)

When Jesus said "Be Ye Perfect as your Father in Heaven is Perfect" to the multitudes in the sermon on the mountain. {Matthew chapters 5,6,& 7} (Imagine that, sitting on top of a Mountain watching and listening to God Himself preach the Message) When Jesus taught us "Be Ye Perfect," He was planting Good Holy seeds to grow up into a strong, powerful, Holy, rocksolid foundation In Your Heart! So that when the storms of sin and temptation come to blow upon your house! (YOU) Your house will STAND and NOT FALL because you have let the Lord dig deep to a Holy Rocksolid foundation IN YOUR HEART!

"Be Ye Perfect, Do Not Sin!" You see Satan's evil lie says,(evil seed) "you can't be perfect, nobody's perfect!" If you BELIEVE this EVIL LIE, and Buy into IT; and it grows up into a wicked tree IN YOUR HEART! When the Storms of sin and temptation come and blow on Your House, (YOU) IT WILL FALL!

It's BUILT ON SAND! Because you believe Satan's evil lie, "You Can't Be Perfect, and You must Sin!" Then you will sin because you will give in to your flesh and sin. Because you believe Satan's lie that you have to sin, and your sand foundation will crumble beneath you! Because it's not built on Jesus's ROCK SOLID FOUNDATION, "BE YE PERFECT!" So tell me, Who are You Going To BELIEVE? That Evil Liar Satan, or GOD'S HOLY SON! WHO CANNOT LIE! For It Is IMPOSSIBLE For GOD To LIE! {Hebrews 6:18}

Don't Forget Jesus' other parable! "Therefore whosoever heareth these sayings of mine, and doeth them, I will liken him unto a wise man, who built his house on a Rock; and the rain descended, and the floods came, and the winds blew, and beat upon that House; and it fell not; for it was founded upon a Rock! And every one that heareth these sayings of mine, and doeth them not, he shall be likened unto a

Foolish man, which built his house upon the sand; and the rain descended, and the floods came, and the winds blew, and beat upon that house; and it fell: and great was the fall of it! Now when I was a young boy growing up. About a mile or so from my house, were some thick woods. Full of many different types of trees. Me and a bunch of friends would go and play in those woods all the time. One certain kind of tree that was very plentiful in these woods were black oak trees. Now there was one particular oak tree, that was very thick and powerful planted near a very old red brick water irrigation structure. Probably built around the early 1900's. Because it was planted right next to the small canal, it had an abundant water source; which made it huge and strong! And since it was such a big tree on the side of the canal, it had grown up slightly slanted. (about a 15 degree angle) So that it was easy for me and my friends to climb up the side of this oak tree, and sit down comfortably in the branches. which we did quite often. 8 or 9 of us (or even 15) could have jumped up and down at the same time, in this strong oak tree! And it wouldn't budge not one inch, it withstood many powerful hurricanes. In fact I think it's there to this day! Now, about a mile or so away; in a big subdivision of brick houses in Chalmette, Louisiana. (a couple blocks from my house) Was a Drainage canal that ran between two streets, in this big subdivision; to drain the rain water away. All along this canal were bunches of flimsy willow trees, all the way down the canal. These trees would blow back and fourth with the slightest wind. (of doctrine?) As young boys, we would grab the limbs we could reach and pull down on them; causing them to bend. But you had to be careful, sometimes they'ed give way and snap off! This type of tree would come down easily under pressure. Now a certain group of boys had tied a rope about twenty feet up onto one of these willow trees. They would hold on to the rope, Get a running head start. And swing out over the canal, Kickin and screamin; and swing around to the other side of the tree. This lasted for a couple of days. (maybe a week or two, I'm not sure) But one day the willow tree gave way to the pressure, and fell! One of the boys fell down into the canal, and broke a couple Ribs on some cypress knees; in the bottom of that canal! Those Boys had chosen to trust in the wrong type of tree, and one of them paid a heavy price for it!

If that boy had landed on his head, he could have easily been killed.

Now, this brings me back to the heart of my message. Getting back to the parable Jesus taught, about the man who planted good seed in his field to grow his crops. But an Evil enemy came in the night, and planted evil seed in the same field to destroy it! This is exactly what happened to <u>us</u>! In <u>our</u> lifetime! Jesus in the Bible Taught Us, "Be Ye Perfect, Go and Sin no More!" Our Precious Lord and Savior was Planting "Good Seed" <u>IN OUR HEARTS</u>! To help us grow strong in God! To Walk Holy, and stand firm against SIN! But at some point in your Lifetime, (probably when you were young) some person told you. "You can't Be Perfect, Nobody's Perfect!" And you Believed It. This is an Evil Lie! And an Evil Seed from Satan Himself! And It grew into an evil tree in your Heart! And it's whole Purpose <u>IS TO WEAKEN YOUR RESOLVE</u> to walk Holy and Sinless; and to Cause You To GIVE IN TO <u>SIN</u>! So You Must Now Let God's Holy Spirit, take God's Holy Sword,(The Word of God) and <u>CUT THIS WICKED TREE DOWN</u>! AND BURN IT UP WITH <u>HOLY GHOST FIRE</u>!!! Because If You Still Believe Satan's Wicked Lie (Evil Seed) That You Can't Be Perfect and You Have To Sin, When the Storms of Sin and Temptation come and beat upon your house! (YOU) Your House Will Fall, Because You Have Bought Into Satan's Sand Foundation of LIES! That You Can't Be Perfect, and that You Have to Sin. Just like the weak and Flimsy Willow Tree, You will Break under the Pressure and <u>GIVE IN</u>!

But If You Believe The Mighty Lord Jesus, (The Holy Son of God) Who cannot Lie! And Let His Good Seed "Be Ye Perfect" Grow up into a Strong Powerful Rocksolid Foundation in Your Heart! When the Storms of Sin and temptation come and Beat upon Your House, You Will Stand! Because You Have let the Lord Dig Deep into Your Heart to Bedrock Foundation Called Jesus Christ! (The Stone That the Builders Rejected) Then the Mountain <u>Built By God</u> of Apostles and Prophets, and Martyrs, Jesus Christ Being the Chief Corner Stone! WILL STAND BY <u>YOU</u>! And If you will let his Good Seed <u>Grow UP</u> In your HEART! Into a Powerful Holy Oak Tree, Then You Won't give in to Every wind and wave of Doctrine. And the Storms of wind and rain, of Sin and Temptation that Beat Upon Your House! Will Not Make You Fall, Because <u>God's Hand</u> Is Upon You!

And you'll Say,"Satan take your Evil seeds and Evil lies, and Get Ye Behind Me" You can take your Sin straight to Hell with You!" Jesus told me "Be Ye Perfect!" And That's Exactly What I'm Going To Do! Brothers and Sisters, Do you think for one minute, that our Precious Lord and Savior Jesus Christ; who loves us would <u>ever</u> give us a commandment, He knew we couldn't <u>Keep</u>! Never! <u>Never</u>! Jesus Was Down Here In This Body! He Knows What You are Going Through! Beloved, I understand That sometimes Good, Sincere Christians Fall down. But The SMART ONES, <u>GET RIGHT BACK UP</u>!!! Put it under the Blood of Jesus! KEEP Walking with God! And NEVER DO IT AGAIN!!! The Apostle Paul Said,"This one thing I Do, FORGETTING THOSE THINGS THAT ARE BEHIND ME!!! I PRESS ON TOWARDS THE MARK, OF THE HIGH CALLING OF GOD; <u>IN CHRIST JESUS</u>! PRESS ON TOWARDS THE LORD! But There are Some who won't Do This! And the reason why? What is really Happening is, In your Evil Heart is some sin that you like, and <u>You Want To Do</u>! It's Not That You Can't Be Perfect!!! IT'S THAT <u>YOU DON'T WANT TO BE PERFECT</u>!!! Because <u>then</u> you would have to <u>give up</u> some Pitiful little <u>Sin</u>, That You <u>Enjoy Doing</u>! <u>THAT'S WHY</u>!!! It's Not That God Doesn't have the Power to Deliver You From It! It's That You Don't <u>Want</u> to Be Delivered from it! <u>Examine</u> Your Own <u>Heart</u>, The Bible Says! The First and Great Commandment is that thou shall Love the Lord Thy God with all thy Heart, and all thine soul, and all thy Mind, and all thine strength! You See the Day that you Love Jesus more than you love your sins, those sins will melt away like wax in God's Holy Ghost fire! And don't forget the second commandment, Thou shall love thy neighbor as much as you love yourself! It's at this point That I want to expose another one of satan's lies. Satan has lied to us about what being Perfect really Is! So he can condemn you and hold you down from doing any thing at all for God! Satan wants you to think that being perfect is never having made a single solitary mistake! <u>IT'S A LIE</u>! Only JESUS Has Ever Done <u>THAT</u>! The Spotless LAMB of GOD, In Whom There Is No Sin! Hallelujah! The Scripture plainly says, "We all like sheep have gone astray, we each have turned to our own way." and again There is None Righteous, No Not One! That is why Jesus Came, to reconcile us to God! We were hellbound sinners, and God reached out with his own powerful hand; and picked us up out of the mire and darkness of a wicked evil world! You are saved by grace, through faith, and not of works lest any man should boast; it is the gift of God! Because NO Flesh shall Glory in his presence! He washed us in the blood of his own son Jesus! He put his holy spirit inside you! ALMIGHTY GOD LIVES <u>INSIDE</u> OF YOU!!!   <u>YOU</u> ARE HIS TEMPLE!!! DO YOU <u>ACT</u> LIKE IT? Do You <u>Now</u> See Why Jesus Said, "Be <u>Ye</u> Perfect"? You <u>represent</u> <u>God</u> here on Earth! <u>You</u> are the temple of the <u>Holy</u> <u>Spirit</u>! He <u>Guides</u> you. He <u>Teaches</u> You. He <u>Loves</u> You! <u>He</u> is the One Who <u>Makes</u> You <u>Perfect</u>! If You Will <u>Let</u> Him! For as many as are <u>Led</u> by the Holy Spirit of God, they are the sons and daughters of God! He is planting His Holy Seeds in your Heart Right Now! Are you going to water and feed them, through Prayer and Studying God's Holy Bible? Do you even spend one hour alone Praying to God every Day? You will if you <u>want</u> to be perfect! There are a lot of people in the Bible that <u>God</u> <u>said</u> were perfect!   Job, Noah, Enoch, God said that David was a Man after his own Heart! You see the <u>Truth</u> is it's <u>YOUR</u> <u>HEART</u> that's Perfect Before God! <u>YOUR</u> <u>HEART</u>!!!   Remember when God sent Samuel to Anoint a King from one of Jesse's sons? Samuel looked at Eliab and said, "surely the lords Anointed is before him." But the Lord said unto Samuel,"Look not on his contanance, or the hight of his stature; because I have refused him: for the Lord seeth not as man seeth; for man looketh on the outward appearance, But the Lord Looketh on <u>The</u> <u>Heart</u>!" You see when you are truly sincere with God. And I Do mean Truly <u>Sincere</u>, Fighting against every sin with 1000 % percent of your Heart; with all your might and strength! Taking every thought into captivity, unto the obedience of Jesus Christ. Watching every single solitary word and syllable that comes out of your mouth, so that "No corupt communication proceeds out of your Mouth!" And you Love and Trust God with all of your Heart, and Soul, and Mind, and Strength! And you Fight with all your Might, Sincerly with every thing thats in you, through constant Prayer and studying his holy word, Day & Night! and you Truely Forgive others from your Heart! And You Love All your Neighbors and your Enemies Fervantly with a Pure Heart!   "<u>God</u> <u>See's</u> <u>That</u>!!!"

And knows You Mean Business! On the other hand, you can put on your best Suit or Dress, trim up, comb your hair, put on some make-up and make the outside of yourself up real nice! Carry your Bible into church, stand up, Praise the Lord, run around the church, hoop and holler, look real pious and holy, quote Scripture, fool the pastor and every single person in the church!
But, If on the INSIDE you are full of dead mens bones and SIN!!! You Will NEVER, EVER, EVER, NEVER FOOL ALMIGHTY GOD!!! EVER! He can See your WHOLE ENTIRE HEART, COMPLETELY AND TOTALLY!!! There is not one atom, of one DNA strand, of one cell; HE DOES NOT SEE!!! If You have one single sin you plan to do once every Ten Years! He Sees IT! If you have unforgiveness or hatred in your Heart, He Sees IT! TRUST ME! YOU CANNOT FOOL GOD!!! You only end up Deceiving your OWN SELF! Because you think that the sin is O.K.! And eventually after the Holy Spirit tells You over and over and over again and again to STOP DOING IT! You Get Turned over TO IT! "Whosoever commitheth Sin is the SERVANT OF SIN!" So that the ONLY person you truly trick is YOURSELF! NOT GOD!!! So cleanse your hands Ye sinners, and Purify your hearts Ye double minded, Draw nigh unto God and He will draw nigh unto YOU! And Give You LIGHT! So Please Know and understand that when Jesus told you "Be Ye Perfect as your Father in Heaven is Perfect," He is telling you the TRUTH! And our Precious Lord and Savior is planting Good Holy Seed in your Heart! That will Grow into a STRONG HOLY LOVE FOR ALMIGHTY GOD!!! And A ROCK SOLID FOUNDATION! So that You can STAND through any storm of Sin and Temptation that Satan, or this Wicked World, or your OWN Flesh! CAN THROW AT YOU! YOU ARE GOD'S CHILD AND HE LOVES YOU! And He will FIGHT FOR YOU! SATAN CANNOT HAVE YOU!!! The Holy Spirit will give you Strength and a way out of every Sin and Temptation! IF YOU WILL LET HIM! So "Be Ye Perfect" and Go and Sin No More, Least A Worst Thing (Hellfire) Come upon You!

        Jesus Christ and Almighty God's Servant,

                Your True Brother in the Lord, Don Diaz

Be Ye Perfect - A Completion, Summation and Conclusion

Beloved, the conclusion or sum total of "Be Ye Perfect" in it's complete entirety; is that a Perfect Christian, a truly sincerely Christ-like person! (which is what the word Christian means, to be Christ-like) Is a person that truly and sincerely <u>Loves God</u> above anything and everything else in the world, on earth, or in the entire universe! A person that loves the Lord thy God, and his only begotten son Jesus Christ, with all his heart, all his soul, all his mind, and all his strength and spirit, fervently, totally, completely, and Forever, above <u>All Else!!!</u> A person who's sacred and utmost desire is to be <u>Well-Pleasing</u> to our Holy Father God who art in Heaven above! To Live a life here on this earth, that will be well pleasing in his sight, give joy to his precious heart, and Glorify God's Hallowed Holy name! A Perfect Christian, is a man or woman who loves God so much that they willingly <u>want to</u> crucify their own flesh, and **<u>Destroy every single SIN in their Life until they are ALL GONE!!!</u>** And they <u>Overcome every Sin</u> that would stand in the way to their getting <u>Closer to their **Father God** whom they **Love Above All Else!!!**</u> And they will <u>Never, Ever, Ever, Stop Fighting to get **CLOSER TO GOD!!!**</u> And His **<u>Precious Son JESUS CHRIST!!!</u>** No matter what part of their Life or Flesh they have to Crucify on the cross, to follow their Awesome Lord and Savior **Jesus Christ** into God's Holy Kingdom in Heaven Above! No matter what Sin or Temptation or Pitfall they may have to Face! Refusing to Stop following Jesus, walking in his footsteps, seeking his face, learning his ways, and conforming their life and will to Jesus Christ's life, and our Father God's Holy will! Always <u>Forgetting</u> those things that are <u>Behind Me</u>, and Reaching Forth to the things that are before me! (**Almighty God in Heaven above**) <u>**I PRESS TOWARD THE MARK OF THE HIGH CALLING OF GOD IN CHRIST JESUS!!! ALWAYS!**</u> That I may know Him, and the power of his Resurrection, and the fellowship of his sufferings, being made conformable unto his death! If <u>By Any Means</u> I might attain unto the Resurrection of the Dead! Not as though I had already attained, either were already perfect: but I follow after, (Jesus) that I may apprehend that for which also I am apprehended of Christ Jesus. (that I may walk the path, and live the life that Jesus already walked and lived for Me!) Let us therefore, as many as be perfect, be thus minded: and if in any thing ye be otherwise minded, God shall reveal even this unto you. Nevertheless, whereto we have already attained, (as ye learn Christ Jesus, walk ye in him) let us walk by the same rule, and let us mind the same thing. Bring forth fruit (a life) worthy of repentance! (Fight the Good Fight of Faith, Lay hold onto Eternal Life and <u>Never</u> Let Go!) Press towards the mark of a Holy Life before God in Christ Jesus, walking in the Holy Spirit, denying and crucifying the lust of the flesh! Fighting to beat down, crucify, overcome and conquer every Sin, through the Power of the Holy Spirit, Faith in Jesus precious Holy Blood that washes us <u>Clean</u> from sins, (when we truly sincerely <u>Repent from and stop doing them</u>) and by the Fire and Love for God that burns within our hearts, because **<u>We Love God and want to Be with Him Forever!!!</u> <u>Because God is our Treasure in Heaven above, and we long to Kneel at Jesus feet and Worship Him because The Mighty Lord Jesus is so Magnificent and Awesome and is much more than Worthy to be Praised!!!</u>** **Jesus Christ** did what <u>no one else could ever Do</u>! Jesus Christ opened a way into Heaven Above, so that <u>We</u> could Be with Almighty God Forever in Heaven! Beloved, there is <u>Nothing</u> in this present evil world that is even worth mentioning next to "Eternal Life" in Christ Jesus, <u>with</u> "Almighty God" (the Author of all Life) <u>in</u> Heaven above!!! **<u>Absolutely nothing!</u>** You may ask, how can you be so <u>absolutely positive</u> in God, Jesus Christ and Heaven above? Because I have already <u>been</u> there! I have <u>walked</u> in Heaven above! I have personally <u>Seen and Touched</u> the clean, pure, Crystal Clear <u>Water</u> that sparkles like Diamonds, and flows from the Throne of Almighty <u>God</u> in Heaven!!! God is <u>Real</u>! Heaven is <u>Real</u>! Jesus Christ <u>is</u> God's Holy <u>Son</u>! <u>Absolutely, Positively, Guaranteed!</u> It is the Truth! God brought <u>me into</u> **Heaven** one night, after praying and seeking his face! By <u>Faith in Jesus Christ</u> and <u>Belief</u> that his Holy Precious <u>Blood, Washes Me Clean from Sin</u>! I didn't even know what <u>God</u> was about to <u>Do</u>! I am always praying and seeking **God's** face! <u>I Love God above all else</u>! Suddenly, I realize I am <u>in</u> a magnificent paradise with many awesome things, and crystal clear Living water is flowing from God's Holy Throne! God's servant, Don Diaz

WARNING! DANGER!

The Lord Jesus shall be Revealed From Heaven with His Mighty Angels, In Flaming Fire Taking Vengeance On Them That Know Not God! And Do Not <u>Obey</u> The Gospel of our Lord Jesus Christ! Who Shall Be Punished With <u>Everlasting</u> <u>Destruction</u> from the Presence of The Lord, And From The Glory of His Power! Because They Recived Not the Love of the <u>Truth</u>, that they Might be Saved!

"The Holy Bible"
{2 Thessalonians 1:7 & 2:10}
"all scripture is given by God" 2 Tim 3:16

Author: Almighty God!!!

www.ingramcontent.com/pod-product-compliance
Lightning Source LLC
Chambersburg PA
CBHW081334080526
44588CB00017B/2614